# Network+™
## Study Guide
### Fourth Edition

David Groth

Toby Skandier

San Francisco • London

Publisher: Neil Edde
Acquisitions Editor: Jeff Kellum
Developmental Editor: Jeff Kellum
Production Editor: Lori Newman
Technical Editor: James Kelly
Copy Editor: Judy Flynn
Compositor: Jeffrey Wilson, Happenstance Type-O-Rama
Graphic Illustrator: Happenstance Type-O-Rama
CD Coordinator: Dan Mummert
CD Technician: Kevin Ly
Proofreaders: Jim Brook, Candace English, Ian Golder, Nancy Riddiough
Indexer: Ted Laux
Book Designer: Bill Gibson, Judy Fung
Cover Designer: Archer Design
Cover Photographer: Photodisc and Victor Arre

SYBEX

To Our Valued Readers:

Thank you for looking to Sybex for your Network+ exam prep needs. We at Sybex are proud of our reputation for providing certification candidates with the practical knowledge and skills needed to succeed in the highly competitive IT marketplace. Certification candidates have come to rely on Sybex for accurate and accessible instruction on today's crucial technologies.

Sybex serves as a participant member of CompTIA's Network+ Advisory Committee, and just as CompTIA is committed to establishing measurable standards for certifying individuals who will support today's complex network systems, Sybex is committed to providing those individuals with the skills needed to meet those standards.

The author and editors have worked hard to ensure that the updated fourth edition of the *Network+ Study Guide* you hold in your hands is comprehensive, in-depth, and pedagogically sound. We're confident that this book will exceed the demanding standards of the certification marketplace and help you, the Network+ certification candidate, succeed in your endeavors.

As always, your feedback is important to us. If you believe you've identified an error in the book, please send a detailed e-mail to support@sybex.com. And if you have general comments or suggestions, feel free to drop me a line directly at nedde@sybex.com. At Sybex we're continually striving to meet the needs of individuals preparing for certification exams.

Good luck in pursuit of your Network+ certification!

Neil Edde
Publisher—Certification
Sybex, Inc.

*To my wonderful book team members. Thanks for your help in making our book a success.*
—*David Groth*

*To my incredibly understanding and supportive wife, Karen, and my wonderful kids, Toby, Tiffani, Trey, and Taylor. Thank you for making such an impossibly odd schedule seem commonplace and acceptable.*
—*Toby Skandier*

# Acknowledgments

It takes many people to put a book together. This will be the fourth edition of this book, so I can safely say that these people know what they're doing and that I can count on working with talented people.

I would first like to thank my co-author Toby Skandier. He has a vast amount of technical knowledge and his contributions to this book helped to make it the best possible. Also, this book would not exist if it weren't for my acquisitions and developmental editor, Jeff Kellum. Thank you for all of your encouragement and support. I appreciate all of the hard work you contribute to each one of my book projects. Additionally, many thanks go to Lori Newman, our book team's tireless production editor. Kudos to you for juggling all sorts of deadlines spanning many projects and for basically keeping your eye on the ball for me all of the time. Kudos should also go to Judy Flynn, editor extraordinaire. Thank you for your careful attention to each of the chapters. Many thanks should also go to Jeffrey Wilson, the compositor at Happenstance Type-O-Rama, for laying out the very pages you see before you. Finally, one last cheer of the proofreaders who checked every last detail before sending the pages to the printer: Jim Brook, Candace English, Ian Golder, and Nancy Riddiough.

I would also like to recognize my wife, family, and friends. My wife, Linda, tirelessly wrote and edited the appendices and kept me on the right track. She was a real trooper because she managed to do that while watching our kids. Thank you to my family and friends who understood when I couldn't go out or help them with projects because I had to work on the book. I really appreciate that.

Finally, thank you, the reader, for purchasing this book. I know that it has all the information in it to help you pass the test. If you have questions about Network+ or this book, feel free to e-mail me at dgroth@cableone.net. All of us involved in the book project have worked very hard to make it the best *Network+ Study Guide* available. I hope you feel the same.
—David Groth

I would like to thank David Groth for laying the foundation in earlier editions that could so easily grow into the modernized work you now hold, based on CompTIA's 2005 objectives for the prized and respected Network+ certification. Thanks also to David for his valuable work on this edition.

My gratitude and respect go out to the wise and professional Sybex team that brought this project together. Any author could shine with the care and polish provided by this wonderful group. A special thanks to Jeff Kellum for spearheading the production of our Study Guide. I really appreciate the support and unerring direction he provided.

I hope you will feel the way we do about this book. I know it will prove to be your most valuable resource in your quest for Network+ certification. Please let me know if there is anything additional you feel we could offer in future editions that will make the candidate's experience more successful and enjoyable. Don't hesitate to send your questions or comments to tskandier@hotmail.com. I am honored by your support for our efforts and hope you realize this book exists solely for you.
—Toby Skandier

# Contents at a Glance

# Contents

**Chapter    3    TCP/IP Fundamentals                              99**

# Introduction

If you are like the rest of the networking community, you probably have many certifications. Certification is one of the best things you can do for your career in the computer or networking field. It proves that you know what you're talking about when it comes to the area in which you are certified.

In this book, you'll find out what the Network+ exam is all about. Each chapter covers a part of the exam. At the end of each chapter, there are review questions to help you prepare for the exam.

# What Is the Network+ Certification?

Network+ is a certification developed by the Computing Technology Industry Association (CompTIA). This organization exists to provide resources and education for the computer and technology community. This is the same body that developed the A+ exam for computer technicians. Back in 1995, members of the organization convened to develop a new certification that tests skills for information technology (IT). To ensure industry-wide support, it was sponsored by many IT industry leaders, including the following:

- Compaq Computers
- Digital Equipment Corporation (a part of Compaq)
- IBM
- Lotus
- Microsoft
- Novell
- TSS
- U.S. Robotics
- US West
- Wave Technologies

The Network+ exam was designed to test the skills of network technicians with 18 to 24 months of experience in the field. It tests areas of networking technologies such as the definition of a protocol, the Open Systems Interconnect (OSI) model and its layers, and the concepts of network design and implementation—such as which items are required for a network and the prerequisites for installation. In addition, it covers troubleshooting concepts and how-tos.

# Why Become Network+ Certified?

The Network+ certification is a relatively new certification, but it is the next certification in a line of CompTIA certifications starting with the A+ certification. Because CompTIA is a well-respected developer of vendor-neutral industry certifications, getting Network+ certified indicates that you are competent in the specific areas tested by Network+.

Three major benefits are associated with becoming Network+ certified:

- Proof of professional achievement
- Opportunity for advancement
- Fulfillment of training requirements

## Proof of Professional Achievement

Networking professionals are competing these days to see who can get the most certifications. And because the Network+ certification is broad and it covers the entire field of networking, technicians want this certification rather than only Microsoft or only Novell, for example. Thus, it can be a challenge to prepare for the Network+ exam. Passing the exam, however, certifies that you have achieved a certain level of knowledge about vendor-independent networking-related subjects.

## Opportunity for Advancement

We all like to get ahead in our careers. With advancement comes more responsibility, to be sure, but usually it means more money and greater opportunities. In the information technology area, this usually can be accomplished by obtaining multiple technology certifications, including Network+.

Network+, because of its wide-reaching industry support, is recognized as a baseline of networking information. Some companies specify that Network+ certification will result in a pay raise at review time. And some companies specify that Network+ certification, in conjunction with A+ certification, is required either before an employee's next review or as a condition of employment.

## Fulfillment of Training Requirements

A training requirement can be mandated by your employer, as just mentioned, or it can be required as part of another certification. There has been talk of using the Network+ certification as a prerequisite to, or as part of, other vendors' certifications. And we think it's a natural fit. For example, training for both the Novell and the Microsoft certification programs (CNE and MCSE) includes a course in the essential networking technologies. Because the Network+ exam covers network fundamentals and is vendor neutral, it may be a good replacement for the Microsoft or the Novell exam.

# How to Become Network+ Certified

The simplest way to find out how to become Network+ certified is to take the exam. It is administered by Pearson VUE and Thomson Prometric, with which most of you are familiar if you have taken other computer certification exams, and it is administered by computer. To register to take the exam, call Thomson Prometric (not the testing center) at 888-895-6116 or Pearson VUE at 877-551-PLUS. You must pay for the exam at registration time with a major credit card (for example, Visa or MasterCard). Check CompTIA's website, as prices may vary.

 You can also register on the Internet through Pearson VUE at www.vue.com or through Thomson Prometric at www.prometric.com or www.2test.com.

The exam itself consists of approximately 72 questions. You have 90 minutes for the test. At the end of the exam, your score report will be displayed on the screen and printed so that you have a hard copy.

# Who Should Buy This Book?

If you are one of the many people who want to pass the Network+ exam, and pass it confidently, then you should buy this book and use it to study for the exam. The Network+ exam is designed to measure the technical knowledge of networking professionals with 18–24 months of experience in the IT industry. This book was written with two goals in mind: to prepare you for passing the Network+ exam, and to prepare you for the challenges of the real IT world. This Study Guide will do that by describing in detail the concepts on which you'll be tested.

# How to Use This Book and CD

This book includes several features that will make studying for the Network+ exam easier. At the beginning of the book (right after this introduction, in fact) is an assessment test that you can use to check your readiness for the actual exam. Take this test before you start reading the book. It will help you to determine the areas you may need to brush up on. You can then focus on these areas while reading the book. The answers to this test appear on a separate page after the last question. Each answer also includes an explanation and a note telling you in which chapter this material appears.

In addition, there are review questions at the end of each chapter. As you finish each chapter, answer the questions and then check your answers, which appear on the page after the last question. You can go back and reread the section in the chapter that deals with each question you got wrong to ensure that you know your stuff.

On the CD-ROM that is included with this book, there are several extras you can use to bolster your exam readiness:

**Electronic Flashcards**    You can use these flashcard-style questions to review your knowledge of Network+ concepts not only on your PC, but also on your handheld devices. You can download the questions right into your Palm device for quick and convenient reviewing anytime, anywhere, without your PC!

**Test Engine**    This portion of the CD-ROM includes all of the questions that appear in this book: the assessment questions at the end of this introduction, all of the chapter review questions, and two bonus exams.

**Full Text of the Book in PDF**    If you are going to travel but still need to study for the Network+ exam—and you have a laptop with a CD-ROM drive—you can take this entire book with you on the CD-ROM. This book is in PDF (Adobe Acrobat) format so it can be easily read on any computer.

# Exam Objectives

In this section, we are going to look at the objectives that the Network+ exam is designed to test. These objectives were developed by a group of networking-industry professionals through the use of an industry-wide job task analysis. CompTIA asked groups of IT professionals to fill out a survey rating the skills they felt were important in their job. The results were grouped into objectives for the exam. The objectives are grouped into four domains. The following table indicates the extent to which they are represented in the actual examination.

| Network+ Certification Domain Areas | % of Examination |
| --- | --- |
| 1.0 Media and Topologies | 20% |
| 2.0 Protocols and Standards | 20% |
| 3.0 Network Implementation | 25% |
| 4.0 Network Support | 35% |
| Total | 100% |

The following sections include the outline of the exam objectives for the Network+ exam and the weighting of each objective category.

The objectives and weighting percentages given in this section can change at any time. Check CompTIA's website at www.comptia.org for a list of the most current objectives.

# Domain 1.0 Media and Topologies (20%)

The objectives for this domain are as follows:

1.1 Recognize the following logical or physical network topologies given a diagram, schematic or description:

- Star
- Bus
- Mesh
- Ring

1.2 Specify the main features of 802.2 (Logical Link Control), 802.3 (Ethernet), 802.5 (Token Ring), 802.11(wireless), and FDDI (Fiber Distributed Data Interface) networking technologies, including:

- Speed
- Access method (CSMA/CA (Carrier Sense Multiple Access/Collision Avoidance) and CSMA/CD (Carrier Sense Multiple Access/Collision Detection))
- Topology
- Media

1.3 Specify the characteristics (For example: speed, length, topology, and cable type) of the following cable standards:

- 10BASE-T and 10BASE-FL
- 100BASE-TX and 100BASE-FX
- 1000BASE-T, 1000BASE-CX, 1000BASE-SX and 1000BASE-LX
- 10 GBASE-SR, 10 GBASE-LR and 10 GBASE-ER

1.4 Recognize the following media connectors and describe their uses:

- RJ-11 (Registered Jack)
- RJ-45 (Registered Jack)
- F-Type
- ST (Straight Tip)
- SC (Subscriber Connector or Standard Connector)
- IEEE 1394 (FireWire)
- Fiber LC (Local Connector)
- MT-RJ (Mechanical Transfer Registered Jack)
- USB (Universal Serial Bus)

1.5 Recognize the following media types and describe their uses:

- Category 3, 5, 5e, and 6
- UTP (Unshielded Twisted Pair)

- STP (Shielded Twisted Pair)
- Coaxial cable
- SMF (Single Mode Fiber) optic cable
- MMF (Multimode Fiber) optic cable

1.6 Identify the purposes, features and functions of the following network components:

- Hubs
- Switches
- Bridges
- Routers
- Gateways
- CSU/DSU (Channel Service Unit/Data Service Unit)
- NICs (Network Interface Card)
- ISDN (Integrated Services Digital Network) adapters
- WAPs (Wireless Access Point)
- Modems
- Transceivers (media converters)
- Firewalls

1.7 Specify the general characteristics (For example: carrier speed, frequency, transmission type and topology) of the following wireless technologies:

- 802.11 (Frequency hopping spread spectrum)
- 802.11$x$ (Direct sequence spread spectrum)
- Infrared
- Bluetooth

1.8 Identify factors which affect the range and speed of wireless service (For example: interference, antenna type and environmental factors).

## Domain 2.0 Protocols and Standards (20%)

The objectives for this domain are as follows:

2.1 Identify a MAC (Media Access Control) address and its parts.

2.2 Identify the seven layers of the OSI (Open Systems Interconnect) model and their functions.

2.3 Identify the OSI (Open Systems Interconnect) layers at which the following network components operate:

- Hubs
- Switches
- Bridges

- Routers
- NICs (Network Interface Card)
- WAPs (Wireless Access Point)

2.4 Differentiate between the following network protocols in terms of routing, addressing schemes, interoperability and naming conventions:

- IPX/SPX (Internetwork Packet eXchange/Sequence Packet eXchange)
- NetBEUI (Network Basic Input/Output System Extended User Interface)
- AppleTalk/AppleTalk over IP (Internet Protocol)
- TCP/IP (Transmission Control Protocol/Internet Protocol)

2.5 Identify the components and structure of IP (Internet Protocol) addresses (IPv4, IPv6) and the required settings for connections across the Internet.

2.6 Identify classful IP (Internet Protocol) ranges and their subnet masks (For example: Class A, B and C).

2.7 Identify the purpose of subnetting.

2.8 Identify the differences between private and public network addressing schemes.

2.9 Identify and differentiate between the following IP (Internet Protocol) addressing methods:

- Static
- Dynamic
- Self-assigned (APIPA (Automatic Private Internet Protocol Addressing))

2.10 Define the purpose, function and use of the following protocols used in the TCP/IP (Transmission Control Protocol/Internet Protocol) suite:

- TCP (Transmission Control Protocol)
- UDP (User Datagram Protocol)
- FTP (File Transfer Protocol)
- SFTP (Secure File Transfer Protocol)
- TFTP (Trivial File Transfer Protocol)
- SMTP (Simple Mail Transfer Protocol)
- HTTP (Hypertext Transfer Protocol)
- HTTPS (Hypertext Transfer Protocol Secure)
- POP3/IMAP4 (Post Office Protocol, version 3/Internet Message Access Protocol, version 4)
- Telnet
- SSH (Secure Shell)
- ICMP (Internet Control Message Protocol)
- ARP/RARP (Address Resolution Protocol/Reverse Address Resolution Protocol)

- NTP (Network Time Protocol)
- NNTP (Network News Transport Protocol)
- SCP (Secure Copy Protocol)
- LDAP (Lightweight Directory Access Protocol)
- IGMP (Internet Group Multicast Protocol)
- LPR (Line Printer Remote)

2.11 Define the function of TCP/UDP (Transmission Control Protocol/User Datagram Protocol) ports.

2.12 Identify the well-known ports associated with the following commonly used services and protocols:

- 20 FTP (File Transfer Protocol)
- 21 FTP (File Transfer Protocol)
- 22 SSH (Secure Shell)
- 23 Telnet
- 25 SMTP (Simple Mail Transfer Protocol)
- 53 DNS (Domain Name Service)
- 69 TFTP (Trivial File Transfer Protocol)
- 80 HTTP (Hypertext Transfer Protocol)
- 110 POP3 (Post Office Protocol, version 3)
- 119 NNTP (Network News Transport Protocol)
- 123 NTP (Network Time Protocol)
- 143 IMAP4 (Internet Messaging Application Protocol, version 4)
- 443 HTTPS (Hypertext Transfer Protocol Secure)

2.13 Identify the purpose of network services and protocols (For example: DNS (Domain Name Service), NAT (Network Address Translation), ICS (Internet Connection Sharing), WINS (Windows Internet Name Service), SNMP (Simple Network Management Protocol), NFS (Network File System), Zeroconf (Zero configuration), SMB (Server Message Block), AFP (Apple File Protocol), LPD (Line Printer Daemon) and Samba).

2.14 Identify the basic characteristics (For example: speed, capacity and media) of the following WAN (Wide Area Networks) technologies:

- Packet switching
- Circuit switching
- ISDN (Integrated Services Digital Network)
- FDDI (Fiber Distributed Data Interface)
- T1 (T Carrier level 1)/E1/J1
- T3 (T Carrier level 3)/E3/J3

- OCx (Optical Carrier)
- X.25

2.15 Identify the basic characteristics of the following Internet access technologies:

- xDSL (Digital Subscriber Line)
- Broadband Cable (Cable modem)
- POTS/PSTN (plain old telephone service/Public Switched Telephone Network)
- Satellite
- Wireless

2.16 Define the function of the following remote access protocols and services:

- RAS (Remote Access Service)
- PPP (Point-to-Point Protocol)
- SLIP (Serial Line Internet Protocol)
- PPPoE (Point-to-Point Protocol over Ethernet)
- PPTP (Point-to-Point Tunneling Protocol)
- VPN (Virtual Private Network)
- RDP (Remote Desktop Protocol)

2.17 Identify the following security protocols and describe their purpose and function:

- IPSec (Internet Protocol Security)
- L2TP (Layer 2 Tunneling Protocol)
- SSL (Secure Sockets Layer)
- WEP (Wired Equivalent Privacy)
- WPA (Wi-Fi Protected Access)
- 802.1x

2.18 Identify authentication protocols (For example: CHAP (Challenge Handshake Authentication Protocol), MS-CHAP (Microsoft Challenge Handshake Authentication Protocol), PAP (Password Authentication Protocol), RADIUS (Remote Authentication Dial-In User Service), Kerberos and EAP (Extensible Authentication Protocol)).

# Domain 3.0 Network Implementation (25%)

The objectives for this domain are as follows:

3.1 Identify the basic capabilities (For example: client support, interoperability, authentication, file and print services, application support and security) of the following server operating systems to access network resources:

- UNIX/Linux/Mac OS X Server
- NetWare

- Windows
- AppleShare IP (Internet Protocol)

3.2 Identify the basic capabilities needed for client workstations to connect to and use network resources (For example: media, network protocols and peer and server services).

3.3 Identify the appropriate tool for a given wiring task (For example: wire crimper, media tester/certifier, punch down tool or tone generator).

3.4 Given a remote connectivity scenario comprised of a protocol, an authentication scheme, and physical connectivity, configure the connection. Includes connection to the following servers:

- UNIX/Linux/MAC OS X Server
- NetWare
- Windows
- AppleShare IP (Internet Protocol)

3.5 Identify the purpose, benefits and characteristics of using a firewall.

3.6 Identify the purpose, benefits and characteristics of using a proxy service.

3.7 Given a connectivity scenario, determine the impact on network functionality of a particular security implementation (For example: port blocking/filtering, authentication and encryption).

3.8 Identify the main characteristics of VLANs (Virtual Local Area Networks).

3.9 Identify the main characteristics and purpose of extranets and intranets.

3.10 Identify the purpose, benefits and characteristics of using antivirus software.

3.11 Identify the purpose and characteristics of fault tolerance:

- Power
- Link redundancy
- Storage
- Services

3.12 Identify the purpose and characteristics of disaster recovery:

- Backup/restore
- Offsite storage
- Hot and cold spares
- Hot, warm and cold sites

# Domain 4.0 Network Support (35%)

The objectives for this domain are as follows:

4.1 Given a troubleshooting scenario, select the appropriate network utility from the following:

- Tracert/traceroute
- ping
- arp
- netstat
- nbtstat
- ipconfig/ifconfig
- winipcfg
- nslookup/dig

4.2 Given output from a network diagnostic utility (For example: those utilities listed in objective 4.1), identify the utility and interpret the output.

4.3 Given a network scenario, interpret visual indicators (For example: link LEDs (Light Emitting Diode) and collision LEDs (Light Emitting Diode)) to determine the nature of a stated problem.

4.4 Given a troubleshooting scenario involving a client accessing remote network services, identify the cause of the problem (For example: file services, print services, authentication failure, protocol configuration, physical connectivity and SOHO (Small Office/Home Office) router).

4.5 Given a troubleshooting scenario between a client and the following server environments, identify the cause of a stated problem:

- UNIX/Linux/Mac OS X Server
- NetWare
- Windows
- AppleShare IP (Internet Protocol)

4.6 Given a scenario, determine the impact of modifying, adding or removing network services (For example: DHCP (Dynamic Host Configuration Protocol), DNS (Domain Name Service) and WINS (Windows Internet Name Service)) for network resources and users.

4.7 Given a troubleshooting scenario involving a network with a particular physical topology (For example: bus, star, mesh or ring) and including a network diagram, identify the network area affected and the cause of the stated failure.

4.8 Given a network troubleshooting scenario involving an infrastructure (For example: wired or wireless) problem, identify the cause of a stated problem (For example: bad media, interference, network hardware or environment).

4.9 Given a network problem scenario, select an appropriate course of action based on a logical troubleshooting strategy. This strategy can include the following steps:

1. Identify the symptoms and potential causes
2. Identify the affected area
3. Establish what has changed
4. Select the most probable cause
5. Implement an action plan and solution including potential effects
6. Test the result
7. Identify the results and effects of the solution
8. Document the solution and process

# Good Luck!

Here are a few things to remember when taking your test:

- Get a good night's sleep before the exam.
- Bring two forms of ID with you. One form must be a photo ID, such as a driver's license. The other can be a major credit card or a passport. Both forms must have a signature.
- Take your time on each question. Don't rush.
- Arrive at the testing center a few minutes early so that you can review your notes.
- Answer all questions, even if you don't know the answer. Unanswered or blank questions are considered wrong. On-screen help allows you to mark a question for answering later or reviewing a previous question.
- There will be questions with multiple correct responses. When there are multiple correct answers, a message at the bottom of the screen will prompt you to "choose all that apply." Be sure to read the messages.
- Read each question twice and make sure you understand it.

Good luck on your Network+ exam and in your future in the IT industry.

# Assessment Test for Network+ Exam

1. Which TCP/IP utility can tell you which server is the mail server for the domain foo.com?

   **A.** FTP

   **B.** nslookup

   **C.** tracert

   **D.** Telnet

2. A user we'll call Bob is experiencing what he calls "weird problems." The computer is constantly crashing and performs very slowly. In addition, people are sending Bob e-mails asking him to stop sending them e-mails when, in fact, he hasn't sent them any in months. What is the most likely cause of this problem?

   **A.** Corrupt operating system

   **B.** Corrupt application software

   **C.** Virus infection

   **D.** Network bottlenecks

3. RSA is a type of which of the following?

   **A.** Data encryption

   **B.** Network protocol

   **C.** Purchase agreement

   **D.** Firewall

4. What is the proper name for the device that connects a PC to an ISDN network?

   **A.** Hub

   **B.** Modem

   **C.** Switch

   **D.** Terminal adapter

5. Which utility does *not* come with Windows 2000?

   **A.** winipcfg

   **B.** tracert

   **C.** Ping

   **D.** ipconfig

6. VLANs are a feature primarily of which type of network device?

   **A.** Hubs

   **B.** Switches

   **C.** NICs

   **D.** Cable

7. Firewalls provide what primary benefit?

   **A.** Increased network performance

   **B.** Elimination of user training

   **C.** Protection from threats on the Internet

   **D.** Complete network security

8. Which part of a network interface card (NIC) identifies whether or not there is basic connectivity from the station to a hub or a switch?

   **A.** Link light

   **B.** Collision light

   **C.** Port

   **D.** Jumper

9. What is the name of the distance vector routing protocol for AppleTalk?

   **A.** RIP

   **B.** OSPF

   **C.** NLSP

   **D.** RTMP

10. Which version is the most current Windows server operating system?

    **A.** Windows NT 3.51

    **B.** Windows NT 4.0

    **C.** Windows 2000 Server

    **D.** Windows Server 2003

11. You are the network administrator for a small company. You come to work one morning and find that the server fails to boot. When it does boot, it has all kinds of configuration errors and data corruption. It was fine yesterday when you left work. You remember that there was a short power failure last night. What device would have prevented these problems?

    **A.** Router

    **B.** Switch

    **C.** NIC

    **D.** UPS

12. IP version 6 (IPv6) uses how many bits in its addressing scheme?

    **A.** 16

    **B.** 32

    **C.** 64

    **D.** 128

**13.** Which of the following network operating systems support(s) the most varied types of client operating systems? (Choose all that apply.)

   **A.** NetWare

   **B.** Unix

   **C.** Windows NT

   **D.** OS/2

**14.** Which network installation tool can be used to connect UTP cable to a 110 block?

   **A.** Cable tester

   **B.** Wire crimper

   **C.** Media installer

   **D.** Punchdown tool

**15.** Which remote access protocol is used to allow remote application execution?

   **A.** PPP

   **B.** PPTP

   **C.** ICA

   **D.** RAS

**16.** Which network device is used to connect dissimilar network technologies at any level of the OSI model?

   **A.** Bridge

   **B.** Router

   **C.** Switch

   **D.** Gateway

**17.** At which level of the OSI model does routing occur?

   **A.** Application

   **B.** Network

   **C.** Data Link

   **D.** Physical

**18.** Which of the following is an example of an IPv6 address?

   **A.** ::000F:ABCD:0003

   **B.** 123456.132455.119499.201333.111111.010111

   **C.** 134.129.51.99

   **D.** 275.13.202.100

**19.** You are the administrator for a 10-station peer-to-peer network that is connected to the Internet. All of the workstations are running TCP/IP, and the server is running IPX/SPX. Unfortunately, your network is having a problem: None of the users can connect to the server. The server can see itself on the network. What do you suspect is the problem?

   **A.** A hacker has changed addresses on the server.

   **B.** The clients' NICs are configured incorrectly.

   **C.** The server is using an incorrect protocol.

   **D.** The Internet connection is configured incorrectly.

**20.** The process of grouping computers for fault tolerance and load balancing is known as _____ _____.

   **A.** grouping

   **B.** clustering

   **C.** loading

   **D.** parceling

**21.** What additional item is required to connect a PC to a DSL modem?

   **A.** NIC

   **B.** Modem

   **C.** Terminal adapter

   **D.** Switch

**22.** Which port number is used for DNS?

   **A.** TCP port 10

   **B.** UDP port 23

   **C.** TCP port 29

   **D.** UDP port 53

**23.** Which Windows operating system(s) has/have local file system security? (Choose all that apply.)

   **A.** Windows 9*x*

   **B.** Windows NT

   **C.** Windows 2000/2003

   **D.** Windows 3.1

**24.** An ISDN B channel typically carries how much data?

   **A.** 4Kbps

   **B.** 16Kbps

   **C.** 32Kbps

   **D.** 64Kbps

**25.** Which network security implementation will decrease the apparent speed of Internet access?

   **A.** Password requirement

   **B.** Firewall

   **C.** Proxy server

   **D.** Blocking the ICMP port

**26.** Which network setting in Windows $9x$ configures a workstation for DHCP?

   **A.** Obtain IP Address Automatically

   **B.** DHCP Enable

   **C.** Use DHCP for Address

   **D.** Get IP Address through DHCP

**27.** Of those listed, which Internet connection type has the most bandwidth?

   **A.** OC-3

   **B.** ISDN

   **C.** T1

   **D.** POTS

**28.** Which protocol is primarily used to provide TCP/IP over dial-up Internet connections?

   **A.** PPP

   **B.** ICA

   **C.** RAS

   **D.** SONET

**29.** Windows 2000 Server has support for which of the following clients?

   **A.** Windows $9x$

   **B.** Macintosh

   **C.** Linux

   **D.** All of the above

**30.** An HTTP proxy cache server will increase the apparent performance of what activity?

   **A.** Bank transactions

   **B.** Web browsing

   **C.** Network login

   **D.** Screen refreshes

# Answers to Assessment Test for Network+ Exam

**1.** B. The only utility listed that can tell which server is acting as the mail exchanger for a domain is the nslookup utility. This is done by setting the query type to MX (mail exchanger). Nslookup will then return the name and IP address of the mail exchanger for the domain foo.com. Please see Chapter 4 for more information.

**2.** C. Many viruses can wreak havoc with a computer system. Many viruses exhibit the behavior described, especially sending e-mails automatically to many people in the infectee's address book. Please see Chapter 9 for more information.

**3.** A. RSA is a type of data encryption used to encrypt data before transmission. Please see Chapter 8 for more information.

**4.** D. Because an ISDN network is an all-digital network, it doesn't use modems but instead uses terminal adapters because they adapt the digital signal from one form to another. Please see Chapter 1 for more information.

**5.** A. The winipcfg utility does not come with Windows 2000 but was instead the IP configuration utility for Windows 9x. All the other utilities come as part of Windows 2000. Please see Chapter 4 for more information.

**6.** B. Virtual LANs are primarily a feature of network switches. Because most true hubs cannot perform segmentation based on MAC addresses, they cannot do VLANs. Although NICs are required in order to use a VLAN, VLANs are not a primary feature of them. And individual cables do not have VLAN features. Please see Chapter 3 for more information.

**7.** C. Firewalls sit between a local network and a public network (such as the Internet) and protect the local network from security threats. It is only a part of a network's security implementation, but a very important part. Please see Chapter 8 for more information.

**8.** A. The link light, when lit, indicates that there is a basic communication between a NIC and a hub or switch (it would also light if two NICs in two different PCs were connected with a cross-over cable). If the cable is severed or wired incorrectly, the link light may not light. Please see Chapter 10 for more information.

**9.** D. AppleTalk uses the Routing Table Maintenance Protocol (RTMP), which is a distance vector routing protocol. RIP is the distance vector protocol for both IP and IPX; OSPF is the link state protocol for TCP/IP; and NLSP is the link state routing protocol for IPX/SPX. Please see Chapter 2 for more information.

**10.** D. Windows Server 2003 is the most current version of a Windows server operating system. Please see Chapter 5 for more information.

**11.** D. The problems are due to the power outage. An Uninterruptible Power Supply (UPS) maintains power to a device that is plugged into it during a power outage. Since the outage was short, it is very likely that a UPS could have maintained power to the server during the outage. If not, it could have at least performed an orderly shutdown of the server. Please see Chapter 9 for more information.

**12.** D.  Because one of the main motivations behind the creation of the IPv6 addressing scheme was the lack of available addresses in IPv4, the length of the address was increased from 32 bits in IPv4 to 128 bits in IPv6. Please see Chapter 3 for more information.

**13.** A, C.  Although all of the NOSes listed can support different client OSes, NetWare and Windows NT support the widest variety of client OSes. Please see Chapter 5 for more information.

**14.** D.  A 110 block is also known as a punchdown block because of its method of installation. Thus, the tool used to install one is a punchdown tool with a 110 blade. Please see Chapter 6 for more information.

**15.** C.  ICA is used with Terminal Server servers to allow remote application execution. The other protocols are used to provide remote access to a host network. Please see Chapter 7 for more information.

**16.** D.  Gateways operate at all levels of the OSI model and connect dissimilar network technologies. While some of the other devices listed may connect dissimilar network technologies, they all operate at only the lower four layers of the OSI model. Please see Chapter 6 for more information.

**17.** B.  The responsibilities of the Network layer include logical network addressing and routing. The Application, Data Link, and Physical layers do not provide any routing functionality. Please see Chapter 2 for more information.

**18.** A.  The only address that is correct is ::000F:ABCD:0003. Option C is an IPv4 address and the other two are bogus addresses. Please see Chapter 3 for more information.

**19.** C.  The server is configured to run only IPX/SPX, but the clients are using only TCP/IP. Changing the protocol to TCP/IP on the server would solve the problem. Please see Chapter 10 for more information.

**20.** B.  Clustering is the method by which multiple copies of a server run together. The load is balanced across all of them. If one should happen to fail, the others continue to run as if nothing happened. Please see Chapter 9 for more information.

**21.** A.  Because DSL operates at speeds higher than typical serial port speeds, a NIC is required in order for the PC to communicate with the DSL modem. None of the other items are required. Please see Chapter 1 for more information.

**22.** D.  UDP (*not* TCP) port 53 is used for DNS. All others, while possibly valid port numbers, are not used for DNS. Please see Chapter 3 for more information.

**23.** B, C.  Because Windows NT and 2000/2003 use NTFS, which has local security properties, they have those properties as well. Please see Chapter 5 for more information.

**24.** D.  An ISDN B channel, or Bearer channel, typically carries 64Kbps. Please see Chapter 7 for more information.

**25.** B.  Because a firewall generally examines every packet and acts on the information in that packet, Internet access will seem to be slower. The other options either have no effect or will increase the apparent speed. Please see Chapter 8 for more information.

**26.** A.   Although all of these answers are saying similar things, the only setting that exists in Windows 9*x* is Obtain IP Address Automatically. Please see Chapter 6 for more information.

**27.** A.   OC-3 has a potential bandwidth of 155Mbps; T1 has a throughput of 1.544Mbps; ISDN is 1.544Mbps; and POTS has 53Kbps. Please see Chapter 7 for more information.

**28.** A.   Of the protocols listed, only the Point-to-Point Protocol (PPP) provides TCP/IP Internet connections over dial-up (modem) connections. Please see Chapter 7 for more information.

**29.** D.   Windows 2000 Server supports many different types of clients, including Windows, Macintosh, and Linux-based clients. Please see Chapter 5 for more information.

**30.** B.   An HTTP proxy cache will cache (or store temporarily) copies of commonly used web page elements on a server on your LAN, thus the common elements will be received directly from the proxy at LAN speeds instead of Internet speeds. Please see Chapter 8 for more information.

# Chapter 1

# Network Fundamentals

---

## THE FOLLOWING NETWORK+ EXAM OBJECTIVES ARE COVERED IN THIS CHAPTER:

✓ **1.1 Recognize the following logical or physical network topologies given a diagram, schematic, or description:**

- Star
- Bus
- Mesh
- Ring

✓ **1.2 Specify the main features of 802.2 (Logical Link Control), 802.3 (Ethernet), 802.5 (Token Ring), 802.11 (wireless), and Fiber Distributed Data Interface (FDDI) networking technologies, including:**

- Speed
- Access method (CSMA/CA [Carrier Sense Multiple Access/Collision Avoidance] and CSMA/CD [Carrier Sense Multiple Access / Collision Detection])
- Topology
- Media

✓ **1.3 Specify the characteristics (for example, speed, length, topology, and cable type) of the following cable standards:**

- 10Base-T and 10Base-FL
- 100Base-TX and 100Base-FX
- 1000Base-TX, 1000Base-CX, 1000Base-SX, and 1000BASE-LX
- 10GBase-SR, 10GBase-LR, and 10GBase-ER

✓ **1.4 Recognize the following media connectors and describe their uses:**

- RJ-11 (Registered Jack)
- RJ-45 (Registered Jack)
- F-Type

- ST (straight tip)
- SC (subscriber connector)
- IEEE1394 (FireWire)
- LC (local connector)
- MTRJ (Mechanical Transfer Registered Jack)
- USB (Universal Serial Bus)

✓ **1.5 Recognize the following media types and describe their uses:**

- Category 3, 5, 5e, and 6
- UTP (unshielded twisted-pair)
- STP (shielded twisted-pair)
- Coaxial cable
- SMF (single-mode fiber) optic cable
- MMF (multimode fiber) optic cable

✓ **1.6 Identify the purposes, features, and functions of the following network components:**

- Hubs
- Switches
- Bridges
- Routers
- Gateways
- CSU/DSU (Channel Service Unit/Data Service Unit)
- NICs (network interface cards)
- ISDN (Integrated Services Digital Network) adapters
- WAPs (wireless access points)
- Modems
- Transceivers (media converters)
- Firewalls

✓ **3.2 Identify the basic capabilities needed for client workstations to connect to and use network resources (for example, media, network protocols, and peer and server services).**

By themselves, computers are powerful tools. When they are connected in a network, they become even more powerful because the functions and tools that each computer provides can be shared with other computers. Networks exist for one major reason: to share information and resources.

Networks can be very simple, such as a small group of computers that share information, or they can be very complex, spanning large geographical areas. Regardless of the type of network, a certain amount of maintenance is always required. Because each network is different and probably utilizes many diverse technologies, it is important to understand the fundamentals of networking and how networking components interact.

This chapter will introduce the components of a network and help you establish a base of knowledge that you can use throughout your networking studies, as well as help you prepare for the Network+ certification exam.

# Network Elements

In the computer world, the term *network* describes two or more connected computers that can share resources such as data, a printer, an Internet connection, applications, or a combination of these. In the following sections, we'll discuss each type of network and describe the situation that is most appropriate for its use.

## Local Area Network

By definition, a *local area network (LAN)* is limited to a specific area, usually an office, and cannot extend beyond the boundaries of a single building. The first LANs were limited to a range (from a central point to the most distant computer) of 185 meters (about 600 feet) and no more than 30 computers. Today's technology allows a larger LAN, but practical administration limitations require dividing it into small, logical areas called workgroups.

A *workgroup* is a collection of individuals (a sales department, for example) who share the same files and databases over the LAN. Figure 1.1 shows an example of a small LAN and its workgroups.

**FIGURE 1.1**    A small LAN

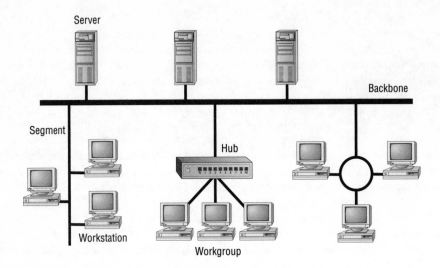

# Wide Area Network

Chances are you are an experienced *wide area network (WAN)* user and don't even know it. If you have ever connected to the Internet, you have used the largest WAN on the planet. A WAN is any network that crosses metropolitan, regional, or national boundaries. Most networking professionals define a WAN as any network that uses routers and public network links. The Internet fits both definitions.

WANs differ from LANs in the following ways:

- WANs cover greater distances.

- WAN speeds are slower.

- WANs can be connected on demand or permanently connected; LANs have permanent connections between stations.

- WANs can use public or private network transports; LANs primarily use private network transports.

- WANs can use either full- or half-duplex communications. LANs have typically used half-duplex communications, although many local area networks today use full-duplex communications (see the sidebar "Full-Duplex vs. Half-Duplex Communications").

The Internet is actually a specific type of WAN. The Internet is a collection of networks that are interconnected and, therefore, is technically an *internetwork* (*Internet* is short for the word *internetwork*).

A WAN can be centralized or distributed. A centralized WAN consists of a central computer (at a central site) to which other computers and dumb terminals connect. The Internet, on the other hand, consists of many interconnected computers in many locations. Thus, it is a distributed WAN.

---

**Full-Duplex vs. Half-Duplex Communications**

All network communications (including LAN and WAN communications) can be categorized as half-duplex or full-duplex. With half-duplex, communications happen in both directions, but in only one direction at a time. When two computers communicate using half-duplex, one computer sends a signal and the other receives; then, at some point, they switch sending and receiving roles. Chances are that you are familiar with half-duplex communications. If you have ever used a push-to-talk technology, such as a CB radio or walkie-talkie, you were communicating via half-duplex: One person talks, and then the other person talks.

Full-duplex, on the other hand, allows communication in both directions simultaneously. Both stations can send and receive signals at the same time. Full-duplex communications are similar to a telephone call, in which both people can talk simultaneously.

---

# Host, Workstation, and Server

Networks are made up of lots of different components, but the three most common network entities are the host, workstation, and server. For the Network+ exam, you need a good understanding of these three primary components of a network. Each one of these items can be found on most networks.

## Understanding Workstations

In the classic sense, a *workstation* is a powerful computer used for drafting or other math-intensive applications. The term is also applied to a computer that has multiple central processing units (CPUs) available to users. In the network environment, the term *workstation* normally refers to any computer that is connected to the network and used by an individual to do work.

It is important to distinguish between workstations and clients. A *client* is any network entity that can request resources from the network; a workstation is a computer that can request resources. Workstations can be clients, but not all clients are workstations. For example, a printer can request resources from the network, but it is a client, not a workstation.

## Understanding Servers

In the truest sense, a *server* does exactly what the name implies: It provides resources to the clients on the network ("serves" them, in other words). Servers are typically powerful computers that run the software that controls and maintains the network. This software is known as the *network operating system.*

We'll discuss this topic in detail in Chapter 3, "TCP/IP Fundamentals."

Servers are often specialized for a single purpose. This is not to say that a single server can't do many jobs, but, more often than not, you'll get better performance if you dedicate a server to a single task. Here are some examples of servers that are dedicated to a single task:

**File Server**    Holds and distributes files.

**Print Server**    Controls and manages one or more printers for the network.

**Proxy Server**    Performs a function on behalf of other computers. (*Proxy* means "on behalf of.")

**Application Server**    Hosts a network application.

**Web Server**    Holds and delivers web pages and other web content using the Hypertext Transfer Protocol (HTTP).

**Mail Server**    Hosts and delivers e-mail. It's the electronic equivalent of a post office.

**Fax Server**    Sends and receives faxes (via a special fax board) for the entire network without the need for paper.

**Remote Access Server**    Listens for inbound requests to connect to the network from the outside. Remote access servers provide remote users (working at home or on the road) with a connection to the network, either via modems or an IP connection.

**Telephony Server**    Functions as a "smart" answering machine for the network. It can also perform call center and call-routing functions.

Notice that each server type's name consists of the type of service the server provides (remote access, for example) followed by the word *server*, which, as you remember, means to serve.

Regardless of the specific role (or roles) these servers play, they should all have the following in common:

- Hardware and/or software for data integrity (such as backup hardware and software)

- The capability to support a large number of clients

Figure 1.1, earlier in this chapter, shows a sample network. Physical resources, such as hard-drive space and memory, must be greater in a server than in a workstation because the server needs to provide services to many clients. Also, a server should be located in a physically secure area. Figure 1.2 shows a sample network that includes both workstations and servers. Note that there are more workstations than servers because a few servers can serve network resources to hundreds of users simultaneously.

**WARNING**    If the physical access to a server is not controlled, you don't have security. Use this guideline: If anybody can touch it, it isn't secure. The value of the company data far exceeds the investment in computer hardware and software. We'll look at network security in detail in Chapter 8, "Network Access and Security."

**FIGURE 1.2**    A sample network including servers and workstations

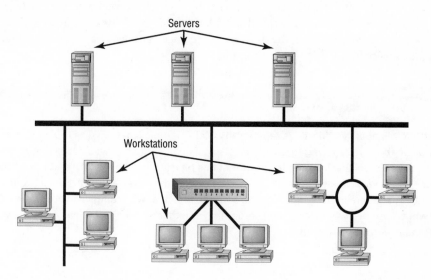

## Understanding Hosts

The term *host* covers pretty much every other networking device, but it can also refer to a workstation and server and is most commonly used when discussing TCP/IP-related services and functions. In fact, a host, in TCP/IP terms, is any network device that has an IP address. Workstations, servers, and any other network device (as long as it has one or more IP addresses) can all be considered hosts. In conversation, you may also hear the word *host* used to describe any minicomputer or server. For the Network+ exam, however, you should stick to the classic definition used here (i.e., workstations, servers, and other network devices).

The term *host* comes from the era when the only intelligent devices on the network were mainframes, which were commonly referred to as hosts regardless of TCP/IP functionality. Nearly all other devices were known as dumb terminals, but no other device had intelligence, only the mainframe. As TCP/IP came into the picture, only the mainframes, or hosts, received IP addresses. This is the same era that produced the term *gateway* to refer to any layer 3 intermediate device, such as a router. Just as the term *gateway* remains in common use today, such as in the very common term *default gateway,* the term *host* is still used, but its use is much broader now that nearly every end and intermediate device is intelligent and has at least one IP address, making them hosts.

## Peer-to-Peer vs. Client/Server Architecture

As you learned earlier in this chapter, the purpose of networking is to share resources. How this is accomplished depends on the architecture of the network operating system software. The two most common network types are peer-to-peer and client/server.

If you were to look at an illustration of a group of computers in a LAN, it would be impossible to determine if the network was a peer-to-peer or a client/server environment. Even a videotape of this same LAN during a typical workday would reveal few clues as to whether it is peer-to-peer or client/server. Yet, the differences are huge. Since you can't see the differences, you might guess correctly that they are not physical but logical.

---

### Physical vs. Logical Concepts

Throughout this book, you'll see us refer to physical and logical networking topics. Generally speaking, when we're referring to the physical aspects of a network, we're referring to some aspect of the network that you can touch or that has physical substance (like electrons, electrical pulses, or the way cables are run). That is, they exist in the physical world. Logical concepts, on the other hand, are more imaginary and esoteric and deal with things like how data flows in a network. So, when we're describing something as either physical or logical in nature, you'll understand how those terms apply.

---

## Peer-to-Peer Network

In *peer-to-peer networks*, the connected computers have no centralized authority. From an authority viewpoint, all of these computers are equal. In other words, they are peers. If a user of one computer wants access to a resource on another computer, the security check for access rights is the responsibility of the computer holding the resource.

Each computer in a peer-to-peer network can be both a client that requests resources and a server that provides resources. This is a great arrangement, provided the following conditions are met:

- Each user is responsible for local backup.
- Security considerations are minimal.
- A limited number of computers are involved.

Networks that run Windows 95/98 as their network operating system and networks using Windows NT, 2000, or XP in a workgroup are considered peer-to-peer networks. Figure 1.3 shows an example of a peer-to-peer network. Peer-to-peer networks present some challenges. For example, backing up company data becomes an iffy proposition. Also, it can be difficult to remember where you stored a file. Finally, because security is not centralized, users and passwords must be maintained separately on each machine, as you can see in Figure 1.3. Passwords may be different for the same users on different machines (or for different resources on Windows 9*x* machines).

## Client/Server Network

In contrast to a peer-to-peer network, a *client/server network* uses a network operating system designed to manage the entire network from a centralized point, which is the server. Clients make requests of the server, and the server responds with the information or access to a resource.

**FIGURE 1.3** A peer-to-peer network

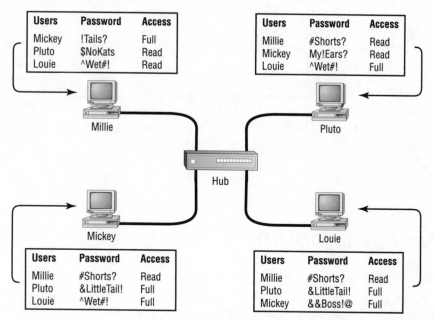

| Users | Password | Access |
|-------|----------|--------|
| Mickey | !Tails? | Full |
| Pluto | $NoKats | Read |
| Louie | ^Wet#! | Read |

| Users | Password | Access |
|-------|----------|--------|
| Millie | #Shorts? | Read |
| Mickey | My!Ears? | Read |
| Louie | ^Wet#! | Full |

Millie

Pluto

Hub

Mickey

Louie

| Users | Password | Access |
|-------|----------|--------|
| Millie | #Shorts? | Read |
| Pluto | &LittleTail! | Full |
| Louie | ^Wet#! | Full |

| Users | Password | Access |
|-------|----------|--------|
| Millie | #Shorts? | Read |
| Pluto | &LittleTail! | Full |
| Mickey | &&Boss!@ | Full |

Client/server networks have some definite advantages over peer-to-peer networks. For one thing, the network is much more organized. It is easier to find files and resources because they are stored on the server. Also, client/server networks generally have much tighter security. All usernames and passwords are stored in the same database (on the server), and individual users can't use the server as a workstation. Finally, client/server networks have better performance and can scale almost infinitely. It is not uncommon to see client/server networks with tens of thousands of workstations. Figure 1.4 shows a sample client/server network. Note that the server now holds the database of user accounts, passwords, and access rights.

Note that today's networks are very often hybrids of the peer-to-peer model and the client/server model. Clients of early Novell NetWare networks, for example, had no ability to share their resources, not that they had many worth sharing, for the most part. Conversely, today's Microsoft and Apple networks, for example, have well-defined servers. They also allow the simultaneous sharing of resources from lesser devices that run what are considered workstation operating systems, which are capable of fewer inbound connections but are running the server service nonetheless. Purists shun the less organized mixture of this resource sharing among servers and clients alike, but the reality is that most networks would be worse off for losing this capability.

**FIGURE 1.4**    A client/server network

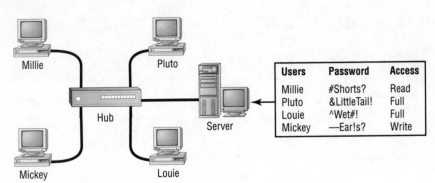

| Users | Password | Access |
|-------|----------|--------|
| Millie | #Shorts? | Read |
| Pluto | &LittleTail! | Full |
| Louie | ^Wet#! | Full |
| Mickey | —Ear!s? | Write |

# Physical Topologies

A topology is basically a map of a network. The physical topology of a network describes the layout of the cables and workstations and the location of all network components. Often, physical topologies are compared to logical topologies, which define how the information or data flows within the network. The topologies are usually similar. It is important to note, however, that a network can have one type of physical topology and a completely different logical topology. This was discussed earlier in the sidebar "Physical vs. Logical Concepts."

The cables or connections in a physical topology are often referred to as network media (or *physical media*). Choosing how computers will be connected in a company's network is critical. A wrong decision in the physical topology makes the media difficult to correct because it is costly and disruptive to change an entire installation once it is in place. The typical organization changes the physical layout and physical media of a network only once about every 10 years, so it is important to choose a configuration that you can live with and that allows for growth.

In the next section, we'll look at physical media. In the following sections, we'll look at the five most common topologies:

- Bus
- Star
- Ring
- Mesh

## Bus Topology

In a *bus topology,* all computers are attached to a single continuous cable that is terminated at both ends, which is the simplest way to create a physical network. Originally, computers were attached to the cable with wire taps. This did not prove practical, so drop cables were used to attach computers to the main cable. In 10Base-2 Ethernet, no drop cables are used, but instead, a "T" is inserted in the main cable wherever a station needs to connect. Figure 1.5 shows an example of a bus network. Notice how the cable runs from computer to computer with several bends and twists.

**FIGURE 1.5**    An example of a physical bus topology

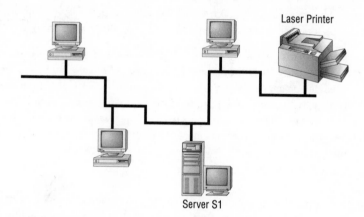

When communicating on a network that uses a bus topology, all computers see the data on the wire. This does not create chaos, though, because the only computer that actually accepts the data is the one to which it is addressed. You can think of a bus network as a small party. David is already there, along with 10 other people. David would like to tell Joe something. David yells out, "Joe! Will you grab me a cup of coffee, please?" Everyone in the party can hear David, but only Joe will respond. A star network with a hub, which you'll read about later, also operates in this manner.

As with most things, there are pros and cons to a bus topology. On the pro side, a bus topology has the following characteristics:

- Is simple to install
- Is relatively inexpensive
- Uses less cable than other topologies

The following characteristics describe the con side of a bus topology:

- Is difficult to move and change
- Has little fault tolerance (a single fault can bring down the entire network)
- Is difficult to troubleshoot

## Star Topology

Unlike those in a bus topology, each computer in a *star topology* is connected to a central point by a separate cable or wireless connection. The central point is a device known by such names as *hub, MAU, concentrator, switch,* and *access point,* depending on the underlying technology.

## Real World Scenario

### A bus sounds good, but . . .

Despite the simplicity of the bus topology, there are some inherent disadvantages to this design. For example, what happens if the wire breaks or is disconnected? Neither side can communicate with the other, and signal bounce occurs on both sides. The result is that the entire network is down. For this reason, bus topologies are considered to have very little fault tolerance.

Sometimes, because a cable is inside a wall, you cannot physically see a break. To determine if a break has occurred, you can use a tool known as a *Time Domain Reflectometer*, or *TDR* (also called a *cable tester*). This device sends out a signal and measures how much time it takes to return. Any break in the cable will cause some portion of the signal to return prematurely, thus indicating the presence of, and the distance to, a break in the cable. Programmed with the specifications of the cable being tested, it determines where the fault lies with a high degree of accuracy. We'll discuss cable testers in Chapter 6, "Wired and Wireless Networks."

Although this setup uses more cable than a bus, a star topology is much more fault tolerant than a bus topology. This means that if a failure occurs along one of the cables connecting to the hub, only that portion of the network is affected, not the entire network. Depending on the type of device at the other end of that cable, this may affect only a single device. It also means that you can add new stations just by running a single new cable. Figure 1.6 shows a typical star topology.

**FIGURE 1.6**    A typical star topology with a hub

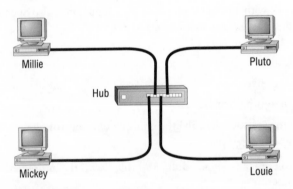

The design of a star topology resembles an old wagon wheel with the wooden spokes extending from the center point. The center point of the wagon wheel would be considered the hub. Like the wagon wheel, the network's most vulnerable point is the hub. If it fails, the whole system collapses. Fortunately, hub failures are extremely rare.

As with the bus topology, the star topology has advantages and disadvantages. The increasing popularity of the star topology is mainly due to the large number of advantages, which include the following:

- New stations can be added easily and quickly.
- A single cable failure won't bring down the entire network.
- It is *relatively* easy to troubleshoot.

The disadvantages of a star topology include the following:

- Total installation cost can be higher because of the larger number of cables, but prices are constantly becoming more and more competitive.
- It has a single point of failure (the hub, or other central device).

There are two subtle special cases for the star topology, the point-to-point link and the wireless access point. If you think of a point-to-point connection as one spoke of a star-wired network, with either end device able to play the role of the hub or spoke device, then you can begin to see the nature of any star-wired topology. What about when there is no wire, though? It takes a firm understanding of what the devices making up the wireless network are capable of to be able to categorize the wireless topology. Wireless access points, discussed in detail in Chapter 6, are nothing more than wireless hubs or switches, depending on capability, that are able to act as wireless bridges by establishing a wireless point-to-point connection to another wireless access point. Either use is reminiscent of the wired star/point-to-point topologies they emulate.

More information about wireless networking can be found in Chapter 6.

## Ring Topology

In the *ring topology,* each computer is connected directly to two other computers in the network. Data moves down a one-way path from one computer to another, as shown in Figure 1.7. The good news about laying out cable in a ring is that the cable design is simple. The bad news is that, as with bus topology, any break, such as adding or removing a computer, disrupts the entire network. Also, because you have to "break" the ring in order to add another station, it is very difficult to reconfigure without bringing down the whole network. For this reason, the physical ring topology is seldom used.

Although its name suggests a relationship, Token Ring does not use a physical ring topology. It instead uses a physical star, logical ring topology (and runs at speeds of either 4Mbps or 16Mbps). You will learn more about logical topologies later in this chapter.

**FIGURE 1.7**   A typical ring topology

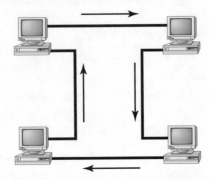

A few pros and many cons are associated with a ring topology. On the pro side, the ring topology is relatively easy to troubleshoot. A station will know when a cable fault has occurred because it will stop receiving data from its upstream neighbor.

On the con side, a ring topology has the following characteristics:

- Expensive, because multiple cables are needed for each workstation.
- Difficult to reconfigure.
- Not fault tolerant. A single cable fault can bring down the entire network.

## Mesh Topology

In a *mesh topology* (as shown in Figure 1.8), a path exists from each station to every other station in the network, resulting in the most physical connections per node of any topology. While not usually seen in LANs, a variation on this type of topology—the hybrid mesh—is used on the Internet and other WANs in a limited fashion. Hybrid mesh topology networks can have multiple connections between some locations, but this is done only for redundancy. In addition, it's called a hybrid because other types of toplogies might be mixed in as well. Also, it is not a full mesh because there is not a connection between each and every node, just a few for backup purposes. Notice in Figure 1.8 how complex the network becomes with four connections.

**FIGURE 1.8**   A typical mesh topology

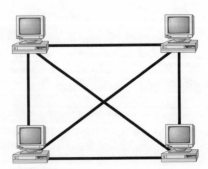

As you can see in Figure 1.8, a mesh topology can become quite complex as wiring and connections increase exponentially. For every *n* stations, you will have *n*(*n*–1)/2 connections. For example, in a network of 4 computers, you will have 4(4–1)/2 connections, or 6 connections. If your network grows to only 10 computers, you will have 45 connections to manage! Given this impossible overhead, only small systems can be connected this way. The payoff for all this work is a more fail-safe, or fault-tolerant, network, at least as far as cabling is concerned.

Today, the mesh topology is rarely used, and then only in a WAN environment and only because the mesh topology is fault tolerant. Computers or network devices can switch between these multiple, redundant connections if the need arises. On the con side, the mesh topology is expensive and, as you have seen, quickly becomes too complex. Using what is known as a partial mesh is a workable compromise between the need for fault tolerance and the cost of a full mesh topology. With a partial mesh, the same technology can be used between all devices, but not all devices are interconnected. Strategy becomes the name of the game when deciding which devices to interconnect.

## Backbones and Segments

With complex networks, we must have a way of intelligently identifying which part of the network we are discussing. For this reason, we commonly break networks into backbones and segments. Figure 1.9 shows a sample network and identifies the backbones and segments. You should refer to this figure when necessary as you read about backbones and segments.

**FIGURE 1.9**    Backbone and segments on a sample network

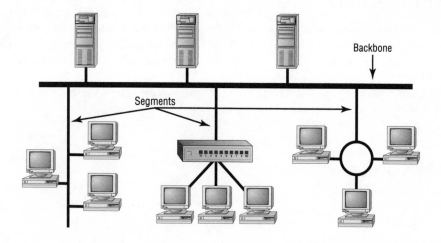

## Understanding the Backbone

A *backbone* is the part of the network to which all segments and servers connect. A backbone provides the structure for a network and is considered the main part of any network. It usually uses a high-speed communications technology of some kind, such as Fiber Distributed Data

Interface (FDDI) or 1 or 10 Gigabit Ethernet. All servers and all network segments typically connect directly to the backbone so that any segment is only one segment away from any server on that backbone. Because all segments are close to the servers, the network is more efficient. Notice in Figure 1.9 that the three servers and three segments connect to the backbone.

### Understanding Segments

*Segment* is a general term for any short section of the network that is not part of the backbone. Just as servers connect to the backbone, workstations connect to segments. Segments are connected to the backbone to allow the workstations on them access to the rest of the network. Figure 1.9 shows three segments.

## Selecting the Right Topology

Each topology has its advantages and drawbacks. The process of selecting a topology can be much like buying a pair of shoes. It's a matter of finding something that fits, feels right, and is within your budget. Instead of asking what your shoe size is, ask questions such as, How much fault tolerance is necessary? and How often will I need to reconfigure the network? Creating a simple network for a handful of computers in a single room is usually done most efficiently by using a wireless access point and wireless network cards because they are simple and easy to install and don'trequire the running of cables. Larger environments are usually wired in a star because moves, adds, and changes to the network are performed more efficiently with a physical star than with any of the other topologies.

If you need uptime to the definition of fault resistant (that is, 99.9-percent uptime or less than 8 hours total downtime per year), you should seriously consider a partial mesh layout. While you are thinking about how fault tolerant a full mesh network is, let the word *maintenance* enter your thoughts. Remember that you will have $n(n-1)/2$ connections to maintain in a full mesh configuration and a subset of that for a partial mesh, which will quickly become a nightmare and could exceed your maintenance budget.

Generally speaking, you should balance the following considerations when choosing a physical topology for your network:

- Cost
- Ease of installation
- Ease of maintenance
- Cable fault tolerance

# Physical Media

Although it is possible to use several forms of wireless networking, such as radio frequency and infrared, the majority of installed LANs today communicate via some sort of cable. In the following sections, we'll look at three types of cables:

- Coaxial
- Twisted pair
- Fiber optic

## Coaxial Cable

*Coaxial* cable (or *coax*) contains a center conductor, made of copper, surrounded by a plastic jacket, with a braided shield over the jacket. A plastic such as polyvinyl chloride (PVC) or fluoroethylenepropylene (FEP, such as DuPont's Teflon) covers this metal shield. The Teflon-type covering is frequently referred to as a *plenum-rated coating.* That simply means that the coating doesn't begin burning until a much higher temperature, doesn't release as many toxic fumes as PVC when it does burn, and is rated for use in air plenums that carry breathable air, usually as nonenclosed fresh-air return pathways that share space with cabling. This type of cable is more expensive but may be mandated by local or municipal fire code whenever cable is hidden in walls or ceilings. Plenum rating applies to all types of cabling and is an approved replacement for all other compositions of cable sheathing and insulation, such as PVC-based assemblies.

As a certified Network+ technician, you no longer need to concern yourself with the Thicknet and RG-58A/U (Radio Grade) types of coaxial cable, unless you would like to do your own research for historical or nostalgic purposes. Today, your focus should migrate from the 50ohm coax of early Ethernet to the 75ohm coax of early (and modern, of course) cable television. The reason for this is that while coax in the Ethernet world is all but a thing of the past, RG-6 or CATV coax is alive and well in the world of broadband cable (cable modem) technology. Chapter 7 will detail the location of 75ohm coaxial cable when used in a cable-modem system. The connectors used with coax in this environment are the same F-Type connectors used for standard cable television connectivity. In fact, the data rides on the same medium, just over different frequencies.

### Using Thin Ethernet

*Thin Ethernet*, also referred to as *Thinnet* or 10Base-2, is a thin coaxial cable. It is basically the same as thick coaxial cable except that the diameter of the cable is smaller (about $1/4''$ in diameter). Thin Ethernet coaxial cable is RG-58. Figure 1.10 shows an example of Thin Ethernet.

With Thinnet cable, you use *BNC* connectors (see Figure 1.11) to attach stations to the network. It is beyond my province to settle the long-standing argument over the meaning of the abbreviation BNC. BNC could mean BayoNet Connector, Bayonet Nut Connector, or British Navel Connector. But it is most commonly referred to as the Bayonet Neill-Concelman connector. What is relevant is that the BNC connector locks securely with a quarter-twist motion.

**FIGURE 1.10** A stripped-back Thinnet

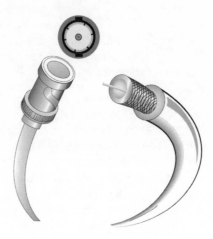

**FIGURE 1.11** A male and female BNC connector

Male

Female

The BNC connector can be attached to a cable in two ways. The first is with a crimper, which looks like funny pliers and has a die to crimp the connector. Pressing the levers crimps the connector to the cable. Choice number two is a screw-on connector, which is very unreliable. If at all possible, avoid the screw-on connector!

In order to attach the backbone cable run to each station, a passive device, known as a T-connector, is used. Picture the uncut backbone cable extending to the back of each device. In order to complete the connection, the cable needs to be cut at the point where the loop is closest to the interface. The two cut ends then need to be terminated with male BNC connectors and plugged into the two female BNC interfaces of the T-connector, with the third, male connector attaching to the female BNC interface on the device's NIC card. It is in violation of the standard to have any sort of drop cable extending from the back of the device, unlike 10Base-5, where such an attachment was customary. This requirement introduces a minimum of two caveats. The first is that any user that gains access to the back of their computer, and that wouldn't be very hard, could disconnect the connectorized ends of the cut backbone, thus producing two unterminated LAN segments, neither one working properly. The second is that so many interconnections introduce failure points and opportunities for noise introduction.

Table 1.1 shows some of the specifications for the different types of coaxial cable.

**TABLE 1.1**    Coaxial Cable Specifications

| RG Rating | Popular Name | Ethernet Implementation | Type of Cable |
|-----------|--------------|-------------------------|---------------|
| RG-58 U | N/A | None | Solid copper |
| RG-58 A/U | Thinnet | 10Base2 | Stranded copper |
| RG-8 | Thicknet | 10Base5 | Solid copper |
| RG-62 | ARCnet | N/A | Solid/stranded |

Although some great advantages are associated with using coax cable, such as the braided shielding that provides fair resistance to electronic pollution like *electromagnetic interference (EMI)* and *radio frequency interference (RFI)*, all types of stray electronic signals can make their way onto a network cable and cause communications problems. Understanding EMI and RFI is critical to your networking success. For this reason, we'll go into greater detail in Chapter 6.

## Using F-Type Connectors

The F-Type connector is a threaded, screw-on connector that differs from the BNC connector of early Ethernet mainly in its method of device attachment. Additionally, as alluded to earlier, you typically find F-Type connectors with 75ohm coaxial media and BNC connectors with 50ohm applications. As with most other coax applications, the F-Type connector uses the center conductor of the coaxial cable as its center connecting point. The other conductor is the metal body of the connector itself, which connects to the shield of the cable. Again, due to the popularity of cable modems, the F-Type coaxial connector has finally made its way into mainstream data networking. Figure 1.12 shows an example of an F-Type coaxial connector.

There is also a twist-on F-Type connector used in fiber-optic cabling, known as the FC connector.

**FIGURE 1.12**    An example of an F-Type coaxial cable connector

# Twisted-Pair Cable

Twisted-pair cable consists of multiple, individually insulated wires that are twisted together in pairs. Sometimes a metallic shield is placed around the twisted pairs. Hence, the name *shielded twisted-pair (STP)*. (You might see this type of cabling in Token Ring installations.) More commonly, you see cable without outer shielding; it's called *unshielded twisted-pair (UTP)*. UTP is commonly used in twisted-pair Ethernet (10Base-T, 100Base-TX, etc.), star-wired networks.

Let's take a look at why the wires in this cable type are twisted. When electromagnetic signals are conducted on copper wires that are in close proximity (such as inside a cable), some electromagnetic interference occurs. In this scenario, this interference is called *crosstalk*. Twisting two wires together as a pair minimizes such interference and also provides some protection against interference from outside sources. This cable type is the most common today. It is popular for several reasons:

- It's cheaper than other types of cabling.

- It's easy to work with.

- It permits transmission rates considered impossible 10 years ago.

UTP cable is rated in the following categories:

**Category 1**    Two twisted wire pairs (four wires). Voice grade (not rated for data communications). The oldest UTP. Frequently referred to as POTS, or plain old telephone service. Before 1983, this was the standard cable used throughout the North American telephone system. POTS cable still exists in parts of the Public Switched Telephone Network (PSTN). Supports signals limited to a frequency of 1MHz.

**Category 2**    Four twisted wire pairs (eight wires). Suitable for up to 4Mbps, with a frequency limitation of 10MHz.

**Category 3**    Four twisted wire pairs (eight wires) with three twists per foot. Acceptable for transmissions up to 16MHz. A popular cable choice since the mid-1980s, but now limited mainly to telecommunication equipment.

**Category 4**    Four twisted wire pairs (eight wires) and rated for 20MHz.

**Category 5**    Four twisted wire pairs (eight wires) and rated for 100MHz .

**Category 5e**   Four twisted wire pairs (eight wires) and rated for 100MHz, but capable of handling the disturbance on each pair caused by transmitting on all four pairs at the same time, which is needed for Gigabit Ethernet.

**Category 6**   Four twisted wire pairs (eight wires) and rated for 250MHz. Became a standard in June 2002.

Frequently, you will hear *Category* shortened to *Cat*. Today, any cable that you install should be a minimum of Cat 5e. This is a minimum because some cable is now certified to carry a bandwidth signal of 350MHz or beyond. This allows unshielded twisted-pair cables to exceed speeds of 1Gbps, which is fast enough to carry broadcast-quality video over a network. A common saying is that there are three ways to do things: the Right way, the Wrong way, and the IBM way. IBM uses types instead of categories when referring to TP (twisted-pair) cabling specifications. Even though a cabling type may seem to correspond to a cabling category (such as Type 1 and Category 1), the two are not the same; IBM defines its own specifications.

Now that you've learned the different types of UTP cables, you will learn how best to connect them to the various pieces of networking equipment using UTP.

 **Real World Scenario**

**Category 5e Cabling Tips**

If you expect data rates faster than 10Mbps over UTP, you should ensure that all components are rated to the category you want to achieve and be very careful when handling all components. For example, pulling too hard on Cat 5e cable will stretch the number of twists inside the jacket, rendering the Cat 5e label on the outside of the cable invalid. Also, be certain to connect and test all four pairs of wire. Although today's wiring usually uses only two pairs, or four wires, the standard for Gigabit Ethernet over UTP requires that all four pairs, or eight wires, be in good condition.

You should also be aware that a true Cat 5e cabling system uses rated components from end to end, patch cables from workstation to wall panel, cable from wall panel to patch panel, and patch cables from patch panel to hub. If any components are missing or if the lengths do not match the Category 5e specification, you don't have a Category 5e cabling installation. Also, installers should certify that the entire installation is Category 5e compliant. However, this requires very expensive test equipment that can make the appropriate measurements.

## Connecting UTP

Clearly, a BNC connector won't fit easily on UTP cable, so you need to use an *RJ (Registered Jack)* connector. You are probably familiar with RJ connectors. Most telephones connect with an RJ-11 connector. The connector used with UTP cable is called RJ-45. The RJ-11 has four wires, or two pairs, and the network connector RJ-45 (also known as an 8P8C connector when referring to the plug instead of the jack) has four pairs, or eight wires, as shown in Figure 1.13.

**FIGURE 1.13**　RJ-11 and RJ-45 connectors

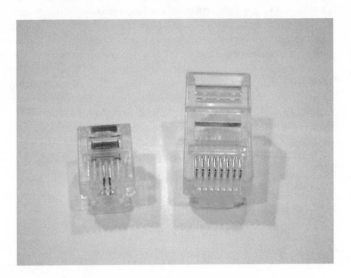

In almost every case, UTP uses RJ connectors. Even the now-extinct ARCnet used RJ connectors. You use a crimper to attach an RJ connector to a cable, just as you use a crimper with the BNC connector. The only difference is that the die that holds the connector is a different shape. Higher-quality crimping tools have interchangeable dies for both types of cables.

## Signaling Methods

The amount of a cable's available bandwidth (overall capacity, such as 10Mbps) that is used by each signal depends on whether the signaling method is baseband or broadband. With baseband, the entire bandwidth of the cable is used for each signal (using one channel). It is typically used with digital signaling. With broadband, on the other hand, the available bandwidth is divided into descrete bands. Multiple signals can then be transmitted within these different bands. Some form of tuning device, or demodulator, is required to choose the specific frequency of interest, as opposed to baseband receiving circuitry, which can be hardwired to a specific frequency. Don't confuse this *broadband* with the term that is the opposite of *narrowband*, which is any bit rate of T1 speeds (1.544Mbps) or slower. That *broadband* refers to speeds in excess of T1/E1 rates, such as Broadband-ISDN (B-ISDN), which has been developed under the ATM specifications.

## Ethernet Cable Descriptions

Ethernet cable types are described using a code that follows this format: *N<Signaling>-X*. Generally speaking, *N* is the signaling rate in megabits per second, and *<Signaling>* is the signaling type, which is either base or broad (baseband or broadband). *X* is a unique identifier for a specific Ethernet cabling scheme.

Let's use a generic example: 10BaseX. The two-digit number 10 indicates that the transmission speed is 10Mb, or 10 megabits. The value *X* can have different meanings. For example, the 5 in 10Base5 indicates the maximum distance that the signal can travel—500 meters. The 2 in 10Base2 is used the same way, but fudges the truth. The real limitation is 185 meters. Only the IEEE committee knows for sure what this was about. We can only guess that it's because 10Base2 seems easier to say than 10Base1.85.

Another 10Base standard is 10Base-T. The *T* is short for *twisted-pair*. This is the standard for running 10-Megabit Ethernet over two pairs (four wires) of Category 4, 5e, or 6 UTP. The fourth, and currently final, 10Base is 10Base-FL. The *F* is short for *fiber,* while the *L* stands for *link*. 10Base-FL is the standard for running 10-Megabit Ethernet over fiber-optic cable to the desktop. Table 1.2, shown a bit later, summarizes this data.

Similarly, there are also standards for 100Base, 1000Base, and 10GBase cabling. Let's take a closer look at these standards:

**100Base-TX**   As network applications increased in complexity, so did their bandwidth requirements. Ten-megabit technologies were too slow. Businesses were clamoring for a higher speed standard so that their data could be transmitted at an acceptable rate of speed. A 100-megabit standard was needed. Thus the 100Base-TX standard was developed.

The 100Base-TX standard is a standard for Ethernet transmission at a data rate of 100Mbps. This Ethernet standard is also known as *Fast Ethernet*. It uses two UTP pairs (four wires) in a minimum of Category 5 UTP cable.

**1000Base-TX**   1000Base-TX, most commonly known as Gigabit Ethernet, allows 1000Mbps throughput on standard twisted-pair, copper cable (rated at Category 5e or higher).

**1000Base-SX**   The implementation of Gigabit Ethernet running over multimode fiber-optic cable (instead of copper, twisted-pair cable) and using short wavelength laser.

**1000Base-LX**   The implementation of Gigabit Ethernet over single-mode and multimode fiber using long wavelength laser.

**1000Base-CX**   An implementation of Gigabit Ethernet over balanced, 150ohm copper cabling and uses a special 9-pin connector known as the *High Speed Serial Data Connector (HSSDC)*.

**10GBase-SR**   An implementation of 10 Gigabit Ethernet that uses short wavelength lasers at 850 nanometers(nm) over multimode fiber. It has a maximum transmission distance of between 2 and 300 meters, depending on the size and quality of the fiber.

**10GBase-LR**   An implementation of 10 Gigabit Ethernet that uses long wavelength lasers at 1310 nm over single-mode fiber. It also has a maximum transmission distance between 2 meters and 10 kilometers, depending on the size and quality of the fiber.

**10GBase-ER**   An implementation of 10 Gigabit Ethernet running over single-mode fiber. It uses extra long wavelength lasers at 1550 nm. It has the longest transmission distances possible of the 10-Gigabit technologies: anywhere from 2 meters up to 40 kilometers, depending on the size and quality of the fiber used.

  See the upcoming section, "Fiber-Optic Cable," in this chapter, for more information on single-mode and multimode fiber and on fiber in general.

## IEEE Standard 1394 (FireWire)

One unique cabling type that is used in a limited sense is IEEE standard 1394, more commonly known as *FireWire* (or as Sony calls it, *i.Link*). Developed by Apple Computer, FireWire runs at 100, 200, 400Mbps (800Mbps in the 1394b standard), but in its standard mode it has a cable length limitation of 15 feet (4.5 meters), which limits it to specialized applications like data transfer between two computers located in close proximity or data transfer between a computer and another device (like an MP3 player).

FireWire uses two types of connectors: the 6 pin and the 4 pin. The 6-pin connector (as shown in Figure 1.14) is for devices that need to be powered from the computer. FireWire cables with the 6-pin connector contain two pairs (four conductors) of copper wire for carrying data and one pair for powering devices, all within a common, braided metal shield. Cables using the 4-pin connector (Figure 1.15) are for data transfer only, and they contain only the four conductors for data, none for power.

**FIGURE 1.14**   Six-pin FireWire connector (male)

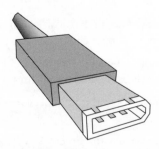

**FIGURE 1.15**   Four-pin FireWire connector (male)

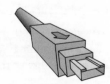

More information about FireWire and its associated standards can be found at the 1394 Trade Association website at www.1394ta.org.

## Universal Serial Bus (USB)

Over the past few years, computer peripherals have been moving away from parallel or serial connection and to a new type of bus. That bus is the *Universal Serial Bus (USB)*. The built-in serial bus of most motherboards generally offers a maximum of 2 external interfaces for connectivity to a PC, although add-on adapters can take that count up to as many as 16 serial interfaces. USB, on the other hand, can connect a maximum of 127 external devices. Also, USB is a much more flexible peripheral bus than either serial or parallel. USB supports connections to printers, scanners, and many other input devices (such as keyboards, joysticks, and mice).

When connecting USB peripherals, you must connect them either directly to one of the USB ports (as shown in Figure 1.16) on the PC or to a USB hub that is connected to one of those USB ports. Hubs can be chained together to provide multiple USB connections. Although you can connect up to 127 devices (each device has a USB plug, as shown in Figure 1.17), it is impractical in reality. Most computers with USB interfaces will support around 12 USB devices.

**FIGURE 1.16**    A USB port

## Fiber-Optic Cable

Because fiber-optic cable transmits digital signals using light impulses rather than electricity, it is immune to Electromagnetic Interference (EMI) and Radio Frequency Interference (RFI).

**FIGURE  1.17**    A USB plug

    You will find a complete discussion of these terms in Chapter 6, but you should know at this point that both could affect network performance.

Anyone who has seen UTP cable for a network run down an elevator shaft would, without doubt, appreciate this feature of fiber. Light is carried on either a glass or a plastic core. Glass can carry the signal a greater distance, but plastic costs less. Regardless of which core is used, the core is surrounded by a glass or plastic cladding, which is more glass or plastic with a different index of refraction that refracts the light back into the core. Around this is a layer of flexible plastic buffer. This can be then wrapped in an armor coating (where necessary), typically Kevlar, and then sheathed in PVC or plenum.

    For more information about fiber-optic cabling, see *Cabling: The Complete Guide to Network Wiring, Third Edition*, by David Barnett, David Groth, and Jim McBee (Sybex, 2004).

The cable itself comes in two different styles: single-mode fiber (SMF) and multimode fiber (MMF). The difference between single-mode fibers and multimode fibers is in the number of light rays (and thus the number of signals) they can carry. Generally speaking, multimode fiber is used for shorter-distance applications and single-mode fiber for longer distances.

If you happen to come across a strand of fiber in the field and want to know if it's single mode or multimode, here are some general guidelines. First of all, if it's got a yellow jacket, it's probably single mode. If it's got an orange jacket, it's most likely multimode. Also, check the writing on the cable itself. You'll find a number like 62.5/125. These are the outside diameters of the core and the cladding (respectively). If the first number is a 8, 9, or 10, it is most likely a single mode. On the other hand, if the numbers read as before (62.5/125), it's most likely a multimode strand of fiber. Use these two tips to help you identify that errant strand of fiber.

Although fiber-optic cable may sound like the solution to many problems, it has pros and cons just as the other cable types. Here are the pros:

- Is completely immune to EMI or RFI
- Can transmit up to 40 kilometers (about 25 miles)

Here are the cons of fiber-optic cable:

- Is difficult to install
- Requires a bigger investment in installation and materials

## Fiber-Optic Connectors

Fiber-optic cables can use a myriad different connectors, but the two most popular and recognizable are the *straight tip (ST)* and *subscriber (or square) connector (SC)* connectors. The ST fiber-optic connector, developed by AT&T, was one of the most widely used fiber-optic connectors. It uses a BNC attachment mechanism similar to the Thinnet connection mechanism, which makes connections and disconnections relatively easy. Its ease of use is one of the attributes that makes this connector so popular. Figure 1.18 shows an example of an ST connector. Notice the BNC attachment mechanism.

The SC connector (sometimes known also as a square connector) is another type of fiber-optic connector. As you can see in Figure 1.19, SC connectors are latched connectors. This latching mechanism holds the connector in securely while in use and prevents it from just falling out.

If data runs are measured in kilometers, fiber optic is your cable of choice because copper cannot reach more than 500 meters (about 1500 feet) without electronics regenerating the signal, and that's for the all-but-obsolete 10Base5 coaxial standard. The standards limit UTP to a mere 100 meters. You may also want to opt for fiber-optic cable if an installation requires high security, because it does not create a readable magnetic field. Although fiber-optic technology was initially very expensive and difficult to work with, it is now being used in some interesting places, such as Gigabit or 10GB Internet backbones. Ethernet running at 10Mbps over fiber-optic cable to the desktop is designated 10Base-FL; the 100Mbps version of this implementation is 100Base-FX. The *L* in the 10Mbps version stands for *link,* as opposed to such other designations as *B* for *backbone* and *P* for *passive.*

SC connectors work with either single-mode or multimode optical fibers, and they will last for around 1000 matings. They are seeing increased use but aren't as popular as ST connectors for LAN connections.

**FIGURE 1.18** An example of an ST connector

**FIGURE 1.19** A sample SC connector

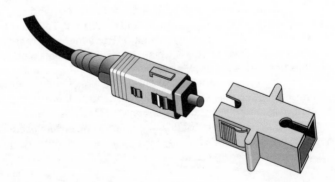

## Small Form Factor Fiber-Optic Connectors

One of the more popular styles of fiber-optic connectors is the *small form factor (SFF)* style of connector. SFF connectors allow more fiber-optic terminations in the same amount of space over their standard-sized counterparts. The two most popular are the *mechanical transfer registered jack (MT-RJ or MTRJ)*, designed by AMP, and the *Local Connector (LC)*, designed by Lucent.

### MT-RJ

The MT-RJ fiber-optic connector was the first small form factor fiber-optic connector to see widespread use. It is one-third the size of the SC and ST connectors it most often replaces. It had the following benefits:

- Small size
- TX and RX strands in one connector
- Keyed for single polarity
- Pre-terminated ends that require no polishing or epoxy
- Easy to use

Figure 1.20 shows an example of an MT-RJ fiber-optic connector

**FIGURE 1.20**    A sample MT-RJ fiber-optic connector

### LC

Local Connector is a newer style of SFF fiber-optic connector that is overtaking MT-RJ as a fiber-optic connector. It is especially popular for use with Fibre Channel adapters and Gigabit Ethernet adapters. It has similar advantages to MT-RJ and other SFF-type connectors but is easier to terminate. It uses a ceramic insert as standard-sized fiber-optic connectors do. Figure 1.21 shows an example of the LC connector.

**FIGURE 1.21**    A sample LC fiber-optic connector

## Cable Type Summary

Table 1.2 summarizes the cable types.

**TABLE 1.2**    Common Ethernet and FDDI Cable Types

| Ethernet Name | Cable Type | Maximum Speed | Maximum Transmis sion Dis tance | Notes |
| --- | --- | --- | --- | --- |
| 10Base5 | Coax | 10Mbps | 500 meters per segment | Also called Thicknet, this cable type uses vampire taps to connect devices to cable. |
| 10Base2 | Coax | 10Mbps | 185 meters per segment | Also called Thinnet, a very popular implementation of Ethernet over coax. |
| 10Base-T | UTP | 10Mbps | 100 meters per segment | One of the most popular net-work cabling schemes. |
| 100Base-TX | UTP, STP | 100Mbps | 100 meters per segment | Two pairs of Category 5 UTP. |
| 10Base-FL | Fiber | 10Mbps | Varies (ranges from 500 meters to 2000 meters) | Ethernet over fiber optics to the desktop. |
| 100Base-FX | Multimode fiber | 100Mbps | 2000 meters | 100Mbps Ethernet over fiber optics. |
| 1000Base-T | UTP | 1000Mbps | 100 meters | Four pairs of Category 5e or higher. |
| 1000Base-SX | Multimode fiber | 1000Mbps | 550 meters | Uses SC fiber connectors. Max length depends on fiber size. |
| 1000Base-CX | Balanced, shielded copper | 1000Mbps | 25 meters | Uses special connector, the HSSDC. |
| 1000Base-LX | Multimode and single-mode fiber | 1000Mbps | 550 meters multi-mode/2000 meters single mode | Uses longer wavelength laser than 1000Base-SX. Uses SC and LC connectors. |

**TABLE 1.2** Common Ethernet and FDDI Cable Types *(continued)*

| Ethernet Name | Cable Type | Maximum Speed | Maximum Transmis sion Dis tance | Notes |
|---|---|---|---|---|
| 10GBase-SR | Multimode fiber | 10Gbps | 300 meters | 850 nm laser. Max length depends on fiber size and quality. |
| 10GBase-LR | Single-mode fiber | 10Gbps | 10 kilometers | 1310 nm laser. Max length depends on fiber size and quality. |
| 10GBase-ER | Single-mode fiber | 10Gpbs | 40 kilometers | 1550 nm laser. Max length depends on fiber size and quality. |
| FDDI | Multimode fiber | 100Mbps | 10 kilometers | Uses MIC connector. |

# Common Network Connectivity Devices

Now that you are familiar with the various types of network media and connections, you should learn about some devices commonly found on today's networks. Because these devices connect network entities, they are known as connectivity devices:

- The network interface card (NIC)
- The hub
- The switch
- The bridge
- The router
- The gateway
- Other devices

These will be discussed in more detail in Chapter 2, "The OSI Model."

## NIC

The *network interface card (NIC)*, as its name suggests, is the expansion card you install in your computer to connect, or interface, your computer to the network. This device provides the physical, electrical, and electronic connections to the network media. A NIC is either an expansion card (the most popular implementation) or built in to the motherboard of the computer. In most cases, a NIC connects to the computer through *expansion slots,* which are special slots located on a computer's motherboard that allow peripherals to be plugged direclty into it. In some notebook computers, NIC adapters can be connected to the printer port or through a PC card slot.

NIC cards generally all have one or two light emitting diodes (LEDs) that help in diagnosing problems with their functionality. If there are two separate LEDs, one of them may be the Link LED, which illuminates when proper connectivity to an active network is detected. This often means that the NIC is receiving a proper signal from the hub/MAU or switch, but it could indicate connectivity to and detection of a carrier on a coax segment or connectivity with a router or other end device using a crossover cable. The other most popular LED is the Activity LED. The Activity LED will tend to flicker, indicating the intermittent transmission or receipt of frames to or from the network.

The first LED you should verify is the Link LED because if it's not illuminated, there will be no chance for the Activity LED to illuminate.

## Hub

As you learned earlier, in a star topology Ethernet network, a hub is the device that connects all the segments of the network together. Every device in the network connects directly to the hub through a single cable. Any transmission received on one port will be sent out all the other ports in the hub, including the receiving pair for the transmitting device, so that CSMA/CD on the transmitter can monitor for collisions. So, if one station sends it, all the others receive it; but based on addressing in the frame, only the intended recipient listens to it. This is to simulate the physical bus that the CSMA/CD standard was based on. It's why we call the use of a hub in an Ethernet environment a physical star/logical bus topology. It is important to note that hubs are nothing more than glorified repeaters, which are incapable of recognizing frame boundaries and data structures; that's why they act with such a lack of intelligence. A broadcast sent out by any device on the hub will be propagated to all devices connected to the hub. Any two or more devices connected to the hub have the capablity of causing a collision with each other, just as in the case of a physical bus.

## Switch

Like a hub, a switch connects multiple segments of a network together, with one important difference. Whereas a hub sends out anything it receives on one port to all the others, a switch recognizes frame boundaries and pays attention to the destination MAC address of the incoming frame as well as the port on which it was received. If the destination is known to be on a different port than the port over which the frame was received, the switch will forward the frame out over only the port on which the destination exists. Otherwise, the frame is silently discarded. If the location of the destination is unknown, then the switch acts much like a hub in that it floods the frame out every port, except for the port over which it was received, unlike a hub. The only way any party not involved in that communication will receive the transmission is if it shares a port with the transmitter or receiver of the frame. This can occur if a hub is attached to the switch port, instead of in a 1:1 relationship of end devices and switch ports. The benefit of a switch over a hub is that the switch increases performance because it is able to support full wire speed on each and every port with a nonblocking backplane, meaning the electronics inside the switch are at least equivalent in speed to the sum of the speeds of all ports.

## Bridge

A *bridge,* specifically a transparent bridge, is a network device that connects two similar network segments together. The primary function of a bridge is to keep traffic separated on both sides of the bridge. Traffic is allowed to pass through the bridge only if the transmission is intended for a station on the opposite side. The main reasons for putting a bridge in a network are to connect two segments together and to divide a busy network into two segments. A switch can be thought of as a hardware-based multiport bridge.

## Router

A *router* is a network device that connects multiple, often dissimilar, network segments into an internetwork. The router, once connected, can make intelligent decisions about how best to get network data to its destination based on network performance data that it gathers from the network itself.

Routers are very complex devices. Often, routers are computers unto themselves with their own complex operating systems to manage the routing functions (Cisco's IOS, for example) and CPUs dedicated to the functions of routing packets. Because of their complexity, it is actually possible to configure routers to perform the functions of other types of network devices (like gateways, firewalls, etc.) by simply implementing the feature within the router's software.

## Gateways

A *gateway* is any hardware and software combination that connects dissimilar network environments. Gateways are the most complex of network devices because they perform translations at multiple layers of the OSI model.

For example, a gateway is the device that connects a LAN environment to a mainframe environment. The two environments are completely different. LAN environments use distributed processing, baseband communications, and the ASCII character set. Mainframe environments use centralized processing, broadband and baseband communications, and the EBCDIC character set. Each of the LAN protocols is translated to its mainframe counterpart by the gateway software.

Another popular example is the e-mail gateway. Most LAN-based e-mail software, such as Novell's GroupWise and Microsoft's Exchange, can't communicate directly with Internet mail servers without the use of a gateway. This gateway translates LAN-based mail messages into the SMTP format that Internet mail uses.

## Other Devices

In addition to these network connectivity devices, there are several devices that, while maybe not directly connected to a network, participate in moving network data:

- Modems
- ISDN terminal adapters
- Wireless access points
- CSU/DSUs
- Transceivers (media converters)
- Firewalls

## Modems

A *modem* is a device that modulates digital data onto an analog carrier for transmission over an analog medium and then demodulates from the analog carrier to a digital signal again at the receiving end. The term *modem* is actually an acronym that stands for MOdulator/DEModulator.

When we hear the term *modem*, three different types should come to mind:

- Traditional (POTS)
- DSL
- Cable

### Traditional (POTS)

Most modems you find in computers today fall into the category of traditional modems. These modems convert the signals from your computer into signals that travel over the plain old telephone service (POTS) lines. The majority of modems that exist today are POTS modems, mainly because PC manufacturers include one with a computer.

### DSL

Digital subscriber line (DSL) is quickly replacing traditional modem access because it offers higher data rates for a reasonable cost. In addition, you can make regular phone calls while online. DSL uses higher frequencies (above 3200Hz) than regular voice phone calls use, which provides greater bandwidth (up to several megabits per second) than regular POTS modems provide while still allowing the standard voice frequency range to travel at its normal frequency to remain compatible with traditional POTS phones and devices, an advantage over ISDN. DSL "modems" are the devices that allow the network signals to pass over phone lines at these higher frequencies.

Most often, when you sign up for DSL service, the company you sign up with will send you a DSL modem for free or for a very low cost. This modem is usually an external modem (although internal DSL modems are available), and it usually has both a phone line and an Ethernet connection. You must connect the phone line to a wall jack and the Ethernet connection to your computer (you must have an Ethernet NIC in your computer in order to connect to the DSL modem). Alternatively, a router, hub, or switch may be connected to the Ethernet port of the DSL modem, increasing the options available for the Ethernet network.

If you have DSL service on the same phone line you use to make voice calls, you must install DSL filters on all the phone jacks where you have a phone. Or, a DSL filter will be installed after the DSL modem for all the phones in a building. Otherwise, you will hear a very annoying hissing noise (the DSL signals) on your voice calls.

### Cable

Another high-speed Internet access technology that is seeing widespread use is cable modem access. Cable modems connect an individual PC or network to the Internet using your cable television cable. The cable TV companies use their existing cable infrastructure to deliver data services on unused frequency bands.

The cable modem itself is a fairly simple device. It has a standard coax connector on the back as well as an Ethernet port. You can connect one PC to a cable modem (the PC will need to have an Ethernet NIC installed), or you can connect the modem to multiple PCs on a network (using a hub or switch). A router may also be used to enhance the Ethernet network's capabilities.

## ISDN Terminal Adapters

Integrated Services Digital Network (ISDN) is another form of high-speed Internet access. It delivers digital services (over 64Kbps channels) over conditioned telephone copper pairs. The device you must hook up to your computer to access ISDN services is properly known as an *ISDN Terminal Adapter*. It's not a modem in the truest sense of the word because a modem changes from digital to analog for transmission. An ISDN TA doesn't change from digital to analog. It just changes between digital transmission formats.

The box itself is about the size of a modem and looks similar to one. But, as with DSL modems, there is a phone jack and an Ethernet jack. You connect a phone cord from the phone jack to the wall jack where your ISDN services are being delivered. Then you connect an Ethernet cable from your PC to the ISDN TA's Ethernet jack. Older, less-capable TAs used an EIA/TIA-232 serial port for PC connectivity.

## Wireless Access Points (WAPs)

A *wireless access point (WAP)* allows mobile users to connect to a wired network wirelessly via radio frequency technologies. WAPs also allow wired networks to connect to each other via wireless technologies. Essentially, they are the wireless equivalent of a hub or a switch in that they can connect multiple wireless (and often wired) devices together to form a network.

One of the most popular use for wireless access points is to provide Internet access in public areas, like libraries, coffee shops, hotels, and airports. WAPs are easy to set up; most often, you just need to plug them in to a wired network and power them up to get them to work. Plus, without the clutter or added expense of cables to hook them up, they make ideal foundations for small business networks.

You'll learn the intricate details of wireless access points that a Network+ technician should know in Chapter 6.

## CSU/DSUs

The Channel Service Unit/Data Service Unit (CSU/DSU) is a common device found in equipment rooms when the network is connected via a T-series data connection or other digital serial technology (e.g., a T1 or Digital Data Server [DDS]). It is essentially two devices in one that are used to connect a digital carrier (the T-series or DDS line) to your network equipment (usually to a router). The *Channel Service Unit (CSU)* terminates the line at the customer's premises. It also provides diagnostics and remote testing, if necessary. The *Data Service Unit (DSU)* does the actual transmission of the signal through the CSU. It can also provide buffering and data flow control.

Both components are required if you are going to connect to a digital transmission medium, such as a T1 line. Sometimes, however, one or both of these components may be built into a router. If both components are built into a router, you only have to plug the T1 line directly into the router. Otherwise, some Physical Layer specification, like V.35 or HSSI, will have to be used to cable the interface on the router to the external CSU/DSU.

## Transceivers (Media Converters)

Another small device that is commonly seen on a network is the external transceiver (also known as a media converter). These are relatively simple devices that allow a NIC or other networking device to connect to a different type of media than it was designed for. Many NICs have special connectors that will allow this, as do hubs and switches.

For example, if you have a 100Base-TX switch and would like to connect it to another switch using fiber-optic cabling, you would connect a fiber transceiver to each switch's transceiver port and then connect the two transceivers together with the appropriate fiber-optic cabling.

With early Ethernet-style DB-15 female Digital-Intel-Xerox (DIX, or more commonly Attachment Unit Interface [AUI]) NIC interfaces, which are still available as medium-independent connectors on more advanced NICs and other networking devices, an external transceiver has to be used to convert the electrical signal from the device to one that is compatible with the cabling medium. Every other popular type of Ethernet technology, such as the xBase-T standards, has a built-in transceiver on the NIC card or device interface. An external transceiver is necessary with these technologies only to act as a media converter.

## Firewalls

A *firewall* is probably the most important device on a network if that network is connected to the Internet. Its job is to protect LAN resources from attackers on the Internet. Similarly, it can prevent computers on the network from accessing various services on the Internet. It can be used to filter packets based on rules that the network administrator sets. These rules state what kinds of information can flow into and out of a network's connection to the Internet.

Firewalls can be either stand-alone "black boxes," or can be set up in software on a server or router. Either way, the firewall will have at least two network connections: one to the Internet (known as the "public" side), and one to the network (known as the "private" side). Sometimes, there is a third network port on a firewall. This port is used to connect servers and equipment that can be considered both public and private (like web and e-mail servers). This intermediary network is known as a *demilitarized zone,* or *DMZ.*

Firewalls are the first line of defense for an Internet-connected network. If a network was directly connected to the Internet without a firewall, an attacker could theoretically gain direct access to the computers and servers on that network with little effort.

# Summary

In this chapter, you learned about the items that can be found on a typical network. You first learned what a network is and the various elements that make up a network, such as servers, workstations, and hosts. Then you learned about the different ways of laying out a network. You learned about bus, star, ring, mesh, and hybrid topologies.

You also learned about the different types of physical media in use on networks today, including coaxial, twisted-pair, and fiber-optic media.

Finally, you learned about some common network devices—including NICs, hubs, switches, bridges, routers, and gateways—seen on a typical network.

# Exam Essentials

**Know how to identify different network topologies.**  A single cable with computers attached to it is a bus. A central hub with cables radiating out to computers is a star. A crisscross, redundant connection to all computers is a mesh. An outer loop connecting all computers is a ring.

**Know the operational characteristics of various cable standards.**  You should know the signaling rate (in Mbps), signaling method (baseband or broadband), media type (copper or fiber), and the other specifics for the various cable standards such as 10Base-T, 10Base-FL, 100Base-TX, 1000Base-T, and 10GBase-SR.

**Be able to recognize different media connectors and describe their uses.**  You should know that RJ-11 is used to connect a phone jack to a telephone; RJ-45 is used for 10Base-T, 100Base-TX, and 1000Base-T twisted-pair Ethernet connections; BNC is used for 10Base2 Ethernet connections; AUI, a DB-15 connector/PC game connector, is used for 10Base5 connections from vampire tap to NIC; ST, the most popular fiber-optic connector, is a barrel connector with a locking ring; and SC, another common fiber connector, is a square-ended connector with a latching mechanism. You should also understand the different types of IEEE 1394 (FireWire) connectors and their different uses.

**Understand the different media types and their uses.**  You should know the different types of commonly used network media (copper cabling and fiber-optic media) and the different applications of each. You must know the differences between Category 3, 5, 5e, and 6 UTP and what the category ratings mean. You should also know the operational characteristics of the different types of fiber-optic cable (single mode and multimode).

**Be able to explain the basic purpose and function of many different network devices.**  You should understand how each network device—including hubs, switches, routers, bridges, firewalls, and wireless access points—functions.

# Review Questions

1. Which of the following are characteristic of a peer-to-peer network? (Choose all that apply.)
   - **A.** It has centralized security and administration.
   - **B.** A computer can be both a client and a server.
   - **C.** A limited number of computers are involved.
   - **D.** It does not require a hub.

2. Which cabling standard can send data at up to 10,000Mbps?
   - **A.** 10Base-T
   - **B.** 100Base-TX
   - **C.** 1000Base-TX
   - **D.** 10GBase-SR

3. Which of the following are not small form factor fiber connectors? (Choose all that apply.)
   - **A.** MT-RJ
   - **B.** LC
   - **C.** FC
   - **D.** SC

4. Which LED on your NIC might save you the most frustration if you start your troubleshooting efforts by monitoring its illumination?
   - **A.** Link
   - **B.** Activity
   - **C.** Collision
   - **D.** 10/100

5. Which of the following is a characteristic of a mesh network?
   - **A.** It controls cable costs.
   - **B.** It offers improved reliability.
   - **C.** It is required by fire code.
   - **D.** It needs a token to operate.

6. Which of the following are advantages of a star-wired topology? (Choose all that apply.)
   - **A.** The star topology uses the least amount of cable.
   - **B.** A cable cut between a lone device and its concentrating device affects only the lone device.
   - **C.** There is a single point of failure in the central concentrating device.
   - **D.** Troubleshooting is simplified compared to the other topologies.

7. Besides the newer high-speed Token Ring, what are the other two standard ring speeds for the Token Ring technology? (Choose all that apply.)

   A. 4Mbps

   B. 16Mbps

   C. 100Mbps

   D. 4Gbps

8. Which of the following is a characteristic of a physical mesh topology?

   A. It has the most physical connections per device.

   B. It is the most common physical LAN topology.

   C. Each device has only an inbound port and an outbound port.

   D. When one device transmits, all other devices hear the transmission.

9. Which of the following FireWire connectors are for devices that need to be powered from the computer?

   A. 4 pin

   B. 6 pin

   C. 8 pin

   D. 10 pin

10. Plenum-rated cable has which of the following characteristics?

    A. It has a lower cost than PVC.

    B. It meets fire codes for installation in suspended ceilings.

    C. It transmits data faster.

    D. All the above.

11. Which of the two following cable, connector, length triples meet the specifications for 1000Base-SX and 1000Base-LX?

    A. UTP, RJ-45, 100m

    B. MMF, LC, 550m

    C. SMF, FC, 2000m

    D. MMF, SC, 550m

12. Which of the following devices would help your laptop communicate with a mainframe on the same LAN segment?

    A. Transceiver

    B. Gateway

    C. Switch

    D. Router

13. Which Ethernet standard is designed to use only two pairs of wires in a UTP cable?

    A.  1000Base-CX

    B.  100Base-FX

    C.  1000Base-T

    D.  100Base-TX

14. A transmission technology that divides that transmission medium into discrete channels so that multiple signals can share the same cable is known as _____.

    A.  duplex communications

    B.  baseband communications

    C.  sideband communications

    D.  broadband communications

15. If you need to change the type of media a NIC is able to connect to, which device would you use?

    A.  Bridge

    B.  Hub

    C.  Transceiver

    D.  All the above

16. An RJ-45 connector should be wired with _____ pairs when used on a Category 5e UTP cable.

    A.  1

    B.  2

    C.  4

    D.  8

17. 10GBase-SR can be extended to _____ meters per segment.

    A.  100

    B.  200

    C.  300

    D.  1000

18. Which network component is used in conjunction with a router to provide access to a T1 circuit?

    A.  Gateway

    B.  T1 modem

    C.  CSU/DSU

    D.  Switch

**19.** If you need to protect internal LAN resources from an external threat, which device can help most?

   **A.** Router

   **B.** Firewall

   **C.** Proxy server

   **D.** HTTPS-compatible NIC card

**20.** Which of the following is a difference between the 100Base-TX and 1000Base-T Ethernet specifications?

   **A.** 1000Base-T is 10 times faster because it uses fiber optics.

   **B.** 100Base-TX requires a minimum of Category 5 UTP, while 1000Base-T must be run over no less than Category 5e UTP.

   **C.** Because it's slower and more stable, 100Base-TX can be run over longer distances.

   **D.** Although both technologies require the same number of pairs for transmitting and receiving, 1000Base-T uses them differently.

# Answers to Review Questions

1. B, C. Computers participating in a peer-to-peer network can be either client or server or both. Additionally, the peer-to-peer model has some practical limitations, including the number of computers involved. Answer A is incorrect because the administration is *not* centralized. Answer D is incorrect because the use of hubs is not related to the implementation of peer-to-peer or client/server networks.

2. D. The 10G in the 10GBase-SR designation can be thought of as standing for 10Gbps or 10,000Mbps, whichever helps you remember.

3. C, D. MT-RJ and LC are both forms of SFF fiber connectors. FC and SC are larger and do not permit the port density afforded by the other two.

4. A. Looking at the Link LED first could save you the frustration of waiting for the Activity LED to light up, which may never happen as long as there are issues with network connectivity (indicated by a dark Link LED).

5. B. The major advantage to mesh networks is their increased reliability. There are multiple redundant connections between all nodes in the network. Answer A is incorrect because the cable costs are much, much more than other networks. Answer C is simply a distracter; mesh is *not* required by fire codes. Answer D is incorrect because most token-based networks could not operate in a mesh environment.

6. B, D. The star topology has the advantage of simplifying the troubleshooting process because, when a device fails, you should check that device and its NIC, the network cable connected to that NIC, and the port on the concentrating device (hub, MAU, switch, etc.) to which the other end of the network cable is connected. Somewhat related to this point, it also has the advantage of localizing problems to the single device or cable segment. While it is true that the central concentrating device is a single point of failure, this is one of the disadvantages of star topologies.

7. A, B. The two early ring speeds of Token Ring were 4Mbps and 16Mbps

8. A. Of the physical topologies, the mesh has the most physical connections per device. This complete interconnection is what creates the mesh. The mesh is not used in the majority of LAN implementations, mostly with WAN links. The most common physical LAN topology is the star topology. Answer C describes a physical ring topology, and D describes a logical bus topology.

9. B. There are only two main types of FireWire connectors, the 4 pin and the 6 pin. The 6-pin connector has two extra pins that provide power from the computer to the device.

10. B. Answer B is the only correct answer because plenum-rated cable meets fire codes for installation in suspended ceilings, raised floors, and any other open area through which ventilation-system air is returned. Plenum cable actually has a higher cost than PVC. Additionally, because the conductors are also made of copper, it doesn't conduct data any faster than PVC-coated cable.

11. B, D. Both the SX and LX standards of gigabit Ethernet are based on fiber-optic cable, not copper. However, while 1000Base-LX permits the use of single-mode fiber over distances of 2000m, it does not use the FC connector. Both it and the SX standard allow the use of SC or LC connectors on multimode fiber over a distance of 550m.

**12.** B. If your PC does not have native connectivity, say via TCP/IP, with a mainframe, none of the devices will assist you in communicating with the mainframe. The only help a router would be is if the mainframe were not on the same LAN segment, but it would have to speak the same protocol as your laptop or a gateway would still be necessary. Of all the answers, gateway is decidedly the best.

**13.** D. 100Base-FX can be ruled out immediately because the *F* indicates a fiber-optic media dependency, while more subtly, 1000Base-CX can be quickly eliminated due to its media dependency on STP, not UTP. 1000Base-T is incorrect because, although it calls for the use of Category 5e UTP, it requires all four pairs for both transmit and receive use.

**14.** D. In broadband communications (television communications, for example), the communications medium is divided into discrete channels. Each channel can carry its own signal. In baseband communications, the transmission takes up the whole communications channel. Full duplex communications give a sender and receiver the ability to each send and receive signals simultaneously. Sideband is a distracter.

**15.** C. Although all the devices listed can be purchased with the variety of interfaces necessary to satisfy the objective, an external transceiver's sole purpose is to change the type of media a NIC or device interface connects to (provided there is a transceiver port available on the NIC or that you purchase a transceiver with the appropriate interconnections).

**16.** C. Although you can wire any combination of pairs in an RJ-45 connector, you should wire all four pairs in a Category 5 UTP into an RJ-45 connector to support those network technologies that may need all four pairs (such as 1000Base-T), even if you aren't currently using them. Additionally, this habit supports all currently available technologies. So, in case you decide to change from Token Ring to Ethernet, if you create a straight-through wired channel, there is no reason to rewire any cables because the popular wire pairing standards will cover both of these technologies and many more.

**17.** C. The maximum segment length for 10GBase-SR is 300 meters.

**18.** C. The Channel Service Unit/Data Service Unit (CSU/DSU) translates LAN signals into signals that are used on T1 lines. Some people incorrectly call it a "T1 modem." It's not a modem because it doesn't translate data into analog and back. Every signal stays in the digital format.

**19.** B. Although a router possesses certain access control capabilities, a firewall's hardened configuration set makes it a superior choice for establishing a secure entryway into a LAN, blocking malicious traffic with pinpoint accuracy while allowing trusted traffic access to the internal resources. A proxy server may include some firewall capabilities, but not to the level of a stand-alone firewall. Besides, in the end, the proxy component that provides this functionality is a firewall, making it the best answer here. HTTPS is not a function of NIC cards, nor would hardening a NIC card help guard an entire LAN against outside threats.

**20.** B. 100Base-TX works fine with two pairs of at least Category 5 UTP, but due to the fact that 1000Base-T uses all four pairs simultaneously (a reason D is incorrect), a minimum of Category 5e UTP is required for proper functioning. Both of these standards are specified over twisted-pair copper (the *T* in their name signifies this), not fiber optics. Both standards are limited to the same 100m segment length.

# Chapter 2

# The OSI Model

## THE FOLLOWING NETWORK+ EXAM OBJECTIVES ARE COVERED IN THIS CHAPTER:

✓ **1.2 Specify the main features of 802.2 (Logical Link Control), 802.3 (Ethernet), 802.5 (Token Ting), 802.11 (wireless), and Fiber Distributed Data Interface (FDDI) networking technologies, including:**

- Speed
- Access method (CSMA/CA [Carrier Sense Multiple Access/Collision Avoidance] and CSMA/CD [Carrier Sense Multiple Access/Collision Detection])
- Topology
- Media

✓ **2.1 Identify a MAC (Media Access Control) address and its parts.**

✓ **2.2 Identify the seven layers of the OSI (Open Systems Interconnect) model and their functions.**

✓ **2.3 Identify the OSI (Open Systems Interconnect) layers at which the following network components operate:**

- Hubs
- Switches
- Bridges
- Routers
- NICs (network interface cards)
- WAPs (wireless access points)

✓ **2.4 Differentiate between the following network protocols in terms of routing, addressing schemes, interoperability, and naming conventions:**

- IPX/SPX (Internetwork Packet Exchange/Sequenced Packet Exchange)
- NetBEUI (Network Basic Input/Output System Extended User Interface)
- AppleTalk/AppleTalk over IP (Internet Protocol)
- TCP/IP (Transmission Control Protocol/Internet Protocol)

You can't open a book on networking technologies without reading about the Open Systems Interconnect (OSI) model. This book is no exception, and for good reason. The OSI model helps us understand the fundamentals of network data transmission by offering a guideline for sending data from one computer to another. In this chapter, we will discuss the OSI model, the most commonly discussed network model. We'll also discuss the most popular and pertinent protocols that function at the different layers of these models.

# Introducing the OSI Model

The OSI model was designed to promote interoperability by creating a guideline for network data transmission between computers and components that have different hardware vendors, software, operating systems, and protocols. For example, look at the simple process of transferring a file. From a user's perspective, a single operation has been performed to transfer the file. In reality, however, many different procedures had to take place behind the scenes to accomplish this seemingly simple task. Network data transmission (like the file transfer) is performed through the use of a protocol suite, also known as a protocol stack, especially when installed in a given device.

A *protocol* is most easily defined as a set of rules used to determine how devices communicate with each other. It is similar to language. If one person speaks English and another speaks English, they can communicate. But if one person speaks only Spanish and the other speaks only English, they won't be able to communicate. A *protocol suite* is a set of similar protocols that work together to make sure communications happen properly.

The OSI model is used to describe what tasks a protocol suite performs as you explore how data moves from the user interface of a transmitter down to its physical network access, across a network, and then up the layers of the receiving device to its user interface. Keep in mind that not all protocols map directly to the guideline provided for us through the OSI model, but there are enough similarities so that you can use the OSI model to examine how these protocols function. This is one of the OSI model's greatest advantages. It is at once very specific in the separation of functionality within a device (specifying more layers than most other models) and very generic in how it explains what happens at each layer. With this duality, networking engineers and administrators are able to make both broad comparisons and precise distinctions between the functionality and interoperability of different protocol stacks. There are a myriad of protocol suites in use today, including IPX/SPX, NetBIOS, and TCP/IP, with the first two being quite a bit less prolific in today's market than the last one. Each performs a specific function. Many of these functions that are provided through the use of a protocol stack and its components are standard functions performed by other components in other protocol stacks, thus paving the way for devices and software that can enable the interoperation between differing stacks.

The most commonly referenced protocol model, the OSI model, was developed in 1977 by the International Organization for Standardization (commonly referred to as ISO) to provide "common ground" when describing any network protocol.

 ISO is not an acronym for the International Organization for Standardization but is instead derived from the Greek word *isos,* which means "equal," and was adopted by the organization. For more information, go to www.iso.ch.

As you can see in Figure 2.1, the OSI model consists of seven layers. Each layer performs a specific function and then passes on the result to another layer. When a sending station has data to send, it formats a network request and then passes that request to the network protocol at the top layer, the Application layer. The protocol that runs at the Application layer performs an operation on the request and then passes it to the next (lower) layer. Each protocol at each layer below the Application layer performs its own calculations and appends its own information to the data sent from the layer above it. At the receiving station, the process happens in reverse. Figure 2.2 illustrates this basic process.

As you can see from the diagram, it is possible to have communication between two devices with vastly differing personalities (operating systems), as long as the protocols they are running for network access and communication are compatible (both TCP/IP, for example). Here we have a DOS-compatible PC and a Macintosh talking together over what could be a common network medium, like Ethernet over copper. The term *peer communication* comes from the fact that, through the use of headers, equivalent protocols in each stack appear to talk directly with one another. Because the header that one protocol creates means something only to that protocol, and because this control information is encapsulated deeper with each successive lower-layer protocol, only the compatible protocol on the receiving device, or perhaps an intermediate device like a router, will be able to access the control information found in the header created by the corresponding process on the transmitting device.

**FIGURE 2.1**    The Open Systems Interconnect (OSI) model

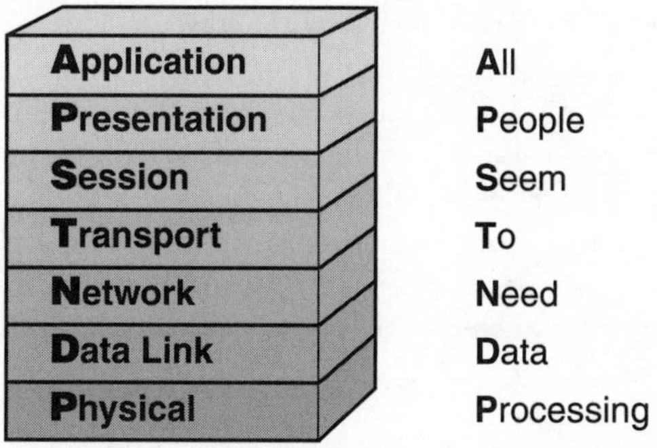

| | |
|---|---|
| **Application** | All |
| **Presentation** | People |
| **Session** | Seem |
| **Transport** | To |
| **Network** | Need |
| **Data Link** | Data |
| **Physical** | Processing |

**FIGURE 2.2**    How data travels through the layers of the OSI model

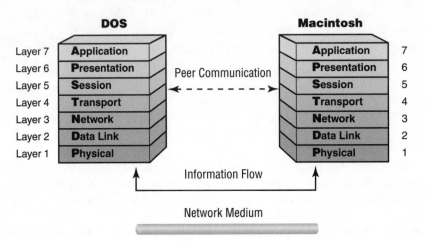

As an example, if TCP on the DOS device creates a TCP header, then this header will be passed transparently by all intermediate devices to the Macintosh device, which will be the only device capable of de-encapsulating the incoming frame far enough to access the TCP header, as well as the only device along the way running TCP because intermediate devices such as routers, switches, and hubs are involved with only the bottom three layers for through traffic and TCP is a layer 4 protocol. Even if this were not true, it is the peer communication between the IP protocol of the DOS device and the IP protocol of every device in between, including the Macintosh device, that tells each one that this IP packet traversing the network is destined for the Macintosh. This alone would be enough to discourage any intermediate device from trying to process the encapsulated TCP header.

Peer communication can be seen in operation at every layer of any protocol or reference model from the way that two devices communicating on a shared segment have to use a common cabling protocol with agreed-upon pin configurations and encoding methods at the Physical layer all the way up to the Application layer, where one device will be able to send a message—written, graphical, or otherwise—to another device and rightly expect that message to come across as intended. These two devices with Application layer peer communication could have considerably more degrees of separation from one another than two devices with peer communication at the Physical layer, allowing any number of devices along the way to produce a path for this message to make it from one end to the other. This example also illustrates the importance of having different protocols in each protocol stack because each layer provides a different scope or diameter of communication; lower-layer protocols require that communicating devices be neighbors, whereas higher-layer protocols don't require any such adjacency. This difference in the scope of the layers allows highly advanced protocol suites to be developed and implemented as stacks.

You can use mnemonic devices to help you remember the order of the OSI model layers: APSTNDP (from top to bottom). The most popular mnemonic for this arrangement is All People Seem To Need Data Processing. A reverse mnemonic (from Physical to Application, bottom to top) is Please Do Not Throw Sausage Pizza Away. (Good advice, don't you think?)

The OSI model is mainly a reference model as opposed to a mainstream protocol suite. Although the ISO has created protocols that operate at each of the higher layers of its model, very few entities have standardizaed on the OSI protocol suite, due mainly to the overbearing popularity of the TCP/IP protocol suite. Let's take a brief look at the layers of the OSI model and the basic protocol functions they describe:

**The Application Layer**    The Application layer, the top layer of the OSI model, does not refer to applications such as word processors, but rather to a set of tools that an application can use to accomplish a task such as a word processor application requesting a file transfer. This layer is responsible for defining how interactions occur between network services (applications) and the network. Services that function at the Application layer include, but are not limited to, file, print, and messaging services. The Application layer may also support error recovery.

As an example, a web browsing application may appear, at first glance, to exist at the Application layer because it is indeed an application and it is involved, most often, with network communication. While the browser software is an application, it is not a protocol because the web services it connects to do not have to operate exactly the same way that the browser operates. The fact that one application is a server application and the other is a client application speaks to their differences and need for underlying compatible protocols. The Application layer protocol in common between the two applications is most likely HTTP, which allows the server to deliver an HTML file to the client for display in its browser window. The same browser could speak FTP to an FTP server. HTTP and FTP are the Application layer protocols here, not the browser software. These protocols give support to the applications that call upon them and offer an entryway into the networking process.

To prove that these functions can be separated from the application itself, open your favorite web browser and surf to your favorite website. On the File menu, save the web page to your Desktop or other favorite local resource. Next, unplug your network connection or shut down your wireless access. You could even pull out your NIC card, for that matter. Open a new instance of your web browser and open the file you saved. Notice that the HTML file displays, even without the support of HTTP and an active network connection. If the application does not need to enter the network process to get its job done, then no Application layer protocol's services will be required. Said another way, if an Application layer protocol is used at one end, then a corresponding Application layer protocol must be used at the other end, and because your web browser can be used independently of a network connection, it is not an Application layer process, as is HTTP, for example.

**The Presentation Layer**    The Presentation layer is responsible for the formatting and code conversion of data being passed up to the Application layer. In this layer, character sets are converted (e.g., from ASCII to Unicode or EBCDIC) and data is encrypted. Data may also be compressed in this layer. Of course, anything that is done to the data on the transmitting device must be undone on the receiving device.

Note that character-set conversion is not a result of the transmitting device's having done anything to the data and is only performed on the receiving device, in response to the Presentation layer's recognizing that incoming data is not based on the same character set that its own upper-layer processes require. On the other hand, compression and encryption services must be supported by both end devices in the conversation, one to add these features, the other to remove them.

It is the Presentation layer that is responsible for recognizing file types in an incoming data stream and performing any massaging to the data to make a file presentable to the Application protocol. Think of this function as providing a common syntax for data and using this syntax to convert to and from the application data. The Multipurpose Internet Mail Extensions (MIME) system denotes the file type of incoming data, helping the Presentation layer know what to do with the incoming stream. File types like MIDI, MPEG, JPEG, and GIF are considered to be Presentation layer entities.

**The Session Layer**    The Session layer defines how two computers establish, synchronize, maintain, and end a session. Practical functions such as security authentication, connection ID establishment, data transfer, acknowledgments, and connection release take place here. This list is not all-inclusive. Any communications that require milestones—or, put another way, require an answer to "Have you got that data I sent?"—are performed here. Typically these milestones are called *checkpoints*. Once a checkpoint has been crossed, any data not received needs retransmission only from the last good checkpoint. Adjusting checkpoints to account for very reliable or unreliable connections can greatly improve the actual throughput of data transmission.

**The Transport Layer**    The Transport layer is responsible for checking that the data was delivered error-free. It is also used to divide a message that is too long into smaller segments and, in the reverse, take a series of short messages and combine them into one longer segment. These smaller or combined segments must later be correctly reassembled. This is accomplished through segment sequencing (usually by appending a number to each of the segments).

This layer also handles logical address/name resolution. Additionally, this layer can send an acknowledgment that it got the data packet. Frequently you will see this referred to as an ACK, which is short for acknowledgment. This layer is responsible for the majority of error and flow control in network communications.

The major difference in the sessions that the Session layer deals with and the connections that a connection-oriented Transport layer protocol (such as TCP) will create lies with the size or scope of the communication. The Session layer is responsible for the ordered bidirectional communication of entire messages, in the form of a dialog, while a connection-oriented Transport layer protocol is only responsible for the ordered transmission of segments of these messages. Session layer functionality will have to be called upon to salvage a session that is broken before a normal end can occur, while Transport layer functionality is fine to reestablish lost segments or broken virtual circuits while the session itself is still established.

**The Network Layer**    The Network layer is responsible for logical addressing and translating logical addresses into physical addresses. A little-known function of the Network layer is prioritizing data. Not all data is of equal importance. Nobody is hurt if an e-mail message is delayed a fraction of a second. Delaying audio or video data a fraction of a second could be disastrous to the message. This prioritization is known as *quality of service (QoS)*.

In addition, the Network layer controls congestion, routes data from source to destination, and builds and tears down packets. Most routing protocols perform their function on packets native to this layer.

**The Data Link Layer**    The Data Link layer takes raw data from the Physical layer and gives it a logical structure, known as a frame. In the opposite direction of flow, the Data Link layer hands frames down to the Physical layer for bit-level encoding onto the networking medium. Frames include information about where the data is meant to go, which device on the local link sent the data, and the overall validity of the bytes sent. In legacy technologies used over less-dependable links, such as X.25 and LLC2 used in an SNA environment, after a data frame is sent, the Data Link layer waits for a positive ACK. If one is not received or if the frame is damaged, another frame is sent. These days, such acknowledgment and retransmission is left to higher layers to perform.

The Data Link layer also controls functions of logical network topologies and physical addressing as well as data transmission synchronization and connection.

**The Physical Layer**    The Physical layer is responsible for controlling the functional interface, such as transmission technique, encoding scheme, cable specifications, pin layout, and connector type.

# The OSI Model's Lower Layers

Now that you have a broad overview of the OSI model and its seven layers, you will learn about the functions of each layer in a little more detail, starting with the lower layers. In addition to the functions, you'll read about some of the devices that operate at those layers and some of their installation concepts. Much of this information is similar to what you may find in other chapters.

## The Physical Layer

The easiest way to think about the Physical layer is that it deals with measurable, physical entities (like electrons, electricity, etc.). Any protocol or device that operates at the Physical layer deals with the physical concepts of a network and knows nothing of the meaning of the individual bits that it transmits or deals with.

## Physical Layer Concepts

Generally speaking, Physical layer concepts involve a network component that is tangible or measurable. For example, when a protocol at the Physical layer receives information from the upper layers, it translates all the data into signals that can be transmitted on a transmission medium. This process is known as *signal encoding* (or *encoding*, for short). With cable media (also called *bounded media*), the protocols that operate at the Physical layer translate the bits of the data into electrical ons and offs, often using pulses of electricity or light for one or both of these states.

Additionally, the Physical layer specifies how much of the media will be used (in other words, its *signaling method*) during data transmission. If a network signal uses all available signal frequencies (or, to put it differently, the entire bandwidth), the technology is said to use *baseband* signaling. Most LAN technologies, such as Ethernet, use baseband signaling. On the other hand, if a signal uses only one frequency (or only part of the bandwidth), the technology is said to use *broadband* signaling. This means multiple signals can be transmitted on the media simultaneously, and one or more of these channels must be "tuned" to in order for device-to-device communication to occur across them. Television signals use broadband signaling.

Finally, the Physical layer specifies the layout of the transmission media (its topology, in other words). A physical topology describes the way the cabling is physically laid out (as opposed to a logical topology, discussed later in the section titled "The Data Link Layer"). The physical topologies include the following:

- Bus
- Star
- Ring
- Mesh

### The Bus Topology

In a physical bus topology, every computer is directly connected to a common medium. A physical bus network uses one network cable that runs from one end of the network to the other. Workstations connect at various points along this cable. The main advantage to this topology is simplicity: Only one cable is used, and a physical bus topology typically requires less cable than other physical topologies. However, a cable fault can bring down the entire network, thus making a physical bus topology the least fault tolerant of all the physical topologies. Figure 2.3 shows a sample physical bus network.

**FIGURE 2.3**   A sample physical bus topology

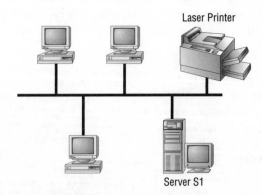

## The Star Topology

In a physical star topology, a cable runs from each network entity to a central device. This central device (called a *hub*) allows all devices to communicate as if they were all directly connected. The main advantage to a physical star topology is its fault tolerance. If one node or cable malfunctions, the rest of the network is not affected. The hub simply won't be able to communicate with the station attached to that port. An Ethernet 10Base-T network is one example of a network type that requires a physical star topology. Figure 2.4 shows a sample network that uses a physical star topology.

**FIGURE 2.4**    A sample physical star topology

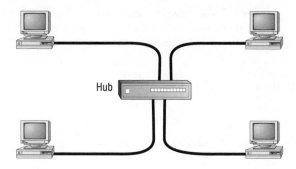

## The Ring Topology

A physical ring topology isn't seen much in the computer-networking world. If you do see it, it's usually in a wide area network (WAN) environment. In a physical ring topology, every network entity connects directly to only two other network entities (the one immediately preceding it and the one immediately following it). The vulnerability of the physical ring topology to disruption of service due to the failure of a single node makes it a poor choice in most network environments. As a result, LANs only ever have implemented the ring as a logical topology, as in physical star/logical ring Token Ring. Figure 2.5 shows a physical ring network.

**FIGURE 2.5**    A sample physical ring topology

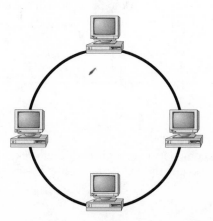

### The Mesh Topology

A physical mesh topology is another physical topology that isn't widely used in computer networks (except in special WAN cases). In a physical mesh topology, every computer is directly connected to every other computer in the network. The more computers there are on a mesh network, the more cables make up the network. If a mesh network has $n$ computers, there will be $n(n-1)/2$ cables. With 10 computers, there would be $10(10-1)/2$, or 45 cables. As you can see, this topology quickly becomes unmanageable with only a few computers. Figure 2.6 shows a sample mesh network.

It is possible to have a *partial* mesh network, where there are multiple connections between network entities but not between all of them. This reduces costs associated with leased circuits by reducing the number of circuits.

**FIGURE 2.6**    A physical mesh topology

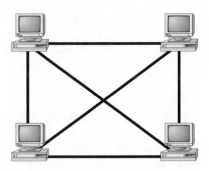

## Physical Layer Devices

Several devices operate primarily at the Physical layer of the OSI model. These devices manipulate mainly the physical aspects of a network data stream (such as the voltages, signal direction, and signal strength). Let's take a quick look at some of the most popular:

- NIC
- Transceivers
- Repeaters
- Hubs
- MAUs

### The Network Interface Card (NIC)

Probably the most common component on any network is the *network interface card (NIC)*. A NIC is the component that provides the connection between a computer's internal bus and the network media. NICs come in many shapes and sizes. They vary by the type of bus connection they employ and their network media connection ports. More than any other Physical layer device, a NIC is recognized for both its layer 2 and its layer 1 personality. Think about it this way: Where in your PC is the Ethernet protocol? We know Ethernet is a layer 2 protocol, but your computer, not the NIC, is the layer 2 device, right? Not really. All you have to do to enable a PC or Macintosh to communicate using Ethernet is to install the physical NIC card and the driver that gets the operating system familiar with the new hardware. None of that was the installation of Ethernet software. Conversely, when you remove a NIC card, you don't have to go into an Add/Remove applet to remove Ethernet from the computer. It goes away with the NIC card. As a result, we can surmise that the NIC card supplies both the Physical layer and the Data Link layer (at least the MAC sublayer) Ethernet functionality of your PC. Figure 2.7 shows an example of a network interface card.

**FIGURE 2.7**    A sample network interface card

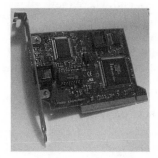

### The Transceiver

In the strictest definition, a *transceiver* is the part of any network interface that transmits and receives network signals (transmitter/receiver). Every functioning network interface has a transceiver, internal or external. Those that do not have a built-in transceiver (for example, NICs with only a DIX/AUI port) will require an external transceiver, but every interface requires some form of transceiver to convert the device's digital signal to one that is compatible with the network medium. The appearance and function of the external transceiver vary with the type of network cable and topology in use.

Some network interface cards have an Attachment Unit Interface (AUI) port (typically a 15-pin D-shell [DB-15] connector), with no internal transceiver, that allows an external transceiver to be used, thus changing the media types to which the NIC can connect. This port is more accurately known as a DIX port because AUI was originally reserved for the drop cable that connected to the DIX port, but through common use, AUI surpassed DIX in popularity. For example, if you are using an Ethernet 10Base2 network interface card with an AUI port, you can connect to an Ethernet 10Base-T network by using an external transceiver attached to the AUI port.

## The Repeater

The simplest of all the Physical layer devices is the repeater, which simply regenerates the signals it receives on one port and sends (or "repeats") them on another as if it were the original physical source of the transmission. Contrast this functionality to an analog amplifier, sometimes referred to inaccurately as an analog repeater. The analog device is unable to completely discern what part of the incoming signal is intentional and what part of it is noise. As a result, except for with high-end models that can incompletely mitigate the noise to some degree, all of the interference is amplified, along with the intended signal. Digital repeaters used in early networking, and still seen in various outposts today, were not subject to such noise reproduction.

Repeaters are used to extend the maximum length of a network segment. They are often used if a few network devices are located far from the rest of the network. Figure 2.8 shows a network that uses a repeater.

There is a limit to the number of 10Mbps repeaters that can be used in serial on a network without separating them by at least a layer 2 device. The *5-4-3 Rule* dictates how many repeaters can be used on a network and where they can be placed. According to this rule, a single network can have five network segments connected by four repeaters, with three of the segments populated. The other two segments are simply for inter-repeater connectivity. The 5-4-3 Rule ensured that the minimum-sized Ethernet frame of 64 bytes could begin being received by the destination device before the last bit was transmitted by the source device. If this rule is violated, two devices may not be able to reach one another across the network. Furthermore, a phenomenon known as late collisions becomes more prominent, resulting in improper recovery behavior by the transmitter, which already believes the frame has made it across the network safely and does not hear the collision. Errored frames known as runts are often the product of late collisions. Today's faster hubs are not bound by the 5-4-3 Rule but actually by stricter guidelines because the data appears compressed by 10Mbps standards and cannot tolerate as long of an electrical distance between transmitting and receiving devices. Figure 2.9 illustrates the 5-4-3 Rule.

**FIGURE 2.8**   A repeater installed on a network

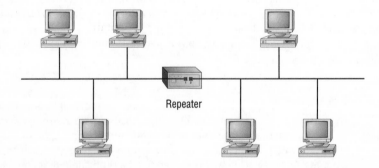

Repeater

**FIGURE 2.9**    The 5-4-3 Rule for network repeaters

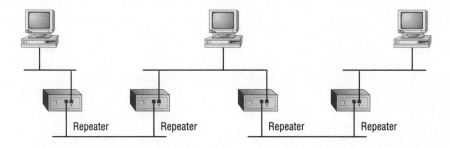

**FIGURE 2.10**    A standard hub

## The Hub

After the NIC, a hub is probably the most common Physical layer device found on networks today. A *hub* (also called an Ethernet *concentrator*) serves as a central connection point for several network devices. At its basic level, an active hub is nothing more than a multiport repeater. A hub repeats what it receives on one port to all other ports, including the port on which the signal was received, so that the transmitting device may monitor and recover from collisions. 10Mbps hubs are, therefore, also subject to the 5-4-3 Rule.

There are many classifications of hubs, but two of the most important are active and passive:

- An active hub is usually powered and it actually regenerates and cleans up the signal it receives, thus doubling the effective segment distance limitation for the specific topology (for example, extending a twisted-pair Ethernet segment another 100 meters).

- A passive hub is typically unpowered and makes only physical, electrical connections. Typically, the maximum segment distance of a particular topology is shortened because the hub takes some power away from the signal strength in order to do its job. You should not expect to see these in service anymore.

## The Multistation Access Unit (MAU)

The Multistation Access Unit (MAU) is a Physical layer device that is unique to Token Ring networks. Token Ring networks use a physical star topology, yet they use a logical ring topology. Logical topologies are discussed in the upcoming section "Data Link Layer." The central device on an Ethernet star topology network is a hub, but on a Token Ring network, the central device is a MAU (sometimes called MSAU, for those who prefer to represent the word *station* separately in the acronym).

The functionality of the MAU is similar to that of a hub in that active MAUs regenerate the signal they receive as they send it out, but the MAU provides the data path that creates the logical "ring" in a Token Ring network. Unlike a hub, the MAU passes the bits received on one port to the port that the MAU deems the nearest active downstream port. In doing so, the MAU recognizes which ports have active stations attached and bypasses any inactive ports in its search for the next active downstream port. The data can travel in an endless loop between stations. MAUs are chained together by connecting the Ring Out port of one MAU to the Ring In port of another and connecting the last Ring Out port to the Ring In of the first MAU in the chain, thus forming a complete loop. MAUs on the market since the mid '90s were found fairly reliably to have a feature that allowed the ring to be completed internally, without the last MAU connecting back to the first. Such flexibility resulted in considerably more expansive rings, without the restriction of that potentially longer run back to the beginning if expansion had occurred in a straight line. In a Token Ring network, you can have up to 33 MAUs chained together. MAUs are shown in Figure 2.11.

**FIGURE 2.11**   MAUs in a Token Ring network

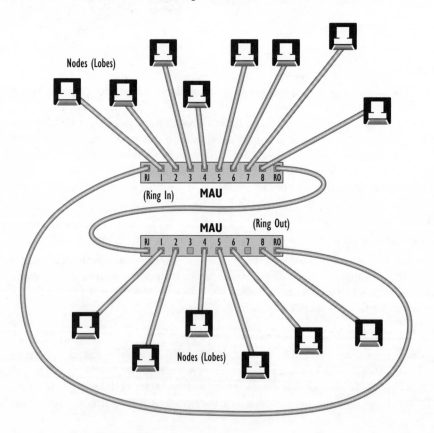

# The Data Link Layer

The Data Link layer is actually made up of two sublayers:

- The Media Access Control (MAC) sublayer
- The Logical Link Control (LLC) sublayer

    Figure 2.12 illustrates this arrangement.

**FIGURE  2.12**    Sublayers of the Data Link layer

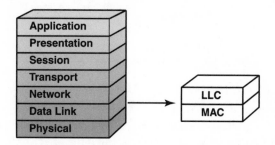

In the following sections, you will be introduced to various topics that all have one major thread in common: each topic is a separate piece of the Data Link puzzle. You will be presented with concepts from the definition of a frame to the format of a MAC address and with details of some of the most popular Data Link protocols on the market today. We'll finish up with a survey of the most popular layer 2 devices in the industry.

## Data Link Layer Concepts

Protocols that operate at the Data Link layer have several responsibilities, including creating, transmitting, and receiving frames. Additionally, the Data Link layer is responsible for physical (MAC) addressing and logical link control (LLC) processing, creating logical topologies, and controlling media access.

### Frames

At the Data Link layer, data coming from upper-layer protocols are divided into logical chunks called *frames*. A frame is a unit of data transmission. The size and format of these frames depend on the transmission technology. In other words, Ethernet frames differ greatly from Token Ring frames and Frame Relay frames, and the three are not compatible (without some sort of intermediary device to translate). Table 2.1 shows the names of the protocol data units (PDUs) at the layers that have distinctive data structures. Just as frames are presented here, the others will be discussed further in their related sections.

**TABLE 2.1**   PDUs by Layer

| Layer | Protocol Data Unit |
| --- | --- |
| Application | Message, datagram, or user data |
| Transport | Segment |
| Network | Packet |
| Data Link | Frame |
| Physical | Bits |

### The Hardware (MAC) Address

Every interface that communincates over a LAN segment has a globally unique address, typically assigned at the factory. This address is protocol independent and is often called the hardware address. It's technically accurate, however, to call it the *MAC address* because it exists at the MAC sublayer of the Data Link layer.

The hardware address is also called the *Ethernet address* or the *physical address*.

The MAC address itself is a 48-bit value, commonly represented as a 12-digit hexadecimal number. As you may remember, the hexadecimal numbering system uses all digits from 0 through 9 and adds *A* through *F*. Each two-digit set is separated by colons, like so:

07:57:AC:1F:B2:76

Or some manufacturers display it with dashes, like so:

07-57-AC-1F-B2-76

The first three sets of digits (07-57-AC in the preceding example) are known as the *Organizationally Unique Identifier (OUI)*, which is administered by the IEEE and uniquely identifies the manufacturer of the interface. The last three sets (1F-B2-76 in this example) form a value, sometimes referred to as the *device ID*, that the manufacturer must ensure exists only on a single manufactured interface that bears that OUI, making the entire 48-bit value unique worldwide. The OUI and the serialized suffix together make up a MAC address. Because the MAC address is almost universally permanently embedded in a ROM chip on the device, it is often referred to as a *burned-in address (BIA)*.

Normally, the MAC address of an interface is set at the factory and cannot be changed. For this purpose, all NIC manufacturers keep track of the MAC addresses they use so they don't duplicate addresses internally among their products. The IEEE ensures that no two manufacturers legally use the same OUI. Again, this creates a globally unique identifier for each interface manufactured by any registered vendor, barring rogue manufacturers from randomly creating their own OUI. Administrators are able to change the MAC addresses of the cards they receive (using a factory-supplied program), so if they discover a rare duplicate MAC address, they can resolve the conflict, or if they have an unrecommended locally administered addressing system, they can implement it. To that end, many operating systems (including Linux and Windows XP) allow a locally administered address (LAA) to overide the factory MAC address. The configuration procedure varies according to the software used, but it is usally a simple procedure.

## Logical Topology

The Data Link layer also bears the responsibility of dictating the logical topology of a network, or the way the devices perceive the topology of the network. A logical topology differs from a physical topology in that the physical topology dictates the way the cables are laid out, whereas the logical topology dictates the way the information flows. The types of logical topologies are the same as the physical topologies except that the information flow specifies the type of logical topology in use. For example, in the early days of Ethernet, networks were physically wired using a bus topology. The MAC sublayer of the Data Link layer of the equipment attached to this physical bus was designed to envision the network as a bus, making the logical topology a bus as well. Thus, that configuration is known as a physical bus/logical bus. Once twisted pair and fiber were introduced into the Ethernet Physical layer, hubs were designed to allow the network to be wired as a physical star while allowing the devices attached to the hub to continue to believe they were part of a bus, making this configuration a physical star/logical bus.

Finally, the Data Link layer can describe the method of media access. There are three main classifications of media access methods:

**Contention**   Every device "competes" with other devices for the opportunity to transmit, and each has an equal chance at transmitting. If two devices transmit at the same time, an error, referred to as a *collision,* occurs and the devices try again.

**Polling**   A central device, called a *controller,* polls each device in turn and asks if it has data to transmit. This type of media access virtually eliminates collisions.

**Token Passing**   This uses a special data packet called a *token.* When a device has the token, it can transmit. If it doesn't have the token, it can't transmit. This media access technology also eliminates collision problems.

## Media Access Methods

With many devices on the same piece of network media, there has to be a way of vying for time on the cable. This process is called media access, and there are three main methods:

**Carrier Sense/Multiple Access with Collision Detection (CSMA/CD)**   This media access technology is probably the most common. When a protocol that uses CSMA/CD has data to transmit, it first senses if a signal is already on the wire (a *carrier*), indicating that someone is transmitting currently. That's the "Carrier Sense" part. If no one else is transmitting, it attempts a transmission and then listens to hear if someone else tried to transmit at the same time. If someone else transmits at the exact same time, a collision occurs. Both senders "back off" and don't transmit until some random period of time has passed. Then they both retry. That's the

"Collision Detection" part. The final part ("Multiple Access") just means that more than one station can be on the network at the same time. CSMA/CD is the access method used in Ethernet and wireless Ethernet networks.

**Token Passing**    In addition to being a broad classification of media access methods, token passing is actually a specific method of media acess unto itself. This media access method uses a special packet called a token. The first computer that is turned on creates the token. It then passes on the token to the next computer. The token passes around the network until a computer that has data to send takes the token off the network, modifies it, and puts it back on the network along with the data it has to send. Each station between the sender and the receiver along the network reads the destination address in the token. If the destination address doesn't match its own, the station simply sends the package on its way. When the destination station recognizes its address in the destination address of the token, the NIC copies the data into the station's memory and modifies the token, indicating that it has received the data and recognized its own address in the frame. The token continues around the network until the original sender receives the token again. If the original sender has more data to send, the process repeats itself (for a specific amount of time). If not, the sender modifies the token to indicate that the token is "free" for anyone else to use. With this method, there are no collisions (as in CSMA/CD networks) because everyone has to have "permission" to transmit (via the token).

**Carrier Sense/Multiple Access with Collision Avoidance (CSMA/CA)**    This technology works almost identically to CSMA/CD, but instead of sending the whole data chunk and then listening to hear if it was transmitted, the sender transmits a request to send (RTS) packet and waits for a clear to send (CTS) before sending. When it receives the CTS, the sender sends the chunk. AppleTalk networks use this method of media access. The difference between CSMA/CD and CSMA/CA has been described like this: Say you want to cross a busy street and you want to use one of these protocols to cross it. If you are using CSMA/CD, you just cross the street. If you get hit, you go back to the curb and try again. If you're using CSMA/CA, you send your little brother across. If he makes it, it's probably OK for you to go.

While there does exist another media access method that had early promise, its timing on the market couldn't have been worse. The method is demand priority, and it was used with the 100VGAnyLAN technology from HP. Today, it is nothing more than an aside in the annals of history, much as it is treated as an aside here. Demand priority was a polling class of media access methods, leaving a large amount of the decision concerning whose turn it was to talk to the concentrator, as opposed to the NIC, which governs such choices in Ethernet and Token Ring. This is similar to the effect of attaching a NIC to a Layer 2 Switch and turning off CSMA/CD on the NIC, which allows the NIC to transmit at will. The switch is then responsible for deciding when the frame gets forwarded to the rest of the network.

## Project 802

One of the major components of the Data Link layer is the result of the Institute of Electrical and Electronics Engineers's (IEEE's) 802 subcommittees and their work on standards for local area and metropolitan area networks (LANs/MANs). The committee met in February 1980, so they used the "80" from 1980 and the "2" from the second month to create the name Project 802. The designation for an 802 standard always includes a dot (.) followed by either a single or a double digit. These numeric digits specify particular categories within the 802 standard. Currently, there are 12 standards. These standards, shown in Figure 2.13, are listed in Table 2.2 and described in more detail in the following sections.

**T A B L E  2 . 2**    IEEE 802 Networking Standards

| Standard | Topic |
|---|---|
| 802.1 | LAN/MAN Management (and Media Access Control Bridges) |
| 802.2 | Logical Link Control |
| 802.3 | CSMA/CD |
| 802.4 | Token Bus |
| 802.5 | Token Ring |
| 802.6 | Distributed Queue Dual Bus (DQDB) Metropolitan Area Network (MAN) |
| 802.7 | Broadband Local Area Networks |
| 802.8 | Fiber-Optic LANs and MANs |
| 802.9 | Isochronous LANs |
| 802.10 | LAN/MAN Security |
| 802.11 | Wireless LAN |
| 802.12 | Demand Priority Access Method |
| 802.15 | Wireless Personal Area Network |
| 802.16 | Wireless Metropolitain Area Network |
| 802.17 | Resilient Packet Ring |
| 802.18 | LAN/MAN Standards Committee |

Some standards have a letter to further distinguish the standard (e.g., 802.11b). The letters usually refer to different versions or interpretations of the standard.

**FIGURE 2.13**    The IEEE standards' relationship to the OSI model

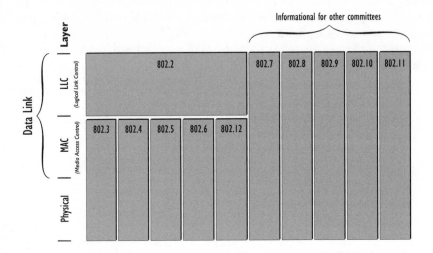

## The 802.1 LAN/MAN Management (and Media Access Control Bridges)

IEEE 802.1 discusses standards for LAN and MAN management, as well as for MAC bridges. One of the derivatives of 802.1 is the spanning tree algorithm for network bridges and switches, 802.1d (bridges and switches are discussed later in this chapter). The spanning tree algorithm helps to prevent switching loops in a switched network. See the upcoming section on 802.10 for its comparison with another popular 802.1 specification.

## The 802.2 Logical Link Control

This standard specifies the operation of the Logical Link Control (LLC) sublayer of the Data Link layer of the OSI model. The LLC sublayer provides an interface between the MAC sublayer and the Network layer. The 802.2 standard is used by the IEEE 802.3 Ethernet specification (discussed next) but not by the earlier Ethernet 2 specifications (used in early implementations of Ethernet).

## The 802.3 CSMA/CD

This standard specifies a network that uses a bus topology, baseband signaling, and a CSMA/CD network access method. This standard was developed to match the Digital, Intel, and Xerox (DIX) Ethernet networking technology. So many people implemented the 802.3 standard, which resembles the DIX Ethernet, that people just started calling it Ethernet. It is the most widely implemented of all the 802 standards because of its simplicity and low cost.

Recently the 802.3ae working group updated 802.3 to include Gigabit Ethernet implementations.

## The 802.5 Token Ring

This standard is one example of a commonly used product becoming a documented standard. Typically, a standard is developed and then products are written to conform to the standard. Token Ring was developed by IBM in 1984, and the 802.5 standard soon followed. The 802.5 standard and Token Ring are almost identical.

Like Ethernet, Token Ring can use several cable types. Most often, it is installed using *twisted-pair* cabling, which can be either *shielded* or *unshielded*. Shielding adds to the cable investment but offers the advantage of resistance to unwanted electrical signals that could impair the network signal.

Possible transmission rates for Token Ring have increased with time; after 4Mbps Token Ring came 16Mbps Token Ring. Token Ring uses a physical star, logical ring topology with token-passing media access. If you install 4Mbps NICs on a network that otherwise uses 16Mbps NICs, your entire ring speed is reduced to 4Mbps. Unlike with Ethernet, a computer cannot talk unless it has a token. This can cause some grief if a token gets "stuck."

Although nowhere near as popular as Ethernet, Token Ring is still used in a number of locations for two reasons:

- IBM made sure that Token Ring did a fine job of talking to IBM mainframes, which are still used.

- Token Ring network performance "degrades with grace."

The latter means that as network traffic increases, the network slowly gets slower because the single token, which can travel in only one direction, gets busy servicing all that demand. Ethernet, on the other hand, can become so flooded as network traffic increases that the entire network collapses. Now, suppose you were wiring a computerized fire alarm system for a large building. Which would you rather use: Ethernet or Token Ring? To increase performance, some Token Ring technologies implement early token release, whereby the sending station doesn't hog the token. It simply grabs the token, sends its data, and frees the token.

In Token Ring, just as in most Ethernet schemes, there is a central device to which stations connect. It isn't, however, called a hub. IBM calls it a MAU. IBM often has a different name for things. Even its name for Token Ring cabling is different. In telephone and computer networks, twisted cable is rated by *categories*. IBM rates Token Ring cable by *type*.

One final difference between Token Ring and the others is the *regeneration process*. Data signals are read, amplified, and repeated by every device on the network to reduce degradation. This includes MAUs and NICs and is one reason that Token Ring was once so much more expensive than Ethernet.

## The 802.10 LAN/MAN Security

The 802.10 Standards for Interoperable LAN/MAN Security (SILS), ratified in late 1992, were originally designed to provide security within shared LAN/metropolitan-area network (MAN) environments. The 802.10 protocol incorporates a mechanism whereby LAN traffic can carry a virtual LAN (VLAN) identifier in the header of its frames, allowing selective switching of frames based on their identifier. Interfaces that were members of one VLAN could not exchange frames with interfaces in another VLAN, creating security. 802.10 incorporates authentication and encryption to ensure data confidentiality, further enhancing security. 802.10 enjoyed some success in FDDI environments but has waned in popularity in recent years in favor of other frame-tagging protocols, such as IEEE 802.1Q and Cisco's proprietary Inter-Switch Link (ISL) protocol.

### The 802.11 Wireless LAN

Wireless networking usually requires a higher up-front investment than cable-based networking. Still, the cost can be justified if an office is rearranged with any regularity or must be moved from location to location to satisfy business requirements. A famous example of this is the Red Cross. This agency would not be effective if it had to wire computers together before assisting at each disaster area.

Recently, 802.11 was updated to include the 802.11a, b, and g standards, which specify higher wireless speeds compared to the original 1Mbps of 802.11. 802.11b is the next faster specification, with bit rates of 11Mbps. Both 802.11a and 802.11g post speeds of 54Mbps, but they do so in different ways. 802.11a uses a 5GHz signal, which makes it effective only at shorter distances, as well as incompatible with 802.11b's 2.4GHz signal, but places it in a much less-crowded bandwidth. Neither one interferes with the other at least. 802.11g, however, shares the lower 2.4GHz frequency of 802.11b, making interoperation of the faster 802.11g end devices with the slower 802.11b access points rather easy through simple rate adaption over the same frequency. Nevertheless, some manufacturers offer NIC cards, for example, that combine all three technologies and allow the device to autosense the capability of the strongest access point in order to allow the modest installed base of more expensive 802.11a access points to play successfully with the others. But the bottom line is that 802.11a is incompatible with the other two specifications.

### The 802.12 Demand Priority Access Method

First developed by Hewlett-Packard, this standard combines the concepts of Ethernet and Token Ring. The communication scheme used is called Demand Priority (thus, the name of the standard). It uses "intelligent" hubs that allocate more bandwidth to frames that have been assigned a higher priority by the sending computer. The hub scans its ports and then allocates bandwidth according to each frame's priority. This is extremely valuable for real-time audio and video transmissions.

The 802.12 standard is also known as *100VG (Voice Grade), 100VG-AnyLAN, 100Base-VG,* and *AnyLAN*. The 100 is short for 100Mbps, or 10 times faster than the original Ethernet speeds. Other manufacturers didn't buy into the ideas of 100VG, perhaps in part because of the higher overhead of demand priority due to port scanning. Instead, they updated the original Ethernet to *Fast Ethernet,* which also supports 100Mbps while maintaining the 802.3 standards.

Table 2.3 summarizes the main features—including speed, access method, topology, and media—of various network standards, such as the most common 802 MAC standards and FDDI.

## Data Link Layer Devices

Three main devices manipulate data at the Data Link layer:

- Bridges
- Switches
- Wireless access points (WAPs)

They are more complex than their Physical layer counterparts and thus are more expensive and more difficult to implement. But they each bring unique advantages to the network.

**TABLE 2.3**   Main Features of Various Network Technologies

| Technol ogy | Speed(s) | Access Method | Topologies | Media |
| --- | --- | --- | --- | --- |
| IEEE 802.3 | 10, 100, 1000, 10,000Mbps | CSMA/CD | Logical bus | Coax or UTP |
| IEEE 802.5 | 4, 16, 100Mbps | Token passing | Physical star, logical ring | STP or UTP |
| IEEE 802.11 | 1, 11, 54Mbps | CSMA/CA | Cellular | RF through air |
| FDDI | 100Mbps | Token passing | Physical star, logical ring | Fiber optic (UTP implemented as TP-PMD) |

## The Bridge

A *bridge* is a network device, operating at the Data Link layer, that logically separates a single network into two segments, but it lets the two segments appear to be one network to higher-layer protocols. The primary use for a bridge is to keep traffic meant for devices on one side of the bridge from passing to the other side. For example, if you have a group of workstations that constantly exchange data on the same network segment as a group of workstations that don't use the network much at all, the busy group will slow down the performance of the network for the other users. If you put in a bridge to separate the two groups, however, only traffic destined for a workstation on the other side of the bridge will pass to the other side. All other traffic stays local. Figure 2.14 shows a network before and after bridging.

Bridges can connect dissimilar network types (for example, Token Ring and Ethernet) as long as the bridge operates at the LLC sublayer of the Data Link layer. If the bridge operates only at the lower sublayer (the MAC sublayer), the bridge can connect only similar network types (Token Ring to Token Ring and Ethernet to Ethernet).

## The Switch

The *switch* is more intelligent than a hub in that it can actually understand the frames that pass through it.

A switch (also known as a Layer 2 switch) builds a table of the MAC addresses of all the devices connected to it (see Figure 2.15).

**FIGURE 2.14**    A sample network before and after bridging

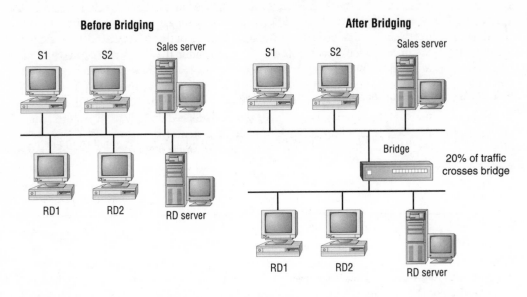

**FIGURE 2.15**    A switch builds a table of all MAC addresses of all connected stations.

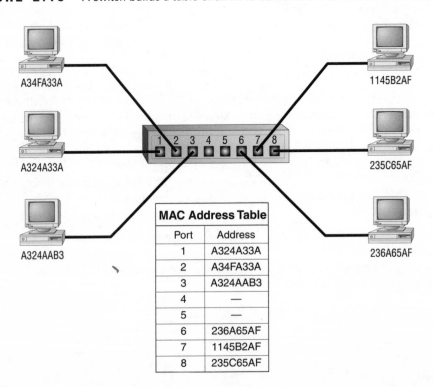

When two devices attached to the switch want to communicate, the sending device sends its data on to its local segment. This data is heard by the switch (similar to the way a hub functions). However, when the switch receives the data, rather than duplicating it out to all the ports as a hub would, it examines the Data Link header for the MAC address of the destination device and forwards it to the correct port. This process triggers a function within the switch that opens a virtual pipe between ports that can use the full bandwidth of the topology because the switch has a non-blocking backplane, able to support the collective bandwidth offered by the sum of its ports.

Switches have risen to the high level of popularity they enjoy today because of their ability to prevent collisions from occurring between the devices attached directly to their ports, thus increasing overall network throughput and efficiency. This stems from the fact that every port on a switch is in a different collision domain. A *collision domain* is that group of devices whose frames could potentially collide with one another. If a server were connected to a 100Mbps port on an Ethernet switch and 10 workstations were directly and individually connected (not through a hub connected to the switch) to 10Mbps ports on the same switch, each workstation would effectively have a dedicated, non-blocking 10Mbps channel to the server and there would never be any collisions. Thus, the inclusion of a switch in a network serves the function of increasing the number of collision domains while reducing the average population of all collision domains for the same number of nodes.

Layer 2 Switches differ from their layer 3 counterparts, which are able to operate on the layer 3 packets by routing the first packet between a source and destination because it stores the actual header required to build the outbound frame. It then rapidly switches subsequent packets between the same two devices in software or even hardware without looking up the layer 3 routing information again.

## The Wireless Access Point

If you are going to connect multiple wireless computers to an existing wired network, you will need at least one *wireless access point (WAP)*. The WAP is essentially a wireless bridge (or switch, as multiple end devices can connect simultaneously). It operates by connecting wireless clients together. In addition, it can connect those wireless clients to a wired network. As with a bridge or switch, the WAP indiscriminately propagates all broadcasts to all wireless and wired devices while allowing filtering based on MAC addresses.

The WAP contains at least one radio antenna that it uses to communicate with its clients via *radio frequency (RF)* signals. The WAP can (depending on software settings) act as either an access point, which allows a wireless user transparent access to a wired network, or a wireless bridge, which will connect a wireless network to a wired network yet only pass traffic it knows belongs on the other side.

Wireless networks will be covered in more detail in Chapter 6.

# The OSI Model's Middle Layers

As you move up the OSI model, the protocols at each successive layer get more complex and have more responsibilities. At the middle are the Network and Transport layers, which perform the bulk of the work for a protocol stack. You'll see why in the sections to follow.

## The Network Layer

The Network layer of the OSI model defines protocols that ensure that the data arrives at the correct destination. This is probably the most commonly discussed layer of the OSI model.

### Network Layer Concepts

The following concepts are the most important Network layer concepts:

- Logical network addressing
- Routing

### Logical Network Addressing

Earlier, you learned that every communicating LAN interface has an address (the MAC address) assigned at the factory and that this address is protocol independent. But as you know, most networks communicate using protocols that must have their own addressing scheme. If the MAC address is the Data Link layer physical address, the protocol-addressing scheme at the Network layer defines the logical address.

Each logical network address is protocol dependent, which is why you may have heard them referred to generically as *protocol addresses*. For example, a TCP/IP address is not the same as an IPX address. Additionally, the two protocols can coexist on the same interface without conflict, each simultaneously binding itself to the protocol-independent MAC address for the associated interface. However, two different interfaces using the same protocol cannot have the same logical network address on the same network. If that happens, neither interface can be seen on the network (see Figure 2.16).

**FIGURE 2.16**    Address conflicts on a network

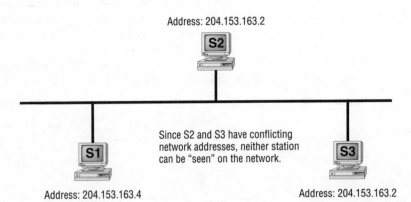

Address: 204.153.163.2

**S2**

Since S2 and S3 have conflicting network addresses, neither station can be "seen" on the network.

**S1**

Address: 204.153.163.4

**S3**

Address: 204.153.163.2

## Understanding Network Address Formats

Whenever you have to set up a network or add a device, it is important to have an understanding of how network addresses work. Every network address in either TCP/IP or IPX has both a network portion and a node, or host, portion. The network portion is the number that is assigned to the network segment to which one of the device's interfaces is connected. The node portion is the unique number that identifies that device on the segment. Together, the network portion and the node portion of an address ensure that a network address will be unique across the entire network.

IPX addresses use a 32-bit value represented as an eight-digit hexadecimal number for the network portion. This number, called the IPX network address, can be assigned randomly by the installation program or manually by the network administrator. The node portion is the 12-digit hexadecimal MAC address assigned by the manufacturer. A colon separates the two portions. Here is a sample IPX address:

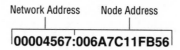

Network Address     Node Address

**00004567:006A7C11FB56**

TCP/IP addresses, on the other hand, use a dotted decimal notation in the format *xxx.xxx.xxx.xxx* as shown in the following:

**199.217.67.34**   IP Address

**255.255.255.0**   Subnet Mask

The address is a 32-bit value represented as four groups of eight-digit binary numbers (or, more commonly, up to three decimal digits, depending on the value of the bits) called octets, separated by periods. Each decimal number in an IP address can range from 0 through 255. Which portion is the network and which portion is the node depends on the class of the address if the default separation is used, but the subnet mask assigned with the address configures that separation, which may not adhere to the default classful boundary. A subnet mask is also a dotted decimal number with numbers in the range of 0 through 255. If a subnet mask contains 255 in any position (corresponding to a binary number of all ones), the corresponding part of the IP address is the network address. For example, if you have the mask 255.255.255.0, the first three octets are the network portion and the last portion is the node. It is possible to have one octet in the mask set to one of a small choice of other values, but that's beyond the scope of this study guide. The term *subnetwork,* or *subnet* for short, is generally used to mean network (when only default subnetting is used), segment, or immediate link, when IP routing is used.

Address conflicts can be common with TCP/IP because an administrator often needs to assign IP addresses. IPX addresses don't suffer from conflict nearly as often because the MAC address is used as part of the IPX address. The MAC address is unique and normally can't be changed (although some utilities are available on some systems). For more information on network addresses, see Chapter 4, "TCP/IP Utilities."

## Packets

At the Network layer, data coming from upper-layer protocols are divided into logical chunks called *packets*. A packet is a unit of data transmission. The size and format of these packets depend on the Network layer protocol in use. In other words, IP packets differ greatly from IPX packets and Apple-Talk DDP packets, and the three are not compatible. Refer back to Table 2.1, which shows the names of the protocol data units (PDUs) at the layers that have distinctive data structures.

## Routing

*Routing* is the process of moving data throughout an internetwork, passing through several network segments using devices called routers, which select the path the data takes. Placing routers in a network to break the network into several smaller subnets turns a network into an entity known as an *internetwork*. Routers determine which paths to take from internal databases called routing tables. These tables contain information about which router network interface (or port) to place information on in order to send it to a particular subnet. Routers will not pass unknown or broadcast packets by default. A router will route a packet only if it has a specific destination. Even if a default route is configured, the default route is, in fact, a specific destination where the router simply sends everything that doesn't match any other entry in the routing table to the default route address. Figure 2.17 illustrates conceptual views of routers and their interconnection.

**FIGURE 2.17** An internetwork

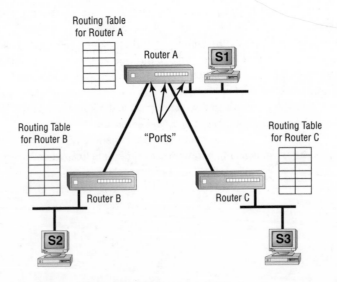

Information gets into routing tables in two ways:

- Through static routing
- Through dynamic routing

In *static routing*, the network administrator manually updates the router's routing table. The administrator enters every subnet into the routing table and selects the port on which the router should place data when the router receives data destined for that subnet from any other port. Unfortunately, on networks with more than a few segments, manually updating routing tables is time intensive and prohibitive.

> When using a Windows server as a router, use the ROUTE command at a command prompt in order to add, change, or remove static routes. This same utility is available for non-server Windows devices in case you would prefer to use individual static routes or manually set up a default route. For assistance using this command, simply open a command prompt and enter ROUTE /?.

*Dynamic routing*, on the other hand, uses route discovery protocols (better known as *routing protocols*) to talk to other routers and find out which networks they are attached to. Routers that use dynamic routing send out special packets to request updates of the other routers in the internetwork as well as to send their own updates.

With dynamic routing, the two categories of routing protocols are distance vector and link state. Older routing protocols, such as Routing Information Protocol (RIP) for TCP/IP and RIP for IPX, use the distance vector method. In distance vector routing, a router sends out its routing table when the router is brought online and every minute or so thereafter. When another router receives the contents of the first router's table, it adds 1 to the hop count of each route in the list of routes and then re-advertises the list. A *hop* is one pass through a router. The main downside to distance vector routing is the overhead required in advertising the entire routing table every 30 seconds, in the case of IP RIP.

Link state routing is more efficient than distance vector routing. Routers using link state routing protocols send out their routing table updates via multicast or unicast, not broadcast, and then only when necessary. If there is an update, only the update is sent. In the worst case, Open Shortest Path First (OSPF) performs a database synchronization about every 30 minutes, hardly a bandwidth hit.

> NetWare Link Services Protocol (NLSP) for IPX and OSPF for TCP/IP are two link state routing protocols.

Several protocols can be routed, but a few protocols can't be routed. It is important to know which protocols are routable and which aren't so that you can choose the appropriate protocol when it comes time to design an internetwork. Table 2.4 shows a few of the most common routable and nonroutable protocols and the routing protocols they use, if any.

**TABLE 2.4**    Routable and Nonroutable Protocols

| Protocol | Routing Protocol | Routable? |
| --- | --- | --- |
| IPX | RIP | Yes |
| IPX | NLSP | Yes |
| NetBEUI | None | No |
| TCP/IP | RIP | Yes |
| TCP/IP | OSPF | Yes |
| XNS | RIP | Yes |

When setting up routing on your network, you may have to configure a default gateway. A *default gateway*, when configured on a workstation, is the router interface on the workstation's subnet that a packet is sent to when the workstation doesn't know the specific path to the intended recipient. TCP/IP subnets sometimes have multiple routers as well and must use this parameter to specify which router is the default.

One important topic to understand is how to configure a default gateway address when configuring TCP/IP. This involves setting up both the router to actually be the default gateway, and set up the workstation to use that address as the default gateway. The following will walk you through setting up a default gateway on a Windows workstation and a Cisco router, switch, or other device running Cisco Internetwork Operating System (IOS). Occasionally, you will need to be able to establish or change this feature on one of these devices. You'll find, by going through these steps on live equipment, that you become more comfortable with an array of other tasks as well, such as altering the routing table and creating static routes.

Microsoft Windows allows manual adjustment of the computer's routing table, which can be quite advanced depending upon such factors as routing protocols being enabled on the computer and any manual configurations that have been made. The following steps establish a default gateway that forwards all traffic that does not otherwise match any entries in the routing table to the IP address you configure

1.  Open up a command prompt session. One way to do this is to click the Start button and then click Run. Type in **cmd** and press Enter.

2.  At the command prompt, enter the command **route print** to view the current routing table.

3.  Make a note of the current default gateway, if any. The default gateway appears on the line that says, "Default Gateway: *current_default_gateway*."

4.  In order to minimize disruption of service, use the same IP address from step 3 in the command **route add 0.0.0.0 mask 0.0.0.0** *current_default_gateway*. If none existed, any address will be fine, although for production configuration, you would want to use the actual IP address of the device to which traffic destined for unknown networks should be forwarded. If you receive an error message, it is probably because you chose an IP address that is not on your local IP subnet. Microsoft requires that the default gateway reside on the same IP subnet as your computer's interface.

5.  To remove a default route, enter the command **route delete 0.0.0.0 mask 0.0.0.0** *current_default_gateway*. Receiving the error message "The route specified was not found" means that you entered the wrong IP address for the current default gateway or that you likely received an error, as described in step 4.

Cisco's (IOS) allows you to create a default gateway for the device you are configuring in much the same way you did for Microsoft Windows, with minor differences. A Cisco router (an example of a device that runs Cisco's IOS) maintains a potentially more complex routing table because the use of dynamic routing protocols tends to be more prevalent on these devices. The following steps establish a gateway of last resort (Cisco's term for a default gateway) out the serial interface Serial0 toward whatever device lies across the serial link from the router being configured. One caveat: if your router currently has no interface called, or no configuration on, Serial0, then the following procedure will create an entry in your running configuration but no result will be seen in the routing table. It is still necessary to perform the removal in the last step or else when and if the interface does become active, the default gateway will activate as well. Feel free to substitute an actual live serial interface for Serial0, if need be, such as Serial1, Serial0/0, and so on. The privileged EXEC mode command `show ip interface brief` can help you determine the available IP interfaces your device possesses. Choose one with an IP address. One more thing: this procedure assumes you are able to find your way to privileged EXEC mode on a Cisco device and begins with the command to enter global configuration mode:

1.  Issue the command **show ip route** and make sure you see the line `Gateway of last resort is not set` after the codes and before the routing entries begin.

2.  If step 1 did not give the expected results, it would be best to find a device that does give such results. Once you get the results requested for step 1, issue the following command to enter global configuration mode:

    ```
    Router#configure terminal
    Router(config)#
    ```

3.  Enter the following commands to establish the default gateway through interface Serial0 and return to privileged EXEC mode, noting the space in the middle of the series of zeros:

    ```
    Router(config)#ip route 0.0.0.0 0.0.0.0 serial0
    Router(config)#end
    Router#
    ```

4.  Enter the command **show ip route** and confirm that the line described in step 1 has changed to `Gateway of last resort is 0.0.0.0 to network 0.0.0.0`.

**5.** Enter the following sequence of commands to remove the default gateway you just created:

```
Router#configure terminal
Router(config)#no ip route 0.0.0.0 0.0.0.0 serial0
Router(config)#end
Router#
```

In both Windows and the Cisco IOS, the default gateway was created with a routing table entry of network 0.0.0.0 with a mask of 0.0.0.0. The reason this entry works as the least desirable routing table entry is because the last series of 0s (zeros) ANDs with any IP address and produces 0.0.0.0, which matches the network number 0.0.0.0 for the default route. Because this works for any IP address, this entry will never fail, but because the number of 1s in the mask is zero, it will be the least desirable entry in the routing table, with matched entries having masks with one or more 1s being preferred. Nevertheless, if the default route is the only matching entry, then it will be used. The AND operation is a Boolean algebra operand that produces a 0 when any pair of bits other than two 1s are ANDed. This means that with a mask of all 0s, the result will always be all 0s, and that will always match the network entry of all 0s, making the default gateway work in every case as long as a better match does not exist.

## Network Layer Devices

Two devices operate at the Network layer:

- Routers
- Layer 3 Switches

### The Router

Routers are Network layer devices that connect multiple networks or segments to form a larger internetwork. They are also the devices that facilitate communication within this internetwork. They make the choices about how best to send packets within the internetwork so that they arrive at their destination. Routers do not propagate broadcasts from one of their ports to another, meaning that each port on a router is in a different broadcast domain. A *broadcast domain* is the collection of all devices that will receive each others' broadcast frames.

Several companies manufacture routers, but probably three of the biggest names in the business are Nortel Networks, Juniper Networks, and Cisco Systems. Nortel Networks is the resulting corporation from the merger of Nortel and Bay Networks, which itself was once separately Welfleet and Synoptics. Cisco has always been a built-from-the-ground-up router company. These companies make other products as well, and even though Nortel Networks concentrates on large-scale telephony equipment, it manages to provide adequate competition for Cisco and Juniper in the router and switch market. Cisco has even moved into Nortel Networks's arena by using its AVVID product line to compete in the growing Voice over IP (VoIP) market.

Routers have many functions other than simply routing packets. They can connect many small segments into an internetwork as well as connect internetworks to a much larger network, such as a corporate intranet or the Internet. Routers can also connect dissimilar lower-layer topologies. For example, you can connect an Ethernet and a Token Ring network using a router. Additionally, with added software, routers can perform firewall functions and packet filtering.

Routers are some of the most complex devices on a network today. Consequently, they are likely to be some of the most expensive But simple low-end routers that make Internet connectivity more affordable have been introduced by Nortel Networks, Cisco, and other companies.

### Layer 3 Switches

A Network layer device that has received much media attention of late is the Layer 3 Switch. The Layer 3 part of the name corresponds to the Network layer of the OSI model. It performs the multiport, virtual LAN, data-pipelining functions of a standard Layer 2 Switch, but it can also perform basic routing functions between virtual LANs.

# The Transport Layer

The Transport layer defines the protocols for structuring messages and checks the validity of transmissions.

## Transport Layer Concepts

The Transport layer is remenescent of the old saying Net Tech instructors used to pound into their students' heads: "Reliable end-to-end error and flow control." The Transport layer does other things as well, but the protocols that operate at the Transport layer mainly ensure reliable communications between upper peer layers. That's not to say there are no Transport layer protocols that provide none of this. In fact, UDP, as you will see, is a stripped-down protocol that has one job only, to connect the upper layers with the Network layer. It doesn't concern itself with such things as reliability, connection establishment, and flow control. Nevertheless, if those things are to be offered, the Transport layer is generally where you need to look for such support.

The following sections strive to demystify the intricacies of one of the more complex layers in the OSI model. Discussions center around connection orientation and caomparisons of the best-known Transport layer protocols.

### The Connection Type

To provide error and flow control services, protocols at the Transport layer use connection services. There are two types of connection services:

- Connection-oriented
- Connectionless

*Connection-oriented services* use acknowledgments and responses to establish a virtual circuit between sending and receiving end devices. The acknowledgments are also used to ensure that the connection is maintained. Alternatively, as in the case of protocols such as Frame Relay and ATM, virtual circuits may be configured manually by administrators or engineers at each switch along a path from one end device to the other. The one thing all connection-oriented protocols have in common, however, is that no user data will be sent into the network without a virtual circuit already having been established.

Connections are similar to phone calls. You dial the intended recipient and the recipient picks up and says hello. You then identify yourself and say that you'd like to talk about something, and the conversation begins. If you hear silence for a while, you might ask, "Are you still there?" to make sure the recipient is still on the line. When finished, you both agree to end the connection by hanging up. Connection-oriented services work in the same way, except that instead of mouths, phones, and words, they use computers, NICs, and special datagrams. Figure 2.18 shows an example of the beginning of communications between two computers using connection-oriented services.

*Connectionless services*, on the other hand, don't have error recovery or flow control because most connectionless services are also unreliable. They do have one simple advantage: speed. Because connectionless services don't have the overhead of maintaining the connection, the sacrifice in error control is more than made up for in speed. To make another analogy, connectionless services are similar to a postcard. Each message is considered singular and not related to any other by the receiving peer layer. The error control and delivery confirmation are left up to higher layers.

## Transport Layer Implementations

Before we discuss the other layers of the OSI model, let's take a look at the IPX/SPX, TCP/IP, and NetBEUI implementations of the Transport layer.

 We will look closer at these protocols, as well as AppleTalk and AppleTalk over IP, in the section "Networking Protocols" later in this chapter.

### The IPX/SPX Protocol

As far as the connection services of IPX/SPX are concerned, there are two transport protocols:

- Internetwork Packet Exchange (IPX))
- Sequenced Packet Exchange (SPX)

**FIGURE 2.18**    Initiating communications using a connection-oriented service

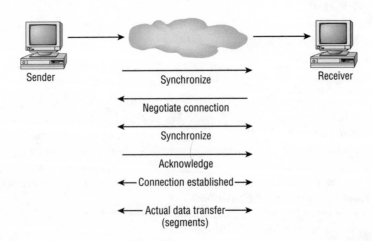

IPX is connectionless and thus enjoys the benefits of connectionless transports, including increased speed. SPX, on the other hand, uses connection-oriented services. SPX always uses the Network layer services of IPX. IPX, however, can operate independently of SPX, as if it were both a Network and Transport layer entity, as represented in Figure 2.19. Notice the way IPX wraps around SPX, taking up space in both the Network and Transport layers, able to interact with higher-layer protocols and services, without the use of SPX. In this way, IPX without SPX is similar to the combination of UDP and IP, in contrast to TCP with IP, which is more akin to the combination of SPX and IPX. While IP will always answer to TCP or UDP, never taking on Transport layer functionality on its own, IPX is capable of just such a feat.

**FIGURE 2.19**    The IPX/SPX protocol model

| OSI Reference Model | NetWare | | | | |
|---|---|---|---|---|---|
| Application | Applications | | NetWare core protocol (NCP) | RPC-based application | LU 6.2 support |
| Presentation | NetBIOS emulator | NetWare shell (client) | | | |
| Session | | | | RPC | |
| Transport | SPX | | | | |
| Network | IPX | | | | |
| Data Link | Ethernet IEEE 802.3 | Token Ring/ IEEE 802.5 | FDDI | ARCnet | PPP |
| Physical | | | | | |

IPX/SPX has no name resolution system by default. That functionality is employed when a NetWare server is running Novell Directory Services (NDS) and the NDS directory requester (which runs at the Session, Presentation, and Application layers) can make requests of an NDS database.

**NOTE**    Directory services databases fall into two broad categories: hierarchical and nonhierarchical. NDS, unlike the NetWare Bindery it was intended to replace, is a hierarchically designed directory service, as is the Active Directory (AD) of Microsoft Windows. Another example of a hierarchical database is the password shadow file of Linux, which contains more information than a standard world-readable password file and is only readable by the root account, making it more secure. The Novell NetWare Bindery is a flat database that contains definitions for objects, such as users, groups, and workgroups. Other nonhierarchical databases are non-AD NT domains and non-shadow Linux password files.

### The TCP/IP Protocol

Like the IPX/SPX protocol stack, the TCP/IP protocol stack has two Transport layer protocols:

- Transmission Control Protocol (TCP)

- User Datagram Protocol (UDP)

TCP is connection oriented, and UDP is connectionless. Some upper-layer protocols, such as FTP and HTTP, require reliable connection-oriented service and, therefore, use TCP. Other upper-layer protocols, such as Trivial File Transfer Protocol (TFTP) and Network File System (NFS), require increased speed and will trade reliability for that speed. They, therefore, use UDP.

A Fully Qualified Domain Name (FQDN) is the type of name that you use when surfing the Web. It consists of a top-level domain name, such as .com, for example, preceded by a second-level domain name, such as comptia, preceded by a server name or subdomain string, such as www. For FQDN-to-IP address resolution, TCP/IP uses Domain Name Service (DNS). Many operating systems use DNS for name resolution, but Unix (whose networking is based on TCP/IP) uses DNS almost exclusively, and today, so does Microsoft Windows. DNS is probably the most cross-platform name resolution method available. Chapter 4 discusses the function and operation of DNS.

### The NetBEUI Protocol

Because it is based on the NetBIOS protocol, NetBIOS Extended User Interface (NetBEUI) has datagram support and, thus, has support for connectionless transmission. It doesn't, however, have support for connection-oriented services. NetBIOS does allow hosts to have logical names, but the naming service, as with NDS and DNS, functions at the upper layers of the OSI model.

# The OSI Model's Upper Layers

The upper layers of the OSI model deal with less esoteric concepts. Even though we're still discussing computer networking, the top three layers (Session, Presentation, and Application) seem easier to understand. Because the Network+ exam doesn't cover the upper layers (and many times these top three layers are grouped together), the following sections will give only a brief overview.

## The Session Layer

Protocols that operate at the Session layer of the OSI model are responsible for establishing, maintaining, and breaking sessions, or *dialogs*. This is different from the connection services provided at the Transport layer because the Session layer operates at a higher level and looks at the bigger picture—the entire conversation, not just one sentence. Many gateways operate at the Session layer. Novell's Service Advertisement Protocol (SAP) is a Session layer protocol, as well as NetBIOS.

# The Presentation Layer

The Presentation layer does what you might think it does: It changes the look, or *presentation,* of the data from the lower layers into a format that the upper-layer processes can work with. Among other services, the Presentation layer deals with encryption, data compression, and network redirectors.

In addition, the Presentation layer deals with character-set translation. Not all computer systems use the same table to convert binary numbers into text. Most standard computer systems use the American Standard Code for Information Interchange (ASCII). Mainframe computers (and some IBM networking systems) use the Extended Binary Coded Decimal Interchange Code (EBCDIC) and Unicode, which is popular on the Internet as one character set that assigns a unique number to every character regardless of the language or the operating system used to display the character. The three are totally different. Protocols at the Presentation layer can translate between the three.

# The Application Layer

Now, you might be thinking, "This layer is for my programs, right?" Wrong. The Application layer defines several standard network services that fall into categories such as file transfer, print access, and e-mail relay. The applications that access these network services are located above the Application layer and are not even part of the layered model.

# Upper-Layer Devices

There are only a few upper-layer devices, none of which operate at any specific layer. Because they perform a range of functions for the network, they fall into the class of devices known as *gateways.* A gateway translates one type of network data into another. Gateways can be either hardware or software, but the most popular way to run a gateway is as a software program on a dedicated computer.

There are many, many types of gateways, but the one most people think of is an e-mail gateway. E-mail gateways translate e-mail messages from one type of e-mail system so that they can be transmitted on another (for example, from GroupWise e-mail to SMTP mail for the Internet).

# Networking Protocols

Now that you have a basic understanding of the OSI model and its related concepts, you can use these concepts to understand how the major protocols work and how each of the protocols within each protocol stack maps to the OSI model, thus describing its function.

In the following sections, you will learn about four major protocol stacks and how each one handles the concepts of addressing, routing, interoperability, and naming:

- TCP/IP
- IPX/SPX

- NetBEUI
- AppleTalk/AppleTalk over IP

# TCP/IP

Transmission Control Protocol/Internet Protocol (TCP/IP) is the protocol suite of choice today. It, like other protocols suites, is used to allow local network devices to communicate over a network. However, TCP/IP is used not only on LANs, but also over WANs and the Internet. Actually, TCP/IP is the only protocol suite in use on the Internet.

 You'll learn more about TCP/IP in Chapter 3, "TCP/IP Fundamentals."

In the following sections, TCP/IP addressing, routing, interoperability, and naming concepts will be presented. This is a consolidation of similar information from other parts of the chapter with a few additional points of interest.

## Addressing

As mentioned earlier in the chapter, each host is given (either manually or automatically) a dotted decimal IP address in the format *xxx.xxx.xxx.xxx*, where *xxx* is a number from 0 to 255.

 There are several addressing rules, which you will learn more about in Chapter 3.

Because addressing is a Network layer concept, the protocols that deal with addressing can be found at this layer. The Address Resolution Protocol (ARP) is responsible for resolving an IP address to the MAC address of the receiving host. The MAC address is a Data Link layer address hard-coded to each network interface by the manufacturer. When a TCP/IP packet is sent, at some point a router will need to determine exactly which device the packet is intended for. On Ethernet networks, the router will use an ARP request broadcast. Any device that wants a specific physical address will send an ARP broadcast on to the immediate link with the IP address of the interface for which it wants the MAC address in the packet header. The device whose interface has the matching IP address will respond with its interface's MAC address. Whenever a device sends an ARP request and receives a response, it notes that resolution in a table known as the ARP cache. When a router receives packets and needs to send them to a particular device on one of its own segments, it examines the IP address of the destination, looks up the MAC address of that device's interface using ARP, and forwards the packet via Ethernet to the intended destination.

 You'll learn more about ARP in Chapter 3.

# Routing

On TCP/IP networks, routing is a fairly involved process. In order to send a packet through an internetwork (like the Internet), the router must have three pieces of information:

- The IP address of the sender
- The IP address of the destination
- The IP address of the next router to which the packet should be sent

The first two are part of the IP datagram being sent, but the router must figure out the last item itself. The router uses information it receives from other routers about what IP networks their interfaces are members of, as well as other networks they have learned about from their neighbors, in order to build a logical "map" of the network (called a *routing table*). Then the router can determine the best way to get the datagram to its destination and send the information on to the next router.

Routers build routing tables using dynamic routing protocols, such as RIP and Open Shortest Path First (OSPF), or by having static routes entered manually. The major difference between the two dynamic routing protocols mentioned is that RIP is a distance vector routing protocol and OSPF is a link state routing protocol. The difference between them is pretty simple. Distance vector protocols (like RIP) are used by routers to gather information about the hosts connected to them and to build a table of the addresses and the segment they are on (called a routing table). The router then sends out this information to all the routers it is connected to. All of the routers that receive this information add the route information to their own routing tables and continute to propagate them. Approximately every 30 seconds (varies depending on the protocol), distance vector protocol routers will re-advertise their entire routing table, with each interface having its own independent timer. Eventually, all routers in the internetwork know about all the other routers and the networks they serve.

Link state routing protocols (like OSPF) work slightly differently. Whereas IP RIP routers will advertise their entire routing table every 30 seconds, a link state router will send out to its "neighbors" only the changes to its routing table, as they occur. Additionally, link state routers have a more directed relationship with their neighbors. Instead of blindly advertising all of their information to their neighbors, link state protocols (like OSPF) prefer to more intentionally send updates only to a specific list of addresses via unicast or multicast.

# Interoperability

Of all the protocols listed in this chapter, no protocol is more flexible or more interoperable than TCP/IP. As the Internet gained popularity, everyone wanted to "get on the Net." As such, almost every computer had to have two things: a web browser and some form of TCP/IP connection. Therefore, every computer that is connected to the Internet is running TCP/IP in one way or another. Many companies use the TCP/IP protocol suite to communicate with one another over the Internet.

Additionally, because of this phenomenon, every operating system has some form of TCP/IP protocol stack and, as such, can communicate with other operating systems on some fundamental level.

## Naming

TCP/IP hosts are named according to the DNS convention. DNS is a service that resolves FQDNs to IP addresses. For instance, you can use friendly names like www.trainsolutions.com to refer to computers instead of unfriendly IP addresses like 192.168.24.31.

There are two parts to a DNS name: the host name (e.g., www) and the domain name (e.g., trainsolutions.com). Each of these components is separated by a period. Typically, you would assign a host name that says what the computer's function is (e.g., www for a web server). The domain name, on the other hand, is usually the name of the company in which the computer resides, or some related name, followed by .com, .edu, .net, or any other top-level domain suffix.

You'll learn more about DNS in Chapter 3.

# IPX/SPX

When Novell NetWare was introduced, it was designed to be a server platform for a local area and wide area networks. To that end, Novell designed a protocol stack that was very efficient over local area networks and that would also work on wide area networks. That protocol stack was the Internetwork Packet Exchange/Sequenced Packet Exchange (IPX/SPX).

In the following sections similar information to that presented for TCP/IP will be presented so that you may compare similar features, including addressing, routing, and naming, between the two.

## Addressing

IPX is the Network layer protocol that handles addressing and routing for the IPX/SPX protocol stack. IPX addressing is actually very simple. It takes the 12-digit hexadecimal address because that is the address for the individual node on that network segment. The network segment is referred to by its own unique 8-digit hexadecimal address. For example, the address 0001ABF3:12AB341FF414 would correspond to an interface with a MAC address of 12-AB-34-1F-F4-14 on the network segment labeled 0001ABF3. Every network segment is assigned its own, unique IPX network address. Since the MAC address is burned in to the NIC at the factory and, for the most part, shouldn't be changed, it doesn't have to be configured. The only configuration that must be done is to assign the IPX network address and configure the server with that address.

In addition to a station address, routers are given an internal IPX address. This address uniquely identifies a router to the rest of a network. NetWare servers always have an internal IPX address because they can function as routers.

## Routing

Most routers that route TCP/IP traffic can also route IPX traffic (although they may require additional software or configuration). IPX/SPX is a routable protocol stack because its address strucure is hierarchical, with a network portion and a node portion. As a result and to increase functionality, IPX/SPX has routing protocols designed into it. The routing protocols for IPX/SPX are RIP and NLSP.

IPX RIP is very similar to the RIP protocol in TCP/IP in that it is the distance vector routing protocol for IPX. Similarly, NLSP is the link state routing protocol for IPX/SPX. Both work similarly to their TCP/IP counterparts. RIP uses broadcasts of the entire IPX routing tables to keep all IPX routers updated, although every 60 seconds, not 30 as with IP RIP, and just as OSPF does, NLSP sends out only the changes to the routing tables and then only to a select group of network addresses. NLSP is actually based on another link state routing protocol, ISO's Intermediate Sytem to Intermediate System (IS-IS).

## Interoperability

IPX/SPX isn't as ubiquitous as TCP/IP (which can even be found running on Coke machines), but it holds its own when it comes to allowing many different platforms to talk. Windows 9*x*, NT, Me, 2000, XP, and2003 as well as NetWare, and a few versions of Linux come "out of the box" with support for communicating with other entities via the IPX/SPX protocol stack, although Microsoft calls its completely compatible version NWLink. Before the popularity explosion of the Internet in the mid-1990s, the IPX/SPX protocol stack was the only protocol stack many companies would run.

The only downside to interoperability using IPX/SPX is that many versions of Unix and other high-end operating systems like OS/400 don't come with built-in support for the IPX/SPX protocol stack or even with an option for support.

## Naming

Really, the only devices that have names are the NetWare servers. Generally speaking, you can name a NetWare server anything you want, as long as you follow these rules:

- The name must not include any of the "illegal" characters, including a period (.), a comma (,), a plus sign (+), an equal sign (=), and a backslash (\).

- Names must have fewer than 64 characters.

- Names are not case sensitive.

These names are resolved using either Bindery Services or Novell Directory Services.

These will be discussed more in Chapter 5, "Major Network Operating Systems."

# NetBEUI

NetBEUI is a Network layer protocol designed to provide support for NetBIOS networks. Net-BIOS is a protocol that was developed by IBM (and later enhanced by Microsoft and Novell) for use with network-aware operating systems like LAN Manager/LAN Server, Windows 9*x*, and Windows NT, 2000, XP, and 2003. It is a very fast and efficient protocol with low over-head. Because NetBIOS is small and efficient, it works well on small LANs with between 10 and 200 nodes. The two protocols are often referred to together as NetBEUI/NetBIOS.

In the following sections, naming, addressing, routing, and interoperability will be presented for NetBEUI, as it was for IPX/SPX and TCP/IP.

## Naming and Addressing

There is very little network addressing with NetBEUI/NetBIOS. Actually, for NetBEUI, naming and addressing are the same thing. Each device, not interface, is configured with a unique name (called the *NetBIOS name*) that is used for all communications. It's simple and quick. The only item that must be configured on the workstation is the name of the workstation. NetBIOS names can be up to 15 characters in length and must adhere to special-character exclusions similar to those listed for IPX/SPX (NetWare).

## Routing

Because the NetBEUI/NetBIOS protocol stack does not have an address structure with a hier-archical format and has no network and host boundaries, it is not a routable protocol. Routers will drop NetBEUI/NetBIOS packets by default. Some routers, however, may be configured to bridge these packets to all segments or to unicast them to a specific IP address, which must be configured on the receiving interface.

## Interoperability

Only a few operating systems run NetBEUI/NetBIOS. The operating systems for IBM and Microsoft are the primary supporters of this protocol. Windows 9*x*, NT, and 2000/2003 and LAN Manager and OS/2 support NetBEUI/NetBIOS. These operating systems can therefore communicate using NetBEUI/NetBIOS. The Macintosh operating system, however, does not support NetBEUI natively, nor do the latest implementations of Microsoft Windows, but you can add it back in, which, unless a strong case exists in favor of doing so, is highly frowned upon due to compatibility issues.

Note that the Apple Filing Protocol should be your certification focus and the overall structure of the AppleTalk suite of protocols is provided for context.

## AppleTalk and AppleTalk over IP

When Apple introduced the Macintosh in 1984, the Mac included networking software. This networking software used a protocol known as AppleTalk and a cabling system known as LocalTalk. It is a very simple and elegant protocol in that the computer takes care of most of the configuration. You simply plug it in and it works. Because of its simplicity and popularity with Mac users, and because the Mac users wanted a faster version, Apple developed AppleTalk version 2 with support for Ethernet (EtherTalk). Figure 2.20 illustrates the interrelationships between these components of AppleTalk, as well as others we'll discuss. Table 2.5 descibes the protocols shown in Figure 2.20.

**FIGURE 2.20**    The AppleTalk protocol model

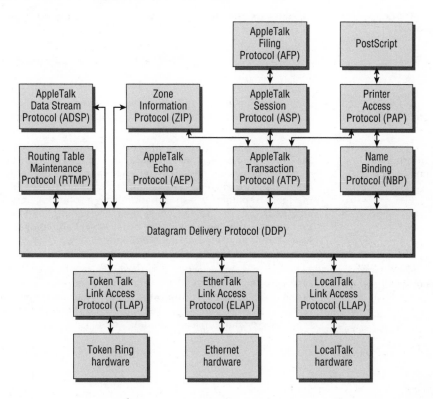

**TABLE 2.5** AppleTalk Protocols Defined

| Protocol | Description |
|---|---|
| Datagram Delivery Protocol (DDP) | Delivers data in discrete packets. DDP is unreliable, not acknowledging data delivery or guaranteeing the order of its delivery. |
| Routing Table Maintenance Protocol (RTMP) | Establishes and maintains routing tables through the exchange of routing information between routers. |
| AppleTalk Echo Protocol (AEP) | Provides a way to test for responsiveness and round-trip transmission times. Similar to using ICMP for Pinging remote devices. |
| AppleTalk Transaction Protocol (ATP) | Provides reliable data transmission, similar to the way in which TCP does so for TCP/IP. |
| Name Binding Protocol (NBP) | Translates an AppleTalk device name into an AppleTalk network address. |
| AppleTalk Data Stream Protocol (ADSP) | Establishes an end-to-end full-duplex session to exchange data between two network applications in which both endpoints have equal control over the communication. |
| Zone Information Protocol (ZIP) | Maintains AppleTalk internetwork-wide mappings of zone names to network number ranges on routers. While ZIP is primarily implemented by routers, end devices implement a portion of ZIP, allowing them to obtain zone information from a router. A zone is similar, in purpose, to a VLAN in layer 2 switching, unifying nodes by departmental membership or other logical affiliations regardless of their physical LAN segment connectivity. |
| AppleTalk Session Protocol (ASP) | Establishes reliable sessions that provide for non-duplicate transmissions between an ASP workstation process and an ASP server process. Unlike those formed in ADSP, ASP sessions are asymmetrical in that an ASP server never initiates communication but only responds to communication initiated by the ASP workstation. |
| Printer Access Protocol | Handles connection setup, maintenance, and termination of reliable transmission of messages to printers. |
| AppleTalk Filing Protocol (AFP) | Provides the interface between an application and a file server. Allows an application on an AppleTalk workstation to access and manipulate files on an AFP file server, such as an AppleShare server or a Microsoft Windows server running AFP, in the form of Services for Macintosh. |

Apple's Mac OS X and OS X Panther (versions 10.3.*x*) can communicate with any server running the AFP service, whether over TCP/IP, which is preferred by Apple, or over the legacy AppleTalk protocol. On Macintosh servers, the AFP service is implemented as *AppleShare*. You can use IP to connect to Macintosh file services running on Mac OS X Server, AppleShare IP, and Windows 2000 and later servers. *AppleShare IP* has been an add-on service available since the Mac OS 8 days, necessary for IP connectivity with AFP resources before this functionality became available natively in Mac OS X. Of course, Mac OS X still is capable of communicating with AFP servers over AppleTalk instead of IP, supporting legacy access to older AppleShare servers and Windows NT servers that only provide Mac file services over AppleTalk. However, Apple recommends migrating to TCP/IP as the transport method between clients and AFP servers.

One note about Mac OS X and AppleTalk: While Mac OS X clients can still use AppleTalk to communicate with older AppleShare servers, Mac OS X servers do not support client communication to their Apple File Services (the server's instance of AFP) via AppleTalk. While the Mac OS X server advertises its services over AppleTalk for older clients to be able to show the server in their Chooser, connection to the server must be via TCP/IP.

In addition to using AppleTalk for service browsing, you can use Mac OS X Server's Server Admin utility to enable Apple File Service browsing via Network Service Locator (NSL) and Rendezvous. *Rendezvous* is an IP-based open service discovery protocol, allowing devices to be added to and removed from networks without configuration. Rendezvous is mentioned in Chapter 3's Zero-Conf discussion.

## Services for Macintosh

Although the Windows 2000 file system is fairly different from the Macintosh file system, files on a Windows 2000 Server machine are accessible by both Windows 2000 clients and Macintosh clients. Services for Macintosh works in the background on a Windows 2000 Server machine to make this multiclient support possible by establishing an AFP-compatible server service. Files can be made to appear as they usually do for both Macintosh and Microsoft clients. A Microsoft client sees files represented as a directory tree, while a Macintosh client sees files represented as a Macintosh folder. In this environment, files may be stored in *shared folders* or *Macintosh volumes*. Macintosh volumes that are shared to the network are seen only by Macintosh clients, not by the Windows 2000 clients. Conversely, in order for a Macintosh client to gain access to a Microsoft shared folder, the administrator must designate the folder as a Macintosh-accessible volume.

For folders that are both a Microsoft shared folder and a Macintosh-accessible volume, both Microsoft clients and Macintosh clients have access to the resource. However, while Microsoft clients see folders and files as they are stored on the server's hard disk beneath the root of the share, Macintosh clients see the volume as containing Macintosh files and folders.

The following sections cover AppleTalk's methods of addressing and naming as well as its ability to be routed over internetworks.

## Addressing

Each station on an AppleTalk network uses an address that is 24 bits long. Sixteen of those bits are given to the network, and each network can support 254 nodes. Each network segment can be given either a single 16-bit network number or a range of 16-bit network numbers. If a network is assigned a range of numbers, that network is considered an *Extended AppleTalk network* because it can support more than 254 nodes. The node address is automatically assigned by the computer itself.

In addition to network numbers, AppleTalk networks use areas called zones. Zones allow an administrator to divide a network into logical areas for easier administration and to make it easier for a user to find resources.

Although you can have multiple zones on an AppleTalk network, an AppleTalk node can belong to only one zone.

## Routing

AppleTalk wasn't originally designed to be routed over a WAN, but with the release of AppleTalk version 2, Apple included routing functionality with the introduction of the Routing Table Maintenance Protocol (RTMP). RTMP is a distance vector routing protocol, like RIP, for both IP and IPX.

## Interoperability

The only computer that comes with AppleTalk installed by default is the Macintosh. Most Windows operating systems are able to use the AppleTalk protocol but require that additional software be installed. By using AppleTalk over IP, it is possible to tunnel AppleTalk conversations over the very Internet itself. Two AppleTalk speakers can package their AppleTalk packets in such a way that they are transmissible through IP intermediate systems, being stripped back down to the original AppleTalk packet by the receiving AppleTalk-speaking device.

## Naming

AppleTalk uses the Name Binding Protocol (NBP) to associate the name of the computer with its network address. It is broadcast based. Every station broadcasts its name when it comes up on a network. The AppleTalk router on a network will cache these names and respond when a node requests a name resolution; the local router will answer with information it has obtained from this NBP cache.

If an AppleTalk network doesn't have a router, each node will perform both its normal NBP requests and any NBP responses to broadcasted requests for its own AppleTalk address.

# Summary

In this chapter, you learned about the OSI model and had an introduction to a few of the most popular protocols in use today. You also learned about the seven layers that make up the OSI model, which are (from top to bottom) the Application, Presentation, Session, Transport, Network, Data Link, and Physical layers. In addition, you learned what each layer's primary responsibility is and in what layer certain popular protocols function. This chapter also reiterated at which layers certain common devices operate.

This chapter included discussions of some of the major protocol suites, including TCP/IP, IPX/SPX, NetBEUI/NetBIOS, and AppleTalk, and how the different protocols of each suite work together. For each protocol, you learned which parts of the protocol stack handle the concepts of addressing, routing, interoperability, and naming.

Also in this chapter, you were introduced to popular Data Link technologies, including those in the 802 standards track of IEEE, such as Ethernet and Token Ring, as well as their media access methodologies, such as CSMA/CD and token passing. On a related note, you were given the details of the structure and use of the 48-bit MAC address.

# Exam Essentials

**Be able to specify the main features—including speed, access method, topology, and media—of various network technologies, such as 802 standards and FDDI.**   You should be able to differentiate between the various networking technologies when studying for the exam. Refer to Table 2.3 for help.

**Be able to identify a MAC address.**   A MAC address on a network is a 12-digit hexadecimal number in the format *xx:xx:xx:xx:xx:xx*, where *x* is a number from 0 to 9 or a letter from *A* to *F*.

**Be able to identify the seven layers of the OSI model and describe their functions.**   The seven layers of the OSI model (from the bottom to top—or layer 1 to layer 7) are the Physical layer, Data Link layer, Network layer, Transport layer, Session layer, Presentation layer, and Application layer.

**Know how to differentiate between the IP, IPX, NetBEUI, and AppleTalk/AppleTalk over IP protocols when it comes to routing, addressing schemes, interoperability, and naming conventions.**   TCP/IP uses the likes of RIP or OSPF as routing protocols, uses a dotted decimal notation (four sets of numbers, each from 0 to 255) for the addressing, is completely interoperable, and uses DNS for host naming.

IPX, on the other hand, uses IPX RIP and NLSP for routing information, uses a unique 20-digit address (incorporating the MAC address) for the station address, interoperates with several different operating systems (but not as many as TCP/IP), and uses NDS for host naming.

NetBEUI isn't routable or as flexible, nor does it have as many features, but it does offer performance on a LAN segment. Addressing and naming are completely automatic (naming does require a user to enter a computer name).

Finally, AppleTalk does have routing protocols (RTMP) and uses an automatic addressing scheme. It requires only that the user name the computer when enabling AppleTalk. It is by far the simplest protocol, but it has the lowest performance and the least interoperability. Apple-Talk over IP is a form of tunneling for AppleTalk traffic so AppleTalk devices across the Internet can communicate using that public network, but AppleTalk itself is compatible with neither IP nor the Internet.

**Be able to explain the issues that must be considered when multiple protocols are running at the same time.**   When running multiple protocols, not only are you using more memory on a computer, you're adding a level of complexity to the network that is multiplied by the number of stations that you add. It is better to run the fewest protocols possible. Some issues you will see include running out of memory, program confusion, stations unable to communicate (each is running a different protocol), and network congestion.

**Identify the OSI layers at which hubs, switches, bridges, WAPs, routers, and network interface cards operate.**   Hubs operate at the Physical layer for the most part. Switches can operate at many different layers (up to layer 5), but the lowest common denominator for all network switches is OSI layer 2 (Data Link layer). Bridges are relatively simple devices and operate primarily at the Data Link layer. Routers are more complex devices, but because all they do is route packets, they operate at layer 3 (Network layer). Finally, network interface cards (NICs) operate at the Physical and Data Link layers.

# Review Questions

1. Which layer of the OSI model ensures reliable, end-to-end communications?

   **A.** Network

   **B.** Transport

   **C.** Session

   **D.** Presentation

2. Which layer of the OSI model provides routing functionality?

   **A.** Transport

   **B.** Data Link

   **C.** Physical

   **D.** Network

3. Which layer of the OSI model translates the data from upper-layer protocols into electrical signals and places them on the network media?

   **A.** Physical

   **B.** Transport

   **C.** Data Link

   **D.** Network

4. You are a consultant designing a network for a company with more than 1000 users. Which 802 standard would you implement to ensure that bandwidth would be sufficient and equal without bridging or additional segments?

   **A.** 802.1

   **B.** 802.2

   **C.** 802.3

   **D.** 802.5

5. Which one of the following devices will not propagate broadcasts from one of its interfaces to another?

   **A.** Hub

   **B.** Switch

   **C.** Repeater

   **D.** Router

6.  You are installing a Windows XP–based TCP/IP network. You accidentally set workstation B to the same IP address as workstation A. Which workstation(s) will receive an error message?

    **A.** Workstation A

    **B.** Workstation B

    **C.** Neither

    **D.** Both

7.  You are installing a Windows XP–based TCP/IP network. You accidentally set workstation B to the same IP address as workstation A. Which workstation(s) will have a valid IP address?

    **A.** Workstation A

    **B.** Workstation B

    **C.** Neither

    **D.** Both

8.  Which device increases the number of collision domains while decreasing the average number of nodes per collision domain?

    **A.** Hub

    **B.** Transceiver

    **C.** Switch

    **D.** NIC

9.  Which of the following protocols use a connectionless transport? (Choose all that apply.)

    **A.** HTTP

    **B.** TCP

    **C.** TFTP

    **D.** IP

    **E.** NetBIOS

10. Which protocols use a connection-oriented transport?

    **A.** UDP

    **B.** NetBIOS

    **C.** HTTP

    **D.** TFTP

11. Which name resolution system is implemented with TCP/IP by default?

    **A.** DNS

    **B.** NDS

    **C.** SND

    **D.** WINS

**12.** Which OSI model layer has both a MAC sublayer and an LLC sublayer?

   **A.** Physical

   **B.** Transport

   **C.** Network

   **D.** Data Link

**13.** Which OSI model layer is responsible for establishing, maintaining, and breaking down dialog?

   **A.** Application

   **B.** Gateway

   **C.** Session

   **D.** Network

**14.** Which OSI layer is responsible for formatting data based on a standard syntax and for character-set conversion?

   **A.** Transport

   **B.** Network

   **C.** Presentation

   **D.** Session

**15.** Which OSI layer is responsible for building and tearing down packets?

   **A.** Network

   **B.** Transport

   **C.** Data Link

   **D.** Physical

**16.** The two halves of a MAC address are referred to as the _____.

   **A.** TCP and IP

   **B.** OUI and device ID

   **C.** OUI and IP

   **D.** Device ID and IP

**17.** Which of the following directory services are hierarchical in design? (Choose all that apply.)

   **A.** Novell NetWare Bindery

   **B.** Microsoft Windows AD

   **C.** Linux password shadow file

   **D.** NT domain

18. You are the administrator of a 100-node Ethernet network. Your users are complaining of slow network speeds. What could you replace your hub with to increase your network throughput?

    **A.** Router

    **B.** Bridge

    **C.** Switch

    **D.** NIC

19. At which OSI model layer do routers primarily operate?

    **A.** Physical

    **B.** Data Link

    **C.** Transport

    **D.** Network

20. Which of the following is a MAC address?

    **A.** 199.165.217.45

    **B.** 00076A:01A5BBA7FF60

    **C.** 01:A5:BB:A7:FF:60

    **D.** 311 S. Park St.

# Answers to Review Questions

1. B. Of the layers listed, the only OSI layer that is responsible for reliable end-to-end communications is the Transport layer. The Network layer is responsible for logical network addresses, the Session layer is responsible for opening sessions and maintaining session information, and the Presentation layer is responsible for how data "looks" to the upper layer(s).

2. D. Of the OSI model layers listed, the Network layer is the only one that is responsible for routing information because it contains information for logical network addressing.

3. A. The Physical layer, as its name suggests, is the layer responsible for placing electrical transitions on the physical media. The other layers are all upper layers.

4. D. The 802.5 standard is similar to the Token Ring technology developed by IBM. That technology scales well and could handle more than 1000 users without bridging or additional segments. Also, the performance would be better than that of any of the other technologies listed.

5. D. Routers will not propagate broadcasts from one of their ports to another. The other devices will. Each interface on a router is in a different broadcast domain.

6. D. By sending out packets to their own IP address, both workstations will detect if there is a duplicate IP address on the network and will display error messages to that effect.

7. A. Because workstation A had a valid IP address to begin with, Windows takes a first come, first served approach with the IP addresses and lets workstation A keep its IP address. Workstation B detects that A already has it and just deactivates its own IP stack.

8. C. Each port on a switch belongs to a different collision domain, such that any device attached to one port on the switch cannot be involved in a collision with a device attached to a different port on the switch. Inserting a switch into a LAN segment serves the purpose of increasing the number of collision domains and reducing the average number of nodes per collision domain.

9. C, E. TFTP and NetBIOS both use a connectionless transport (UDP and NetBEUI, respectively). TCP is, in fact, a connection-oriented transport protocol. HTTP uses TCP, so it is therefore connection oriented. And IP is a Network layer protocol.

10. C. Of all the protocols listed, HTTP is the only one that uses a connection-oriented Transport layer protocol (TCP). The others use, or are themselves, connectionless Transport layer protocols.

11. A. Although WINS is a name resolution that does translate NetBIOS names to IP addresses, it works only on Windows-based networks. The only true name resolution system that almost every TCP/IP network uses is DNS.

12. D. The Data Link layer is divided into two sublayers: the MAC sublayer and an LLC sublayer. The other layers aren't normally subdivided.

13. C. The Session layer is responsible for establishing, maintaining, and breaking down dialog.

**14.** C. The Presentation layer handles such services as data formatting, compression, encryption, and data-set conversion, such as from ASCII to Unicode or EBCDIC.

**15.** A. The Network layer is responsible for packaging data into packets. Different terms for data packages (such as *frames*) are used when discussing the other layers.

**16.** B. The first half of the MAC address is the Organizationally Unique Identifier (OUI), and the second half is the device ID.

**17.** B, C. Of the directory services listed, only Microsoft's Active Directory and the Linux password shadow file are hierarchical in design.

**18.** C. A switch would increase performance by making virtual, direct connections between sender and receiver. Bridges and routers actually decrease performance because these devices introduce latency into the communication. Replacing the hub with an NIC just can't be done.

**19.** D. Because routers deal with logical network addresses, they operate at the Network layer.

**20.** C. MAC addresses use a 12-digit hexadecimal number that is separated into six pairs of hex numbers. The only one that corresponds to that format is Answer C.

# Chapter

# 3

# TCP/IP Fundamentals

## THE FOLLOWING NETWORK+ EXAM OBJECTIVES ARE COVERED IN THIS CHAPTER:

- ✓ **2.4 Differentiate between the following network protocols in terms of routing, addressing schemes, interoperability, and naming conventions:**
  - IPX/SPX (Internetwork Packet Exchange/Sequenced Packet Exchange)
  - NetBEUI (Network Basic Input/Output System Extended User Interface)
  - AppleTalk/AppleTalk over IP (Internet Protocol)
  - TCP/IP (Transmission Control Protocol/Internet Protocol)
- ✓ **2.5 Identify the components and structure of IP (Internet Protocol) addresses (IPv4, IPv6) and the required setting for connections across the Internet.**
- ✓ **2.6 Identify classful IP (Internet Protocol) ranges and their subnet masks (for example, Class A, B, and C).**
- ✓ **2.7 Identify the purpose of subnetting.**
- ✓ **2.8 Identify the differences between private and public network addressing schemes.**
- ✓ **2.9 Identify and differentiate between the following IP (Internet protocol) addressing methods:**
  - Static
  - Dynamic
  - Self-assigned (APIPA (Automatic Private Internet Protocol Addressing))
- ✓ **2.10 Define the purpose, function and use of the following protocols used in the TCP/IP (Transmission Control Protocol/Internet Protocol) suite:**
  - TCP (Transmission Control Protocol)
  - UDP (User Datagram Protocol)
  - FTP (File Transfer Protocol)
  - SFTP (Secure File Transfer Protocol)

- TFTP (Trivial File Transfer Protocol)
- SMTP (Simple Mail Transfer Protocol)
- HTTP (Hypertext Transfer Protocol)
- HTTPS (Hypertext Transfer Protocol Secure)
- POP3/IMAP4 (Post Office Protocol, version 3/Internet Message Access Protocol, version 4)
- Telnet
- SSH (Secure Shell)
- ICMP (Internet Control Message Protocol)
- ARP/RARP (Address Resolution Protocol/Reverse Address Resolution Protocol)
- NTP (Network Time Protocol)
- NNTP (Network News Transfer Protocol)
- SCP (Secure Copy Protocol)
- LDAP (Lightweight Directory Access Protocol)
- IGMP (Internet Group Management Protocol)
- LPR (Line Printer Remote)

✓ **2.11 Define the function of TCP/UDP (Transmission Control Protocol/User Datagram Protocol) ports.**

✓ **2.12 Identify the well-known ports associated with the following commonly used services and protocols:**

- 20 FTP (File Transfer Protocol)
- 21 FTP (File Transfer Protocol)
- 22 SSH (Secure Shell)
- 23 Telnet
- 25 SMTP (Simple Mail Transfer Protocol)
- 53 DNS (Domain Name Server)
- 69 TFTP (Trivial File Transfer Protocol)
- 80 HTTP (Hypertext Transfer Protocol)
- 110 POP3 (Post Office Protocol, version 3)
- 119 NNTP (Network News Transfer Protocol)
- 123 NTP (Network Time Protocol)
- 143 IMAP4 (Internet Message Access Protocol, version 4)
- 443 HTTPS (Hypertext Transfer Protocol Secure)

✓ **2.13 Identify the purpose of network services and protocols, for example, DNS (Domain Name Service), NAT (Network Address Translation), ICS (Internet Connection Sharing), WINS (Windows Internet Naming Service), SNMP (Simple Network Management Protocol), NFS (Network File System), ZeroConf (Zero Configuration), SMB (Server Message Block), AFP (Apple File Protocol), and LPD (Line Printer Daemon).**

✓ **3.6 Identify the purpose, benefits, and characteristics of using a proxy service.**

✓ **3.8 Identify the main characteristics of VLANs (Virtual local area networks).**

✓ **3.9 Identify the main characteristics and purpose of extranets and intranets.**

One of the most important elements of Internet technology—and the element that makes intranets so easy to set up and use—is the networking protocol that provides the foundation to the Internet. This protocol is known as *TCP/IP*. It's actually a whole family of protocols, but its name comes from only two of them: the *Transmission Control Protocol (TCP)* and the *Internet Protocol (IP)*. Before you can connect to the Internet or do anything with your intranet, you must first set up TCP/IP on all devices where intercommunication is desired, including workstations, servers, routers, and every other device that is to be the end recipient of IP traffic.

This chapter starts by describing the TCP/IP family of protocols, continues with a description of IP addressing and address classifications, and goes on to describe several of the name-resolution services available. It concludes with a detailed discussion of how to set up and configure TCP/IP on Windows 2000 and a brief discussion of VLAN technologies.

For detailed information on the IPX/SPX and AppleTalk suites of networking protocols, please consult Chapter 2, "The OSI Model."

# Introducing TCP/IP

Because TCP/IP is so central to working with the Internet and with intranets, you should understand it in detail. We'll start with some background on TCP/IP and how it came about and then move on to the descriptions of the technical goals defined by the original designers. Then you'll get a look at how TCP/IP compares to a theoretical model, the Open Systems Interconnect (OSI) model.

## A Brief History of TCP/IP

The first Request for Comments (RFC) was published in April 1969, laying the groundwork for today's Internet, the protocols of which are specified in the numerous RFCs monitored, ratified, and archived by the Internet Engineering Task Force (IETF). TCP/IP was first proposed in 1973 and was split into separate protocols, TCP and IP, in 1978. In 1983, TCP/IP became the official transport mechanism for all connections to ARPAnet, a forerunner of the Internet, replacing the earlier Network Control Protocol (NCP). ARPAnet was developed by the Department of Defense's (DoD's) Advanced Research Projects Agency (ARPA), formed in 1957 in response to the Soviet Union's launch of Sputnik and later renamed the Defense Advanced Research Projects Agency (DARPA), which was split into ARPAnet and MILNET in 1983 and disbanded in 1990.

Much of the original work on TCP/IP was done at the University of California, Berkeley, where computer scientists were also working on the Berkeley version of UNIX (which eventually grew into the Berkeley Software Distribution [BSD] series of UNIX releases). TCP/IP was added to the BSD releases, which in turn was made available to universities and other institutions for the cost of a distribution tape. Thus, TCP/IP began to spread in the academic world, laying the foundation for today's explosive growth of the Internet and of intranets as well.

During this time, the TCP/IP family continued to evolve and add new members. One of the most important aspects of this growth was the continuing development of the certification and testing program carried out by the U.S. government to ensure that the published standards, which were free, were met. Publication ensured that the developers did not change anything or add any features specific to their own needs. This open approach has continued to the present day; use of the TCP/IP family of protocols virtually guarantees a trouble-free connection between many hardware and software platforms.

## TCP/IP Design Goals

When the U.S. Department of Defense began to define the TCP/IP network protocols, their design goals included the following:

- TCP/IP had to be independent of all hardware and software manufacturers. Even today, this is fundamentally why TCP/IP makes such good sense in the corporate world: It is not tied to IBM, Novell, Microsoft, DEC, or any other specific company.

- It had to have good built-in failure recovery. Because TCP/IP was originally a military proposal, the protocol had to be able to continue operating even if large parts of the network suddenly disappeared from view, say, after an enemy attack.

- It had to handle high error rates and still provide completely reliable end-to-end service.

- It had to be efficient and have a low data overhead. The majority of IP packets have a simple, 20-byte header, which means better performance in comparison with other networks. A simple protocol translates directly into faster transmissions, giving more efficient service.

- It had to allow the addition of new networks without any service disruptions.

As a result, TCP/IP was developed with each component performing unique and vital functions that allowed all the problems involved in moving data between machines over networks to be solved in an elegant and efficient way. Before looking at both TCP and IP individually, you should understand where TCP/IP fits into the broader world of network protocols and, particularly, how it compares to the theoretical reference model published by the International Organization for Standardization (ISO) as the OSI model.

The popularity that the TCP/IP family of protocols enjoys today did not arise just because the protocols were there, or even because the U.S. government mandated their use. They are popular because they are robust, solid protocols that solve many of the most difficult networking problems and do so in an elegant and efficient way.

## The Internet, an internet, an intranet, and an extranet

The title of this sidebar may be a bit confusing and look a bit informal with the odd capitalization, but it's for a very good reason. While *internet* is a truncated version of *internetwork,* a lot of play has come from the root of these words. Let's examine the word *internetwork* first, just to make sure we understand where all the variants come from. As you know, a network is a conglomeration of devices tied together with a common technology. Well, once you establish two or more of these networks, work can be started on bringing them together. The interconnection and intercommunication between these autonomous networks is known as an internetwork or just internet. We know we have an internet when we use routers or other layer 3 devices to interconnect the networks. What kind of fun can we have with these words?

First of all, just by capitalizing the word *internet* to form *Internet,* we get the proper name of the global commercial internetwork that is tied together by TCP/IP (actually, all of these entities are) and that has a scope of the planet we call home. If those Mars rovers have IP addresses, the scope suddenly gets a bit grander. That's the flexibility of TCP/IP for you. What if we analyze the meaning of *inter*? An internet is connectivity and communication across network boundaries. Does that mean, then, that an *intranet* is connectivity and communication within a network? Gotcha. An intranet is more an opposite of the Internet, in terms of scope. If the Internet spans many administrative boundaries, encompassing many disparate networks, then an intranet, while often an internet (how's that for a catch?), encompasses only networks under a single administrative domain, a large corporation's internal internetwork. Did you catch that? An intranet can be an internet, but not the Internet. Fun, huh?

Well, then, that just leaves *extranet.* Think of an extranet as an intranet becoming a very controlled Internet. That is, if an intranet is made up of all networks under a single administrative control, then an extranet is the expansion of that to include one, two, or just a few additional outside networks. Said differently, an extranet is an intranet interconnected and intercommunicating with networks that are under separate administrative control. This isn't nearly as unruly as the Internet, because this interconnectivity arose from some sort of partnership or affiliation between the parties. Let's say, for instance, that a manufacturing company wants to have a vendor monitor its inventory so that whenever materials that the vendor supplies reach a minimum threshold, an order can be generated automatically, without personnel from the manufacturing company getting involved. That would require some sort of limited vendor access to internal manufacturing company resources. While the manufacturing company wants the vendor to have access to all that they need to help automate the supply process, they don't want the vendor accessing sensitive financial, personnel, or possibly engineering information. By tweaking the firewalls just so, the vendor's trusted network assets can be allowed access to the manufacturing company's inventory control system but nothing else. That's an extranet. While there's a big difference between them all, they are all very similar. They are all generally TCP/IP internetworks.

### Benefits of Using TCP/IP over Other Networking Protocols

There are several benefits to using the TCP/IP networking protocol:

- TCP/IP is a widely published open standard and is completely independent of any hardware or software manufacturer.

- TCP/IP can send data between different computer systems running completely different operating systems, from small PCs all the way to mainframes and everything in between.

- TCP/IP is separated from the underlying hardware and will run over Ethernet, Token Ring, and X.25 networks, to name a few, and even over dial-up telephone lines.

- TCP/IP is a routable protocol, which means it can send datagrams over a specific route, thus reducing traffic on other parts of the network.

- TCP/IP has reliable and efficient data-delivery mechanisms.

- TCP/IP uses a common addressing scheme. Therefore, any system can address any other system, even in a network as large as the Internet. (We will look at this addressing scheme in the section "Understanding IP Addressing" later in this chapter.)

## TCP/IP and the OSI Model

As you learned in Chapter 2, "The OSI Model," the OSI model divides computer-to-computer communications into seven connected layers; TCP/IP uses the Department of Defense (DoD) model, which describes communications in only four layers, as Figure 3.1 shows. Each successively higher layer builds on the functions provided by the layers below.

The DoD model has fewer layers than the OSI model has, but that does not mean that it has less functionality. We draw the models to the same height because all data communications functionality is there. The DoD model simply combines the functionality of those layers into "larger" layers whose protocols perform all related functions of the equivalent OSI layers. Remember, that's part of the OSI reference model's success. Even though the original protocols never really caught on, the model itself is at once generic in its description of protocol functionality and specific in its separation of communications tasks into more layers than just about any other model.

**FIGURE 3.1**    A comparison of the seven-layer OSI model, the four-layer DoD model, and how TCP/IP maps to each model

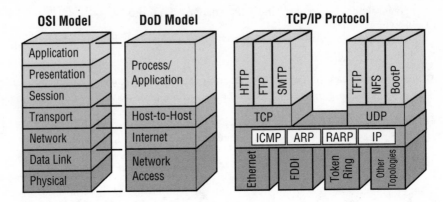

As you may remember from Chapter 2's discussion of the OSI model, the layers are as follows:

**Application Layer**    The highest layer; defines the manner in which applications interact with the network—including databases, e-mail, and terminal-emulation programs using Application layer protocols similar to Lightweight Directory Access Protocol (LDAP), Simple Mail Transfer Protocol (SMTP), and Telnet.

**Presentation Layer**    Defines the way in which data is formatted, presented, converted, and encoded.

**Session Layer**    Coordinates communications and maintains the session for as long as it is needed—performing security, logging, and administrative functions.

**Transport Layer**    Defines protocols for structuring messages and supervises the validity of the transmission by performing error checking.

**Network Layer**    Defines data-routing protocols to increase the likelihood that the information arrives at the correct destination node.

**Data Link Layer**    Validates the integrity of the flow of the data from one node to another by synchronizing blocks of data and controlling the flow.

**Physical Layer**    Defines the mechanism for communicating with the transmission medium and the interface hardware.

    Although no commercially available networking protocol suite follows the OSI model exactly, most perform all the same functions.

In the DoD model, the four layers are as follows:

**Process/Application Layer**    The highest layer; applications such as FTP, Telnet, and others interact through this layer. Corresponds to the top three layers of the OSI model.

**Host-to-Host Layer** TCP and UDP add transport control information to the user data. Corresponds to the Transport layer of the OSI model.

**Internet Layer** Adds IP information to form a packet. Corresponds to the Network layer of the OSI model.

**Network Access Layer** Defines the mechanism for communicating with the transmission medium and the interface hardware. Corresponds to the bottom two layers of the OSI model.

Each layer adds its own header and, in the case of Data Link protocols, trailer control information to the basic data structure and encapsulates the *protocol data unit (PDU)* from the layer above. On the receiving end, this header and trailer information is stripped, one layer at a time, until the equivalent of the original data arrives at its final destination.

> *PDU* is a generic term used to describe the end product of a protocol. It can be thought of as the entire data structure handed down by that protocol to the protocol at the next lowest layer, or the information placed on the network media by the Physical layer. A PDU will consist of the original user data and any upper-layer control information (headers and trailers) imposed by upper-layer protocols encapsulated by the control information of the protocol creating the PDU.

Now let's look at how TCP and IP work together.

# The Transmission Control Protocol

TCP is the Transport layer of the protocol and serves to ensure a reliable, verifiable data exchange between hosts on a network. TCP breaks data into pieces, wraps the pieces with the information needed to identify it as a piece of the original message, and allows the pieces to be reassembled at the receiving end of the communications link. The wrapped and bundled pieces are called *datagrams*. Datagrams are also referred to as *segments* for TCP due to the way it often splits the original data into more manageable chunks. The most important information in the header includes the source and destination port numbers, a sequence number for the datagram, and a checksum.

The *source port number* and the *destination port number* ensure that the data is sent back and forth to the correct application process running on each computer. The *sequence number* allows the datagrams to be rebuilt in the correct order in the receiving device, and the *checksum* allows the protocol to check whether the data sent is the same as the data received. It performs this last feat by running the bits of the segment through a complex polynomial expression and inserting the resulting number in the header. This is when IP enters the picture. Once the header is on the datagram, TCP passes the datagram to IP to be routed to its destination. The receiving device then performs the same calculation, and if the two calculations do not match, an error has occurred somewhere along the line and the datagram is silently discarded by the destination device and resent by the source device after its timer expires waiting for a positive acknowledgment that never arrives.

Figure 3.2 shows the layout of the datagram with the TCP header in place.

**FIGURE 3.2**    A datagram with its TCP header

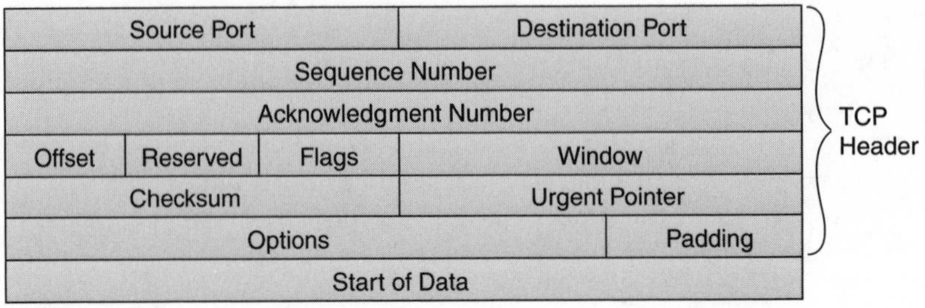

| Source Port | | Destination Port | |
|---|---|---|---|
| Sequence Number | | | |
| Acknowledgment Number | | | |
| Offset | Reserved | Flags | Window |
| Checksum | | Urgent Pointer | |
| Options | | | Padding |
| Start of Data | | | |

TCP Header

In addition to the source and destination port numbers, the sequence number, and the checksum, a TCP header contains the following information:

**Acknowledgment Number**    Indicates that the data was received successfully. If the datagram is damaged in transit, the receiver throws the data away and does not send an acknowledgment back to the sender. After a predefined time-out expires, the sender retransmits the data for which no acknowledgment was received. Only *positive forward acknowledgments* are sent in TCP. *Positive* means that only successful transmissions are acknowledged. *Forward* means that the acknowledgment number represents the next sequence number the destination device expects to receive.

**Offset**    Specifies the length of the header in 32-bit chunks.

**Reserved**    This field specifies variables that are set aside for future use. This field must contain zeros.

**Flags**    These are six one-bit fields that indicate various things, such as whether this segment is the end of the higher-layer message, that the acknowledgment number is significant, that the sender is requesting that a virtual circuit with the receiver be established or torn down, or that the data in the segment is urgent.

**Window**    Provides a way to increase the number of segments transmitted before the sender expects an acknowledgment, which improves efficiency in data transfers. Conversely, decreasing the value of this field can indicate that network problems endanger the integrity of the data so more segments need to be acknowledged until conditions improve.

**Urgent Pointer**    Gives the location in the segment where the urgent data ends, assuming the urgent data begins at the beginning of the segment. This allows out-of-band transmission of special data, signifying to the receiving device that this data should be pushed ahead of any other that it has received but has not yet processed. Special data could include keyboard break sequences in a Telnet session, which should immediately be processed by the receiving device in order to discontinue potentially harmful processing of previously received data. In light of this use, it makes sense that the transmitting device would place such critical control information at the beginning of a new, emerging segment.

**Options**    Communicates various parameters of the TCP virtual circuit. The only option originally specified in the TCP RFC (RFC 793) was maximum segment size, which has to be communicated in the first segment during connection establishment. Later RFCs specify additional options. The latest list of TCP options can be found on the web site for the Internet Assigned Numbers Authority (`www.iana.org/assignments/tcp-parameters`).

**Padding**    Ensures that the header ends on a 32-bit boundary so that the offset field makes sense as a whole number.

The data in the segment immediately follows this header information.

---

### The Actual Use of TCP Communications

The following list summarizes the TCP process:

- Flow control allows two systems to cooperate in datagram transmission to prevent overflows and lost segments.

- Acknowledgment lets the sender know that the recipient has received the information.

- Sequencing ensures that segments arrive in the proper order.

- Checksums allow easy detection of corrupted segments.

- Retransmission of lost or corrupted segments is managed in a timely way.

---

# The Internet Layer Protocols

The Internet layer of the DoD model is made up of various protocols, with the three main protocols being the *Internet Protocol (IP)*, the *Internet Control Message Protocol (ICMP)*, and the *Address Resolution Protocol (ARP)*. The following sections introduce these three protocols and provide more detail. And no discussion of things layer 3 would be complete without mentioning routers and the process of routing.

## The Internet Protocol

The Network layer portion of the DoD model is called the Internet layer. Not surprisingly, the main protocol at this layer is the Internet Protocol (IP). IP is what actually moves the data from point A to point B, a process that is called *routing*.

IP is considered *connectionless*; that is, it does not swap control information (or handshaking information) in order to establish an end-to-end connection before starting a transmission. This is also known as *best effort* transmission. Additionally, if a packet is lost in transmission, IP must rely on TCP to determine if the data did not arrive successfully at its destination and, if not, to retransmit the entire segment, which could be more data than was carried by the lost packet if IP had to fragment the segment. IP's only job is to route the data to its destination. In this effort, IP inserts its own header in the datagram once it is received from TCP (or UDP or another higher-layer protocol). The main contents of the IP header are the source and destination addresses, the protocol number, and a checksum.

> IP is considered *unreliable.* This is because it contains no error detection or recovery capability, not because it is undependable. For these reasons, UDP is also an unreliable protocol. Conversely, TCP is considered *reliable.*

Without the header provided by IP, intermediate routers between the source and destination—originally called *gateways* in the RFCs—would not be able to determine where to route the datagram. Figure 3.3 shows the layout of the datagram with the IP header in place, followed by the upper-layer header and data, which IP sees as just upper-layer information.

**FIGURE 3.3**   A datagram with TCP and IP headers

| Version | IHL | TOS | Total Length | |
|---|---|---|---|---|
| Identification | | Flags | Fragmentation Offset | |
| Time to Live | Protocol | Header Checksum | | IP Header |
| Destination IP Address | | | | |
| Destination IP Address | | | | |
| Options and Padding | | | | |
| TCP Header | | | | |
| Start of Data | | | | |

The fields in the IP header include the following:

**Version**   Defines the IP version number. Version 4 is the current standard. IP version 6 is currently supported by the newest equipment and may quickly become the new standard.

**IHL (Internet Header Length)**   Defines the length of the header information. The header length can vary; the standard header is five 32-bit words, and the sixth and subsequent words are for options and padding.

**TOS (Type of Service)**   Originally, these eight bits were broken into four fields in the first six bits, with 0s in the last two bits. The first three bits are called the precedence bits and allow the specification of eight levels of priority, with 0 being lowest and 7 being highest. The next three bits specify normal or low delay, normal or high throughput, and normal or high reliability, depending on values of 0 or 1, respectively, meaning 0 is normal for each field. Note that a value of 1 for each of these bits would be preferred. In some implementations, the first six bits are collectively used for prioritization of traffic. When used for this purpose, the first six bits are called Differentiated Services Code Point (DSCP) bits. In still other implementations, the last two bits can be used to give TCP the ability to communicate congestion details, in which case they are referred to as Explicit Congestion Notification (ECN) bits.

> While all of this detail is pertinent to the TOS field, only a basic understanding is necessary for Network+ proficiency.

**Total Length**    Specifies the total length of the datagram, which has no specified minimum but should be supported in all implementations up to 576 bytes. Being 16 bits, the length field can specify a maximum packet length of 65,535 bytes.

**Identification**    An identifying number that the receiving system can use to reassemble fragmented datagrams. Each fragment produced from the same datagram will bear the same identifying number in this field.

**Flags**    When set to 1, the second flag bit specifies that the datagram should not be fragmented and must therefore travel over subnetworks that can handle the size without fragmenting it; the third flag bit being set indicates that the packet is the last of a fragmented segment. When reset to 0, these two flags have the opposite meanings. The first flag bit is not used and always must be set to 0.

**Fragmentation Offset**    Indicates, in units of 8 octets (64 bits), the original position of the fragmented data and is used during reassembly. The first fragment of a set of fragmented packets or non-fragmented packets have a value of 0 in this field, as you might expect.

**Time to Live (TTL)**    Originally, the time in seconds that the datagram could be in transit; if this time was exceeded, the datagram was considered lost. Now interpreted as a *hop* count and usually set to the default value of 32 (for 32 hops), this number is decremented by each router through which the packet passes. The router that decrements this field to 0, which is known as the executioner, drops the packet and sends an ICMP time exceeded message back to the original source of the packet.

**Protocol**    Identifies the protocol whose header and data follow the IP header, allowing the interleaving or multiplexing of multiple protocols. For example, a value of 6 indicates TCP, a value of 17 indicates User Datagram Protocol (UDP), and a value of 1 indicates ICMP. Multiplexing of upper-layer information means that one protocol, such as TCP, does not need to finish its transmission before another, such as UDP, begins using the services of IP. Without the use of such a field, only one protocol could be used in any given implementation of IP.

**Header Checksum**    An error-checking value that is recalculated at each packet processing point (for example, each router). Recalculation is necessary because certain IP header fields change, such as TTL. The checksum is computed only on the bits of the IP header, with the checksum field initially set to all 0s before the computation.

**Source Address**    The 32-bit IP address of the original transmitting device. Note that this value can change along the path of transmission if certain technologies, such as Network Address Translation (NAT), are in use.

> NAT is the process of converting between the IP addresses used on a corporate intranet or other private network and Internet IP addresses. This process makes it possible to use a large number of addresses within the private network without depleting the limited number of available registered IP addresses. NAT is usually performed within a router or firewall.

**Destination Address**    The 32-bit IP address of the original destination device. This address can be altered along the transmission path in the same way as noted for the source address.

**Options and Padding**    IP options are a set of variable fields that may or may not be present in each IP packet. While the presence of options is not mandatory, the support of all possible IP options is required by each IP implementation. This means that if an IP host includes an option, all IP devices will understand it. Examples of standards-based options are Security, Record Route, and Internet Timestamp. If any options are included in the IP header, it is necessary to verify that the IP header ends on a 32-bit boundary. If not, it is necessary to pad with 0s at the end of the last option, until the total length of the IP header is a multiple of 32 bits.

**Upper-Layer Information**    The header and user data handed down by a protocol, such as TCP. The header will not appear for non-initial IP fragments.

The data in the packet immediately follows this header information, which may correspond to a complete TCP segment, UDP datagram, or other IP-supported PDU or to a portion thereof when fragmentation has occurred.

## Internet Control Message Protocol (ICMP)

ICMP works at the Network layer and provides the functions used for Network layer management and control. Routers send ICMP messages to respond to undeliverable datagrams by placing an ICMP message in an IP datagram and then sending the datagram back to the original source. The `ping` command—used in network troubleshooting and described in Chapter 5, "Major Network Operating Systems"—uses ICMP.

## Address Resolution Protocol (ARP) and Reverse ARP (RARP)

The Network layer protocol, ARP, associates the physical hardware address of a network node to its already known IP address. Using ARP, an IP process constructs a table (known as the ARP cache) that maps logical addresses to the hardware addresses of nodes on the local network. When a node needs to send a packet to a known IP address on the local subnet, it first checks the ARP cache to see if the physical address information is already present. If so, that address is used and network traffic is reduced; otherwise, a normal ARP request is made to determine the address.

See Chapter 4, "TCP/IP Utilities," for more on ARP.

Reverse ARP (RARP) is nothing more than ARP packets with different codes in the header, indicating to devices receiving RARP packets that these are requests by the source device for its own IP configuration, meaning RARP replies should be handled by a RARP server and that any device not fulfilling this role need not process these requests any further. If, however, the receiving device is a RARP server, it is incumbent upon that device to find the requesting device's MAC address in a configured list (RARP is an older, manual process, unlike DHCP). The server sends the IP address it finds associated with the requesting MAC address back to the requesting device. RARP was adequate for diskless workstation initial IP configuration but fell short as an be-all, end-all supplier of detailed IP-related information, which is why DHCP has supplanted RARP for supplying network-based IP configuration in most modern networks.

## Routers and Routing

As you already know, routing is the process of getting your data from point A to point B. Routing datagrams is similar to driving a car. Before you drive off to your destination, you determine which roads you will take to get there. And sometimes along the way, you may change your mind and alter your route.

The IP portion of the TCP/IP protocol inserts its header in the datagram, but before the datagram can begin its journey, IP determines whether it knows the destination. If it does, it sends the datagram on its way. If it doesn't know and can't find out, IP sends the datagram to the host's default gateway.

One key to understanding some of the original Internet documents, as well as some of the legacy terminology, is to realize that every router in the Internet was once referred to as a gateway. Therefore, a default gateway is really a default router.

Each host on a TCP/IP network can have a default gateway, an off-ramp for datagrams not destined for the local network. They're going somewhere else, and the router's job is to forward them to that destination if it knows where it is. Each router has a defined set of routing tables that tell the router the route to specific destinations.

Because routers don't know the location of every IP address, they have their own default gateways that act just like any TCP/IP host. In the event that the first router doesn't know the way to the destination, it forwards the datagram to its own default gateway. This forwarding, or routing, continues until the datagram reaches its destination. The entire path to the destination is known as the *route*.

Datagrams intended for the same destination may actually take different routes to get there. Many variables determine the route. For example, overloaded routers may not respond in a

---

### All TCP/IP Devices Route

Technically, end devices and routers both work similarly when deciding what to do with an IP packet. In fact, any packet that leaves one of these devices toward a destination does so because the transmitting device knew what to do with it, even if it is sent out to the default gateway address. The default gateway is actually a statically or dynamically learned route entry, just like every other entry in the routing table. Any potential destination address is ANDed (ANDing is a Boolean algebra operator that produces a 0, unless two 1s are ANDed) with each route entry's mask, the result compared to the entry's network address. All matches are then compared for the longest prefix length, which means the most 1s in the mask, which is the one chosen when more than one match is found. Since the default gateway's entry always has a prefix length of 0, it will only be chosen when no other match is found, leading to the use of the word *default.* Therefore, even when the default gateway is used, it is because the destination is "known." Any packet whose destination address produces no matches with the route entries in the routing table is dropped.

---

timely manner or may simply refuse to route traffic and so they time out. That time-out causes the sending router to seek an alternate route for the datagram.

Routes can be predefined and made static, and alternate routes can be predefined, providing a maximum probability that your datagrams travel via the shortest and fastest route.

If you configure the TCP/IP settings for a computer on a LAN that has a router through which the Internet is accessible, there are certain settings that must be made and others that just make life easier but without which reliable Internet access cannot be achieved. These are an IP address for the computer, a common subnet mask for the LAN, a default gateway IP address for the local router interface, and the address of a DNS server. While the last two settings are not technically mandatory, it's easier to consider these four parameters as requirements than it is to explain the extra and meticulous configuration that must be made to get around the last two settings, which includes manual routing table manipulation and the use of hosts files.

# The Application Protocols

Application layer protocols are built on top of and into the TCP/IP protocol suite and are available on most implementations. The following list includes such protocols:

- SNMP
- TFTP
- FTP
- SFTP

- SMTP
- IMAP
- NFS
- SSH
- HTTPS
- NNTP
- LDAP
- LPR
- POP3
- LPD
- Telnet
- HTTP
- NTP
- SCP
- IGMP

## Simple Network Management Protocol (SNMP)

Simple Network Management Protocol (SNMP) allows network administrators to collect information about the network. It is a communications protocol for collecting information about devices on the network, including hubs, routers, and bridges. Each piece of information to be collected about a device is defined in a Management Information Base (MIB). SNMP uses UDP to send and receive messages on the network.

## File Transfer Protocol (FTP)

File Transfer Protocol (FTP) provides a mechanism for single or multiple file transfers between computer systems; when written in lowercase as "ftp," it is also the name of the client software used to access the FTP server running on the remote host. The FTP package provides all the tools needed to look at files and directories, change to other directories, and transfer text and binary files from one system to another. FTP uses TCP to actually move the files.

We'll look at how to transfer files using FTP in detail in the next chapter.

## Trivial File Transfer Protocol (TFTP)

Trivial File Transfer Protocol (TFTP) is a "stripped down" version of FTP, primarily used to boot diskless workstations and to transfer boot images to and from routers. It uses a reduced feature set (fewer commands and a smaller overall program size). In addition to its reduced size, it also uses UDP instead of TCP, which makes for faster transfers but with no reliability.

## Secure File Transfer Protocol (SFTP)

Secure File Transfer Protocol (SFTP) is used when you need to transfer files over an encrypted connection. It uses an SSH session (more on this later) which encrypts the connection. The SFTP protocol then is used to transfer files over this encrypted connection. Apart from that, it functions exactly as the FTP protocol does: It is used to transfer files between computers.

## Simple Mail Transfer Protocol (SMTP)

Simple Mail Transfer Protocol (SMTP) allows for a simple e-mail service and is responsible for moving messages from one e-mail server to another. The e-mail servers run either Post Office Protocol (POP) or Internet Mail Access Protocol (IMAP) to distribute e-mail messages to users.

## Post Office Protocol (POP)

Post Office Protocol (POP) provides a storage mechanism for incoming mail; the latest version of the standard is known as POP3. When a client connects to a POP3 server, all the messages addressed to that client are downloaded; there is no way to download messages selectively. Once the messages are downloaded, the user can delete or modify messages without further interaction with the server. In some locations, POP3 is being replaced by another standard, IMAP.

## Internet Message Access Protocol, Version 4 (IMAP4)

Internet Message Access Protocol (IMAP) allows users to download mail selectively, look at the message header, download just a part of a message, store messages on the e-mail server in a hierarchical structure, and link to documents and Usenet newsgroups. Search commands are also available so that users can locate messages based on their subject, header or content. IMAP has strong authentication features and supports the Kerberos authentication scheme originally developed at MIT. The current version of IMAP is version 4.

## Line Printer Daemon (LPD)

Another TCP/IP upper-layer service that is in widespread use is the Line Printer Daemon (LPD). It resides on a network printer or print server and responds to TCP/IP printing requests from the printing clients (known as *LPR clients*). It was developed as the printing services for UNIX. But, because of the tight marriage between UNIX and TCP/IP, the LPD service became the default print service used with TCP/IP.

 A *daemon* is a program that acts like a terminate and stay resident (TSR) application by loading into memory and lurking there for any trigger that calls upon its services.

# Network File System (NFS)

UNIX systems are unique in the way they access files and are actually fairly elegant. The Network File System (NFS) Application layer protocol was originally designed to allow shared file systems on UNIX servers to appear as local file systems on UNIX clients.

# Telnet

Telnet is a terminal emulation protocol that provides a remote logon to another host over the network. It allows a user to connect to a remote host over a TCP/IP connection as if they were sitting right at that host. Keystrokes typed into a Telnet program will be transmitted over a TCP/IP network to the host. The visual responses are sent back by the host to the Telnet client to be displayed.

# Secure Shell (SSH)

The Secure Shell (SSH) protocol is used to establish a secure Telnet session over a standard TCP/IP connection. It is used to run programs on remote systems, log in to other systems, and move files from one system to another, all while maintaining a strong, encrypted connection. It replaces such utilities as rsh and rlogin as well as Telnet.

# Hypertext Transfer Protocol (HTTP)

Hypertext Transfer Protocol (HTTP) is the command and control protocol used to manage communications between a web browser and a web server. When you access a web page on the Internet or on a corporate intranet, you see a mixture of text, graphics, and links to other documents or other Internet resources. HTTP is the mechanism that opens the related document when you select a link, no matter where that document is actually located.

# Hypertext Transfer Protocol Secure (HTTPS)

Hypertext Transfer Protocol Secure (HTTPS), also referred to as Secure Hypertext Transfer Protocol (which you will see abbreviated as SHTTP or S-HTTP), is a secure version of HTTP that provides a variety of security mechanisms to the transactions between a web browser and the server. HTTPS allows browsers and servers to sign, authenticate, and encrypt an HTTP message.

# Network Time Protocol (NTP)

Network Time Protocol (NTP), originally developed by Professor David Mills at the University of Delaware, is used to synchronize (or set) computer clocks to some standard time source, which is usually a nuclear clock. This protocol (along with synchronization utilities) keeps all computers on a network set to the same time. Time synchronization is important because many transactions are time and date stamped (in a database, for example). If the time on a server is out of synchronization with the time on two different computers, even by just a few seconds, the server will get confused. For example, one computer can seemingly enter a transaction, but the server will indicate that it occurred before it actually did. Because this time problem will crash the database server, it is important that these servers (and workstations) use NTP.

## Network News Transfer Protocol (NNTP)

The Network News Transfer Protocol (NNTP) is the TCP/IP protocol used to access Usenet news servers. Usenet news servers contain thousands of individual message boards known as newsgroups. Each newsgroup is about a particular subject (cars, dating, computers, etc.). Chances are, if you have an interest, there is a newsgroup about it. The details of the NNTP protocol are specified in RFC 977.

NOTE    Because of the relative complexity involved in configuring a news reader program, there are many websites (including google.com) that have made newsgroup access available through the Web.

## Secure Copy Protocol (SCP)

While FTP is easy to use to transfer files, it has a major security problem in that the username and password are sent along with the file request in clear text (i.e., not encrypted). It would be a relatively simple matter for someone to intercept that information and use it for other purposes.

Secure Copy Protocol (SCP) was designed to overcome this limitation. It uses SSH to establish and maintain an encrypted connection between hosts. The file transfer can then take place without fear of password or data interception.

## Lightweight Directory Access Protocol (LDAP)

In large networks, most administrators have set up some kind of directory that keeps track of users and resources (e.g., NDS, Active Directory). In order to have a standard method of accessing directories, the Lightweight Directory Access Protocol (LDAP) was developed. It allows clients to perform object lookups with a directory using a standard method. LDAP was originally specified as RFCs 1487 (version 1) and 1777 (version 2), with RFC 3377 proposing the more commonly used third version, which fixes a number of shortcomings in the protocol.

## Internet Group Management Protocol (IGMP)

The Internet Group Management Protocol (IGMP) is a TCP/IP protocol that is used to manage IP multicast sessions. It uses special IGMP messages to learn the layout of the multicast groups and which hosts belong to which groups. Additionally, the individual hosts in an IP network use IGMP messages to join and leave a multicast group. IGMP messages help keep track of group membership and active multicast streams. IGMP is in its second version, as specified in RFC 2236, with a third version (RFC 3376), currently proposed.

## Line Printer Remote (LPR)

When using pure TCP/IP printing (as with UNIX workstations or when used for cross-platform printing), the LPD/LPR pairing is used most often. The Line Printer Daemon (LPD) is installed on the print device and manages the printer as well as the print jobs. The Line Printer Remote (LPR) software is the printing client that sends the print jobs to the LPD via TCP/IP.

# Other Upper-Layer Protocols

Various other upper-layer protocols play an important role in the success of the TCP/IP protocol suite as a flexible, well-rounded, self-contained group of protocols:

- UDP
- SMB
- AFP
- ICS

## User Datagram Protocol (UDP)

User Datagram Protocol (UDP) is a Transport layer connectionless protocol that does not provide the reliability services available with TCP but instead provides best effort transmission services to application protocols. UDP gives applications a direct interface with IP and the ability to address a specific application protocol running on a host via a port number without setting up an end-to-end virtual circuit or connection. UDP, like TCP, uses IP to deliver its packets.

Figure 3.4 shows how some of these components fit together.

**FIGURE 3.4**     The components in a TCP/IP block diagram

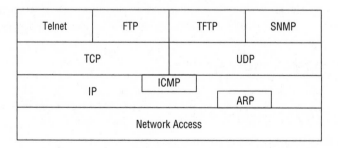

# Server Message Block (SMB)

Server Message Block (SMB) is a Presentation layer protocol developed through the efforts of corporations the likes of Xerox, 3Com, and IBM and further developed by (and currently attributed to) Microsoft, providing a networking command message format used when sending networking commands to servers. These commands allow a client to do things like browse for resources; open connections, access files, printers, and communications ports; and list directories. SMB can be run over any number of lower-layer protocols, such as NetBEUI, NetBIOS over TCP/IP, NetBIOS over IPX/SPX, and others.

## Samba

SMB is not limited to Windows machines (although they are where SMB commands are usually found). SMB is being developed for the world community as the Common Internet File System (CIFS), a term now synonymous with SMB. Through Samba, one popular application of SMB/CIFS for the non-Microsoft market (visit samba.org), UNIX and Linux servers can use SMB commands to communicate with Windows clients. Samba is a free open-source protocol suite that provides file and print services to SMB/CIFS clients. Samba allows for interoperability between Linux/UNIX servers and Windows-based clients by running on a platform other than Microsoft Windows, such as UNIXLinux, IBM OpenVMS, and so on. Samba uses TCP/IP installed on the host server, allowing that host to interact with a Microsoft Windows client or server as if it were a Windows file and print server.

The two primary programs, or daemons, of Samba, called smbd and nmbd, are responsible for two each of the four common CIFS services:

- File and print services
- Authentication and authorization
- Name resolution
- Service announcement (browsing)

Arguably the foundation of CIFS, file and print services are performed by smbd, as are authentication and authorization. The nmbd daemon provides NetBIOS name services to clients, including name resolution and service announcement, often referred to as browsing services.

# AppleTalk Filing Protocol (AFP)

Before there was ever a Windows file sharing system in place, Apple had the AppleTalk Filing Protocol (AFP) for its AppleShare servers. AFP is the Presentation layer protocol that is used to access AppleShare and Mac OS File Sharing files. It is the only protocol that accesses AppleShare servers natively. Any system wanting to access an AppleShare server must be running some version of AFP (or at least AFP over another transport protocol, like TCP/IP).

     See Chapter 2 for more on AFP.

⊕ **Real World Scenario**

**A Better Windows Server?**

I was working at a local networking service establishment when I was presented with a problem. A customer wanted a server capable of doing some file sharing. The server had to be robust and capable of interacting with all of the company's Windows clients. But they were at the end of a budget cycle and the new budget wouldn't be approved for at least a month and they needed the server for one of their workgroups immediately. They had the hardware but couldn't afford the Windows 2000 Server licenses they needed and Windows 98 just wasn't up to par. The solution we came up with was to install Red Hat Linux on one of their machines and then install Samba. It allowed them to have SMB-compatible file sharing and use their existing Windows clients while not having to purchase a Windows server. To my knowledge, that server is still running today.

## Internet Connection Sharing (ICS)

In addition to the standard TCP/IP services provided in Windows, Microsoft includes Internet Connection Sharing (ICS) services in all versions of Windows since Windows 98. What ICS does is to take an Internet connection to one computer and share it with the rest of the computers on a network, essentially turning the computer connected to the Internet into an Internet gateway for the rest of the network. Microsoft states that ICS works mostly at the Network layer of the OSI model, where it facilitates layer 3 access to the Internet on behalf of one or more other devices.

ICS works with just about any Internet connection type. The main benefit to ICS is that you are running an Internet gateway in software so you can avoid the added expense of a router for your small network. However, the software gateway in ICS isn't as efficient as a dedicated hardware router.

# Overview of Ports and Sockets

On a TCP/IP network, data travels from a port on the sending computer to a port on the receiving computer. A *port* is a numerical value that identifies the application associated with the data. The source port number identifies the application that sent the data, and the destination port number identifies the application that receives the data. Each port is assigned a unique 16-bit number in the range of 0 through 65535. Additionally, there are two types of ports—TCP and UDP—which are based on their respective protocols. Both TCP and UDP maintain a separate list of used (reserved and allocated) port numbers. This allows them both to make sure no port is duplicated within each list. A benefit of this mechanism is that multiple application data streams can be multiplexed through each protocol simultaneously. For example, it is no problem for TCP to handle HTTP traffic and FTP traffic simultaneously, nor is it a problem for UDP to allow TFTP and SNMP simultaneous access to the network.

Of course, *simultaneous access* is a figurative expression because, as with all serial data flows, only one data source can be serviced at a time. The appearance of simultaneous operation is achieved through time-division multiplexing, which interleaves the separate flows into one.

The very existence of ports and their numbers is more or less transparent to the users of the network because many server-side ports are standardized. Thus, a client application protocol will know which remote port it should connect to for a specific service. For example, all servers that offer Telnet services usually do so on TCP port 23, and web servers normally run on TCP port 80. This means that when you connect to the Internet to browse to a web server, you automatically connect to port 80, and when you use Telnet, you automatically connect to port 23. The TCP/IP protocol suite uses a modifiable lookup table to determine the correct port for the data type. Table 3.1 lists some of the *well-known port numbers* for common protocols.

**TABLE 3.1**   Well-Known Port Numbers for Common Protocols

| Port | Protocol |
| --- | --- |
| UDP port 15 | NETSTAT |
| TCP port 20 | FTP data |
| TCP port 21 | FTP control |
| TCP port 22 | SSH |
| TCP port 23 | Telnet |
| TCP port 25 | SMTP |
| TCP port 53 | DNS zone transfers |
| UDP port 53 | DNS queries |
| UDP port 69 | TFTP |
| TCP port 70 | Gopher |
| TCP port 79 | Finger |

**TABLE 3.1**    Well-Known Port Numbers for Common Protocols *(continued)*

| Port | Protocol |
| --- | --- |
| TCP port 80 | HTTP |
| TCP port 110 | POP3 |
| UDP port 111 | RPC |
| TCP port 119 | NNTP |
| TCP port 123 | NTP |
| UDP port 137 | NetBIOS name service |
| TCP port 143 | IMAP4 |
| UDP port 161 | SNMP |
| TCP port 443 | HTTPS |
| UDP port 520 | RIP |
| UDP port 2049 | NFS |

Client application protocols require identification by port numbers as well, but they could not possibly each have their own well-known port numbers, which is where *registered port numbers* come in. Registered port numbers begin at 1024 and extend to 49151. These port numbers are used by TCP and UDP alike to be temporarily assigned to client application protocols as they begin their journey to the remote device and its server application protocol. Ports from 49152 to 65535 are considered *dynamic ports* and/or *private ports*.

The combination of an IP address (more on IP addresses in a moment) and a port number is known as a *socket*. A socket identifies a single network process in terms of the entire Internet or other end-to-end IP-based internetwork. Two sockets—one on the sending system and one on the receiving host—are needed to define a connection for connection-oriented protocols, such as TCP. You may hear or see the terms *socket* and *port* used as if they are interchangeable terms, but they are not.

In the Novell NetWare world, a socket is part of an IPX internetwork address and acts as a destination for the IPX data packet. Most socket numbers are allocated dynamically, but a few are associated with specific functions.

Sockets were first developed as a part of the BSD UNIX system kernel, in which they allow processes that are not running at the same time or on the same system to exchange information. You can read data from or write data to a socket just as you can with a file. Socket pairs are bidirectional so that either process can send data to the other.

### The Two Ports and Modes of FTP

You may have noticed in Table 3.1 that FTP has two TCP ports associated with it, one for control and the other for data. Additionally, FTP runs in two modes: active and passive. In every FTP active-mode session, both of these ports are used on the server but in very different capacities. Because the use of the FTP protocol implies that resources will be available across a potentially insecure public infrastructure, it is important that the administrator of those resources have the last word as to their availability. This is where the two ports come into play. Port 21, the FTP control port, is targeted by the client when an FTP session is being requested of the server. In this request directed at the server's TCP port 21, the client issues a PORT command, whereby it communicates to the server the random TCP port it would like the server to send data back to. This randomly assigned port will generally be one greater than the port it was using to source the traffic to port 21. The server then opens a TCP connection sourced from its own port 20, the FTP data port, back to this advertised port on the client. Once this TCP connection is established, data transfer can commence across it. This prevents the client from simply reaching over to the server and grabbing whatever it wants without first being authenticated. The port 20 connection can be postponed, pending proper authentication from the client.

That's how the *active-mode FTP* connection works. What if a firewall local to the user is secure enough not to allow what appears to be an externally initiated TCP connection? Well, then the second half of the FTP process fails because that's exactly what the server's port-20-initiated connection is and data transfer never actually occurs. Why not let the client initiate the data connection to port 20 at will? Well, if the server merely lets any and every client gain immediate access to its resources without authentication, FTP wouldn't last very long as a successful protocol. One solution is for everything to start the same way it does for the active-mode FTP connection, but instead of the server initiating the second session from port 20, it actually opens a random port, as the client did, and asks the client to use that port to effect its data transfers. All of this can be done in the initial port 21 control phase, allowing any authentication the administrator has configured to occur before this random port number is shared with the client. How does the server know the client wishes to start this type of connection and not have the server open a connection of its own from port 20? Instead of issuing the PORT command, as it did in the active-mode connection, the client issues the PASV command, indicating to the server that the client itself needs to open the data connection. This is known as *passive-mode FTP*. Not all client software supports passive-mode FTP, but most modern versions do. A key difference between the modes is that active mode uses both ports 20 and 21 but passive mode only uses port 21, substituting a registered port, greater than 1024, for port 20.

# Understanding IP Addressing

As you know from the section "The Internet Layer Protocols" earlier in this chapter, IP moves data between computer systems in the form of a series of one or more packets, often making up a TCP or UDP datagram, and each datagram is delivered to the IP destination system and to the port number (on that system) that is contained in the encapsulated TCP or UDP header. This destination socket, or port and address combination, is a standard 48-bit number (a 32-bit IP address and a 16-bit port number) that contains enough information to identify the receiving network, the host for which the datagram is intended on that network, and the application running on that host.

In this section, you'll learn what IP addresses are, why they are so necessary, and how they are used in TCP/IP networking. But first, let's clear up a possible source of confusion: Ethernet addresses and IP addresses.

## Overview of Ethernet Addresses

You may remember from an earlier section that TCP/IP is independent of the underlying network hardware. If you are running on an Ethernet-based network, be careful not to confuse the Ethernet hardware address and the IP address required by TCP/IP.

Each Ethernet network card (and any other NIC, for that matter) has its own unique hardware address, known as the media access control (MAC) address. This hardware address is predefined and preprogrammed on the NIC by the manufacturer of the board as a unique 48-bit number.

The first three bytes of this address are called the Organizationally Unique Identifier (OUI) and are assigned by the Institute of Electrical and Electronics Engineers (IEEE). Manufacturers purchase OUIs and then vary the last three bytes of the MAC address for each interface they produce, making each address unique provided no other manufacturer makes unauthorized use of the OUI and related address space. Remember that the Ethernet address is predetermined and is hard-coded onto the NIC. IP addresses, however, are very different.

## Overview of IP Addresses

TCP/IP requires that each interface on a TCP/IP network have its own unique IP address. There are two addressing schemes for TCP/IP: IPv4 and IPv6. You should know how these schemes differ.

### IPv4

An IPv4 address is a 32-bit number, usually represented as a four-part decimal number with each of the four parts separated by a period or decimal point. You may also hear this method of representation called *dotted decimal* or *dotted quad decimal*. In the IPv4 address, each individual byte, or *octet* as it is sometimes called, can have a value in the range of 0 through 255.

The term *octet* is the Internet community's own term for an 8-bit byte. It came into common use because some of the early computers attached to the Internet had bytes of more than 8 bits; for example, DEC's systems had blocks of 18 bits.

The way these addresses are used varies according to the class of the network, so all you can say with certainty is that the 32-bit IPv4 address is divided in some way to create an identifier for the network, which all hosts on that network share, and an identifier for each host, which is unique among all hosts on that network. In general, though, the higher-order bits of the address make up the network part of the address and the rest constitutes the host part of the address. In addition, the host part of the address can be divided further to allow for a *subnetwork address*. For more detail on this addressing scheme, see the sections "IPv4 Address Classifications" and "Understanding Subnets" later in this chapter.

Some host addresses are reserved for special use. For example, in all network addresses, host numbers of all 0s and all 1s are reserved. An IPv4 host address with all host bits set to 0 in binary identifies the network itself, so 10.0.0.0 refers to network 10. An IP address with all host bits set to 1 in binary is known as a *broadcast address*. The broadcast address for network 172.16 is 172.16.255.255. A datagram sent to this address is automatically sent to every individual host on the 172.16 network.

American Registry for Internet Numbers (ARIN) assigns and regulates IP addresses on the Internet; you can get one directly from ARIN, or you can ask your Internet service provider (ISP) to secure an IP address on your behalf. Another strategy is to obtain your address from ARIN and only use it internally until you are ready to connect to the Internet.

If you are setting up an intranet and you don't want to connect to the outside world through the Internet, you don't need to obtain a registered IP address from ARIN. Obtaining registered addresses from ARIN simply ensures that the addresses you use are unique over the entire Internet. If you are never going to connect to the Internet, there's no reason to worry about whether those addresses are the same as an address of a computer that isn't even on your network. Nowadays, however, it is rare to find an individual or organization that implements an IP-based internetwork that does not intend to connect to the Internet. More realistically, you might choose to use private address space (the 10.0.0.0 network, for example) internally while translating to a small pool of ARIN-registered addresses, using NAT, in order to communicate with the Internet, thus conserving public registered address space.

## IPv4 Address Classifications

In an IPv4 address, the default number of bits used to identify the network and the host vary according to the network class of the address. While other methods, such as Classless Inter-Domain Routing, are currently more popular for specifying address space boundaries for entities of various sizes, the following classes of IP addresses originally offered a default set of boundaries for varying sizes of address space and still provide a fallback mechanism for end and intermediate devices in the absence of ample subnetting information:

- Class A was designed for very large networks only. The default network portion for Class A networks is the first 8 bits, leaving 24 bits for host identification. The high-order bit is always binary 0, which leaves 7 bits available for IANA to define 127 networks. The remaining 24 bits of the address allow each Class A network to hold as many as 16,777,214 hosts. Examples of Class A networks include General Electric, IBM, Hewlett-Packard, Apple, Xerox, Compaq, Columbia University, MIT, and the private network 10.0.0.0. All possible Class A networks are in use; no more are available.

- Class B was designed for medium-sized networks. The default network portion for Class B networks is the first 16 bits, leaving 16 bits for host identification. The 2 high-order bits are always binary 10, and the remaining 14 bits are used for IANA to define 16,384 networks, each with as many as 65,534 hosts attached. Examples of Class B networks include Microsoft, Exxon, and the 16 private networks ranging from 172.16.0.0 to 172.31.0.0, inclusive. Class B networks are generally regarded as unavailable, but address conservation techniques have made some of these addresses become available from time to time over the years.

- Class C was designed for smaller networks. The default network portion for Class C networks is the first 24 bits, leaving 8 bits for host identification. The 3 high-order bits are always binary 110, and the remaining 21 bits are used by IANA to define 2,097,152 networks, but each network can have a maximum of only 254 hosts. Examples of Class C networks are the 256 private networks ranging from 192.168.0.0 to 192.168.255.0. Class C networks are still available.

- Class D is the multicast address range and cannot be used for networks. There is no network/host structure to these addresses. They are taken as a complete address and used as destination addresses only, just like broadcast addresses. The 4 high-order bits are always 1110, and the remaining 28 bits allow access to more than 268 million possible addresses.

- Class E is reserved for experimental purposes. The first 4 bits in the address are always 1111.

One trick that works well, when faced with determining the class of an IP address written entirely in binary, is to assign the letters A through D to the first 4 bits, in alphabetical order. Wherever the first 0 falls signifies the class of address with which you are dealing. If none of the first 4 bits are set to 0, then you have a Class E address.

Figure 3.5 illustrates the relationships among these classes and shows how the bits are allocated by the Internet Network Information Center (InterNIC), an Internet Corporation for Assigned Names and Numbers (ICANN) licensed service mark.

**FIGURE 3.5**    The IP address structure

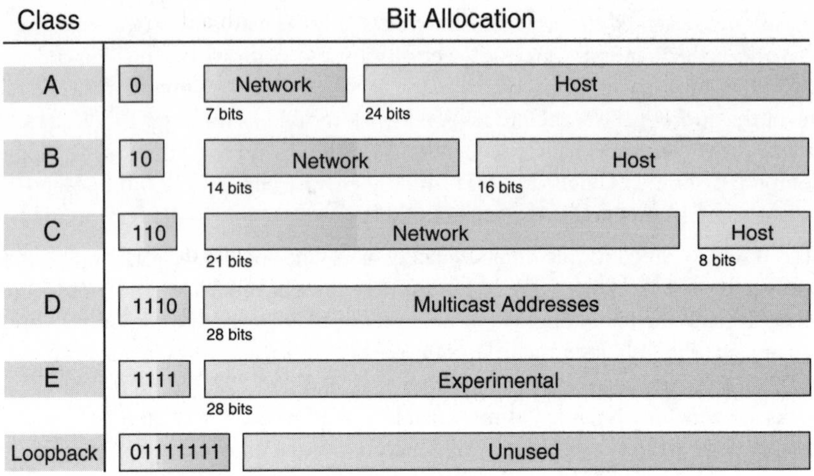

Because the bits used to identify the class are combined with the bits that define the network address, we can draw the following conclusions from the size of the first octet, or byte, of the address:

- A value of 126 or less indicates a Class A address. The first octet is the network number; the next three, the host ID.

- A value of exactly 127, while technically in the Class A range, is reserved as a software loopback test address. If you send an echo request to 127.0.0.1, the ping doesn't actually generate any network traffic. It does, however, test that TCP/IP is installed correctly. Using this number as a special test address has the unfortunate effect of wasting almost 17 million possible IP addresses, a case of early-70s short-sightedness, much like the theory that 64KB of RAM should be enough for PCs.

- A value of 128 through 191 is a Class B address. The first two octets are the network number, and the last two are the host address.

- A value of 192 through 223 is a Class C address. The first three octets are the network address, and the last octet is the host address.

- A value of 224 through 239 is a Class D multicast address. Again, there are no network or host portions to multicast addresses.

- A value greater than 239 indicates a reserved Class E address.

## IPv6

IPv6 was originally designed because the number of available unregistered IPv4 addresses was running low. Because IPv6 uses a 128-bit addressing scheme, it has more than 79 octillion (that's 79,000,000,000,000,000,000,000,000,000 to you and me) times as many available addresses as IPv4. Also, instead of representing the binary digits as decimal digits, IPv6 uses eight sets of four hexadecimal digits, like so:

3FFE:0B00:0800:0002:0000:0000:0000:000C

In addition, you can abbreviate these very long addresses by dropping leading 0s (zeros) (like the 0 before the *B* in "0B00"). You can also drop any single grouping of zero octets (as in the number above) between numbers as long as you replace them with a double colon (::) and they are complete octets (you can't drop the three 0s in the second octet to make it just "B" instead of "0B00," for example). If you apply this rule (known as the zero compression rule) to the above address, it would make the example address look like so:

3FFE:0B00:0800:0002::000C

The private address spaces listed with each class description are specified in RFC 1918 as being available to anyone who wants to use IP addressing on a private network but does not want to connect these networks directly to the Internet. Private addresses are those addresses that are not permitted to be routed by Internet routers. In fact, ISPs can be fined for passing traffic with these addresses as source or destination. Conversely, public addresses are those IP addresses that are allowed to be passed by Internet routers. You can use the private address space without the risk of compromising someone else's registered network address space. If you use a private address and decide to interconnect your intranet with the Internet, you may use NAT to do so.

As with IPv4, there are several addresses that are reserved for special uses. For example, the IPv6 address ::/0 is the default address for a host that has yet to be assigned an address (like 0.0.0.0 in IPv4). The address ::1/128 is reserved for the local loopback (like 127.0.0.1 in IPv4). IPv6 also includes provisions for the old IPv4 hosts so they can be migrated to the new addressing scheme. This is accomplished by using the address ::*xxx.xxx.xxx.xxx*, where the last four sets of digits refer to the old IPv4 address.

The way a host is configured is one very unique aspect of the IPv6 addressing scheme. Instead of an IP address, subnet mask, and default gateway, each station is required to have three different addresses. First of all, the host has an address from each upstream supplier, a local address, and a link-local address. The local address is a number like ::1/128 that defines the local host. The link-local address is the address for the local subnet.

Finally, IPv6 has some other unique addressing concepts, like autoconfiguration (similar to DHCP, but extended further) and neighbor discovery, whereby the IPv6 host discovers its network surroundings.

You can't use the zero compression rule to drop more than one grouping of zero octets. For example, you can't make 3FFE:0000:0000:0002:0000:0000:0000:000C into 3FFE::0002::000C. This is also part of the zero compression rule: There can be only one set of double colons! Otherwise, receiving devices would not be able to reverse-engineer the number of missing zeros. Therefore, since it's up to the human entering the address, compress the longer series of zeros.

For more information on IPv6, check out RFC 2373 at www.ietf.org.

# Understanding Subnets

The IP addressing scheme provides a flexible solution to the task of addressing thousands of networks, but it is not without problems. The original designers did not envision the Internet growing as large as it has; at that time, a 32-bit address seemed so large that they quickly divided it into different classes of networks to facilitate routing rather than reserving more bits to manage the growth in network addresses. To solve this problem, and to create a large number of new network addresses, another way of dividing the 32-bit address was developed, called *subnetting*.

An IP subnet modifies the IP address by using host ID bits as additional network address bits. In other words, the dividing line between the network address and the host ID is moved to the right, thus creating additional networks but reducing the number of hosts that can belong to each network.

When IP networks are subnetted, they can be routed independently, which allows a much better use of address space and available bandwidth. To subnet an IP network, you define a bit mask, known as a *subnet mask,* in which a bit pattern of consecutive 1s followed by consecutive 0s is ANDed with the IP address to produce a network address with all 0s in the host ID.

Working out subnet masks is one of the most complex tasks in network administration and is not for the faint of heart. If your network consists of a single segment (in other words, there are no routers on your network), you will not have to use this type of subnetting, but if you have two or more segments (or subnets), you will have to make some sort of provision for distributing IP addresses appropriately. Using a subnet mask is the way to do just that.

The subnet mask is similar in structure to an IP address in that it has four parts, or octets, but it works a bit like a template that, when superimposed on top of the IP address, indicates which bits in the IP address identify the network and which bits identify the host. In binary, if a bit is on (set to 1) in the mask, the corresponding bit in the address is interpreted as a network bit. If a bit is off (reset to 0) in the mask, the corresponding bit in the address is part of the host ID. The 32-bit value may then be converted to dotted decimal notation for human consumption. Sometimes, you will use only one subnet mask to subnet your network. Variable Length Subnet Masking (VLSM) is the practice of using more appropriate varied subnet masks with the same classful network for the different subnet sizes. A *classful* network is one subnetted to the default boundaries of network and host bits, based on the class of IP address.

A subnet is only known and understood locally; to the rest of the Internet, the address is still interpreted as a classful IP address (and maybe even as a group of classful addresses) if an entity has administrative control over a contiguous block of such addresses. Table 3.2 shows how this works for the standard IP address classes.

Routers then use the subnet mask to extract the network portion of the address so that they can compare the computed network address with the routing table entry corresponding to the mask used and send the data packets along the proper route on the network.

**TABLE 3.2**    Default Subnet Masks for Standard IP Address Classes

| Class | Subnet Mask Bit Pattern | Subnet Mask |
|-------|-------------------------|-------------|
| A | 11111111 00000000 00000000 00000000 | 255.0.0.0 |
| B | 11111111 11111111 00000000 00000000 | 255.255.0.0 |
| C | 11111111 11111111 11111111 00000000 | 255.255.255.0 |

Because pretty much all the Class A and Class B networks are taken, you are most likely to encounter subnet-related issues when working with a Class C network or with any private address space. In the next section, you'll get a detailed look at how to subnet a Class C network.

## Why Subnet?

When faced with the choice of whether or not to subnet your network, you must remember several of the advantages to subnetting. The following list summarizes the advantages of the subnetting solution:

- It minimizes network traffic, decreasing congestion.

- It isolates networks from others.

- It increases performance.

- It optimizes use of IP address space.

- It enhances the ability to secure a network.

## Subnetting a Class C Network

How do you find out the values that you can use for a Class C network subnet mask? Remember from a previous discussion that InterNIC defines the leftmost three octets in a Class C address, leaving you with the rightmost octet for your own host and subnetting use. If your network consists of a single segment, you have the following subnet mask:

```
11111111 11111111 11111111 00000000
```

When expressed as a decimal number, this is

```
255.255.255.0
```

Because all of your addresses must match these leftmost 24 bits, you can do what you'd like with the last 8 bits, given a couple of exceptions that we'll look at in a moment.

You might decide to divide your network into two equally sized segments, with, for example, the numbers 0 through 127 as the first subnet (00000000 through 01111111 in binary) and the numbers 128 through 255 as the second subnet (10000000 through 11111111 in binary). Notice how the numbers within each subnet can vary only in the last seven places. So, placing 1s in the mask where the bits should be identical for all hosts in a subnet, the subnet mask becomes

255.255.255.128

In binary this is

11111111.11111111.11111111.10000000

Use the Windows Calculator in scientific mode (choose View ➤ Scientific) to look at binary-to-decimal and decimal-to-binary conversions. Click the Bin (binary) button and then type the bit pattern that you want to convert. Click the Dec (decimal) button to display its decimal value. You can also go the other way and display a decimal number in binary form. This works great for hexa-decimal and octal numbering systems, as well.

Now let's get back to the exceptions mentioned earlier. The network number is the first number in each range, so the first subnet's network number is X.Y.Z.0 and the second is X.Y.Z.128 (X, Y, and Z are the octets assigned by InterNIC). The default router address is commonly the second number in each range—X.Y.Z.1 and X.Y.Z.129—and the broadcast address is the last address, or X.Y.Z.127 and X.Y.Z.255. You can use all the other addresses within the range as you see fit on your network.

Table 3.3 describes how you can divide a Class C network into four equally sized subnets with a subnet mask of 255.255.255.192. This gives you 62 IP addresses on each subnet once you have accounted for the network and broadcast addresses.

**TABLE 3.3**   Class C Network Divided into Four Subnets

| Network Number | First Address | Broadcast Address |
| --- | --- | --- |
| X.Y.Z.0 | X.Y.Z.1 | X.Y.Z.63 |
| X.Y.Z.64 | X.Y.Z.65 | X.Y.Z.127 |
| X.Y.Z.128 | X.Y.Z.129 | X.Y.Z.191 |
| X.Y.Z.192 | X.Y.Z.193 | X.Y.Z.255 |

Table 3.4 describes how you can divide a Class C network into eight equally sized subnets with a subnet mask of 255.255.255.224. This gives you 30 IP addresses on each subnet once you have accounted for the network and broadcast addresses. You can continue this trend for subnet masks with fourth-octet values of 240, 248, and 252. A fourth-octet value of 254 is widely regarded as unusable because the only possible values in each subnet have only 0s or 1s in the host portion, which are illegal for assignment to hosts.

**TABLE 3.4**    Class C Network Divided into Eight Subnets

| Network Number | First Address | Broadcast Address |
| --- | --- | --- |
| X.Y.Z.0 | X.Y.Z.1 | X.Y.Z.31 |
| X.Y.Z.32 | X.Y.Z.33 | X.Y.Z.63 |
| X.Y.Z.64 | X.Y.Z.65 | X.Y.Z.95 |
| X.Y.Z.96 | X.Y.Z.97 | X.Y.Z.127 |
| X.Y.Z.128 | X.Y.Z.129 | X.Y.Z.159 |
| X.Y.Z.160 | X.Y.Z.161 | X.Y.Z.191 |
| X.Y.Z.192 | X.Y.Z.193 | X.Y.Z.223 |
| X.Y.Z.224 | X.Y.Z.225 | X.Y.Z.255 |

## Classless Inter-Domain Routing (CIDR)

InterNIC no longer gives out addresses under the Class A, B, or C designations. Instead, it uses a method called *Classless Inter-Domain Routing* (or *CIDR*, which is usually pronounced "cider"). CIDR networks are described as "slash *x* (/*x*)" networks; the *x* represents the number of bits in the IP address range that InterNIC controls, more easily seen as the number of bits in the subnet mask set to 1. This allows InterNIC to define networks that fall between the old classifications, which means that you can get a range of addresses much better suited to your needs than in times past. In CIDR terms, a network classified as a Class C network under the old scheme becomes a /24 network because InterNIC controls the leftmost 24 bits and you control the rightmost 8 bits. Table 3.5 shows some examples of /*x* network types.

You can also combine multiple classful networks into a single network using this same designation system. This process is known as *supernetting*.

**TABLE 3.5**    Table 3.5Examples of CIDR Network Types

| InterNIC Network Type | Subnet Mask | Number of Usable IP Addresses |
|---|---|---|
| /8 | 255.0.0.0 | 16,777,214 |
| /12 | 255.240.0.0 | 1,048,574 |
| /16 | 255.255.0.0 | 65,534 |
| /20 | 255.255.240.0 | 4,094 |
| /21 | 255.255.248.0 | 2,046 |
| /22 | 255.255.252.0 | 1,022 |
| /23 | 255.255.254.0 | 510 |
| /24 | 255.255.255.0 | 254 |
| /25 | 255.255.255.128 | 126 |
| /26 | 255.255.255.192 | 62 |
| /27 | 255.255.255.224 | 30 |
| /28 | 255.255.255.240 | 14 |
| /29 | 255.255.255.248 | 6 |
| /30 | 255.255.255.252 | 2 |

# IP Proxy Servers

A *proxy server* is one of several solutions to the problems associated with connecting your intranet or corporate network to the Internet. A proxy server is a program that handles traffic to external host systems on behalf of the client software running on the protected network; this means that clients access the Internet through the proxy server. It's a bit like those one-way mirrors—you can see out, but a potential intruder cannot see in.

**NOTE**  Another mechanism used to monitor and control traffic between the Internet and an internal network is a *firewall*. Although the functions performed by proxy servers and firewalls are related and appear in combination products, they'll be presented in different chapters here. You will find more information on firewalls in Chapter 9, "Fault Tolerance and Disaster Recovery," while additional coverage of various proxies can be found in Chapter 8, "Network Access and Security."

A proxy server sits between a user on your network and a server out on the Internet. Instead of communicating with each other directly, each talks to the proxy (in other words, to a "stand-in"). From the user's point of view, the proxy server presents the illusion that the user is dealing with a genuine Internet server. To the real server on the Internet, the proxy server gives the illusion that the real server is dealing directly with the user on the internal network. So a proxy server can be both a client and a server; it depends on which way you are facing. The point to remember here is that the user is never in direct contact with the Internet server, as Figure 3.6 illustrates.

The proxy server does more than just forward requests from your users to the Internet and back. Because it examines and makes decisions about the requests that it processes, it can control what your users can do. Depending on the details of your security policy, client requests can be approved and forwarded, or they can be denied. And rather than requiring that the same restrictions be enforced for all users, many advanced proxy server packages can offer different capabilities to different users.

**FIGURE 3.6**    How a proxy server works

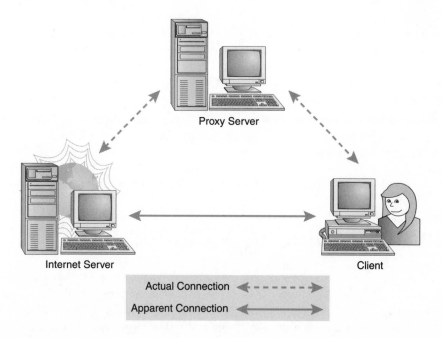

A proxy server can be effective only if it is the only type of connection between an internal network and the Internet. As soon as you allow a connection that does not go through a proxy server, your network is at risk.

## Proxy Server Caching

Many proxy servers can cache documents, which is particularly useful if a number of clients request the same document independently. With caching, the client request is filled more quickly and Internet traffic is reduced. The types of caching are as follows:

**Active Caching**    The proxy server uses periods of low activity to go out and retrieve documents that it thinks will be requested by clients in the near future.

**Passive Caching**    The proxy server waits for a client to make a request, retrieves the document, and then decides whether or not to cache the document.

 Some documents, such as those from a paid subscription service or those that are subject to constant change (for example, documents from financial institutions, documents relating to stock ticker records, and those requiring specific authentication) cannot be cached.

Large companies may have multiple proxy servers, and two caching standards have emerged:

**Internet Cache Protocol (ICP)**    Internet Cache Protocol (ICP) specifies a message format to be used for communications between proxy servers; these messages are used to exchange information about the presence or absence of a specific web page in the proxy server cache. Unfortunately, ICP is not scalable, and the number of ICP messages exchanged between proxy servers climbs rapidly as the number of proxy servers increases.

**Cache Array Routing Protocol (CARP)**    Cache Array Routing Protocol (CARP) offers a solution to the ICP problem by using multiple proxy servers with a single large cache. CARP removes the need for proxy server–to–proxy server communications and also prevents the information in the cache from becoming redundant over time. CARP is referred to as queryless distributed caching and is supported in Netscape and Microsoft proxy server products.

# Name Resolution Methods

Internet host names are used because they are easier to remember than the long dotted decimal IP addresses. A host name is typically the name of a device that has a specific IP address and on the Internet is part of what is known as a *Fully Qualified Domain Name (FQDN)*. An FQDN consists of a host name and a domain name. An example of an FQDN is hostname.company.com.

Although we have phone numbers and can remember them when we need to, life would be difficult if we had to remember the phone numbers of all our friends and associates. We might be able to remember the numbers of as many as 10 friends and relatives, but after that, things would get a bit difficult. Therefore, we remember their names and have directories of names and the phone numbers. Likewise, it's easier to remember `www.microsoft.com` than it is to remember 198.105.232.6 and look up the name to associate the IP address with it.

The process of finding the IP address for any given host name is known as *name resolution,* and it can be performed in several ways: a HOSTS file, a request broadcast on the local network, DNS, and WINS. But before you read about that, you need to first understand Internet domains and how they are organized.

## Internet Domain Organization

On the Internet, domains are arranged in a hierarchical tree structure. The following list includes some of the top-level domains currently in use:

`com`: A commercial organization. Most companies will end up as part of this domain.

`edu`: An educational establishment, such as a university.

`gov`: A branch of the U.S. government.

`int`: An international organization, such as NATO or the United Nations.

`mil`: A branch of the U.S. military.

`net`: A network organization.

`org`: A nonprofit organization.

**WARNING**  Unfortunately, the word *domain* is used in several ways, depending on the context. In talking about the Internet, a domain refers to a collection of network host computers. See Chapter 4, "TCP/IP Utilities," for a discussion of how Microsoft Windows Server products define a domain.

Your local ISP is probably a member of the `.net` domain, and your company is probably part of the `.com` domain. The `.gov` and `.mil` domains are reserved strictly for use by the government and the military within the United States. In other parts of the world, the final part of a domain name represents the country in which the server is located (`.ca` for Canada, `.jp` for Japan, `.uk` for Great Britain, and `.ru` for Russia, for example). Well over 130 countries are represented on the Internet. The `.com` domain is by far the largest, followed by the `.edu` domain.

If you want to contact someone within one of these domains by e-mail, you just add that person's e-mail name to their domain name, separated by an at (@) sign. Generically, it looks like this:

`name@company.com`

To increase the number of domain names available for use—after all, there is only one `mcdonalds.com` domain name available—several alternative top-level domains have been suggested. These include `.firm` for businesses and companies, `.store` for businesses selling goods rather than services, `.arts` for cultural and entertainment organizations, and `.info` for informational services. The domains `.cc`, `.biz`, `.travel`, and `.post` are also in use on the Internet.

ICANN assigns all Internet domain names and makes sure that a name is not duplicated. Names are assigned on a first come, first served basis, but if you try to register a name that infringes on someone else's registered trademark, your use of that name will be rescinded if the trademark holder objects.

## Using HOSTS

Several automatic conversion systems are available to translate an IP address into a host name, and HOSTS is one of the simplest. You create a file called HOSTS, located in a particular folder or directory based on the requirements of the operating system, and enter a line in the file for every system. Here's an example:

```
198.34.56.25 myserver.com #My server's information
198.34.57.03 yourserver.com
```

Now comes the nasty part. You must store this ASCII file on *every single workstation on your network*; when you make a change, you must change the contents of the HOSTS file on *every single workstation on your network*. This is a simple but painful process inside a network. But what happens if you want to go outside of this network to other networks or to the Internet? The file size would be simply enormous. Fortunately, there are better solutions, as you will see in the next two sections.

 Any information entered to the right of a pound sign in a HOSTS file is ignored, so you can use this space for comments.

## Using DNS

The abbreviation DNS stands for *Domain Name Service*. You use DNS to translate host names and domain names to IP addresses, and vice versa, by means of a standardized lookup table that the network administrator defines and configures. The system works just like a giant telephone directory.

Suppose you are using your browser to surf the Web and you enter the URL `http://www.microsoft.com` to go to the Microsoft home page. Your web browser then asks the TCP/IP protocol to ask the DNS server for the IP address of `www.microsoft.com`. When your web browser receives this address, it connects to the Microsoft web server and downloads the home page. DNS is an essential part of any TCP/IP network because it simplifies the task of remembering addresses; all you have to do is simply remember the host name and domain name.

A DNS zone is an administrative area or name space within a DNS domain. For example, `sybex.com` is a DNS domain, but there is a server that is authoritative over the `sybex.com` name space, or zone. An additional level could be added to `sybex.com`, making, for instance, `networkbooks.sybex.com`. The networkbooks zone would be handled by a particular server. The server holds the zone file, or DNS table, for that zone. DNS tables are composed of records. Most records are composed of a host name, a record type, and an IP address. There are several record types, including the address record, the mail exchange record, the CNAME record, and the SOA record.

There are *primary DNS servers,* which are authoritative for the zone for which they carry the zone file, and *secondary DNS servers,* which have a nonauthoritative copy of the zone file updated from the primary server. The DNS zone file must be changed only on the primary server that is authoritative for that zone. If changes are made to the secondary server, the changes will not be propagated elsewhere, and these changes will be lost during the next update from the primary server. What this means is that whenever a change to any record is required, even one as simple as adding the IP address of a new server or changing the IP address of an established one, the change must be performed by the administrator, ISP, or other entity that hosts and has write access to the primary DNS server that is authoritative for the domain/zone in which the change occurs.

The *address record,* commonly known as the A record, maps a host name to an IP address. The following example shows the address record for a host called `mail` in the `company.com` domain:

```
mail.company.com.      IN     A      204.176.47.9
```

The *mail exchange (MX) record* points to the mail exchanger for a particular host. DNS is structured so that you can actually specify several mail exchangers for one host. This feature provides a higher probability that e-mail will actually arrive at its intended destination. The mail exchangers are listed in order in the record, with a priority code that indicates the order in which the mail exchangers should be accessed by other mail delivery systems.

If the first priority doesn't respond in a given amount of time, the mail delivery system tries the second one, and so on. Here are some sample mail exchange records:

```
hostname.company.com.  IN     MX     10 mail.company.com.
hostname.company.com.  IN     MX     20 mail2.company.com.
hostname.company.com.  IN     MX     30 mail3.company.com.
```

In this example, if the first mail exchanger, `mail.company.com`, does not respond, the second one, `mail2.company.com`, is tried, and so on.

The *CNAME record,* or canonical name record, is also commonly known as the *alias record* and allows hosts to have more than one name. For example, your web server has the host name `www`, and you want that machine to also have the name `ftp` so that users can use FTP to access a different portion of the file system as an FTP root. You can accomplish this with a CNAME record. Given that you already have an address record established for the host name `www`, a CNAME record that adds `ftp` as a host name would look something like this:

```
www.company.com.       IN     A      204.176.47.2
ftp.company.com.       IN     CNAME  www.company.com.
```

When you put all these record types together in a zone file, or DNS table, it might look like this:

```
mail.company.com.       IN    A      204.176.47.9
mail2.company.com.      IN    A      204.176.47.21
mail3.company.com.      IN    A      204.176.47.89
yourhost.company.com.   IN    MX     10 mail.company.com.
yourhost.company.com.   IN    MX     20 mail2.company.com.
yourhost.company.com.   IN    MX     30 mail3.company.com.
www.company.com.        IN    A      204.176.47.2
ftp.company.com.        IN    CNAME  www.company.com.
```

The *SOA record,* or start of authority record, contains global parameters for the zone and is easily the most crucial record in the zone file. There can be only one SOA per zone file. The SOA record might look something like this:

```
company.com.    IN    SOA    ns.company.com. dns\.support.company.com. (
                              55281      ; serial number
                              7200       ; refresh = 2h
                              3600       ; update retry = 1h
                              604800     ; expire = 7d
                              1800       ; minimum TTL = 30m
                              )
```

Table 3.6 explains the fields in the preceding SOA record output.

**TABLE 3.6** Fields of the DNS SOA Record

| Field name | Sample value | Description |
| --- | --- | --- |
| Zone name | company.com. | The root name of the zone. May be substituted by @, if the $ORIGIN directive is specified with this value elsewhere in the zone file. Note the final dot. |
| Class | IN | The class of record. IN means Internet. There are no contemporary alternatives for IN worthy of discussion. |
| Resource record type | SOA | Indicates this record is the zone file's one and only SOA record. |
| Name server | ns.company.com. | The primary DNS server for this zone. May be shortened to ns, as long as company.com. is specified by $ORIGIN. If the server is external to the zone, then it must appear as an FQDN with a final dot. A matching NS record should appear elsewhere in the zone file to support this entry. |

**TABLE 3.6** Fields of the DNS SOA Record *(continued)*

| Field name | Sample value | Description |
| --- | --- | --- |
| E-mail address | dns\.support.company.com. | The e-mail address of the administrator or other party responsible for the zone. There is an assumed @ in the place of the first dot. If any dots precede the @ in the actual e-mail address, then a backslash (\) must precede each of these additional dots. The address represented here is dns.support@company.com. This entry may be shortened in the same way as noted for the name server. |
| Serial number | 55281 | This is a manually updated numeric value that *should* be incremented by the editor every time the zone file is changed. Because it is a 32-bit number, you could easily use a system of yyyymmddxx for the year, month, and day the change was made, with a two-digit serial number in case of multiple edits in a single day. |
| Refresh | 7200 | The number of seconds a secondary server uses as an interval between checking with the primary server to see if the zone file has changed. A zone transfer, which may or may not be solicited, resets this timer. Decreasing this timer when making a change to the zone file will cause the secondary servers to be updated with the new information more quickly. |
| Retry | 3600 | The number of seconds between a failed attempt and a subsequent attempt by a primary server to update a secondary slave server. |
| Expire | 604800 | The number of seconds a secondary server waits after receiving an update from the primary server before declaring the zone data nonauthoritative. This value should be as long as you need for the secondary server to remain functional in the event of a primary-server outage. |
| Minimum TTL | 1800 | The number of seconds for which the records in the zone that do not have their own default TTL are valid and should be cached. |

You can establish other types of records for specific purposes, but we won't go into those in this book. DNS can become very complex very quickly, and entire books are dedicated to the DNS system.

The `nslookup` and `dig` commands are discussed further in Chapter 4, but a quick peek at a special function of the utility will help tie together the preceding material. The following output was generated by the nslookup utility. Notice the similarity to the actual SOA record shown earlier. Once nslookup is started, entering the command `set type=SOA`, followed by entering the domain for which you want to view the SOA information for that zone, will produce output similar to this:

```
C:\>nslookup
Default Server:  ns.company.com
Address:  10.184.147.254

> set type=SOA
> company.com
Server:  ns.company.com
Address:  10.184.147.254

Non-authoritative answer:
company.com
        primary name server = ns.company.com
        responsible mail addr = dns\.support.company.com
        serial  = 55281
        refresh = 7200 (2 hours)
        retry   = 3600 (1 hour)
        expire  = 604800 (7 days)
        default TTL = 1800 (30 mins)
[output omitted]
>
```

## Using WINS

*WINS,* or *Windows Internet Naming Service,* is an essential part of the Microsoft networking topology as long as NetBIOS is still in use. But before we get into the discussion of WINS, we must define a few terms, including these two protocols—NetBIOS and NetBEUI.

**NetBIOS**    NetBIOS (pronounced "net-bye-ose") is an acronym formed from *network basic input/output system,* a Session layer network protocol originally developed by IBM and Sytek to manage data exchange and network access. NetBIOS provides an application programming interface (API) with a consistent set of commands for requesting lower-level network services to transmit information from node to node, thus separating the applications from the underlying network operating system. Many vendors once provided either their own version of NetBIOS or an emulation of its communications services in their products.

**NetBEUI**     NetBEUI (pronounced "net-boo-ee") is an acronym formed from *NetBIOS Extended User Interface,* an implementation and extension of IBM's NetBIOS transport protocol from Microsoft. NetBEUI communicates with the network through Microsoft's Network Driver Interface Specification (NDIS). NetBEUI was once shipped with all versions of Microsoft's operating systems and is generally considered to have a lot of overhead. It also has no structure to its addressing format, which does not allow determination of a network and therefore means it has no routing capability, making it suitable only for small networks; you cannot build internetworks with NetBEUI, and so it is often replaced with TCP/IP. Microsoft added extensions to NetBEUI in Windows NT to remove the limitation of 254 sessions per node. This extended version of Net-BEUI is called the NetBIOS Frame (NBF).

WINS is used in conjunction with TCP/IP and maps NetBIOS names to IP addresses. For example, you have a print server on your LAN that you have come to know as PrintServer1. In the past, to print to that server you needed only to remember its name and to select that name from a list. However, TCP/IP is a completely different protocol and doesn't understand Net-BIOS names; it therefore has no way of knowing the location of those servers. That's where WINS comes in.

Each time you access a network resource on a Windows network using TCP/IP, your system needs to know the host name or IP address. If there are no routers in your network, NetBIOS-speaking devices can simply broadcast their presence on the network and broadcast a request for the unknown MAC address of a known NetBIOS name, all without a WINS server. Once routers are introduced, however, the broadcasts that NetBIOS uses for resolution do not make it through the routers, so connectivity is lost to devices not on the same subnet as the requesting device. If WINS is installed in a routed environment, you can continue using the NetBIOS names that you have previously used to access the resources because WINS provides the cross-reference from NetBIOS name to IP address for you. Once the IP address is known, ARP can be used to obtain the MAC address after the packet has been routed to the proper IP subnet.

 A NetBIOS name doesn't always refer to just a machine. Several services on a machine can also have their own NetBIOS names.

When you install and configure TCP/IP, as described later in this chapter, you'll see a place to specify the WINS server addresses. These addresses are stored with the configuration, and TCP/IP uses them to query for host names and addresses when necessary. WINS is similar to DNS in that it cross-references host names to addresses; however, as mentioned earlier, WINS resolves NetBIOS names to IP addresses, but DNS resolves TCP/IP FQDNs to IP addresses.

Another major difference between WINS and DNS is that WINS builds its own reference tables dynamically but you have to configure DNS manually. Dynamic DNS (DDNS) does exist, but it is not yet implemented on the Internet. When a workstation running TCP/IP is booted and attached to the network, it uses the WINS address settings in the TCP/IP configuration to communicate with the WINS server. The workstation gives the WINS server various pieces of information about itself, such as the NetBIOS host name, the actual username logged on to the workstation, and the workstation's IP address. WINS stores this information for use on the network and periodically refreshes it to maintain accuracy.

Microsoft, however, has developed a new DNS record—called DNS Server—that allows the DNS server to work in perfect harmony with a WINS server. The Microsoft DNS Server software was shipped with Windows NT and later server systems. Here's how it works: The host name portion of the DNS FQDN can be looked up on the WINS server for hosts in the local domain. Thus, you need not build complex DNS tables to establish and configure name resolution on your server; Microsoft DNS relies entirely on WINS to tell it the addresses it needs to resolve. And because WINS builds its tables automatically, you don't have to edit the DNS tables when addresses change; WINS takes care of this for you. This feature also is not available on the Internet.

You can use both WINS and DNS on your network, or you can use one without the other. Your choice is determined by whether your network is connected to the Internet and whether your host addresses are dynamically assigned. When you are connected to the Internet, you must use DNS to resolve host names and addresses because TCP/IP depends on DNS service for address resolution. Addresses of both DNS and WINS servers can be supplied to a host with its Dynamic Host Configuration Protocol (DHCP) lease.

## Using DHCP

The primary reason for using DHCP is to centralize the management of IP addresses. When the DHCP service is used, DHCP scopes include pools of IP addresses that are assigned for automatic distribution to client computers on an as-needed basis, in the form of *leases,* which are periods of time for which the DHCP client may keep the configuration assignment. Clients attempt to renew their lease at 50 percent of the lease duration. The address pools are centralized on the DHCP server, allowing all IP addresses on your network to be administered from a single server. It should be apparent that this saves loads of time when changing the IP addresses on your network. Instead of running around to every workstation and server and resetting the IP address to a new address, you simply reset the IP address pool on the DHCP server. The next time the client machines are rebooted, they are assigned new addresses.

If the client workstation cannot locate the DHCP server on the network automatically, either you will see an error message to that effect when you restart the client workstation or Automatic Private IP Addressing (APIPA) running on the machine will assign itself an IP address in the 169.254.0.0/16 address range.

More capable than RARP, DHCP is an update to the Bootstrap Protocol (BootP) and can manage much more than the IP addresses of client computers. It can also assign DNS servers, WINS servers, default gateway addresses, subnet masks, and many other options.

# Configuring TCP/IP on Windows Workstations

Being able to configure your operating system to use TCP/IP is a must for any network administrator. Because Microsoft Windows is the dominant operating system, we will show you how to configure a Windows client to use TCP/IP. The information in this section assumes that you already have Windows 2000 running on the client.

Because you are likely using Plug and Play network interface cards, Microsoft Windows 2000 automatically installs TCP/IP on your machine. In this case, you can skip ahead to the discussion in Chapter 4 on how to use the TCP/IP utilities to confirm that your system is up and running properly.

If, however, you want to look at or change some of the configuration settings or if TCP/IP doesn't seem to be installed on your system for whatever reason, stay with this chapter.

There is very little difference between configuring TCP/IP on a Windows 2000 device regardless of the exact version or function, such as Server or Professional. The dialog boxes you use are virtually identical. Windows 2000 Professional is used in the discussion that follows. Windows XP and 2003 are slightly different in appearance, but still very similar.

To begin configuring TCP/IP, follow these steps:

1. Choose Start ➤ Settings ➤ Control Panel ➤ Network and Dial-Up Connections to open the Network and Dial-Up Connections dialog box, which lists all of the currently installed network components.

You can also right-click the My Network Places icon on the Windows Desktop and select Properties from the pop-up menu to open the Network and Dial-Up Connections dialog box.

2. Right-click one of your network adapters and select Properties to open the Properties dialog box for your adapter.

**3.** If you do not see Internet Protocol (TCP/IP) in the scrolling list (assuming you have enough entries to scroll), follow the next three steps. If you do see it, skip to step 7.

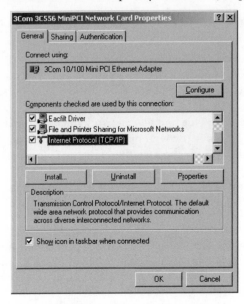

**4.** Click the Install button, which brings up the Select Network Component Type window.

**5.** Click Protocol in the list and click the Add button to bring up the Select Network Protocol dialog box.

**6.** Select Microsoft from the left frame and Internet Protocol (TCP/IP) from the right frame and click the OK button. This will take you back to the Properties dialog box for your adapter. Now Internet Protocol (TCP/IP) should appear in the scrolling list.

**7.** Click Internet Protocol (TCP/IP) and click the Properties button, which brings up the Internet Protocol (TCP/IP) Properties window.

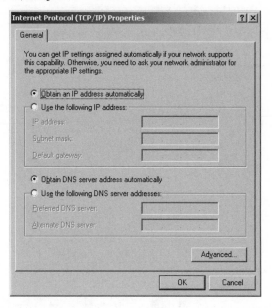

**8.** Initially, you see the General tab, which is set to obtain your IP address, subnet mask, default gateway, and DNS server(s) via DHCP. You may select the alternate radio buttons to manually enter this information.

**9.** Click the Advanced button, which brings up the Advanced TCP/IP Settings dialog box.

**10.** Notice the IP Settings, DNS, WINS, and Options tabs along the top of the Advanced TCP/IP Settings dialog box (shown in Figure 3.7 in the next section).

In the following sections, we will look at these four tabs. In addition, we will cover key information regarding the configuration database of Windows, known as the Registry, and the open set of protocols, known as ZeroConf, designed to reduce the amount of manual TCP/IP configuration necessary to bring up a small network.

## The IP Settings Tab

You use the IP Settings tab, shown in Figure 3.7, to specify, edit, or remove additional IP addresses for this device when you are not using DHCP. This can be helpful when the device is acting as more than one type of server. Using an IP address for each type of server aids in clarity during configuration and troubleshooting. Additionally, you can make the same kinds of adjustments to the statically configured default gateway(s). The interface metric can be used to cause the device to favor one interface over another for otherwise equivalent routes. This is most helpful when the device is acting as a router with multiple NIC cards and possibly a dynamic routing protocol (such as RIP or OSPF) running.

**FIGURE 3.7** The IP Settings tab of the Advanced TCP/IP Settings dialog box

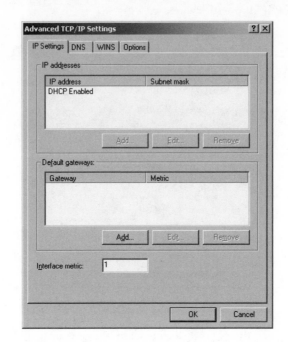

## The DNS Tab

You use the DNS tab, shown in Figure 3.8, to add, edit, or remove DNS server addresses and adjust the order in which they will be queried. You also have quite a bit of granularity with how you can control the use of DNS suffixes, which refer to the part of FQDNs that should be used when you're trying to resolve a name to an IP address and the entered name alone does not produce a match. Dynamic DNS settings are adjusted in this tab as well.

You know from earlier in this chapter that an FQDN consists of the name of the host followed by the domain name. For example, if the name of the local computer is `wallaby` and the domain is `sybex.com`, the FQDN is `wallaby.sybex.com`.

## The WINS Tab

By adding the IP addresses of WINS servers in the WINS tab, shown in Figure 3.9, you specify that those servers be used in order to resolve a NetBIOS name to an IP address. The order can be adjusted after address entry.

**FIGURE  3.8**   The DNS tab of the Advanced TCP/IP Settings dialog box

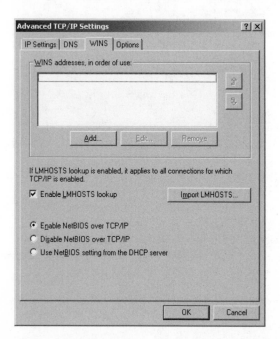

**FIGURE  3.9**   The WINS tab of the Advanced TCP/IP Settings dialog box

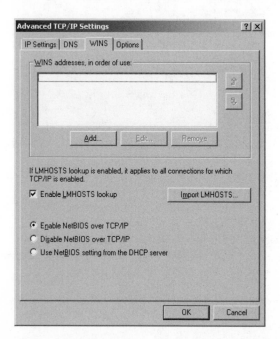

On this tab, you can enable the use of the local LMHOSTS file in the %SystemRoot%\system32\ drivers\etc folder of the Windows 2000 family of operating systems. You can also make choices concerning the use of NetBIOS over TCP/IP.

For the value of variables, such as %SystemRoot%, execute the set command from a command prompt on your Microsoft Windows machine.

## The Options Tab

The Options tab allows you to adjust IP security and TCP/IP filtering settings (see Figure 3.10).

**FIGURE 3.10** The Options tab of the Advanced TCP/IP Settings dialog box

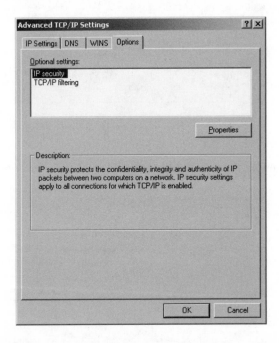

Highlighting the IP Security option and clicking the Properties button leads to the ability to turn off IPSec functionality or set it to one of three modes of varying aggressiveness, beginning with simply responding to requests for IP security, then progressing to requesting IP security, and finally to requiring it.

The TCP/IP filtering option allows you to exercise quite a bit of control over which protocols are allowed to communicate with the computer. Filtering may be performed on any combination of TCP and UDP port numbers and IP protocol number.

## The Windows Registry

All of this TCP/IP configuration information is stored in the Windows Registry database, along with lots of other hardware and software configuration information. You can change most of the TCP/IP parameters by using the Network applet in Control Panel as you have just seen. Certain parameters, however, such as Time to Live and the default Type of Service, can be changed only by using the Registry Editor (regedit.exe or regedit32, depending on your preference). If you change some of these Registry parameters without detailed knowledge of TCP/IP configuration, you may affect the performance of TCP/IP on your system in an adverse and unexpected way.

If you are configuring TCP/IP on a Windows NT or 2000 device and you want to know more, check out the Microsoft Knowledge Base article 120642 on the Microsoft website at www.microsoft.com. This article covers all the standard, optional, and nonconfigurable TCP/IP parameters and describes which parameters are updated by using the Network applet in Control Panel and which are changed using the Registry Editor. If you want to see the equivalent article for Windows XP, check out article 314053.

In the next chapter, you'll get a look at some of the utilities in the TCP/IP toolkit that you can use to view and troubleshoot your TCP/IP network. All of these tools are based on the original UNIX tools, but these days they are available in one form or another for all operating systems, including all versions of UNIX, Novell NetWare, and Microsoft Windows.

## Zero Configuration (ZeroConf)

As anyone who's ever tried to hook their laptop to someone else's to use TCP/IP to play video games, transfer files, or whatever, will tell you…it's a pain. Even though computer manufacturer's and software programmers will tell you that networking is supposed to be simple, it really isn't. You need to configure several parameters (IP address, DNS or host name, etc.) properly or you won't be able to communicate. These parameters are usually no problem for network technicians, but what about the average person? Configuring peer-to-peer or small network networking usually involves a game of "What should my IP address be?" between the people that want to network.

Enter the Internet Engineering Task Force (IETF) and the Zero Configuration (ZeroConf) initiative. The primary goal was to make networking via TCP/IP extremely easy and "hands off" for small networks. Ideally, two computers could be connected through Ethernet jacks with only a crossover cable and be able to communicate without any further configuration. In order to accomplish this, the ZeroConf working group of the IETF had four main areas of focus:

1. Automatic Interface address configuration

2. Automatic Multicast address configuration

3. Translation of addresses to names and names to addresses

4. Service location

In order for the ZeroConf initiative to be successful, each of these components must be implemented in the ZeroConf protocol.

> Apple Computer has been a large participant in the design of the ZeroConf protocol. It has its own protocol, called Rendezvous, which itself is an open ZeroConf protocol that has been submitted to the IETF for approval.

## Automatic Local Interface Configuration

As you may already know, a computer must have a local IP address in order to communicate. Instead of relying on static addressing (too much work and too much to know) or dynamic addressing (other hardware required), ZeroConf allows for automatic configuration by the two communicating entities themselves. In the absence of a manually configured address or a DHCP server, the communicating entities will "figure out" their own local IP addresses (known as *link-local addresses*) as follows: First, for each interface, each computer chooses a random TCP/IP address somewhere in the address space 169.254.1.0 to 169.254.254.255 (that is 169.254.0.0/16 with the top and bottom 256 addresses reserved for future use). Then, the computer configures its local interface with this address.

Of course, it wouldn't do any good if both computers chose the same address. So, two things happen to prevent that. First of all, the random number used to select the IP address is based on several computer-specific items (including the MAC address, real time clock, etc.) so that each computer is guaranteed a unique address. In addition, after the unique address is selected, it must be tested to ensure that no other device is using the same link-local address. To do this, the computer uses ARP to tell the other computers on the network segment connected to the interface being configured what IP address it intends to use. If no devices respond that they are already using that address, the interface is configured with the chosen address and communication can take place.

> Windows has had this capability since Windows 98. Microsoft calls it Automatic Private IP Addressing, or APIPA. The basics of this capability have been incorporated into the ZeroConf proposed standard.

## Multicast Address Selection

Another requirement of the ZeroConf initiative is that there is a mechanism for automatically choosing multicast addresses for the network. The IETF has defined the standard for the *ZeroConf Multicast Address Allocation Protocol (ZMAAP)*. This protocol is used to allocate multicast addresses among the various peers in small, peer-to-peer networks.

This protocol is the polar opposite of the multicast address assignment protocol known as *MADCAP*, which stands for *Multicast Address Dynamic Client Allocation Protocol*. Where MADCAP is a client-server multicast address allocation scheme, ZMAAP is a peer-to-peer allocation scheme. Essentially, each node on a ZeroConf network is running its own little multicast allocation service (called a *mini-MAAS* in ZeroConf parlance). Any entity that needs a multicast address will make a request to its local mini-MAAS, which will then select an address and, before permanently allocating it, inform the other local mini-MAASs of its choice. If there are any objections, the originating mini-MAAS will rechoose the address. Otherwise, it will go ahead and allocate the address.

## Name Resolution

You might think that there isn't a way around name resolution, apart from constantly exchanging HOSTS files or some other silliness. In actuality, ZeroConf relies on standard TCP/IP protocols, including one known as Multicast DNS. Traditional DNS relies on centralized servers to answer DNS queries. But the addresses of these servers must be configured (and the goal is zero configuration), so the designers of ZeroConf decided to use Multicast DNS. Multicast DNS was a little-used protocol until ZeroConf came along.

Traditional name resolution works much like asking the host at a party to introduce you to the people in the party you don't know. Let's say you wanted to know which person in the room was named John. With the traditional DNS model, you would ask the party host (the "DNS server" in our scenario). If you were to use Multicast DNS in the same scenario, you would simply shout in the room, "Hey, is there a John in here?"

Multicast DNS essentially puts out a multicast transmission that asks for the address of the network name being requested. This works great in small networks, but the amount of traffic required and the introduced delays make Multicast DNS impractical for larger networks, such as the Internet.

## Service Location

The final aspect of ZeroConf is service location. It is important on networks to be able to locate services. AppleTalk is the master of finding services on a network without configuration. Apple designed it so that whenever you plugged a printer into an AppleTalk network, it would advertise itself on the network and you could just choose it. This traditionally has been difficult on TCP/IP networks. Furthermore, the chatty nature of such services would not be welcome on large networks.

The IETF has designed a protocol specifically for locating services on a ZeroConf network. That protocol is known as *DNS Service Discovery,* or *DNS-SD*. DNS-SD allows clients to use regular DNS queries, without the need for a new DNS message structure, to find a list of names of particular types of services provided within a particular domain.

# Virtual LANs (VLANs)

With the introduction of Ethernet switches, and their subsequent replacement of Ethernet hubs in corporate LAN environments, came the power to manage traffic flow much more efficiently and in many different ways. One of those ways was to allow users on different switch ports to participate in their own network separate from, but still connected to, the other stations on the same or connected switch. This "network-within-a-network" concept became known as *Virtual LAN (VLAN)* technology.

Let's say, for example, that you have a 24-port Ethernet switch. If you have a group of users that constantly use a particular server and produce very large amounts of broadcast traffic, you might want to separate them into their own segment. But, with VLAN-capable switches, you are able to modify the segmentation within the switch itself regardless of geographical proximity of the VLAN members, thus saving you the expense of additional network hardware or recabling. To do this, you would use the switch management software to assign the ports on which those users and their server were working to their own VLAN. The VLAN for this group could be VLAN #2, for example, and the VLAN everyone else is assigned to could be the default management VLAN #1. Users would still be able to communicate with each other and their respective servers (assuming a router was installed), but broadcast traffic would be isolated.

With large, enterprise-capable switches, this benefit is realized even more so. With hundreds of ports, you can segment the network any way you'd like, even on-the-fly and into many different segments.

Let's say, for example, a company's network is divided into VLANs based on the departmental affiliation of the users. Bob transfers from the finance department to the accounting department but keeps his same office. Susan moves from one building to another but remains in the marketing department. The administrator needs simply to configure Bob's switch port to be in the Accounting VLAN and Bob immediately enters the Accounting broadcast domain. Of course, Bob's computer must be reconfigured for the subnet related to the Accounting VLAN, which can be done centrally by rescinding his DHCP lease. Once his system requests a new DHCP lease, the DHCP server with the scope for his new subnet will offer him the proper IP information. The administrator can then configure the new port on the new switch that Susan is now plugged into for the marketing department, and regardless of her physical move, Susan never notices that she is connected to different switch hardware and her IP configuration can remain the same.

In practice, each VLAN corresponds to a different IP subnet, which is why a router is required to change the VLAN affiliation of a frame. The underlying packet has to be routed to the destination subnet, even if the intended recipient happens to be connected to the switch port right beside the port leading from the source device.

# Summary

In this chapter, you learned the basics of the Transmission Control Protocol/Internet Protocol (TCP/IP) suite. First of all, you learned how TCP/IP works and about the various parts that make up TCP/IP. Then you learned about the Transport Control Protocol, the first part of TCP/IP, and how it is used to transport data within TCP/IP. Following that, you learned how the Network layer protocol IP is used.

In addition to these two protocols, you learned of the various application protocols (like SMTP, FTP, and HTTP) and how they work. Relating very closely to that was the idea of ports and sockets for each protocol and how each port is mapped to a specific protocol or is specified for each.

One concept that gives many people trouble is the concept of TCP/IP addressing, which was covered in this chapter for both IPv4 and IPv6. Also, those addresses must be resolved into "friendly" names, a detail which was covered in the section "Name Resolution Methods."

Also in this chapter, you learned how to configure TCP/IP on a Windows-based workstation. Finally, you learned about Virtual LAN (VLAN) technologies and how they work within a network.

# Exam Essentials

**Be able to recognize the different protocols within TCP/IP and be able to define their purpose and function.**    The TCP/IP stack is made up of several protocols, which perform such functions as protocol transport, file access, file transfer, and mail transfer. These protocols include TCP, SMTP, IP, NNTP, HTTP, and FTP.

**Be able to differentiate between the Internet, an internet, an intranet, and an extranet.** When *Internet* is capitalized, it refers to the worldwide TCP/IP internetwork that we all know and love or hate, whereas *internet* is a more generic term referring to a network in which routers or other layer 3 devices are present. An intranet is an internetwork with well-defined administrative boundaries, while an extranet expands the intranet to include trusted outside networks.

**Be able to define the function of common TCP and UDP ports.**    You should know how to coordinate protocol name and function with port number. (Refer to Table 3.1 for specific examples.)

**Know how to identify IP addresses (IPv4, IPv6) and their default subnet masks.**    IPv4 = *xxx.xxx.xxx.xxx*, where *xxx* is a number from 0 to 255. The default subnet mask is 255.0.0.0 for a Class A address (IP range is 0.*x.x.x* to 127.*x.x.x*), 255.255.0.0 for a Class B (IP range is 128.*x.x.x* to 191.*x.x.x*), and 255.255.255.0 for a Class C (192.*x.x.x* to 223.*x.x.x*).

IPv6 = *xxxx:xxxx:xxxx:xxxx:xxxx:xxxx:xxxx:xxxx*, where *x* is a hexadecimal digit. IPv6 has no address classes and thus no default subnet mask.

**Know how to identify the purpose of subnetting and of default gateways.**    The purpose of subnetting is to divide a network into two or more segments, gaining more addressable segments from a single address space and reducing congestion. Default gateways are configured so that a host has an address to send an encapsulated packet to when it doesn't know a specific route to the destination address.

**Know how to identify the difference between public and private networks.**    Public networks are networks that are open to the general public and, as such, use valid IP addresses that can be "seen" by the general public. The Internet is an example of a public network. Private networks, on the other hand, use addresses that cannot be seen by the general public and are not available for public use or allowed onto the Internet in any way. Your company's LAN is an example of a private network. These addresses must be translated to public addresses in order to allow the internal devices to communicate on the Internet.

**Identify the purpose, benefits, and characteristics of using a proxy service.**   A proxy server keeps a LAN somewhat separated from the Internet. Doing so increases security and filtering control and has the tendency to speed up Internet access through caching of recently used web pages.

**Be able to describe the main characteristics of VLANs.**   Virtual LANs (VLANs) are a feature of network switches that allow machines on different physical network segments to be organized into a virtual segment, or VLAN.

# Review Questions

1.  Where should Samba be installed to allow a Microsoft operating system access to a UNIX operating system?

    **A.** On the Microsoft client

    **B.** On the Microsoft server

    **C.** On the UNIX client

    **D.** On the UNIX server

2.  Which feature is not available in NetBEUI/NetBIOS?

    **A.** It is self-tuning.

    **B.** It is fast in small networks.

    **C.** It requires little configuration.

    **D.** It is routable.

3.  The Class B address range for the first octet is _____.

    **A.** 1–127

    **B.** 128–191

    **C.** 192–223

    **D.** 224–255

4.  What does a subnet mask allow a TCP/IP device to differentiate?

    **A.** Network ID and host ID

    **B.** Workgroups from each other

    **C.** Host IDs

    **D.** All the above

5.  HTTP usually connects to a web server on port number _____.

    **A.** 21

    **B.** 25

    **C.** 80

    **D.** 443

6.  The port number for POP3 mail is _____.

    **A.** 25

    **B.** 80

    **C.** 100

    **D.** 110

**7.** FTP usually connects to the server on port number _____.

   **A.** 21

   **B.** 25

   **C.** 80

   **D.** 110

**8.** Internet mail is sent between mail servers via which protocol?

   **A.** SNMP

   **B.** SMTP

   **C.** POP

   **D.** Telnet

**9.** What is the default subnet mask for a Class C address?

   **A.** 255.0.0.0

   **B.** 255.255.0.0

   **C.** 255.255.255.0

   **D.** 255.255.255.255

**10.** Network Address Translation, or NAT, is found in _____.

   **A.** Hubs

   **B.** Transceivers

   **C.** NIC protocol drivers

   **D.** Routers

**11.** Joe's computer has been configured with an IP address in which the host bits are all binary 1s. Joe can't seem to communicate on the network at all. What is the most likely problem?

   **A.** Joe's computer is configured with an IP address that conflicts with another device.

   **B.** Joe's computer is configured with the broadcast address for his subnet.

   **C.** Joe's computer needs to be configured with the IP address of a DNS server.

   **D.** Joe's computer needs to be configured with the address of the default gateway.

**12.** Which protocol is considered connection-oriented?

   **A.** DDP

   **B.** TCP

   **C.** NetBEUI

   **D.** UDP

**13.** What type of network includes limited outside access to internal corporate resources?

   **A.** The Internet

   **B.** An internet

   **C.** An intranet

   **D.** An extranet

**14.** SMTP normally operates through port number _____.

   **A.** 21

   **B.** 25

   **C.** 80

   **D.** 110

**15.** FQDN is an acronym for _____.

   **A.** Fully Qualified Division Name

   **B.** Fully Qualified DNS Name

   **C.** Fully Qualified Dynamic Name

   **D.** Fully Qualified Domain Name

**16.** What is the result of increasing the refresh value in the SOA record of a zone file on a primary DNS server?

   **A.** The secondary DNS servers will be updated with changes to the zone file more quickly and more often.

   **B.** The minimum time to live for resource records without a TTL setting will be increased.

   **C.** The time after a secondary DNS server receives a zone transfer when it considers the zone information to be invalid increases.

   **D.** The secondary DNS servers will be updated with changes to the zone file less quickly and less often.

**17.** Which of the following changes would require an administrator to contact the service provider that hosts the primary DNS server for the administrator's DNS domain? (Choose all that apply.)

   **A.** The company changed IP addressing schemes, and the web server's address changed as a result.

   **B.** The company added 15 new client PCs to the network.

   **C.** The company added a new mail server.

   **D.** The company upgraded from Category 3 cabling to Category 5e.

**18.** FTP is the abbreviation for _____.

   **A.** Formal Transfer Protocol

   **B.** Full Transfer Protocol

   **C.** Final Transfer Protocol

   **D.** File Transfer Protocol

**19.** Which of the following is not a feature of a proxy server?

  **A.** It can reduce Internet traffic requests.

  **B.** It can assist with security.

  **C.** It can reduce user wait time for a request.

  **D.** It can convert a nonroutable protocol to a routable protocol.

**20.** What is the primary purpose of a VLAN?

  **A.** Demonstrating the proper layout for a network

  **B.** Simulating a network

  **C.** Segmenting a network inside a switch or device

# Answers to Review Questions

1. D. Samba is installed on a UNIX server to allow Windows clients to be able to see the UNIX device as a server on the Windows network.

2. D. The NetBEUI/NetBIOS protocol stack does not contain a Network layer routing protocol because it was intended for LAN use only and, as such, cannot be routed.

3. B. The range of the numbers for the first octet in a Class B IP addressing scheme is 128–191. The range of 0–127 is for Class A, 192–223 is for Class C, and 224–255 is reserved for other classes and purposes.

4. A. The purpose of a subnet mask is to separate the network portion and the host portion of an IP address. In the Internet Protocol addressing scheme, it is a group of selected bits whose values serve to identify a subnet. All members of the subnet share the mask value. Once each portion is identified using the mask, members of each subnet can be referenced more easily.

5. C. Port 80 is the TCP port number used to initiate HTTP connections between web client (browser) and web server. Port 23 is used for Telnet, port 25 is used for SMTP, and port 443 is used for less common secure web server access using HTTPS.

6. D. The TCP port number used to initiate connections between POP3 clients and servers is 110. As previously mentioned, port 25 is used for SMTP, and port 80 is used for HTTP connections. Port 100 is not normally used in typical Internet communications.

7. A. FTP clients connect to FTP servers using TCP port 21. As already mentioned, port 25 is used for SMTP, port 80 is used for HTTP, and port 110 is used for POP3 mail communications.

8. B. Internet e-mail servers send mail between themselves using the SMTP protocol. The SNMP protocol is used for the management and monitoring of various network devices. The POP protocol is used to download e-mail from mail servers. Telnet is used for remote terminal emulation.

9. C. 255.255.255.0 is the default subnet mask for a Class C address, 255.0.0.0 is the default for a Class A, 255.255.0.0 is the default for Class B, and 255.255.255.255 is the universal broadcast address.

10. D. Most often, NAT is used in routers and firewalls to translate between two different IP addresses.

11. B. All 1s in the host portion of an IP address represent the broadcast address for the corresponding subnet. All 0s in the host portion represent the identification of the network or subnet itself. Not being configured with the IP address of a DNS server or the default gateway will not completely disable network communications.

12. B. Of those listed, the only one that maintains a virtual "connection" is TCP. UDP and NetBEUI are both connectionless, and DDP is AppleTalk's connectionless Datagram Delivery Protocol.

13. D. An extranet is basically an intranet with limited outside access granted to suppliers and affiliates. The Internet and an internet are far too broad to describe this type of network. Intranets, by definition, do not allow any outside access.

**14.** B. SMTP initiates connections between servers using TCP port number 25.

**15.** D. The correct acronym expansion for FQDN is Fully Qualified Domain Name. The FQDN is the complete name of an Internet host (e.g., www.sybex.com) that is used when referencing a host from outside that host's LAN.

**16.** D. The refresh value in the SOA record of a zone file indicates how many seconds the secondary DNS server will wait before asking the primary server if the zone file has changed. Increasing this value will cause the secondary server to contain invalid information longer, but decreasing the refresh value, as in option A, by too much will generate unnecessary traffic. Option B would occur by increasing the minimum TTL value in the SOA record and will simply cause resource records to expire less frequently, also increasing the likelihood that cached information will be invalid. However, decreasing this value does not necessarily trigger a zone transfer for updated information, as decreasing the refresh value would.

**17.** A, C. Any time the IP address of a server that needs to be accessible from the Internet changes or is added, the entity responsible for maintaining the authoritative zone file for the domain that the server is on must be contacted to make changes to such records as the A record, the MX record, and the SOA record. Changing cabling or adding devices that do not need to be accessed by name from the Internet are not situations that require a change to the DNS zone file.

**18.** D. The proper expansion of FTP is File Transfer Protocol. The abbreviation is more commonly used when referring to file-transferring protocols. There can be several protocols for transferring files between machines and/or networks. For example, FTAM provides file-transfer service for networks that use the OSI reference model, and FTP provides these services for TCP/IP protocols.

**19.** D. Proxy servers act on behalf of clients to provide Internet access and other Internet services. Generally speaking, however, a proxy server does not convert a nonroutable protocol to a routable protocol.

**20.** C. Virtual LANs allow a network to be segmented virtually, inside a network switch, so that several ports are grouped together and function collectively as a network segment, possibly by departmental or other logical groupings.

# Chapter

# 4

# TCP/IP Utilities

**THE FOLLOWING NETWORK+ EXAM OBJEC-
TIVES ARE COVERED IN THIS CHAPTER:**

✓ **4.1 Given a troubleshooting scenario, select the appropriate
network utility from the following:**

- tracert/traceroute
- ping
- arp
- netstat
- nbtstat
- ipconfig/ifconfig
- winipcfg
- nslookup/dig

✓ **4.2 Given output from a network diagnostic utility (for
example, those utilities listed in objective 4.1), identify the
utility and interpret the output.**

With the vast array of people using TCP/IP on their networks, we must have a way to test IP connectivity. Because Microsoft makes the majority of client platforms, the Network+ exam tests the basic concepts of the function and use of the TCP/IP utilities that come with Windows. You can use several utilities to verify TCP/IP function on Windows workstations:

- arp
- netstat
- nbtstat
- ftp
- ping
- ipconfig/winipcfg (ifconfig in UNIX)
- tracert (traceroute in other environments)
- Telnet
- nslookup (dig in UNIX)

# Using the Address Resolution Protocol (ARP)

The Address Resolution Protocol, or ARP, is part of the Transmission Control Protocol/Internet Protocol (TCP/IP) protocol stack; it is used to translate TCP/IP addresses to MAC (media access control) addresses using broadcasts. When a machine running TCP/IP wants to know which machine on an Ethernet network uses a particular IP address, it will send an ARP broadcast that says, in effect, "Hey! Who is IP address *xxx.xxx.xxx.xxx*?" The machine that owns the specific address will respond with its own MAC address. The machine that made the inquiry then adds that information to its own ARP table.

In addition to the normal usage, the ARP designation refers to a utility in Windows that you can use to manipulate and view the local workstation's ARP table.

## The Windows ARP Table

The *ARP table* in Windows is a list of TCP/IP addresses and their associated physical (MAC) addresses. This table is cached in memory so that Windows doesn't have to perform ARP lookups for frequently accessed TCP/IP addresses (for example, servers and default gateways). Each entry contains not only an IP address and a MAC address, but a value for Time to Live (TTL), which indicates how long each entry stays in the ARP table.

The ARP table contains two kinds of entries:

- Dynamic
- Static

*Dynamic ARP table entries* are created whenever the Windows TCP/IP stack performs an ARP lookup and the MAC address is not found in the ARP table. The ARP request is broadcast on the local segment. When the MAC address of the requested IP address is found, that information is added to the ARP table as a dynamic entry.

The ARP table is cleared of dynamic entries whose TTL has expired to ensure that the entries are current.

*Static ARP table entries* serve the same function as dynamic entries, but are made manually using the arp utility, which is discussed next.

## Using The *arp* Utility

ARP is a protocol in the TCP/IP suite. ARP is used by IP to ascertain the MAC address of a device on the same subnet as the requester. When a TCP/IP device needs to forward a packet to a device on the local subnet, it first looks in its own table, called an ARP cache (*cache* because the contents are periodically aged out), for an association between the known IP address of the destination device on the local subnet and the same device's MAC address. If no association that includes the destination IP address can be located, the device sends out an ARP broadcast that includes its own MAC and IP information as well as the IP address of the target device and a blank MAC address field, which is the object of the whole operation. It is this one unknown value that the source device requests be returned in an ARP reply. Windows includes a utility called arp, which allows viewing of the operating system's ARP cache.

To start the arp utility in Windows 2000, follow these steps:

1. Choose Start ➢ Run and enter **cmd** to open the MS-DOS Prompt window. Or, you can choose Start ➢ Programs ➢ Accessories ➢ Command Prompt.
2. At the command prompt, type **arp** and any switches you need, as discussed later in this section.

Entered alone, the arp command lists only the switches you must use in order to use the arp utility correctly.

The arp utility is primarily useful for resolving duplicate IP addresses. For example, your workstation receives its IP address from a Dynamic Host Configuration Protocol (DHCP) server, but it accidentally receives the same address as another workstation. When you try to ping it, you get no response. Your workstation is trying to determine the MAC address, and it can't do so because two machines are reporting that they have the same IP address. To solve this problem, you can use the arp utility to view your local ARP table and see which TCP/IP address is resolved to which MAC address. To display the entire current ARP table, use the arp command with the −a switch, like this:

```
arp −a
```

You'll see something similar to the following:

```
Interface: 204.153.163.3 on Interface 2
Internet Address        Physical Address        Type
204.153.163.2           00−a0−c9−d4−bc−dc        dynamic
204.153.163.4           00−a0−c0−aa−b1−45        dynamic
```

The −g switch will produce the same result.

From this output, you can tell which MAC address is assigned to which IP address. Then, for static assignments, by examining your network documentation (you do have it, don't you?), you can tell which workstation has the IP address and if it is indeed supposed to have it. For DHCP-assigned addresses, you can begin to uncover problems with multiple DHCP scopes or servers giving out identical addresses and other somewhat common configuration issues. Note that, under normal circumstances, you should not see IP addresses in the ARP table for a given interface that are not members of the same IP subnet as the interface, and each other for that matter.

If the machine has more than one network card (as may happen in Windows servers), each interface will be listed separately.

In addition to displaying the ARP table, you can use the arp utility to manipulate the table. To add static entries to the ARP table, use the arp command with the −s switch. These entries stay in the ARP table until the machine is rebooted. A static entry hard-wires a specific IP address to a specific MAC address so that when a packet needs to be sent to that IP address, it is sent automatically to that MAC address. Here's the syntax:

```
arp −s [IP Address] [MAC Address]
```

Simply replace the [IP Address] and [MAC Address] sections with the appropriate entries, like so:

```
arp −s 204.153.163.5 00−a0−c0−ab−c3−11
```

You can now take a look at your new ARP table by using the `arp -a` command. You should see something like this:

```
Interface: 204.153.163.3 on Interface 2
Internet Address        Physical Address        Type
204.153.163.2           00-a0-c9-d4-bc-dc       dynamic
204.153.163.4           00-a0-c0-aa-b1-45       dynamic
204.153.163.5           00-a0-c0-ab-c3-11       static
```

Finally, if you want to delete entries from the ARP table, you can either wait until the dynamic entries time out, or you can use the –d switch with the IP address of the static entry you'd like to delete, like so:

```
arp -d 204.153.163.5
```

This deletes the entry from the ARP table in memory.

> The arp utility doesn't confirm successful additions or deletions (use arp -a or arp -g for that), but it will give you an error message if you use incorrect syntax.

# Using the *netstat* Utility

Using `netstat` is a great way to see the TCP/IP connections (both inbound and outbound) on your machine. You can also use it to view packet statistics (similar to the `MONITOR.NLM` utility on a NetWare server console), such as how many packets have been sent and received, the number of errors, and so on.

When used without any options, `netstat` produces output similar to that in Figure 4.1, which shows all the outbound TCP/IP connections (in the case of Figure 4.1, a Web connection). The `netstat` utility, used without any options, is particularly useful in determining the status of outbound Web connections.

The Proto column lists the protocol being used. Because this is a Web connection, the protocol is TCP. The Local Address column lists the source address and the source port (source socket). In this case, *default* indicates that the PC has no NetBIOS name configured and refers to the local IP address, which is followed by the source ports, four separate dynamically registered TCP ports used to open four separate TCP connections. The Foreign Address item for all four connections is 204.153.163.2:80, indicating that for all four connections, the address of the destination machine is 204.153.163.2 and that the destination port is TCP port 80 (in other words, HTTP for the Web). The State column indicates the status of each connection. This column shows statistics only for TCP connections because UDP establishes no virtual circuit to the remote device. Usually, this column indicates ESTABLISHED once a TCP connection between your computer and the destination computer is established.

**FIGURE 4.1** Output of the `netstat` command without any switches

```
C:\NETSTAT
Active Connections

Proto     Local Address      Foreign Address      State
TCP       default:1026       204.153.163.2:80     ESTABLISHED
TCP       default:1027       204.153.163.2:80     ESTABLISHED
TCP       default:1028       204.153.163.2:80     ESTABLISHED
TCP       default:1029       204.153.163.2:80     ESTABLISHED
```

If the address of either your computer or the destination computer can be found in the HOSTS file on your computer, the destination computer's name, rather than the IP address, will show up in either the Local Address or Foreign Address column.

The output of the `netstat` utility depends on the switch. You can use the following :

- −a
- −e
- −r
- −s
- −n
- −p

Simply type **netstat** followed by a space and then the switch. Some switches have options, but the syntax is basically the same. Note the UNIX style of the switches, where the hyphen must be included. This is common in Microsoft operating systems for TCP/IP utilities, which stem from original use in UNIX systems.

## The −a Switch

When you use the −a switch, the `netstat` utility displays all TCP/IP connections and all User Datagram Protocol (UDP) connections. Figure 4.2 shows a sample output produced by the `netstat −a` command.

The last two entries in Figure 4.2 show a protocol type of UDP and the source port nicknames of nbname and nbdatagram, which are the well-known port numbers of 137 and 138, respectively. These port numbers are commonly seen on networks that broadcast the NetBIOS name of a workstation on the TCP/IP network. You can tell that this is a broadcast because the destination address is listed as *:* (meaning "any address, any port").

**FIGURE 4.2**   Sample output of the netstat -a command

```
C:\ NETSTAT -a

Active Connections

Proto     Local Address        Foreign Address        State
TCP       default:1026         204.153.163.2:80       ESTABLISHED
TCP       default:1027         204.153.163.2:80       ESTABLISHED
TCP       default:1028         204.153.163.2:80       ESTABLISHED
TCP       default:1029         204.153.163.2:80       ESTABLISHED
UDP       default:nbname       *:*
UDP       default:nbdatagram   *:*
```

The State column has no entry because UDP is not a connection-oriented protocol and, therefore, has no connection state.

The most common use for the -a switch is to check the status of a TCP/IP connection that appears to be hung. You can determine if the connection is simply busy or is actually hung and no longer responding.

## The –*e* Switch

The -e switch displays a summary of all the packets that have been sent over the network interface card (NIC) as of that instant. The two columns in Figure 4.3 show packets coming in as well as being sent.

**FIGURE 4.3**   Sample output of the netstat -e command

```
C:\NETSTAT -e

Interface Statistics

                          Received      Sent

Bytes                     3126759       648563
Unicast packets           4688          4233
Non-unicast packets       226           193
Discards                  0             0
Errors                    0             0
Unknown protocols         487
```

You can use the -e switch to display the following categories of statistics:

**Bytes**   The number of bytes transmitted or received since the computer was turned on. This statistic is useful in helping to determine if data is actually being transmitted and received or if the network interface isn't doing anything.

**Unicast Packets**   The number of packets sent from or received at this computer. To register in one of these columns, the packet must be addressed directly from one computer to another and the computer's address must be in either the source or destination address section of the packet.

**Non-unicast Packets**   The number of packets not directly sent from one workstation to another. For example, a broadcast packet is a non-unicast packet. The number of non-unicast packets should be smaller than the number of unicast packets. If the number of non-unicast packets is as high as or higher than that of unicast packets, too many broadcast packets are being sent on your network. You should find the source of these packets and make any necessary adjustments.

**Discards**   The number of packets that were discarded by the NIC during either transmission or reception because they weren't assembled correctly.

**Errors**   The number of errors that occur during transmission or reception. These numbers may indicate problems with the network card.

**Unknown Protocols**   The number of received packets that the Windows networking stack couldn't interpret. This statistic shows up only in the Received column because, if the computer sent them, they wouldn't be unknown, would they?

Unfortunately, statistics don't mean much unless they can be colored with time information. For example, if the Errors column shows 100 errors, is that a problem? It might be if the computer has been on for only a few minutes. But 100 errors could be par for the course if the computer has been operating for several days. Unfortunately, the `netstat` utility doesn't have a way of indicating how much time has elapsed for these statistics.

---

 **Real World Scenario**

**Outsmarting *netstat***

On occasion, you may need to have netstat occur every few seconds. Try placing a number after the `netstat -e` command, like so:

```
netstat -e 15
```

The command executes, waits the number of seconds specified by the number (in this case, 15), and then repeats until you press Ctrl+C.

You can use the interval parameter with any combination of switches for the same effect.

---

## The –r Switch

You use the –r switch to display the current route table for a workstation so that you can see how TCP/IP information is being routed. Figure 4.4 shows sample output using this switch. You can tell from this output which interface is being used to route to a particular network (useful if computers have multiple NICs).

**FIGURE  4.4**    Sample output of the `netstat -r` command

```
C:\NETSTAT -r
  Route Table

Active Routes:

        Network Address         Netmask  Gateway Address    Interface  Metric
              127.0.0.0        255.0.0.0        127.0.0.1    127.0.0.1      1
          204.153.163.0    255.255.255.0    204.153.163.4  204.153.163.4    1
          204.153.163.4  255.255.255.255        127.0.0.1    127.0.0.1      1
        204.153.163.255  255.255.255.255    204.153.163.4  204.153.163.4    1
              224.0.0.0        224.0.0.0    204.153.163.4  204.153.163.4    1
        255.255.255.255  255.255.255.255    204.153.163.4      0.0.0.0      1


  Active Connections

    Proto    Local Address      Foreign Address        State
    TCP      default:1026       204.153.163.2:80       ESTABLISHED
    TCP      default:1027       204.153.163.2:80       ESTABLISHED
    TCP      default:1028       204.153.163.2:80       ESTABLISHED
    TCP      default:1029       204.153.163.2:80       ESTABLISHED
```

# The *–s* Switch

Using the –s switch displays a variety of TCP, UDP, IP, and ICMP protocol statistics. The following is some sample output using this switch.

```
C:\netstat -s

IP Statistics

    Packets Received              = 17455
    Received Header Errors        = 0
    Received Address Errors       = 108
    Datagrams Forwarded           = 0
    Unknown Protocols Received    = 0
    Received Packets Discarded    = 0
    Received Packets Delivered    = 17346
    Output Requests               = 16374
    Routing Discards              = 255
    Discarded Output Packets      = 0
    Output Packet No Route        = 0
    Reassembly Required           = 2
    Reassembly Successful         = 1
```

```
Reassembly Failures              = 0
Datagrams Successfully Fragmented = 0
Datagrams Failing Fragmentation  = 0
Fragments Created                = 0
```

ICMP Statistics

|                        | Received | Sent |
|------------------------|----------|------|
| Messages               | 12       | 19   |
| Errors                 | 0        | 0    |
| Destination Unreachable | 0       | 7    |
| Time Exceeded          | 0        | 0    |
| Parameter Problems     | 0        | 0    |
| Source Quenchs         | 0        | 0    |
| Redirects              | 0        | 0    |
| Echos                  | 4        | 8    |
| Echo Replies           | 8        | 4    |
| Timestamps             | 0        | 0    |
| Timestamp Replies      | 0        | 0    |
| Address Masks          | 0        | 0    |
| Address Mask Replies   | 0        | 0    |

TCP Statistics

```
Active Opens                = 715
Passive Opens               = 0
Failed Connection Attempts  = 35
Reset Connections           = 638
Current Connections         = 1
Segments Received           = 15815
Segments Sent               = 15806
Segments Retransmitted      = 61
```

UDP Statistics

```
Datagrams Received  = 573
No Ports            = 946
Receive Errors      = 0
Datagrams Sent      = 492
```

> Because the Network+ exam doesn't cover them, we won't go into detail on what all these statistics mean. You can probably figure out some of them, such as Packets Received. For details, go to Microsoft's support website at www.microsoft.com/support/.

## The *–n* Switch

The -n switch is a modifier for the other switches. When used with other switches, it reverses the natural tendency of netstat to use names instead of network addresses. In other words, when you use the –n switch, the output always displays network addresses instead of their associated network names. Following is output from the netstat command and then the netstat -n command, showing the same information but with IP addresses instead of names:

```
C:\>netstat

Active Connections

  Proto  Local Address           Foreign Address           State
  TCP    f0194063:2082           PKDWA005.company.com:5000  ESTABLISHED
  TCP    f0194063:2091           PKDWB02C.company.com:1312  ESTABLISHED
  TCP    f0194063:2164           firewall.company.com:http  TIME_WAIT
  TCP    f0194063:2173           firewall.company.com:http  TIME_WAIT

C:\>netstat -n

Active Connections

  Proto  Local Address           Foreign Address           State
  TCP    10.188.152.116:2082     10.185.12.100:5000         ESTABLISHED
  TCP    10.188.152.116:2091     10.185.12.28:1312          ESTABLISHED
  TCP    10.188.152.116:2164     172.16.83.31:80            TIME_WAIT
  TCP    10.188.152.116:2173     172.16.83.31:80            TIME_WAIT

C:\>
```

## The –p Switch

Like the –n switch, the –p switch is a modifier. Typically used with the –s switch (discussed earlier), it specifies which protocol statistics to list in the output (IP, TCP, UDP, or ICMP). For example, if you want to view only ICMP statistics, you use the –p switch like so:

```
netstat -s -p ICMP
```

The netstat utility then displays the ICMP statistics instead of the gamut of TCP/IP statistics that the –s switch normally produces.

---

 **Real World Scenario**

### Uses for *netstat*

You might be saying to yourself, "OK. Fine...I can use lots of cool switches with netstat, but what is it good for, really?" I'm always finding uses for netstat. One time, I found a particularly nasty worm on my PC using netstat. Being the geek that I am, I just happened to run netstat for giggles one day and noticed a very large number of outbound connections to various places on the Internet. It was sending out SYN packets to a large number of hosts (an indication that my computer was involved—unknowingly—in a large-scale denial of service attack). Upon further examination, I noticed that this activity would start shortly after bootup.

I tried running netstat after bootup and noticed that the first outbound connection was to TCP port 6667 to some IRC server I'd never heard of (I didn't even have an IRC client on my machine at the time). It was particularly nasty to try to get rid of while active, so I turned off port 6667 on my firewall. That prevented the initial connection to the IRC server (and, as I found out later, prevented the worm from getting its instructions from the IRC server) and I was then able to remove it. I would have never found out that this worm was working without netstat. My antivirus program even missed it.

---

# Using the *nbtstat* Utility

You'll remember from the last chapter that NetBIOS associates names with workstations. But NetBIOS is only an upper-layer interface and requires a transport protocol. In many cases, TCP/IP is used. You use the nbtstat utility to do the following:

- Track NetBIOS over TCP/IP statistics
- Show the details of incoming and outgoing NetBIOS over TCP/IP connections
- Resolve NetBIOS names

Because NetBIOS name resolution is primarily a Windows network issue, the `nbtstat` command is available only in Windows-based operating systems.

To display a basic description of `nbtstat` and its associated options, type **nbtstat** at the command line. You'll use these options to configure the display of information about NetBIOS over TCP/IP hosts. Here are some of the switches you can use:

- −a
- −c
- −r
- −S

- −A
- −n
- −R
- −s

All `nbtstat` switches are case sensitive. Generally speaking, lowercase switches deal with NetBIOS names of hosts, and uppercase switches deal with the TCP/IP addresses of hosts.

## The −*a* Switch

The −a switch displays a remote machine's NetBIOS name table, which is a list of all the Net-BIOS names that that particular machine "knows about." The following command produced the output for the server S1 shown in Figure 4.5:

```
nbtstat -a S1
```

**FIGURE 4.5**    Sample output of the `nbtstat -a` command

C:\>nbtstat -a s1

NetBIOS Remote Machine Name Table

| Name | Type | | Status |
|------|------|------|--------|
| S1 | <20> | UNIQUE | Registered |
| S1 | <00> | UNIQUE | Registered |
| ACME | <00> | GROUP | Registered |
| ACME | <1C> | GROUP | Registered |
| ACME | <1B> | UNIQUE | Registered |
| S1 | <03> | UNIQUE | Registered |
| ACME | <1E> | GROUP | Registered |
| ACME | <1D> | UNIQUE | Registered |
| .._MSBROWSE__.| <01> | GROUP | Registered |
| INet~Services | <1C> | GROUP | Registered |
| IS~S1.................. | <00> | UNIQUE | Registered |

MAC Address = 00-A0-C9-D4-BC-DC

**TABLE 4.1**   Last Byte Identifiers for Unique Names

| Hex ID | Description |
| --- | --- |
| 00 | The general name for the computer. |
| 03 | Messenger service ID used to send messages between a WINS server and a workstation. This is the ID registered with a WINS server. |
| 06 | Remote Access Server (RAS) server service ID. |
| 20 | File-serving service ID. |
| 21 | RAS client. |
| 53 | Domain Name Service (DNS). |
| 123 | Network Time Protocol (NTP). |
| 1B | Domain master browser ID. A NetBIOS name with this ID indicates the domain master browser. |
| 1F | NetDDE service ID. |
| BE | Network monitor agent ID. |
| BF | Network monitor utility ID. |

**TABLE 4.2**   Last Byte Identifiers for Group Names

| Hex ID | Description |
| --- | --- |
| 01 | Indicates the master browser for a domain to other master browsers. |
| 20 | The Internet group name ID. This ID is registered with the WINS server to indicate which computers are used for administrative purposes. |
| 1C | The domain group name ID. |
| 1D | The master browser name. |
| 1E | The normal group name. |

As you can see, using this switch produces an output with four columns. The Name column gives the NetBIOS name entry of the host in the NetBIOS name table of the remote machine. The next column displays a unique two-digit hexadecimal identifier for the NetBIOS name. This identifier represents the last byte of the NetBIOS name shown in the Name column and is necessary because the same name might be used several times on the same station. It uniquely identifies which service on the host the name is referencing. Tables 4.1 and 4.2 list the hexadecimal identifiers for unique and group host names.

The Type column refers to the type of NetBIOS name being referenced:

- Unique NetBIOS names refer to individual hosts.
- Group names refer to the names of logical groupings of workstations, either domains or workgroups.

The Status column refers to the status of the NetBIOS name for the specified host, regardless of whether the name has been registered with the rest of the network.

## The –*A* Switch

The –A switch works exactly as the –a switch and produces the same output; only the syntax of the command is different. First, you use an uppercase *A* instead of a lowercase *a*. Second, you use the IP address of the host whose NetBIOS name table you want to view instead of the NetBIOS name. The syntax includes the `nbtstat` command followed by the –A switch and finally the IP address of the host whose NetBIOS table you want to view:

```
nbtstat -A 199.153.163.2
```

## The –*c* Switch

The function of the –c switch is to display the local NetBIOS name cache on the workstation on which it is run. Figure 4.6 shows sample output of the `nbtstat -c` command.

**FIGURE 4.6**    Sample output of the `nbtstat -c` command

```
Node IpAddress: [204.153.163.4] Scope Id: []

          NetBIOS Remote Cache Name Table

    Name              Type      Host Address    Life [sec]
    ---------------------------------------------------------
S1              <00>  UNIQUE    204.153.163.2      420
```

Each entry in this display shows the NetBIOS name, the hex ID for the service that was accessed, the type of NetBIOS name (unique or group), the IP address that the name resolves to, and its Life (in seconds). The Life amount dictates how long (in seconds) each entry will live in the cache. When this time expires, the entry is deleted from the cache.

If you run nbtstat to display the cache and you get the result "No names in the cache," all entries in the cache have expired. This will happen often if you don't regularly access machines or services with NetBIOS names.

## The *–n* Switch

You use the –n switch to display the local NetBIOS name table on a Windows device. The output (shown in Figure 4.7) is similar to the output of the –a switch, except that instead of displaying the NetBIOS name table of another host, you are displaying it for the machine on which you are running the command.

**FIGURE 4.7**    Sample output of the nbtstat –n command

```
C:\NBTSTAT -n

Node IpAddress: [204.153.163.4] Scope Id: []

          NetBIOS Local Name Table

     Name              Type        Status
------------------------------------------------
   DEFAULT      <00>   UNIQUE     Registered
   WORKGROUP    <00>   GROUP      Registered
   DEFAULT      <03>   UNIQUE     Registered
   DEFAULT      <20>   UNIQUE     Registered
   WORKGROUP    <1E>   GROUP      Registered
   WORKGROUP    <1D>   UNIQUE     Registered
   .._MSBROWSE__.<01>  GROUP      Registered
   ADMINISTRATOR<03>   UNIQUE     Registered
```

## The *–r* Switch

This switch is probably the most commonly used switch when NetBIOS over TCP/IP (NBT) statistics are checked. The –r switch displays the statistics of how many NetBIOS names have been resolved to TCP/IP addresses. Figure 4.8 shows sample output of the nbtstat –r command.

As you can see, the statistics are divided into categories. The first category is NetBIOS Names Resolution and Registration Statistics, which shows how many names have been resolved or registered either by broadcasts on the local segment or by lookup from a WINS name server. The second category gives the NetBIOS unique and group names and their associated hex IDs that were resolved or registered. In Figure 4.8, the output shows that no WINS server is operating, so all NetBIOS names were resolved by broadcast only. This is evident from the lack of statistics of names resolved by a name server.

**FIGURE 4.8**   Sample output of the nbtstat -r command

```
C:\>nbtstat -r


NetBIOS Names Resolution and Registration Statistics
----------------------------------------------------

Resolved By Broadcast    = 2
Resolved By Name Server  = 0

Registered By Broadcast  = 12
Registered By Name Server = 0

   NetBIOS Names Resolved By Broadcast
   ----------------------------------------------
         ACME          <1B>
         ACME          <00>
```

The -r switch is useful in determining how a workstation is resolving NetBIOS names and whether WINS is configured correctly. If WINS is not configured correctly or is simply not being used, the numbers in the Resolved by Name Server and Registered by Name Server categories will always be zero.

## The -R Switch

The -R switch is the exception that proves the rule because it has nothing to do with the -r switch. Let's say that you have a bad name in the NetBIOS name cache but the right name is in the LMHOSTS file. The LMHOSTS file contains NetBIOS names of stations and their associated IP addresses. Also, the cache is consulted before the LMHOSTS file is. The problem here is that the bad address will be in the cache (until it expires). To purge the NetBIOS name table cache and reload the LMHOSTS file into memory, simply use the nbtstat command with the -R switch, like so:

nbtstat -R

## The -S Switch

You use the -S switch to display the NetBIOS sessions table, which lists all the NetBIOS sessions, incoming and outgoing, to and from the host where you issue the command. The -S switch displays both workstation and server sessions but lists remote addresses by IP address only.

Figure 4.9 shows sample output of the nbtstat -S command. The NetBIOS name is displayed along with its hex ID. The state of each session is also shown. An entry in the In/Out column determines whether the connection has been initiated from the computer on which you are running nbtstat (outbound) or whether another computer has initiated the connection to this computer (inbound). The numbers in the Input and Output columns indicate (in bytes) the amount of data transferred between this station and the station listed in that entry.

**FIGURE 4.9**    Sample output of the nbtstat –S command

```
C:\NBTSTAT -S

              NetBIOS Connection Table
Local Name           State      In/Out  Remote Host          Input   Output
-----------------------------------------------------------------------------
S1           <00>    Connected  Out     204.153.163.4        256B    432B
S1           <03>    Listening
```

## The –s Switch

As with the –A and –a switches, the lowercase –s switch is similar to its uppercase sibling. The nbtstat –s command produces the same output as nbtstat –S except that it tries to resolve remote host IP addresses into host names, if possible. Figure 4.10 shows sample output from the nbtstat –s command. Note the similarities between Figure 4.10 and Figure 4.9.

**FIGURE 4.10**    Sample output of the nbtstat –s command

```
C:\NBTSTAT -s

              NetBIOS Connection Table

Local Name           State      In/Out  Remote Host          Input   Output
-----------------------------------------------------------------------------
S1           <00>    Connected  Out     DEFAULT      <20>    256B    432B
S1           <03>    Listening
```

As you can do with the netstat command, you can place a number for an interval at the end of any nbtstat command to indicate that the command should execute once every so many seconds (as specified by the number) until you press Ctrl+C.

# Using The File Transfer Protocol (FTP)

From Chapter 3, "TCP/IP Fundamentals," you know that *File Transfer Protocol (FTP)* is a subset of TCP/IP and that FTP is used during the transfer of files between UNIX boxes. In recent years, FTP has become a truly cross-platform protocol for file transfer. Because the Internet, and thus TCP/IP, use has skyrocketed, almost every client (and server) platform has implemented FTP. Windows is no exception. Its TCP/IP stack comes with a command-line ftp utility.

To start the ftp utility, enter **ftp** at a command prompt. The result is an ftp command prompt:

ftp>

From this command prompt, you can open a connection to an FTP server and upload and download files as well as change the way FTP operates. To display a list of all the commands you can use at the `ftp` command prompt, type **help** or **?** and press Enter. To get help on a specific command, type **help**, a space, and then the name of the command.

In the following sections, you will get an introduction to uploading and downloading files because every network technician and administrator needs to know how to do this. As they come up, the specific commands necessary to perform those two operations will be discussed, as well as commands that relate to those processes. But first, let's look at how to start the process.

## Starting FTP and Logging In to an FTP Server

Of the two FTP file operations (download and upload), the ability to download files is the more important skill for a network technician or administrator to master because network and client operating system drivers and patches are located on FTP servers throughout the Internet.

The first steps in starting an FTP download session are to determine the address of the FTP site and start the `ftp` utility. The FTP site typically has the same name as the website except that the first three characters are `ftp` instead of www. For example, Microsoft's website is www.microsoft.com. Its FTP site, on the other hand, is `ftp.microsoft.com`. We'll use this FTP site as an example for the rest of this section.

First, start the `ftp` utility as discussed earlier, and then follow these steps:

1.  At the `ftp` command prompt, type **open**, a space, and the name of the FTP server as in the following example:

    `ftp>`**open ftp.microsoft.com**

    If the FTP server is available and running, you will receive a response welcoming you to the server and asking you for a username:

    `ftp>`**open ftp.microsoft.com**
    `Connected to ftp.microsoft.com.`
    `220 Microsoft FTP Service`
    `User (ftp.microsoft.com:(none)):`

You can also start an FTP session by typing **ftp**, a space, and the address of the FTP server (for example, **ftp ftp.microsoft.com**). This allows you to start the ftp utility and open a connection in one step.

2.  Enter a valid username and press Enter.
3.  Enter your password and press Enter.

Most Internet web servers that allow just about anyone to download files also allow the username anonymous. Remember to type the username exactly and to double-check as you enter it because usernames are case sensitive. In addition to anonymous, you can use the username ftp to gain access to a public FTP server. They are both anonymous usernames. Remember that FTP (and UNIX) usernames are case sensitive.

If you are accessing a private FTP server, you should use the username and password given to you by the administrator. If you are accessing a public FTP server with a username such as anonymous, you can use your e-mail address as the password.

You don't have to enter your entire e-mail address to log in with the anonymous username. Most FTP server software doesn't verify the actual e-mail address, just that it is, in fact, an e-mail address. To do this, it checks for an @ sign and two words separated by a period. You just need to enter a very short e-mail address to bypass the password (like u@me.com). This is especially helpful if you have a long e-mail address. It's also more secure if you don't want lots of junk e-mail.

If you enter the wrong username and/or password, the server will tell you so by displaying the following and leaving you at the `ftp` command prompt:

```
530 Login Incorrect
Login failed.
```

You must now start over with the login process. If you are successful, the FTP server will welcome you and drop you back at the `ftp` command prompt. You're now ready to start uploading or downloading files.

## Downloading Files

After you log in to the FTP server, you'll navigate to the directory that contains the files you want. Thankfully, the FTP command-line interface is similar to the DOS command-line interface. This is no surprise since DOS is based on UNIX and FTP is a UNIX utility. Table 4.3 lists and describes the common navigation commands for FTP. Remember that these are also case sensitive.

After you navigate to the directory and find the file you want to download, you must set the parameters for the type of file. Files come in two types:

- ASCII, which contains text

- Binary, which is all other files

If you set `ftp` to the wrong type, the file you download will contain gibberish. When in doubt, set `ftp` to download files as binary files.

**TABLE 4.3**    Common FTP Navigation Commands

| Command | Description |
| --- | --- |
| ls | Short for list, this command displays a directory listing. Very similar to the DIR command in MS-DOS. |
| cd | Short for change directory, this command works almost identically to the MS-DOS CD command. Use it to change to a different directory and navigate the server's directory structure. |
| pwd | Short for print working directory, this command displays the current directory on the server. Useful if you forget where you are when changing to several locations on the server. |
| lcd | Short for local change directory, this command displays and changes the current directory on the local machine. Useful when you are downloading a file and aren't in the directory where you want to put the file. |

To set the file type to ASCII, type **ascii** at the ftp command prompt. Ftp will respond by telling you that the file type has been set to A (ASCII):

```
ftp>ascii
Type set to A
```

To set the file type to binary, type **binary** at the ftp command prompt. Ftp will respond by telling you that the file type has been set to I (binary):

```
ftp>binary
Type set to I
```

To download the file, you use the get command, like so:

```
ftp>get scrsav.exe
200 PORT command successful.
150 Opening BINARY mode data connection for 'scrsav.exe'
   (567018 bytes).
```

The file will start downloading to your hard drive. Unfortunately, with its default settings, the ftp utility doesn't give you any indication of the progress of the transfer. When the file has downloaded, the ftp utility will display the following message and return you to the ftp command prompt:

```
226 Transfer complete.
567018 bytes received in 116.27 seconds (4.88 Kbytes/sec)
```

You can download multiple files by using the mget command. Simply type **mget**, a space, and then a wildcard that specifies the files you want to get. For example, to download all the text files in a directory, type **mget** **\*.txt**.

## Uploading Files

To upload a file to an FTP server, you must have rights on that server. These rights are assigned on a directory-by-directory basis. To upload a file, log in and then follow these steps:

1.   At the ftp command prompt, type **lcd** to navigate to the directory on the local machine where the file resides.

2.   Type **cd** to navigate to the destination directory.

3.   Set the file type to ASCII or binary.

4.   Use the put command to upload the file.

The syntax of the put command is as follows:

ftp>put *local file destination file*

For example, if you want to upload a file that is called 1.txt on the local server but you want it to be called my.txt on the destination server, use the following command:

ftp>put 1.txt my.txt

You'll see the following response:

```
200 PORT command successful.
150 Opening BINARY mode data connection for collwin.zip
226 Transfer complete.
743622 bytes sent in 0.55 seconds (1352.04 Kbytes/sec)
```

You can upload multiple files using the mput command. Simply type **mput**, a space, and then a wildcard that specifies the files. For example, to upload all the text files in a directory, type **mput** **\*.txt**.

When you're finished with the ftp utility, simply type **quit** to return to the command prompt.

# Using the *ping* Utility

*Ping* is the most basic TCP/IP utility and is included with most TCP/IP stacks for most platforms. Windows, again, is no exception. In most cases, `ping` is a command-line utility (although there have been some GUI implementations). You use the `ping` utility for two primary purposes:

- To find out if you can reach a host
- To find out if a host is responding

Here is the syntax:

```
ping hostname or IP address
```

If you ping any station that has an IP address, the ICMP that is part of that host's TCP/IP stack will respond to the request. This ICMP test and response might look something like this:

```
ping 204.153.163.2

Pinging 204.153.163.2 with 32 bytes of data:

Reply from 204.153.163.2: bytes=32 time<10ms TTL=128
Reply from 204.153.163.2: bytes=32 time=1ms TTL=128
Reply from 204.153.163.2: bytes=32 time<10ms TTL=128
Reply from 204.153.163.2: bytes=32 time<10ms TTL=128
```

Because you receive a reply from the destination station (204.153.163.2 in this case), you know that you can reach the host and that it is responding to basic IP requests.

Most versions of `ping` work in the same fashion, although there are some switches you can use to specify certain information—for example, the number of packets to send, how big a packet to send, and so on. If you are running the Windows command-line version of `ping`, use the -? switch to display a list of the available switches, like so:

```
ping -?
```

Table 4.4 lists and describes some of the most common switches for the Windows `ping` utility.

You can ping your local TCP/IP interface by typing **ping 127.0.0.1** or **ping localhost**. Both addresses represent the local interface.

**TABLE 4.4**    Windows *ping* Utility Switches

| Switch | Description |
|--------|-------------|
| −? | Displays a list of switches that can be used with ping. |
| −a | Resolves the pinged address to a host name simultaneously. |
| −n # | Pings the specified host multiple times (the number of times is specified by the number, #). |
| −t | Pings the host continually until you press Ctrl+C. |
| −r # | Records the route taken during the ping hops. Requires a number (#) to indicate the number of hops to record. Similar to the tracert command (discussed later in this chapter). |

# Using *winipcfg, ipconfig,* and *ifconfig*

Of all the TCP/IP utilities that come with Windows, the IP configuration utilities are probably the most overlooked. These utilities display the current configuration of TCP/IP on that workstation, including the current IP address, DNS configuration, WINS configuration, and default gateway.

## Using the *winipcfg* Utility

The IP configuration utility for Windows 95/98 is winipcfg. You use it to display the current TCP/IP configuration on a Windows 95/98 workstation. Follow these two steps to display the IP configuration information using winipcfg

**1.**    Choose Start ➢ Run, type **winipcfg**, and click OK to display the IP Configuration dialog box.

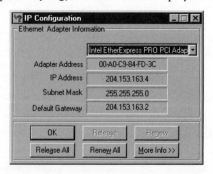

Click the down arrow to choose the network interface for which you want to view statistics. The screen in the graphic above shows this information for the Intel EtherExpress.

**2.** To display more detailed configuration information, click the More Info button to open the IP Configuration dialog box shown here.

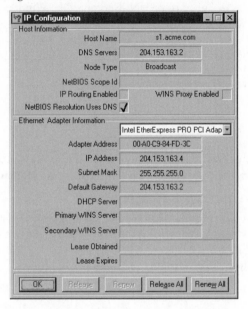

 Even thought `ifconfig` is not a Windows utility, it is a TCP/IP configuration util-ity and it naturally fits here. Its use is very similar to the other Windows config-uration utilities.

 If you are using DHCP to get IP address information, click the Release All button to remove all information obtained from a DHCP server (including an IP address). Click the Renew All button to release all DHCP information and request new TCP/IP configuration information.

The top of this screen shows the DNS name of the machine and the IP address of the DNS server that this workstation is using. Below that are several lines of NetBIOS over TCP/IP infor-mation. The bottom section contains the same information shown in the first screen but includes such additional information as the addresses of the DHCP and WINS servers (if present) and the lease information (how long the DHCP information is current) for the addresses obtained from a DHCP server.

The `winipcfg` utility comes in handy when you're resolving TCP/IP address conflicts and configuring a workstation. For example, if this workstation is experiencing duplicate IP address errors, you can run `winipcfg` to determine the IP address of this station. Also, if the address was obtained from a DHCP server, you can release it and obtain a new IP address by clicking the Renew All button.

## Using the *ipconfig* Utility

Because Windows NT was designed to be UNIX compatible, Windows NT (as well as its later incarnations, including Windows 2000 Server and Windows Server 2003) and UNIX have several functions and utilities in common. You can use many UNIX command-line utilities at the command prompt of Windows NT and later operating systems, including these:

- ftp
- ping
- tracert
- ipconfig

The Windows utility ipconfig does roughly the same job as its Windows 95/98 counterpart, winipcfg. With Windows ipconfig, however, the display is command-line based.

You can also use the ipconfig utility in Windows 98, with slightly diminished features. winipcfg still remains the most useful of the two utilities in Windows 98.

To use ipconfig, follow these steps:

1.  Choose Start ➢ Programs ➢ Accessories ➢ Command Prompt to display the command prompt.

2.  Type **ipconfig**, which produces output similar to the following:

```
C:>ipconfig

Windows 2000 IP Configuration

Ethernet adapter E100B1:

        Connection-specific DNS Suffix  . :
        IP Address. . . . . . . . . . . : 192.168.1.101
        Subnet Mask . . . . . . . . . . : 255.255.255.0
        Default Gateway . . . . . . . . : 192.168.1.1

C:\>
```

As you can see, this output is similar to the information in the Windows 95/98 IP Configuration dialog box except that the MAC address is not listed, although with the /all switch you can obtain that as well.

Only four switches can be used with the ipconfig command. Table 4.5 lists and describes all four switches, and the output that follows Table 4.5 shows the results of using the /all switch with ipconfig.

**TABLE 4.5**    *ipconfig* Switches

| Switch | Description |
|--------|-------------|
| /? | Displays the available switches and a description of each. |
| /all | Displays all TCP/IP configuration information; similar to clicking the More Info button in the Windows 95/98 IP Configuration dialog box. |
| /release | Releases all TCP/IP configuration information obtained from DHCP; similar to clicking the Release All button in the Windows 95/98 IP Configuration dialog box. |
| /renew | Releases and then renews all TCP/IP configuration information obtained from a DHCP server. |

The following shows sample output produced by using the ipconfig /all switch:

```
C:\>ipconfig/all

Windows 2000 IP Configuration

        Host Name . . . . . . . . . . . . : f0194063
        Primary DNS Suffix  . . . . . . . : company.com
        Node Type . . . . . . . . . . . . : Hybrid
        IP Routing Enabled. . . . . . . . : No
        WINS Proxy Enabled. . . . . . . . : No
        DNS Suffix Search List. . . . . . :

Ethernet adapter Wireless-G Notebook Adapter:

        Connection-specific DNS Suffix  :
        Description . . . . . . . . . . : E100B1
        Physical Address. . . . . . . . : 00-A0-C9-D8-7F-17
        DHCP Enabled. . . . . . . . . . : Yes
        Autoconfiguration Enabled . . . : Yes
        IP Address. . . . . . . . . . . : 192.168.1.101
        Subnet Mask . . . . . . . . . . : 255.255.255.0
        Default Gateway . . . . . . . . : 192.168.1.1
        DHCP Server . . . . . . . . . . : 192.168.1.254
        DNS Servers . . . . . . . . . . : 192.168.1.253
                                          192.168.1.252
        Lease Obtained. . : Wednesday, January 19, 2005 ~CA2:35:07 PM
        Lease Expires . . : Thursday, January 20, 2005 ~CA2:35:07 PM

C:\>
```

Because Windows servers can (and often do) have more than one TCP/IP interface, you can specify which interface you want to view statistics for by placing its address on the command line with the switches. If you don't specify, ipconfig displays information for all interfaces.

## Using the *ifconfig* Utility

There is a utility in Linux/UNIX that shows information similar to what ipconfig shows. This utility is called ifconfig (short for "interface configuration"). Although ipconfig and ifconfig show similar information, there are major differences between these two utilities. The ipconfig utility is used mainly to view TCP/IP configuration for a computer. You can use ifconfig to do the same thing, but ifconfig can also be used to configure a protocol or a particular network interface.

The general syntax of the ifconfig command is as follows:

ifconfig *interface* [address [*parameters*]]

The interface parameter is the UNIX name of the interface, such as eth0. If the optional address parameter is specified, the ifconfig command sets the IP address for the interface to the address specified. When the ifconfig command is used by itself with no parameters, all configured interfaces are reported on. If only the interface name is specified, output similar to the following is produced:

**# ifconfig eth0**

```
eth0   Link encap 10Mbps Ethernet   HWaddr 00:00:C0:90:B3:42
       inet addr 172.16.0.2 Bcast 172.16.0.255 Mask 255.255.255.0
       UP BROADCAST RUNNING   MTU 1500   Metric 0
       RX packets 3136 errors 217 dropped 7 overrun 26
       TX packets 1752 errors 25 dropped 0 overrun 0
```

The output shows that the eth0 interface is a 10Mbps Ethernet interface. The interface's MAC and IP address information is displayed in this output as well. The third line of the output begins by listing the state of the various flags an interface can have. The optional parameters field at the end of the ifconfig command can be used to change the state of these flags. The MTU and metric fields are used in making routing decisions, just as they would be used in any router. The values on the RX (receive) and TX (transmit) lines represent, in order, the number of packets that were transmitted or received without errors, how many packets were transmitted or received with errors, how many packets were dropped due to insufficient buffer space, and how many packets were lost due to the packets overrunning the capacity of the kernel to process them. Often the receive value will be higher than the transmit value for these last two properties because transmitted packets can be controlled much more easily than inbound packets.

# Using the *tracert* Utility

Have you ever wondered where the packets go when you send them over the Internet? The TCP/IP traceroute (tracert) command-line utility will show you every router interface a TCP/IP packet passes through on its way to a destination.

To use tracert, at a Windows command prompt, type **tracert**, a space, and the DNS name or IP address of the host for which you want to find the route. The tracert utility responds with a list of all the DNS names and IP addresses of the routers that the packet is passing through on its way. Additionally, tracert indicates the time it takes for each attempt. Figure 4.11 shows sample tracert output from a workstation connected to an ISP (Corporate Communications, in Fargo, North Dakota, in this case) in the search engine Yahoo!.

**FIGURE 4.11**    Sample tracert output

```
C:\>tracert www.yahoo.com
Tracing route to www10.yahoo.com [204.71.200.75]
over a maximum of 30 hops:

  1    110 ms     96 ms    107 ms  fgo1.corpcomm.net [209.74.93.10]
  2     96 ms    126 ms     95 ms  someone.corpcomm.net [209.74.93.1]
  3    113 ms    119 ms    112 ms  Serial5-1-1.GW2.MSP1.alter.net [157.130.100.185]
  4    133 ms    123 ms    126 ms  152.ATM3-0.XR2.CHI6.ALTER.NET [146.188.209.126]
  5    176 ms    133 ms    129 ms  290.ATM2-0.TR2.CHI4.ALTER.NET [146.188.209.10]
  6    196 ms    184 ms    218 ms  106.ATM7-0.TR2.SCL1.ALTER.NET [146.188.136.162]
  7    182 ms    187 ms    187 ms  298.ATM7-0.XR2.SJC1.ALTER.NET [146.188.146.61]
  8    204 ms    176 ms    186 ms  192.ATM3-0-0.SAN-JOSE9-GW.ALTER.NET [146.188.144.133]
  9    202 ms    198 ms    212 ms  atm3-0-622M.cr1.sjc.globalcenter.net [206.57.16.17]
 10    209 ms    202 ms    195 ms  pos3-1-155M.br4.SJC.globalcenter.net [206.132.150.98]
 11    190 ms      *       191 ms  pos0-0-0-155M.hr3.SNV.globalcenter.net [206.251.5.93]
 12    195 ms    188 ms    188 ms  pos4-1-0-155M.hr2.SNV.globalcenter.net [206.132.150.206]
 13    198 ms    202 ms    197 ms  www10.yahoo.com [204.71.200.75]

Trace complete.
```

As you can see, the packet bounces through several routers before arriving at its destination. This utility is useful if you are having problems reaching a web server on the Internet and you want to know if a WAN link is down or if the server just isn't responding. Figure 4.11 shows that every router is up and is, in fact, responding. The asterisk indicates that the attempt for that router took longer than the default time-out value. This usually means that either the router is extremely busy or that particular link is slow.

You can use tracert to ascertain how many hops a particular host is from your workstation. This is useful in determining how fast a link should be. Usually if a host is only a couple of hops away, access should be relatively quick.

# Using the *Telnet* Utility

*Telnet* is an acronym formed from Terminal EmuLation for NETworks. It was originally developed to open terminal sessions from remote UNIX workstations to UNIX servers. Although still used for that purpose, it has evolved into a troubleshooting tool. Figure 4.12 shows the basic Telnet interface as it is being used to start a terminal session on a remote UNIX host.

**FIGURE 4.12**    The Telnet utility

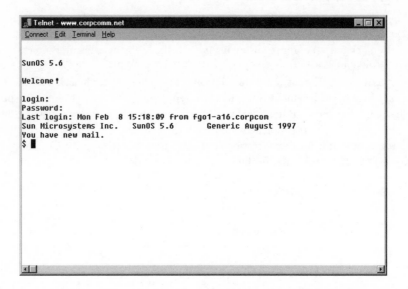

```
Telnet - www.corpcomm.net                              _ □ ✕
Connect  Edit  Terminal  Help


SunOS 5.6

Welcome !

login:
Password:
Last login: Mon Feb  8 15:18:09 from fgo1-a16.corpcom
Sun Microsystems Inc.    SunOS 5.6        Generic August 1997
You have new mail.
$ █
```

In today's Windows environments, Telnet is a basic command-line tool for testing TCP connections. You can Telnet to any TCP port to see if it is responding, which is especially useful when checking SMTP and HTTP (Web) ports. If you'll remember from Chapter 3, each upper-layer service in a TCP stack has a number for its address. Each network service that uses a particular address will respond to a TCP request on this port (if the defaults are used). Table 4.6 lists the most commonly referenced port numbers and their associated services.

**TABLE 4.6**    TCP Port Numbers and Services

| Port | TCP/IP Service |
| --- | --- |
| 21 | FTP |
| 23 | Telnet |
| 25 | SMTP |
| 80 | HTTP Session Start |
| 110 | POP3 Mail Transfer Protocol |

This list is by no means comprehensive. For a complete list, go to
www.iana.org/assignments/port-numbers.

To find out if a TCP service is responding, follow these steps:

1. Choose Start ➢ Run.

2. Type **Telnet** and click OK to open the Telnet utility.

3. At the prompt, enter a question mark (?) to display the valid commands for this interface.

```
C:\WINNT\system32\telnet.exe                                    _|□|×|
Microsoft (R) Windows 2000 (TM) Version 5.00 (Build 2195)
Welcome to Microsoft Telnet Client
Telnet Client Build 5.00.99206.1

Escape Character is 'CTRL+]'

Microsoft Telnet> ?

Commands may be abbreviated. Supported commands are:

close           close current connection
display         display operating parameters
open            connect to a site
quit            exit telnet
set             set options (type 'set ?' for a list)
status          print status information
unset           unset options (type 'unset ?' for a list)
?/help          print help information
Microsoft Telnet> open www.sybex.com 80_
```

4. At the prompt, type **open** and the IP address or DNS host name of the device running the TCP service to which you want to connect, followed by the TCP port number (one from Table 4.6, for instance).

   For example, to find out if the Sybex web server is responding to TCP port 80 (its default port), enter the IP address or DNS host name of the server (**www.sybex.com**, in this case) followed by the TCP port number (**80**, in this case).

If you successfully connect to the web server, you won't be notified that this is
the case. If the web server doesn't respond, you'll receive a Connect Failed
message.

5. If the procedure was successful, you can simply close the Telnet window or key in **Ctrl+]** to return to the Telnet prompt.

# Using the *nslookup* Utility

Whenever you are configuring a server or workstation to connect to the Internet, you will always have to configure DNS if you want name resolution to happen (i.e., if you want to be able to type **www.sybex.com** instead of an IP address). When configuring DNS, it is very advantageous to be able to test what IP address DNS is returning to ensure that it is working properly. The nslookup utility allows you to query a name server and quickly find out which name resolves to which IP address.

> The UNIX dig (short for domain information groper) utility does the exact same thing as nslookup. It is primarily a command-line utility that allows you to perform a single DNS lookup for a specific entity, but it may also be operated in batch mode for a series of lookups. While detailed information on this command is beyond the scope of this study guide, more information can be found on the Web by searching for "unix dig".

The nslookup utility comes with Windows NT and later, as well as most versions of UNIX and Linux. It did *not*, however, come with Windows 95/98. You can run it from a Windows command prompt. Once you are at the command prompt, you can start the nslookup utility by simply typing **nslookup** and pressing Enter. Once you're inside this utility, the command prompt will change from something similar to C:\> sign to a shorter > sign. It will also display the name and IP address of the default DNS server you will be querying (you can change it, if necessary). Once here, you can start using nslookup. The following output shows a sample of the display after the nslookup command has been entered at the C:\> prompt.

```
Microsoft Windows 2000 [Version 5.00.2195]
(C) Copyright 1985-2000 Microsoft Corp.

C:\>nslookup
Default Server:  ns.company.com
Address:  10.89.155.68

>
```

The primary job of nslookup is to tell you the many different features of a particular domain name, the name servers that serve it, and how they are configured. For example, you can simply type in a domain name at the > prompt, like so:

```
>sybex.com
```

The nslookup utility would return this information:

```
Server:  ns.company.com
Address:  10.89.155.68
```

```
Non-authoritative answer:
name: sybex.com
address: 10.0.0.1
```

This tells you that the server that returned the information was not responsible (authoritative) for the zone information of the domain for which you requested an address and that the name server for the domain sybex.com is located at the IP address 10.0.0.1. This means that when your computer wants to talk to www.sybex.com, it must talk to the name server at 10.0.0.1 to find out the IP address of the host called www on the sybex.com domain.

You can also ask nslookup for other information by setting a different option within nslookup. Just type **set *option*** at the > prompt and replace *option* with the actual option you want to use. Table 4.7 gives some of the common options and their uses.

**TABLE 4.7**    The *nslookup* Options and Their Uses

| Option | Use |
| --- | --- |
| type=mx | Sets future query type to e-mail servers (mail exchangers) for that domain |
| Domain=*domain name* | Sets the default domain name for lookups to *domain name* |
| Retry=*X* | Specifies the number of retries (the number of retries is specified by *X*) |

# Summary

In this chapter you learned about many of the utilities for using and troubleshooting TCP/IP. These utilities include tracert, ping, arp, netstat, nbtstat, ipconfig, winipcfg, ifconfig, dig, and nslookup. You also learned how these utilities are used, including their various options and switches and how they affect the use of these utilities. Finally, you learned about how these utilities work within the TCP/IP suite.

# Exam Essentials

**Know how to describe and use the troubleshooting information and statistics that** arp, nbtstat, **and** netstat **provide for you.**    The arp utility shows whether an IP address is being resolved to your MAC address (or someone else's in case of conflicts). The netstat utility produces TCP/IP statistics, and nbtstat produces NetBIOS over TCP/IP statistics.

**Know how to diagnose a network by using TCP/IP's troubleshooting commands.**   Ping echoes back if a machine is alive and active on a network. Tracert shows the path that the ping packets take from source to target. And Telnet enables a user to participate in a remote text-based session.

**Know what the tracert utility does.**   The tracert utility finds the route from your computer to any computer on a network.

**Know what the ping utility does.**   Ping determines if a particular IP host is responding.

**Know what the ftp utility does.**   The ftp utility allows you to reliably download and upload files from and to an FTP server across the Internet.

**Know what the ipconfig and ifconfig utilities do.**   Ipconfig displays TCP/IP configuration information for Windows NT and later operating systems. The ifconfig utility performs a similar function in UNIX environments, in addition to performing certain interface configuration tasks.

**Know what the winipcfg utility does.**   Winipcfg displays TCP/IP configuration information for Windows 95/98.

**Know what the nslookup and dig utilities do.**   Nslookup and dig allow you to look up DNS resolution information.

# Review Questions

1. Which TCP/IP utility is most often used to test whether an IP host is up and functional?

   **A.** ftp

   **B.** Telnet

   **C.** ping

   **D.** netstat

2. Which TCP/IP utility will produce the following result?

   ```
   Interface: 199.102.30.152
   Internet Address    Physical Address    Type
   199.102.30.152      A0-ee-00-5b-0e-ac   dynamic
   ```

   **A.** arp

   **B.** netstat

   **C.** tracert

   **D.** nbtstat

3. Which Windows utility can you use to display NetBIOS over TCP/IP statistics?

   **A.** nbtstat

   **B.** netstat

   **C.** arp

   **D.** ipconfig

4. Which TCP/IP utility might produce the following output?

   ```
   Pinging 204.153.163.2 with 32 bytes of data:
   Reply from 204.153.163.2: bytes=32 time=1ms TTL=128
   Reply from 204.153.163.2: bytes=32 time=1ms TTL=128
   Reply from 204.153.163.2: bytes=32 time=1ms TTL=128
   Reply from 204.153.163.2: bytes=32 time<10ms TTL=128
   ```

   **A.** tracert

   **B.** ping

   **C.** WINS

   **D.** winipcfg

5. Which utility can you use to find the MAC and TCP/IP address of your Windows 95/98 workstation?

   **A.** ping

   **B.** winipcfg

   **C.** ipconfig

   **D.** tracert

   **E.** Telnet

6.  Which `ping` commands will verify that your local TCP/IP interface is working? (Choose all that apply.)

    **A.** `ping 204.153.163.2`

    **B.** `ping 127.0.0.1`

    **C.** `ping localif`

    **D.** `ping localhost`

    **E.** `ping iphost`

7.  Which switch for the Windows `nbtstat` utility will display all NetBIOS name resolution statistics?

    **A.** `-r`

    **B.** `/r`

    **C.** `-R`

    **D.** `/R`

8.  Which program can you use to download files from a UNIX server?

    **A.** `nbtstat`

    **B.** `netstat`

    **C.** `arp`

    **D.** `ftp`

9.  Which `nbtstat` utility switch will purge and reload the remote NetBIOS name table cache?

    **A.** `-r`

    **B.** `-R`

    **C.** `/r`

    **D.** `/R`

10. Which Windows 2000 utility will display the current TCP/IP configuration of the host it is executed on?

    **A.** `arp`

    **B.** `ipconfig`

    **C.** `winipcfg`

    **D.** `winipconfig`

11. Which utility produces an output similar to the following?

    ```
    1  110 ms   96 ms   107 ms  fgo1.corpcomm.net [209.74.93.10]
    2   96 ms  126 ms    95 ms  someone.corpcomm.net [209.74.93.1]
    3  113 ms  119 ms   112 ms  Serial5-1-1.GW2.MSP1.alter.net    [157.130.100.185]
    4  133 ms  123 ms   126 ms  152.ATM3-0.XR2.CHI6.ALTER.NET     [146.188.209.126]
    5  176 ms  133 ms   129 ms  290.ATM2-0.TR2.CHI4.ALTER.NET    [146.188.209.10]
    6  196 ms  184 ms   218 ms  106.ATM7-0.TR2.SCL1.ALTER.NET    [146.188.136.162]
    7  182 ms  187 ms   187 ms  298.ATM7-0.XR2.SJC1.ALTER.NET    [146.188.146.61]
    ```

```
8   204 ms   176 ms   186 ms  192.ATM3-0-0.SAN-JOSE9- GW.ALTER.NET
[146.188.144.133]
9   202 ms   198 ms   212 ms  atm3-0-622M.cr1.sjc.globalcenter.net [206.57.16.17]
10 209 ms   202 ms   195 ms  pos3-1-155M.br4.SJC.globalcenter.net
[206.132.150.98]
11 190 ms     *      191 ms  pos0-0-0-155M.hr3.SNV.globalcenter.net [206.251.5.93]
12 195 ms   188 ms   188 ms  pos4-1-0-   155M.hr2.SNV.globalcenter.net
[206.132.150.206]
13 198 ms   202 ms   197 ms  www10.yahoo.com [204.71.200.75]
```

  **A.** arp

  **B.** tracert

  **C.** nbtstat

  **D.** netstat

**12.** You are the network administrator. A user calls you complaining that the performance of the intranet web server is sluggish. When you try to ping the server, it takes several seconds for the server to respond. You suspect that the problem is related to a router that is seriously overloaded. Which workstation utility could you use to find out which router is causing this problem?

  **A.** netstat

  **B.** nbtstat

  **C.** tracert

  **D.** ping

  **E.** arp

**13.** Which ipconfig switch will display the most complete listing of IP configuration information for a station?

  **A.** /all

  **B.** /renew

  **C.** /release

  **D.** /?

**14.** Which utility will display a list of all the routers that a packet passes through on the way to an IP destination?

  **A.** netstat

  **B.** nbtstat

  **C.** tracert

  **D.** ping

  **E.** arp

**15.** Which Windows TCP/IP utility could you use to find out if a server is responding on TCP port 21?

    **A.** tcp

    **B.** port

    **C.** ping

    **D.** netstat

    **E.** Telnet

**16.** Which arp command can you use to display the currently cached ARP entries?

    **A.** arp

    **B.** arp -A

    **C.** arp -a

    **D.** arp /A

    **E.** arp /a

**17.** Which ftp command-line command will initiate the download of a file?

    **A.** arp

    **B.** get

    **C.** put

    **D.** lcd

**18.** Which two arp utility switches perform the same function? (Choose all that apply.)

    **A.** -g

    **B.** -A

    **C.** -d

    **D.** -a

**19.** Which netstat switch will enable you to view the number of ICMP packets your workstation has sent and received?

    **A.** -a

    **B.** -r

    **C.** -s

    **D.** -I

**20.** Which nbtstat switch displays a list of all the NetBIOS sessions currently active on the local workstation?

    **A.** -a

    **B.** -r

    **C.** -s

    **D.** -I

# Answers to Review Questions

1. C. Although all utilities can be used to test the functionality of an IP host in one way or another, the ping utility is used specifically to test whether an IP host is up and responding.

2. A. The ARP utility is used to display the contents of the ARP cache, which tracks the resolution of IP addresses to physical (MAC) addresses and will produce the displayed output.

3. A. The *nbt* in nbtstat stands for "NetBIOS over TCP/IP." The purpose of nbtstat is to display the NetBIOS over TCP/IP statistics for a computer running both protocols.

4. B. The purpose of the ping utility is to test the communications channel between two IP hosts as well as how long it takes the packets to get from one host to another.

5. B. The winipcfg utility is for Windows 95/98. It displays information like the MAC and TCP/IP address of your workstation as well as other TCP/IP configuration information for your workstation.

6. B, D. The address 127.0.0.1 is the special IP address designated for the local TCP/IP interface. The host name localhost is the host name given to the local interface. Therefore, pinging either the IP address or the host name for the local interface will tell you whether or not the local interface is working.

7. A. The command nbtstat –r displays all the name resolutions performed by the local client as well as their associated IP addresses. The –R switch will reload the cache.

8. D. The only utility listed that can be used to download files from a UNIX server is the ftp utility.

9. B. To purge and reload the remote NetBIOS name cache, you must use nbtstat –R. Remember that the *R* must be uppercase and it will not work correctly without the hyphen before it.

10. B. The ipconfig utility is similar to the Windows 95/98 utility winipcfg in that it displays the current TCP/IP configuration of a station. However, ipconfig is a Windows NT based–only utility, with a limited version available for 98.

11. B. The tracert utility traces the route from the source IP host to the destination host.

12. C. The tracert utility will tell you which router is having the performance problem and how long it takes to move between each host. Tracert can be used to locate problem areas in a network.

13. A. The ipconfig /all switch will display the most complete listing of TCP/IP configuration information for a Windows NT computer.

14. C. The tracert utility returns all router names and addresses through which a packet passes on its way to a destination host.

15. E. The Telnet utility can be used to test if a particular IP host is responding on a particular TCP port.

16. C. The arp –a command will display the current contents of the ARP cache on the local workstation.

**17.** B. The `get` command, followed by the name of the file you want to download, will initiate the download of that particular file.

**18.** A, D. The `arp` utility's –a and –g switches perform the same function. They both show the current ARP cache.

**19.** C. The –s switch will enable you to view the statistics about how many of a particular TCP/IP protocol's packets have been sent and received.

**20.** C. `nbtstat` –s will list all NetBIOS sessions, incoming and outgoing, from that PC.

# Chapter 5

# Network Operating Systems

---

**THE FOLLOWING NETWORK+ EXAM OBJEC-TIVES ARE COVERED IN THIS CHAPTER:**

✓ **3.1 Identify the basic capabilities (for example, client support, interoperability, authentication, file and print services, application support, and security) of the following server operating systems to access network resources:**

 ▪ UNIX/Linux/Mac OS X Server

 ▪ NetWare

 ▪ Windows

 ▪ AppleShare IP (Internet Protocol)

Every network today has some form of software to manage its resources. This software runs on a special, high-powered computer and is called a *network operating system* (or *NOS,* for short). The NOS is one of the most important components of the network. In this chapter, we will look at four of the most popular network operating systems:

- Microsoft Windows
- Novell NetWare
- UNIX/Linux
- Macintosh

NetWare, developed by Novell, was the first network operating system to gain wide acceptance in the PC market. Windows, although introduced by Microsoft in 1993, still has market share as a server platform as of late because of its ease of use. UNIX, while being the oldest network operating system, is only starting to gain popularity with PC users through PC-based flavors of UNIX, such as Linux. This rise in popularity is due in part to the Internet, which is based on UNIX standards and protocols. The fourth network operating system in use today—though used in a much smaller part of the networking market—is Apple's AppleShare IP, for use on the Mac OS, which we will cover briefly.

# Microsoft Windows

With the same graphical interface as other versions of Windows and simple administration possible from the server console, Windows 2003 Server is possibly the most popular NOS in use today. Microsoft introduced Windows NT in 1993 with version 3.1 (about the same time Windows 3.1 was taking off as a desktop graphical interface for DOS). This NOS went pretty much unnoticed until version 3.51 was introduced about a year later. Windows NT 3.51 was quite stable, and by this time, hardware vendors had met the challenge with the 486 and Pentium processors. Because of its similarity to Windows 3.1 and its powerful networking features, Windows NT gained popularity. Microsoft began to put its significant marketing muscle behind it, and Windows NT started to become a viable alternative in the network operating system market previously dominated by Novell NetWare and the various flavors of UNIX. Windows NT was followed closely by Windows 2000, then 2003 Server, and the Windows platform has become a dominant force in the NOS market.

For more information on Windows server OSes, check out Microsoft's website at www.microsoft.com.

In the following sections, you will learn about the features, inner workings, administration, application support, and security of Windows Server.

# Features

The Windows server platform is the first choice of developers because of the similarity in programming for all Windows platforms. Additionally, the installation CD includes a complete Internet server suite (including WWW, FTP, and DNS [Domain Name Service] server programs). Finally, because the look and feel of all Windows platforms is almost identical to that of Microsoft's desktop operating systems, training administrators requires much less time. These features along with many others have skyrocketed Windows Server use in the corporate network infrastructure. Let's take a look at a couple of the more popular features of Windows 2003 Server: the user interface and third-party support.

## The Windows User Interface

The Windows Server interface is basically the same as the Windows interface we've come to love (or hate, depending on your view). Windows NT 3.1 and 3.5x use the same basic look and feel as the Windows 3.1 desktop operating system. Windows NT 4 and Windows 2000 use the interface from Windows 95 and Windows 98.

Although there might be subtle differences between the desktop operating systems and their Server counterparts, the basic look and feel is the same. Because of this, a novice administrator can easily learn to use Windows Server. Analysts refer to this as a shallow learning curve.

## Third-Party Support

Because of its ease of use and relatively inexpensive cost, Windows Server sells well. Third-party vendors write thousands of software titles for Windows. Currently the number of third-party network programs for Windows far surpasses the number for NetWare.

One reason for the range of software available for Windows Server is that developers can create these programs using many of the development tools they use to write Windows programs. Additionally, Microsoft makes much of the code available to developers for little or no charge. Other vendors often charge to download their development tools, although that trend is rapidly changing. Finally, a program that is certified as Windows Compatible must work on all Windows platforms, both Server and desktop, including Windows 95/98/Me/NT/2000/XP/2003 Server. Because it's so easy to develop programs for all versions and because Microsoft requires it for Windows certification, the number of programs available for Windows Server is constantly growing. That isn't to say that all programs are network enabled, but when given the choice, developers usually choose to create programs for Windows rather than for other network operating system platforms.

## Client Support

One of Windows' shortcomings is its relative single-mindedness when it comes to clients. Windows as a server platform mainly supports Windows clients with the majority of its features. It is possible to support Mac and UNIX clients, but only with special add-on software, and even then, some client features and security are limited. But, it is possible to support all versions of Windows Operating Systems as clients for all of the Windows Server platforms.

## Interoperability

With the vast diversity of client operating systems out there, any network operating system must be able to provide services to multiple clients. Windows never used to "play well with the other children" in terms of interoperating with other platforms. Historically speaking, a NOS other than Windows Server would have limited interoperability with Windows Server. These days, Windows Server has many tools for platform interoperability.

One of the coolest interoperability tools for Windows is Windows Services for Unix (SFU), which provides a framework for UNIX scripts as well as UNIX services like NFS to run on Windows. You can download it from www.microsoft.com. With SFU, an administrator can port network services and scripts to a Windows Server machine and run them on the Interix subsystem (a sort of "mini-Unix" part of Windows that comes with SFU).

In addition, Windows can interoperate with NetWare. When Windows NT Server was first introduced in 1993, NetWare was the primary network operating system available. As a matter of fact, it had more than 75 percent of the installed network operating system base. For this reason, Microsoft created software for Windows that allows it to coexist in a NetWare environment. Three main programs facilitate the integration of Windows and NetWare:

- Gateway Services for NetWare (GSNW)
- Client Services for NetWare (CSNW)
- File and Print Services for NetWare (FPNW)

### Gateway Services for NetWare (GSNW)

GSNW installs as a service on a Windows Server machine and translates requests for Windows resources into NetWare requests. At a lower level, GSNW is translating Server Message Block (SMB) protocol requests into NetWare Core Protocol (NCP) requests. GSNW allows multiple Windows NT clients to connect through a Windows NT server to NetWare servers using only Windows NT client software and protocols. Figure 5.1 illustrates this arrangement.

**NOTE**   GSNW has a relatively undocumented feature: Any number of Windows clients can connect to NetWare resources through GSNW and use only one license on the NetWare server being accessed. With this capability, it is theoretically possible to build a network of mostly NetWare servers but license all of them for five users or fewer. Novell is understandably peeved. However, GSNW performance is very poor in this application. Microsoft doesn't recommend GSNW for environments with high NetWare traffic.

**FIGURE 5.1**    Gateway Services for NetWare (GSNW) operation

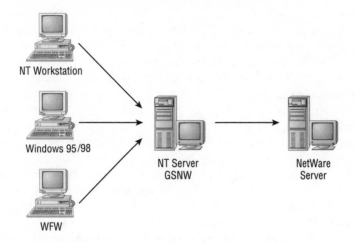

## Client Services for NetWare (CSNW)

CSNW is probably the simplest of all the software, but it requires the most overhead to implement. You must install CSNW on every Windows workstation computer that needs access to NetWare resources. Client services for NetWare allows a user sitting at a Windows workstation to access the services of NetWare servers. Additionally, all users who want to access NetWare resources need user accounts and rights on the NetWare servers they access.

## File and Print Services for NetWare (FPNW)

FPNW is really a method for providing files and printers hosted by Windows Server to Novell clients. When installed and configured on a Windows server, this service makes a Windows server look like a NetWare server to Novell clients. This service is good when you have a small number of NT servers and a large number of NetWare servers.

# Authentication

Since Windows 2000 Server, all Windows products have been able to use Kerberos for authentication. Authentication also works in conjunction with Microsoft's own directory service, which is similar to NDS and known as Active Directory (AD). Kerberos is a technology that is used for authentication. Essentially, a unique identifier known as a *ticket* is given to every user that successfully authenticates to AD. From then on, that ticket is sent along with all transmissions to indicate exactly who sent the information. One important note: for Kerberos to be used as an authentication mechanism, all applications that are to use it must be modified to include authentication information. This process is known as kerberization.

## File and Print Services

Windows Server's file and print services, while not as robust as some, are completely adequate for the small-to-medium size network and, if scaled properly, can service large numbers of clients equally well. The major advantage to Windows Server over other server platforms is that it uses the familiar Windows interface and terminology.

Windows Server uses the concept of folders and shares for its file sharing. Individual documents are stored in folders on the server's hard disk. To make them accessible to network users, these folders are "shared." A share is any folder on a computer that has been shared (by changing its properties from "not shared" to "shared") with the rest of the network. Once a folder is shared, a client can access all the files within it (depending on the security settings, of course) and any folders within it as well.

Additionally, Windows Server supports the sharing of printers in the same manner. A printer, once configured on the server, can be shared with the rest of the network like any folder. As a matter of fact, sharing printers is not only easy, but cool as well. When configured correctly, a printer shared under Windows NT, 2000, XP, or 2003 Server can be automatically installed by connecting to it. The client can automatically download the appropriate driver from the server the first time it connects.

## Application Support

Application support is one area where Windows really shines. It is arguably the platform with the most developer support. Almost any application that will run on the desktop Windows (e.g., Windows $9x$, NT, 2000, XP, etc.) will run on Windows 2003 Server. Plus, Windows 2003 Server network applications are extremely easy to configure and run because there is a very shallow learning curve. People already understand the Windows interface.

By far, Windows has the greatest number of software packages available for it. You can run these packages on Windows Servers in addition to running them on a desktop operating system.

## Security

Although Windows Server has many advantages, its security is not as robust as it should be. In fact, most of the patches released by Microsoft for Windows Server are security patches. It is extremely vulnerable to Internet attacks because of its sheer design. The same features that make Windows Server easy to use also make it more vulnerable to hacker attacks.

In addition, to meet marketing deadlines, Windows is often put into distribution before it's ready and then fixed and patched after the fact. This rush allows potential security flaws to remain unfixed until after they have been discovered. These flaws have been the source of many security problems over the years.

That isn't to say that Windows Server as a platform can't be made secure; it just requires more work. You must make sure that the server is patched to the most current patch levels, and you need to take common-sense precautions like having a firewall (but you'd need these protections for the other platforms as well, just as a precaution). Once patched properly, Windows can be as secure as any of the other NOS platforms.

# Novell NetWare

NetWare is one of the more powerful network operating systems on the market today. It is almost infinitely scalable and has support for multiple client platforms. Although many companies larger than a few hundred stations are running NetWare, this NOS enjoys success in many different types of networks.

As this book goes to press, the current version of NetWare is version 6.5 and includes workstation management support, Internet connectivity, web proxy, native Transmission Control Protocol/Internet Protocol (TCP/IP) support, and continued support for its award-winning directory service, NDS.

 For more information on NetWare, check out Novell's website at www.novell.com.

In the following sections, we will look at the features of NetWare and how it functions as well as how it interoperates with other operating systems.

Specifically, you will learn about the following topics:

- Features
- Client support
- Interoperability
- Authentication
- Directory structure
- File and print services
- Application support
- Security

## Features

NetWare is popular in large networks (more than 20 servers) because of features such as centralized administration of all users and their properties. The most important features of Net-Ware 4.*x* and later are the following:

- The directory service
- The simple user interface
- Fairly minimal hardware requirements
- Scalable hardware support
- Third-party support
- Interoperability with many types of computer systems

NetWare has always been an excellent directory, file, and print server, but with its acquisition of many Java technologies (including the Java graphical user interface [GUI] on the server introduced with NetWare 5), it is starting to encroach on the application server market. These features make NetWare an excellent choice in the directory, file, and print environments.

## Client Support

Novell supports a wide range of diverse clients. To facilitate this, Novell developed client software that allows many client operating systems to take advantage of all NetWare features. Specifically, Novell's clients (sometimes called NDS clients) enable access to the NDS database. Even though some clients are included with various operating systems and the vendors themselves design them, you should implement Novell's client on the client operating systems you are running to get the most functionality out of NetWare—including being able to administer NetWare. The NetWare client written by Novell for a particular operating system provides full NDS functionality and is therefore the best choice for connecting that operating system to a NetWare network.

Table 5.1 lists the Novell clients that are available for NetWare and the special feature(s) of each.

There are NDS clients for UNIX, but the UNIX vendor usually develops them. One rare exception is UNIXWare, a product Novell developed several years ago. This rather cool version of UNIX has been completely integrated with NetWare.

**TABLE 5.1**    Available Novell Clients

| Operating System | Client | Special Features |
|---|---|---|
| Windows 95/98 | Novell Client for Windows 95/98 | Fully integrated with the Windows 95/98 Explorer. Included with NetWare versions after 4.11. |
| Windows NT/2000/XP | Novell Client for Windows NT/2000/XP | Replaces graphical login screen with an interface that allows you to simultaneously log in to both NetWare and Windows NT/2000/XP. |

## Interoperability

NetWare is one of the most flexible NOSes and can communicate with just about any computing environment, including the following:

- Windows 95/98/Me
- Windows NT/2000/XP
- Mac OS

- VMS
- OS/400
- UNIX
- OS/2

When each of these operating systems tries to communicate with a NetWare server, the server appears as though it were a member of that type of network. For example, on a Mac OS network, a NetWare server can appear to be just another Macintosh server, but in reality it's a Pentium-class box running NetWare. I have found that a NetWare server makes a better server for Macs than Apple's own servers running the AppleShare network operating system.

# Authentication

Authentication is the process by which a user proves they are who they say they are to the network operating system. All NetWare versions since version 4.0 use Novell Directory Services (NDS) for resource access and authentication. A *directory service* is a feature of a network operating system that enables users to find network resources. There are three main types of directory services for NetWare:

**Bindery**    The bindery (pronounced with a long *i*) is a simple, flat database of users, groups, and security information that resides on a server. It is available in versions of NetWare prior to version 4.

**Novell Directory Services (NDS)**    This provides access to a global, hierarchical database of network entities (called *objects*). It is available in version 4 and later. Based on the X.500 Internet directory standard (a standard way of naming network entities), this database (called the Directory with a capital *D*, not to be confused with a DOS directory) is distributed and replicated to all NetWare servers on the network. Each server contains a part of the directory database. Additionally, all servers know about one another and the directory information that each contains.

**EDirectory**    This is just an extension of NDS. It allows NDS trees to be connected over the Internet, essentially creating a meta directory. The current version of NDS is known as eDirectory.

A major advantage of NDS over the bindery is that with NDS, the entire network is organized into a hierarchical structure, called an NDS tree. This tree is a logical representation of a network. It includes objects that represent the network's users, servers, printers, and other resources (see Figure 5.2). On the other hand, the bindery contains user information for only the server on which it resides. NDS is described as a *network-centric* directory service, whereas the bindery is *server-centric*.

**FIGURE  5.2**    A sample NDS Tree

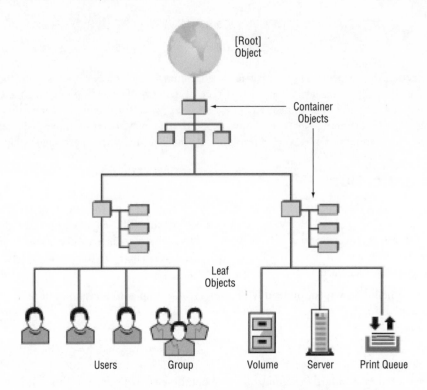

To contrast these two directory services, let's look at an example. If a user on a NetWare 3.*x* network wants to log in to multiple servers, the administrator must create users on every server. If there are 20 servers on the network, the administrator must create that user 20 times, once on each server. With NDS, however, the administrator simply creates a single user object in the Directory. The user can then log in to the network on any server. The administrator simply assigns rights to the resources that the user needs to access.

To change the Directory database, a NetWare network administrator uses a program called NetWare Administrator. Although this graphical Windows utility has gone through several iterations in the past six years since its introduction, it is the only administrative utility you need to modify NDS objects and their properties. Many utilities are available for specific functions, but NetWare Administrator is the one utility that can do it all. Figure 5.3 shows a sample NetWare Administrator screen. From this one screen, an administrator can modify any object's properties, including security settings, object names, and network parameters. You can manage your entire network from this one program.

Each iteration of NetWare Administrator included new features and a new filename. Table 5.2 lists the myriad versions and their associated filenames.

**FIGURE 5.3**    A NetWare Administrator screen

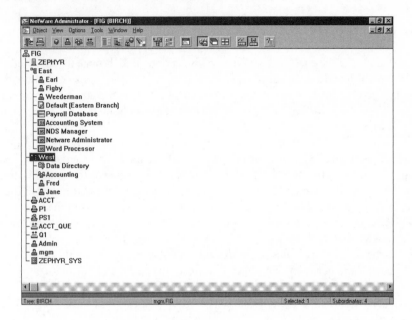

**TABLE 5.2**    NetWare Administrator Filenames

| Version | Filename |
| --- | --- |
| NetWare Administrator (original version) | NWADMIN.EXE |
| NetWare Administrator for Windows 3.*x* | NWADMN3X.EXE] |
| NetWare Administrator for Windows 95 | NWADMN95.EXE |
| NetWare Administrator for Windows NT | NWADMNNT.EXE |
| NetWare Administrator for Windows (32-bit) | NWADMN32.EXE |

# Directory Structure

Directories like Novell's that use the X.500 standard are hierarchical in nature and use a structure called the *Directory Information Tree (DIT)*. In a DIT, the top level of the structure is called the *[Root],* which leads to the fact that the DIT is commonly referred to as an *inverted tree.*

Making up the structure below the [Root] are *intermediate objects* and *leaf objects.*

Leaf objects are also called terminating objects because they are at the "ends" of the tree.

To easily find objects in the Directory, it must be further organized through the use of intermediate objects. They can be likened to alphabetized subsections of a telephone book (A, B, C, and so on).

Leaf objects represent resources in your organization (such as people, devices, applications, services, and so on) and can be likened to each name in a telephone book (Smith, Chang, Moreau, and so on).

Each object in the tree has *attributes,* which are properties that define the object. Information stored in an attribute is called a *value.* An example of an attribute in a telephone book is phone number, and the value is the number itself. Objects can have many different attributes.

Each object (depending on its type) can be located only in certain places within the DIT. Labels are used to identify object types and thus their possible locations in the tree. Each label is a one- or two-character abbreviation of the object type or of an object attribute. Each object is also graphically represented in the tree. A Leaf Object's graphical representation varies depending on the type of Leaf Object (for example, user, printer, and application).

Object types, where in the tree an object is allowed to reside, and object attributes follow rules called the *schema.*

Table 5.3 describes each of the possible object labels in an NDS tree, the associated object type, and the possible location of the object in the tree.

**TABLE 5.3**    Labels, Object Types, and Object Locations in the Tree

| Label | Object Type | Location in the Tree |
|-------|-------------|----------------------|
| C | Country | Below [Root] |
| O | Organization | Below [Root] or below Country objects |
| OU | Organizational Unit | Below Organization or Organizational Unit objects (intermediate grouping object) |
| CN | Leaf (CN is an abbreviation for Common Name, a leaf object attribute.) | Below Organization or Organizational Unit objects |

When accessing a particular object, you must understand the idea of context. An object's context is its exact location within the tree, taking into account all of the containers that it is in. For example, if a user, Connie, was in the sales organizational unit, which in turn was in the Acme organization, the user object Connie would have the context of

OU=SALES.O=ACME

Because it has the OU= and O= labels, this name is known as a typefull context. This type of name is used when there must be no doubt about the type of container that exists at a particular level. In addition, Connie's typefull *distinguished name* (the name of an object plus its context) would be

.CN=CONNIE.OU=SALES.O=ACME.

**Make note of the leading period; this denotes a distinguished name.**

Contexts and names can also be used without their container labels, like so:

SALES.ACME (for a context)

.CONNIE.SALES.ACME (for an object's distinguished name)

This is known as a typeless context and is used most often because it's easier to remember.

## File and Print Services

NetWare is known for its file and print services, that is, the network services that serve out files to client computers and allow printers to be shared over the network. NetWare was the first NOS to provide file and print services for PCs and it arguably is the best at it. As a matter of fact, the file services are so advanced that NetWare can be made to appear as any kind of file server. For example, a NetWare server can be made to look like an AppleShare server to Macintosh clients, an NFS server to UNIX clients, and so on.

## Application Support

Application support is one major downfall for NetWare. NetWare is a server-only platform. Novell's view is that a server should run only services, not desktop-type applications. To that end, NetWare servers run services very well. But NetWare does not run desktop applications (like word processing programs, spreadsheets, or what have you) at all.

## Security

NetWare is arguably the most secure NOS. It uses public key encryption during the login process (passwords are never sent in cleartext between client and server). Plus, you cannot get access to the local files unless you are logged in with a proper client. NetWare is the only NOS that has been certified by the National Security Agency (NSA) as C2 Red Book secure, which means that it is secure enough for U.S. government use.

In addition, NetWare uses NDS for the back-end authentication. Clients will send authentication requests to NDS and NDS will look up the user in the Directory and verify that the attempted login is an appropriate request and that the user information is valid.

# UNIX/Linux

Of the other network operating systems available, the various forms of UNIX are probably the most popular. It is definitely the oldest of the network operating systems. Bell Labs developed UNIX, in part, in 1969. We say "in part" because there are now so many iterations, commonly called *flavors*, of UNIX that it is almost a completely different operating system.

Although the basic architecture of all flavors is the same (32-bit kernel, command-line based, capable of having a graphical interface, as in X Window System), the subtle details of each make one flavor better in a particular situation than another.

In the following sections, you will learn about these UNIX/Linux topics:

- Features
- Client support and interoperability
- Authentication
- File and print services
- Security

## Features

UNIX flavors incorporate a kernel, which constitutes the core of the operating system. The kernel can access hardware and communicate with various types of user interfaces. The two most popular user interfaces are the command-line interface (called a *shell*) and the graphical interface (X Window System). The UNIX kernel is similar to the core operating system components of Windows Server and NetWare. In UNIX, the kernel is typically simple and, therefore, powerful. Additionally, the kernel can be recompiled to include support for more devices. As a matter of fact, some flavors (like Linux) include the source code so that you can create your own flavor of UNIX.

The UNIX flavor that has been receiving the most attention lately is Linux. Linux is a fairly easy-to-use (as UNIX goes, anyway) flavor developed by Linus Torvalds at the University of Helsinki, Finland. He started his work in 1991 and released version 1 of the Linux kernel in 1994. As this book is being written, the current Linux kernel is version 2.2. Since Linux development teams add features daily, it's only a matter of time before a new release.

Linux runs mainly on the Intel platform, although some distributions run on Rapid Instruction Set Computing (RISC) processors such as the MIPS and Alpha. Attempts have been made, successfully, to run the RISC version on other platforms, such as the Macintosh. Linux is easy to install, and most distributions are free and include the source code. Hardware requirements can vary widely with each distribution.

And there are various flavors of Linux. People acquire Linux, come up with a new feature, recompile Linux with the new feature, and then redistribute it. According to Linux's distribution agreement (called the GNU public license), any sale or distribution must include the source code so that others can also develop custom Linux applications.

Most Linux distributions include a full suite of applications, such as a word processor, the X Window System graphical interface, and source code compilers. Additionally, most UNIX applications that comply with the POSIX standard should run on Linux with little or no modification.

Because Linux is a flavor of UNIX, it comes with network support for TCP/IP. In particular, Caldera's OpenLinux is making its mark in the networking world. OpenLinux was developed for corporate networking, so it supports multiple protocols (including Point-to-Point Protocol [PPP], Apple-Talk, IPX, and SMB). It also includes support for integration with other network operating systems.

Two other distributions of Linux should be noted: Red Hat and Slackware. Red Hat Linux is the most portable version of Linux, with code that runs natively on the Intel, Alpha, and SPARC processors. The Slackware distribution was specifically designed for the Intel platform and, as such, supports many PC hardware devices, including Ethernet and multiple (up to 16) processors.

For more detailed information on Linux, as well as locations to download it, check out www.linux.org. For a list of the various English Linux distributions, check out www.linux.org/dist/english.html.

## Client Support and Interoperability

UNIX servers use primarily Internet standard protocols, like TCP/IP, FTP, HTTP, LPR, and so on. Therefore, just about any client that can be configured with TCP/IP and a web browser is a potential client. Most other NOS platforms are moving to this idea of using TCP/IP and Internet standard protocols for all communications and network services, but it's been difficult because each vendor has a lot invested in its own proprietary systems.

## Authentication

UNIX can use multiple methods of authentication. It depends on whether the OS is UNIX or Linux and what kind of software is running for authentication, although remember that UNIX generally uses Internet standard protocols. So, UNIX can use Lightweight Directory Access Protocol (LDAP) or Kerberos for authentication. But there are clients for NDS and AD as well. It just depends on what kind of software is running on the server or how it has been configured. For example, you can set up a Linux box with an NDS client so it can work with other NetWare servers. Or, you can set up a UNIX box with its own LDAP server.

## File and Print Services

As you might expect, UNIX file and print services are TCP/IP based. Therefore, protocols like FTP, NFS, and HTTP are used with standard file sharing. As discussed in Chapter 3, UNIX printing uses the LPD/LPR combination. But there is UNIX software available that makes UNIX appear as a Windows server. This software is known as Samba. It uses the standard Server Message Block (SMB) protocol—the same protocol that Windows networking uses. Samba is freely available on the Internet.

You can check out Samba at the Samba website located at www.samba.org.

## Application Support

UNIX has plenty of application support because it is the oldest of the NOSes discussed in this chapter. However, it is important to note that applications are usually made to run on the specific version and flavor of UNIX. For example, an application written for Sun Solaris may not run on SCO UNIX, even though they are both UNIX.

Also, a large amount of UNIX software is available for free on the Internet. It can be downloaded and installed, but there may not be any technical support available for it if you get it for free.

## Security

Most UNIX flavors have existed for quite some time, and therefore many of the security issues have been discovered and their causes fixed. Even though new security issues are always popping up, the large installed user base means that fixes are always easy to come by. Plus, many of the users can come up with fixes themselves because the average UNIX administrator is extremely well versed at fixing their own problems.

### Real World Scenario

#### Running Windows on Linux

Let's face it, Linux has made its way into the enterprise and has finally arrived. In fact, many companies are using it more and more for mission-critical applications. Over the last several years, a need has arisen for companies to be able to run Windows applications on Linux-based computers. Microsoft would have you believe that it isn't necessary to switch to Linux (www.microsoft.com/windowsserversystem/facts/default.mspx), but the fact is, in many cases, people already have.

The first product to allow Windows programs to run on Linux is known as Wine. Wine is an open-source (meaning it's free) implementation of the APIs that allow Windows programs to run on Windows, except these APIs run on Linux (and X Window System). Wine allows you to install a Windows program right into Linux and run it from within X Window System. There is even a special Linux distribution that includes many of the Wine components. This distribution is called Lindows. Although it allows most applications to run, there may be compatibility issues. More information of Wine can be found at its website at www.winehq.com.

Another product that allows the marriage of Windows and Linux is Win4Lin. Win4Lin is an emulator. It essentially emulates another computing environment (in this case an x86 environment) inside an X Window System window. You can then install Windows into this environment and run most Windows applications. Compatibility is not as much of an issue, but performance is. You are essentially doubling up on the amount of system resources your computer is using just to run one program because you are running two operating systems. You can find more information on Win4Lin at www.netraverse.com.

# Macintosh

The Macintosh interface is considered to be the easiest to use of all graphical user interfaces. Developed in 1983 by Apple, the Macintosh Operating System (or Mac OS) is seeing a resurgence of popularity with the introduction of several new models, like the iMac, the G4 Cube, and the Titanium PowerBook G4 Macintosh. Macintosh has always had a very loyal following, and with good reason. The Macintosh OS (combined with the Macintosh hardware platform) is a very user-friendly computer. As such, many people who have never used computers before are buying Macs.

 With very few exceptions, the Mac OS will not run on any hardware platform except the Macintosh.

In the following sections, you will learn about these topics as they apply to the Mac OS:

- Features
- Client support
- Interoperability
- Authentication
- File and print services
- Application support
- Security

## Features

The Mac OS has gone through several major revisions so far, with each version having many more features than the one before it. No discussion of the Mac OS would be complete without a brief discussion of the major releases of the Mac OS:

**System 1**   When the original Macintosh was released in 1984, the Mac OS interface (simply called the Finder in those days) was pretty bare (similar to Figure 5.4). It contained the basic elements of the current Mac OS, but in non-color form. It had no support for color, but it did have a very powerful graphical user interface (GUI) that made many people go out and buy it.

**System 6**   System 6 was introduced around 1986 and quickly made the Macintosh world even more exciting with the introduction of color to the operating system. Depending on the video card, a Mac with System 6 could display thousands, even millions, of colors. This was very exciting stuff for the time.

**System 7**   As good as System 6 was, it didn't have good support for multitasking. (It could switch between programs using a product known as Multifinder, but it wasn't great.) Macintosh System 7, therefore, gave Mac users the ability to run multiple programs at once. In addition, it gave users support for TrueType fonts (automatically scalable fonts) and the ability to share out a disk onto the network so that other Mac users could access it. It also gave users the ability to use virtual memory (using a portion of the hard disk as memory).

**FIGURE 5.4**    The basic Macintosh GUI

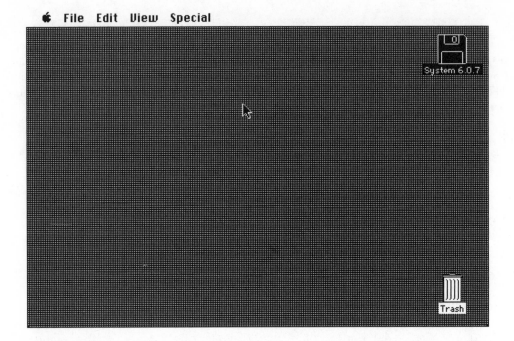

**Mac OS 8**    In 1997, Apple made a few changes with the operating system. First of all, it now actively promoted the fact that the Macintosh system software was to be known as Mac OS. Also, due to a partnership with Microsoft (and an infusion of capital from the same), Internet Explorer was installed as the default browser. Apple also increased its cross-platform connectivity with the introduction of an updated version of its PC Exchange product, which now had support for Windows 9 x long file-names. Finally, the OS contained its own Java Virtual Machine for running Java applications.

**Mac OS 9**    With Mac OS 9, Apple brought the Mac OS up to speed with Microsoft's multiuser offerings. It was now possible to specify different settings and environments for multiple users of the same Macintosh. Along with that, Apple introduced the Keychain, which stored the various online passwords for a user so that only one password was required when a user went online. Finally, it included a network browser so that a user could browse the network easily for a network server.

**Mac OS X (OS 10)**    Amid much hoopla, Apple introduced OS X, the current version and first major rewrite of the Mac OS in years, in 2001. The basic interface still looks the same; however, the use of color, graphics, and moving graphics is much improved over previous versions (as shown in Figure 5.5). Also, it is based on a UNIX kernel (BSD with a Mach Kernel), which makes it more stable, more scalable, and generally more powerful than previous versions. Windows "fly" open and get "squished" onto a bar (called the Dock) when minimized. Also, for the first time, you can save directly to PDF format in most applications. This new OS, in addition to being extremely powerful, is also extremely user- and Internet-friendly.

**FIGURE 5.5**    Mac OS X

## Client Support

The Mac OS on the whole as a server platform is only somewhat limited in its client support. As you would expect, the Mac OS X Server supports Mac clients but, with its latest versions, includes Samba so that Windows clients can authenticate to a Mac OS X Server. Also, the Mac OS X Server can function beautifully as an Internet server because the core of Mac OS X is UNIX. And, as you might well expect, a UNIX server of any kind makes an excellent Internet server because of the close ties with TCP/IP.

## Interoperability

As a server platform, the Mac OS is reliable and fairly scalable. It really can't compete with the largest UNIX and high-end server platforms in the enterprise, but it makes for a good workgroup web server platform. In that respect, the Mac OS is compatible with many different clients. As a client, though, there is one major problem with the Mac OS: The predominant business client platform is the Windows platform. As such, most business applications are written for that platform, and translations of all those applications for the Mac OS are few and far between. Still, there are translations of the most popular business applications (e.g., Microsoft Word) for the Mac OS that make it viable to use in the workplace.

Another compatibility and interoperability benefit is the support of other server operating systems for Mac OS clients. Windows NT and 2000 have built-in support for Mac OS clients. In fact, the support is so good that Mac OS clients can't tell the difference between a Windows server with Mac OS file and print support and an actual Macintosh server. Novell NetWare has similar support for Mac OS clients, as previously mentioned in this chapter.

## Authentication

Authentication for Mac OS X is handled through the Kerberos authentication mechanism, which makes Mac OS X ideal in a networked environment. Additionally, Mac OS X includes a feature known as the keychain. The keychain is a storage location for all the passwords you might use on the Internet (website passwords, FTP passwords, etc.) or anywhere. When a user authenticates to the system, that procedure unlocks the keychain. From then on, any time the user revisits a location that has credentials stored in the keychain, the keychain will automatically provide them on behalf of the user.

In addition to Kerberos and the keychain, Mac OS X and newer versions include support for Apple's Open Directory. Open Directory is a directory much like Microsoft's Active Directory and Novell's eDirectory. It allows all users to authenticate to a central database of users so a user has to authenticate only once to the Directory. From then on, the security settings stored in the Directory for that user dictate what parts of the network can be accessed and under which conditions.

## File and Print Services

The Mac OS can perform many functions on a network. In addition to being a client, a Macintosh can be a file and print server using AppleShare (Apple's proprietary networking software) as well as an Internet server using various Apple and third-party software. The advantage of having a Macintosh as a server is that it is extremely easy to administer. It is so easy, in fact, that many first-time users have no problems networking Macs and making them into file (or other) servers. Also, in small companies where there isn't a budget for an IT staff or money for outsourced support, a Mac OS server can be managed by existing staff.

## Application Support

Mac OS X has a unique position as far as application support is concerned. It can run older Mac OS applications as well as those written specifically for Mac OS X. Plus, it can run some UNIX and X Window System applications, provided they support the Mac OS kernel.

The Mac OS X platform, because of its UNIX underpinnings, makes for a very reliable workgroup and small business server. Therefore, many application developers are making small business suite packages for Mac OS X Server. In addition, Mac OS X Server comes with the Apache web server and MySQL 4, a very powerful open source web platform for developing database-driven websites.

## Security

The Mac OS offers reliable security. Mac OS X has local user account security built in as part of the OS. Network security has also been taken into account. Many services that would be susceptible to a hack are turned off by default, so a Mac is more secure than other OSes right out of the box. Additionally, there are many third-party security products (including some that implement Kerberos security, which is the type used by Windows 2000) that can make the Mac OS extremely secure over the network.

---

### AppleShare IP: History

No discussion of Mac OS X Server would be complete without at least a brief discussion of AppleShare IP. AppleShare IP is basically the file and printer services of AppleShare (which traditionally ran over AppleTalk) configured to run over TCP/IP for cross-platform file sharing. It was released with AppleTalk version 5 and was developed as a response to the networking and computer industries' move toward TCP/IP as the standard networking protocol and away from NOS-specific protocols like IPX/SPX and AppleTalk. AppleShare IP has been upgraded several times and has now been incorporated into Mac OS X Server

---

# Summary

In this chapter, you learned about the various client- and server-related topics for four main network operating systems: Windows, NetWare, UNIX, and the Mac OS. For each, you learned about client support, interoperability, authentication, file and print services, application support, and security.

First, you learned about Windows Server and its prevalent use as an application server platform. You learned of its extreme ease of administration and shallow learning curve. Next, you learned about Novell NetWare and its former dominance in the networking market. You learned of its flexibility in client support, ease of administration (using eDirectory), and scalability. Then you learned that UNIX (and Linux) has great power but more complex administration. You also learned of its different flavors and their main applications. Finally, you learned about the Mac OS X and its ease of use as well as its presence in the networking arena. Although it is easy to use, the enterprise has not yet adopted it as a standard client platform.

# Exam Essentials

**Be able to describe the basic capabilities UNIX/Linux.**   UNIX/Linux is the NOS with the longest history. It consists of a core (called a kernel) and a user interface called a shell. Linux is an operating system based on UNIX and developed by Linus Torvalds that primarily runs on the Intel platform and is in widespread use. UNIX/Linux uses standard TCP/IP protocol for communications and network services. You can use multiple methods of authentication by simply installing different software packages.

**Be able to describe the basic capabilities of NetWare.**    NetWare is the most widespread NOS in use today. It was the first NOS to be used for PC LANs. It is popular with administrators of large networks. It has excellent client support for multiple client platforms. Additionally, it has software to interoperate with other computing platforms natively. NetWare 4.*x* and above uses NDS for authentication. NDS is a directory service that keeps track of all of the network entities and performs authentication for them. Although NetWare makes a great server platform, there aren't as many applications for NetWare as there are for Windows or other NOS platforms. However, it is the most secure NOS. Government agencies all use NetWare as their core NOS.

**Be able to describe the basic capabilities of Windows.**    Windows Server is the NOS with the most application support. It uses the same interface and, to some extent, the same software as the desktop Windows versions. It has limited client support but does support interoperability with other NOS platforms, like NetWare and UNIX. The most current version of Windows Server uses Kerberos and Active Directory for authentication. Kerberos is the method of authentication and Active Directory is the directory that holds the authentication information (like usernames, passwords, etc.). Windows Server uses folders and shares to provide file and print services to clients, thus making it easy to use. Windows main challenge is the amount of security problems it has, but these are overcome by keeping the NOS patched to the most current levels at all times.

**Be able to describe the basic capabilities of Macintosh.**    The Mac OS platform is the easiest platform to use. The newest version is based on a UNIX kernel, so essentially it is a UNIX server. In addition to Mac clients, a Mac server can support UNIX clients and Windows clients (through Samba). Authentication is handled through Kerberos (similar to UNIX and Windows Server) and Open Directory. File and print services are handled through AppleShare and other open protocols and utilities (like FTP and HTTP). Mac OS has limited application support; it has the fewest native applications of any of the listed NOSes, but it can run some of the UNIX applications (although they may require recompiling).

# Review Questions

**1.** Which directory service is based mainly on the Internet directory standard X.500?

 **A.** NTDS

 **B.** NDS

 **C.** X.25

 **D.** IETF

**2.** Which of the following network operating systems has a graphical interface? (Choose all that apply.)

 **A.** UNIX

 **B.** NetWare 5

 **C.** NetWare 4

 **D.** Windows 2003 Server

**3.** Which client would you install on a Windows 98 machine to allow access to all features and services of a NetWare server?

 **A.** Microsoft Client for NetWare Networks

 **B.** Novell Client for Windows

 **C.** Microsoft Client for Microsoft Networks

 **D.** Novell Client for NetWare Networks

**4.** On a Windows Server network with a few NetWare 4 servers, which Windows XP clients would you install on a workstation to allow a user to access the greatest number of network services? (Choose all that apply.)

 **A.** Microsoft Client for NetWare Networks

 **B.** Novell Client for Windows

 **C.** Microsoft Client for Microsoft Networks

 **D.** Novell Client for NetWare Networks

**5.** What is the name of the authentication technology for Windows Server?

 **A.** NDS

 **B.** Kerberos

 **C.** Active Directory

 **D.** NT Domain Manager (NTDM)

**6.** What utility allows an administrator to modify NDS objects and their properties?

   **A.** User Manager

   **B.** syscon

   **C.** NetWare Administrator

   **D.** nwconfig

**7.** Of the following, which name is an example of a typefull distinguished name?

   **A.** .SERVER1.MKTG.ACME

   **B.** .CN=SERVER1.OU=MKTG.O=ACME

   **C.** CN=SERVER1.OU=MKTG.O=ACME

   **D.** SERVER1.MKTG.ACME

**8.** By default, on which directory service does Windows Server 2003 rely?

   **A.** NDS

   **B.** AD

   **C.** SCO

   **D.** NTDS

**9.** By default, which directory service is used by NetWare 4 and later?

   **A.** NDS

   **B.** AD

   **C.** SCO

   **D.** NTDS

**10.** Which of the following network operating systems can run on an Intel Pentium? (Choose all that apply.)

   **A.** NetWare

   **B.** Windows NT Server

   **C.** Linux

   **D.** Solaris

**11.** Which of the following is a typeless distinguished name?

   **A.** .SERVER1.MKTG.ACME

   **B.** .CN=SERVER1.OU=MKTG.O=ACME

   **C.** CN=SERVER1.OU=MKTG.O=ACME

   **D.** SERVER1.MKTG.ACME

12. The many flavors of UNIX can use which types of interfaces? (Choose all that apply.)

   **A.** Biometric

   **B.** Command line

   **C.** Graphical

   **D.** Psychic

13. What is the context of the object known as `.RogerU.Admin.ACME`?

   **A.** `RogerU`

   **B.** `Admin.ACME`

   **C.** `ACME`

   **D.** `RogerU.Admin.ACME`

14. On which platforms does NDS run natively? (Choose all that apply.)

   **A.** NetWare 3.*x*

   **B.** NetWare 4.*x*

   **C.** NetWare 5.*x*

   **D.** Netware 6.*x*

15. Which of the following is not a currently implemented operating system?

   **A.** Windows Server 2003

   **B.** Windows XP Server

   **C.** Windows XP Professional

   **D.** Mac OS X

16. Which software is included with Mac OS X Server (as well as available for many Linux versions) that allows Windows clients to connect to a Mac OS server?

   **A.** Windows for Macs

   **B.** MacDrive

   **C.** OSShare

   **D.** Samba

17. What is the name of the directory technology developed by Apple and used by Mac OS X?

   **A.** iDirectory

   **B.** eDirectory

   **C.** Kerberos

   **D.** Open Directory

**18.** The set of rules that dictate what types of objects can exist in a directory is known as a what?

    **A.** Law

    **B.** Schema

    **C.** Specification

    **D.** Directory code

**19.** Which distribution of Linux was designed specifically for the Intel platform and supports many of its features, including multiple (up to 16) processors?

    **A.** Red Hat

    **B.** Slackware

    **C.** OpenLinux

    **D.** Yggdrasil

**20.** The command-line interface to UNIX is known as a what?

    **A.** Linux

    **B.** Shell

    **C.** Window

    **D.** NIC

# Answers to Review Questions

1.  B. The only two options listed that are directory services are NTDS and NDS. Of those two, the only one that is an X.500-compliant directory service is NDS.

2.  A, B, D. All of the NOSes listed, except NetWare 4, have a graphical interface. UNIX has X Window, NetWare 5 has the Graphical Java Console, and Windows Server uses a Windows-based interface.

3.  B. Novell Client for Windows is Novell's NetWare client for the Windows platform, including Windows 98. It enables a Windows 98 machine to access the full range of NetWare (and NDS) services.

4.  B, C. Novell Client for Windows (as previously mentioned) and Microsoft Client for Microsoft Networks will allow the station to access Windows servers.

5.  B. Windows Server uses Active Directory to store the names of users and groups, but it uses Kerberos during the authentication process to verify the authenticity of those users.

6.  C. Although all of the listed utilities are administration utilities of some type, the name of the administration program for modifying NDS objects in NetWare 4 and above is NetWare Administrator.

7.  B. Typefull distinguished names always have leading periods and call out the object types with their appropriate prefixes (`CN=`, `OU=`, etc.).

8.  B. Active Directory (AD) is the directory service used by default by Windows Server 2003.

9.  A. Novell Directory Services (NDS) is the default directory service used by NetWare 4 and later.

10.  A, B, C, D. All the operating systems listed are available in one form or another for the Intel platform.

11.  A. Typeless distinguished names still include the leading period, but without the object type identifiers (`CN=`, `OU=`, etc.).

12.  B, C. There are two main methods users can use to interact with UNIX: through a text-based command line and through a graphical interface.

13.  B. An object's context is the complete name of all the containers in which it resides, so `Admin.ACME` is the only correct response.

14.  B, C, D. The only platforms that NDS runs on natively are NetWare 4.*x*, 5.*x*, and 6.*x*. NDS will *not* run natively on NetWare 3.*x*.

15.  B. There is no such thing as Windows XP Server. Windows XP is a desktop operating system.

16.  D. Samba is the technology that allows Mac OS X Server to respond to Windows SMB network calls and will make a Mac appear as another Windows server.

17.  D. Apple's own directory, similar to NDS and Active Directory, is known as Open Directory.

**18.** B. The schema defines what types of objects can exist in a directory.

**19.** B. Although all of the listed distributions have ports to the Intel platform, the Slackware distribution was developed specifically for the Intel platform.

**20.** B. The main command-line interface in UNIX is known as a shell.

# Chapter 6

# Wired and Wireless Networks

---

**THE FOLLOWING NETWORK+ EXAM OBJECTIVES ARE COVERED IN THIS CHAPTER:**

✓ **1.7 Specify the general characteristics (for example, carrier speed, frequency, transmission type, and topology) of the following wireless technologies:**

- 802.11 (frequency hopping spread spectrum), 802.11x (direct sequence spread spectrum)
- Infrared
- Bluetooth

✓ **1.8 Identify factors which affect the range and speed of wireless service (for example, interference, antenna type, and environmental factors).**

✓ **3.3 Identify the appropriate tool for a given wiring task (for example, wire crimper, media tester/certifier, punchdown tool, or tone generator).**

This chapter brings you to the most important test of all: your ability to install new network hardware and software. The Network+ exam tests your knowledge of the basic network hardware components that you might install as well as how to successfully upgrade outdated hardware or software. In this chapter, we're going to examine what you should consider before you upgrade, some common network components you might install, whether they should be wired or wireless, and how you connect them.

# Before Installing New Hardware or Software

Before you add a new hardware component to a network, upgrade the operating system, install a new application, or make any other such change, you need a clear picture of the current condition of the network. Additionally, you need to have an understanding of how a network behaves when it is functioning normally so that you will be able to tell when the network is malfunctioning. This includes an understanding of standard operating procedures and how they are being implemented and an awareness of any environmental issues that affect the way the network is set up. You also need to take a close look at error messages and log files, which will give you a lot of information about the health of the network, and be sure you are familiar with the current configuration and baselines. In addition, don't forget to review the manufacturers' documentation that you should have at hand. A 15-minute perusal of the documentation beforehand could save you hours of work later.

## Standard Operating Procedures

Standard operating procedures (SOPs) are part of company policy and typically cover everything from sick-day accrual to how the computer systems are used. In particular, network administrators need to be aware of company policies regarding the following:

- Internet access
- Printing
- Storage allocation
- E-mail usage
- User administration

Policies about these issues will be reflected in the network's naming conventions, protocol standards, and workstation configuration and will affect the location of network devices.

## Naming Conventions

Naming conventions specify how network entities are named within the guidelines of the network operating system being used. Each entity name must be unique on the network, including the names you give to the following:

- Servers
- Printers
- User accounts
- Group accounts
- Test and service accounts

### Naming Servers

In general, you name servers according to their location or function; sometimes it makes sense to use a combination. For example, a server located in Seattle might be named SEATTLE, or a server in the sales department might be named SALES. Or you might name a server that stores data DATA1, a server that stores applications APPS1, a server that stores a database DB1, and so on.

Another common practice is to name file servers FS followed by a number, such as FS1, FS2, FS3, and so on. Unfortunately, this naming convention doesn't provide the user with any information about what the server stores.

The most common naming convention in use today is a combination of location and function. Using this approach, you might specify that the first four characters of the name identify the server's location; the next two, the server's function; and the last two, the server's rank for that type of server. For example, the FRGOFS02 server is located in Fargo, it's a file server, and it is the second server of that type in Fargo.

### Naming Printers

As with server names, printer names are often derived from their function, location, or both. Naming a printer after its function or location makes the printer easier to locate for the users. If, for example, your dot-matrix printer is used to print multiple-part forms, you might name it Forms. If you have more than one forms printer, you might need to use two-word names, such as Forms-Ship or Forms-Finance. You might name high-quality printers Laser or Laser-Legal, indicating that this printer is always loaded with legal-size paper.

This is not intended to reflect a right or a wrong way to address naming conventions. There is only one right way for any organization—the method it follows.

## The X.500 Standard

As an aside, it may interest you to understand where the directory services that you use today come from. Novell Directory Services (NDS) and Active Directory (included with Windows 2000 Server) are modeled after a standard known as X.500. X.500 is a type of global phone book. The period (.) is the delimiter for NDS, Active Directory, and X.500 entries. Suppose, for example, a user's name is Bob. Bob works in the accounts department of the finance division at a company known as YourCo. His full address would be Bob.Accounts.Finance.YourCo.

In NDS and Active Directory, each name is known as an *object*. A graphical tree displays each object. Thus, it is efficient to begin at a higher level and administer policies to an entire network, for example, at YourCo. Furthermore, it is possible to drill down and work on a smaller unit level. Additional policy information can be applied to the Finance level.

Using periods as the delimiter, NDS and Active Directory look similar to DNS, or the Domain Name Service.

DNS is an Internet standard. This standard is like NDS in that it is based on X.500 and the period is used as a delimiter. But it's time to put one misconception to rest here and now: Not all Internet addresses need www. Try http://research.Microsoft.com to prove this to yourself.

Another point needs to be made about DNS entries. All URLs don't end with .com, .org, or .edu. *Country codes* are common final entries in a *URL*. Here are some of them:

- .tw (Taiwan)
- .tz (Tanzania)
- .ua (Ukraine)
- .ug (Uganda)
- .uk (United Kingdom)
- .um (U.S. Minor Outlying Islands)
- .us (United States of America)
- .uy (Uruguay)
- .uz (Uzbekistan)
- .va (Vatican City State)

As you use the Internet, NDS, and Active Directory, notice the commonalities between them. When you do, you will see how their common lineage ties them together.

### Naming User Accounts

Generally speaking, the simplest username is the user's first name. This method works well in a company with only a few users and fits the informality often found in a small office. It is fairly insecure, however, because hackers could easily guess a username. It also won't work in a larger organization that could easily include two people with the same first name.

The user-naming convention you use should allow for unique IDs and ensure that there are no duplicates. Larger firms typically use a first initial followed by part of or the entire last name. For example, Rebecca Messersmitt-Kazlowski would be RMessersmittKazlowski. This is still a long username and might even cause a problem with maximum character lengths allowed in some operating systems. In this example, Rmesser might be used as a short, yet unique, login name.

### Naming Groups

Groups are network entities that logically associate users by function. They are designed to make network administration easier: You can assign rights to a group of users all at once rather than to each individual. Because the group of users is organized by function, it would stand to reason that groups should be named by function. Additionally, the names should be short, fewer than 15 characters if possible. For example, if you have a group of users from the sales department that all use the same printer, you might name the group SALES_PRN. On the other hand, if you just want a general group for security and rights assignment purposes, you might name that group of users SALES.

 We'll discuss groups in detail in Chapter 8, "Network Access and Security."

### Naming Test and Service Accounts

When you install new services on the network, such as printers, applications, and so on, it is always a good idea to test their functionality first. It is not good practice to do this testing while logged in using an administrative account because administrative accounts usually have all-encompassing rights to the network. Thus, problems related to accessing the service are more likely to occur when an administrative account is not used for testing. It is better to use a user account that is equivalent to one who will be using the service. For this reason, it makes sense to create *test accounts* that you can use to test access to and the functionality of new services.

*Service accounts,* on the other hand, give outside network maintenance personnel the ability to perform administrator-level functions on your network. This is necessary whenever you must call in outside personnel.

The naming conventions document should also specify naming conventions for these accounts and define their security rights.

## Protocol Standards

You have already learned that protocols have different properties. If your firm has nothing but NetWare servers that are either version 3.*x* or 4.*x*, using Internet Packet eXchange (IPX) as the standard protocol would make sense. Alternatively, suppose there is a small group called New Product Development. Because of the sensitive nature of this group's work and because data should not leave the department, a routable protocol might be forbidden. In this case, NetBIOS Enhanced User Interface (NetBEUI) would be a wise choice because it cannot be routed and serves a small group without much maintenance. Today, because of its prevalence and to reduce training and operational expenses, a great number of companies are standardizing on Transmission Control Protocol/Internet Protocol (TCP/IP).

Regardless of the protocol you choose, you must obtain all network addresses before installing or upgrading a network device. This brings its own set of considerations. As you saw in Chapter 4, "TCP/IP Utilities," using TCP/IP as an example, each IP address must be unique, and just guessing at one is bound to create havoc. Clearly, you need a well-documented IP address and associated parameters, such as where the IP address comes from. Your SOPs should specify how network addresses are to be formatted and distributed.

## Workstation Configuration

A standardized workstation configuration serves a company well for a couple of reasons:

- You can narrow the scope of problems at a client station.
- You can more easily troubleshoot if everyone uses the same operating system, network client, and productivity software.

This is not to say that everyone in the office has to have the exact same software. The engineering group would most likely need a computer-aided design (CAD) program, along with the appropriate horsepower and RAM. Giving everyone in the company a CAD program, however, would waste resources, and it would be difficult for the accounting department to use a CAD program to create a paycheck for each employee. Therefore, a standard for workstation configuration is usually mandated by a group's function. However, once an application is chosen, only that application (preferably the same version) should be used by anyone who requires access to that type of program. Which applications and which versions of each application can be used on the network should be documented in your SOPs.

 Some network management applications simplify the process of distributing unique applications to those users who need them while maintaining the same basic workstation software configuration. Examples of these include Microsoft's Systems Management Server (SMS) and Novell's ZENworks.

It is also important to define minimum workstation hardware standards. Typically, the minimum requirement is one or two generations behind what is considered the hottest, fastest new system. A standards document might specify the following:

- Type, brand, and speed of CPU
- Minimum RAM
- Minimum hard-disk size
- Type and brand of NIC
- Minimum monitor size (14″, 15″, or 17″)

## Network Device Placement

The network SOP may also specify where network devices are to be placed. Many of these specifications relate to safety—for example, where cables are to be run and where to place network devices so that they are immune to sources of extreme heat or cold. Also, critical network components (such as servers and routers) should be placed in a room away from "busy fingers."

You should also consider the needs of users when you are deciding where to place network devices. For example, although placing a printer in the middle of the office might seem logical, it probably makes more sense to place it near the employees who use it the most.

---

 **Real World Scenario**

### Network Documentation

I don't know how many times I've gone into a place and asked where their documentation was only to be met with a blank stare. I was recently at a small business that was experiencing network problems. The first question I had was, "Do you have any kind of network documentation?" I got the blank stare. So, we proceeded to search through lots of receipts and other paperwork to try to work out the network layout and figure out exactly what was on the network. As it turns out, they had recently bought a wireless access point and it was having trouble connecting, which was causing the aforementioned problems. However, to solve the problem, I had to take two hours to answer a fairly simple question that would have taken five minutes had the network documentation been readily available.

Documentation doesn't have to be anything fancy; it can start with a three-ring binder filled with a simple network map, any receipts for network equipment, and a stack of loose-leaf paper to record services, changes, network addressing assignments, and so on. Just this little bit of documentation can save the owner lots of steps, especially in the critical first few months of a new network install.

---

# Environmental Issues

Environmental conditions, as they relate to installing or upgrading a network and its components, are important. Just like human beings, computers require a proper environment in order to function correctly. If the environment is harsh, the device will not function at peak efficiency. Surprisingly, environmental conditions and their consequences may be the most overlooked topic in the entire industry of networking. Often problems that seem to appear out of nowhere and appear to make no sense are caused by environmental conditions. Let's examine the frequently elusive challenges that we all face at one time or another:

- Power problems
- ESD problems

- EMI problems
- RFI problems
- Climate problems

## Power Problems

Alternating current (AC), which is "food" to PCs and other network devices, is normally 110 volts and changes polarity 60 times a second (or 60 Hertz). These values are referred to as *line voltage*. Any deviation from these values can create problems for a PC or other network device. Power problems fall into three categories:

- Overage
- Underage
- Quality

### Power Overage Problems

During a power overage, too much power is coming into the computer. Power overage can take two forms:

- A *power spike* occurs when the power level rises above normal levels and then drops back to normal in less than one second.
- A *power surge* occurs when the power level rises above normal levels and stays there for more than one or two seconds.

**FIGURE 6.1**    Comparing a power spike and a power surge

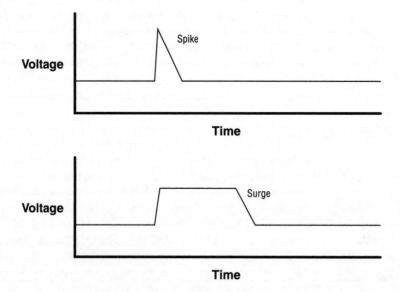

Typically, power surges last longer than a second or two, and they may last for several minutes. For this reason, surges are usually more damaging than spikes (although a very large spike can damage a computer's power supply just as much as a surge). Figure 6.1 shows the difference between a spike and a surge.

Two types of devices are used to protect computers and other network devices from power overage problems:

- Surge protectors
- Line conditioners

A *surge protector* contains a special electronic circuit that monitors the incoming voltage level and trips a circuit breaker when the overvoltage reaches a certain level (called the *overvoltage threshold*). The problem with surge protectors is that the threshold is set too high to be safe. By the time the circuit breaker trips, some overvoltage has gotten to the power supply of the computer, possibly damaging it. Nor does a surge protector protect against power surges and spikes that are lower than the threshold. For the most part, a surge protector is better than nothing, but not by much. It is really only a multiple-outlet strip and should not be considered anything more.

Surge protectors with a very low overvoltage threshold cost upward of $50. They sacrifice themselves in the event of any significant overvoltage but are smart enough not to trip for just a small amount over the standard power levels. Additionally, most of these protectors contain electronic circuits that can "shave off" any overvoltage and ensure that the powered devices receive only the voltage they need.

*Line conditioners* are a much better choice for protecting against surges and spikes. Line conditioners use several electronic methods to "clean" all power coming into them. The best models can be prohibitively expensive, but there is a way to get a kind of "natural" line conditioner. An *Uninterruptible Power Supply (UPS)* uses a battery and power inverter to run the computer equipment that plugs into it. A battery charger continuously charges the battery. The battery charger is the only thing that runs off line voltage. The computer itself runs off steady voltage supplied by the UPS. When power problems occur, the battery charger stops operating and the equipment continues to run off the battery. The power coming from the UPS is always a continuous 110 volts, 60 Hertz. Because the AC power from the wall never crosses over the battery charger to run the computer components, it's considered a "natural" line conditioner. As you will see, the UPS is the solution for a number of power problems.

## Power Underage Problems

Power underages occur when power levels drop below the standard, and they are almost as common as power overages. There are three types of power underages:

- A *sag* is an inverted spike. Sags occur when power levels drop below normal and rise back to normal within a brief period of time (usually less than one second). It is doubtful that you would be aware of sags (you might see a light flicker off and then on), although your computer might reboot.

- A *brownout,* on the other hand, occurs when power drops below normal levels for several seconds or longer. In other words, a brownout is an inverted surge. The lights in the room will dim for a short period of time and then come back to full brightness.

- A *blackout* is a total loss of power for several seconds, several minutes, or several hours.

Any one of these problems will cause your computers and other network devices to malfunction. Figure 6.2 contrasts these power problems.

To ward off power underage problems, you need only one device: a UPS, which allows network devices to continue to function even in the complete absence of power. Some are intelligent and can shut down your computer in the case of a blackout.

**FIGURE 6.2**    Comparing power underage problems

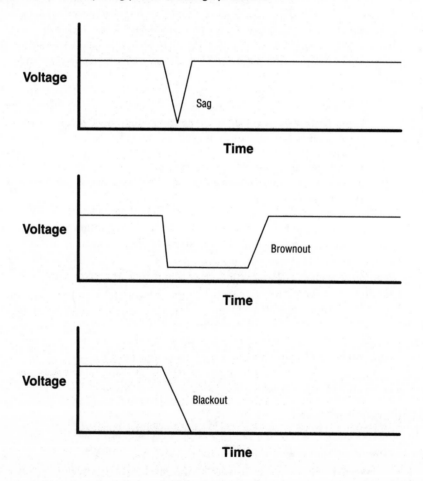

### Power Quality Problems

Power quality problems generally indicate that stray frequencies have entered the power supply through the power cord. Stray frequencies can cause strange problems (such as intermittent reboots or hangs) and can damage a device's power supply. You can detect problems in power quality only with an oscilloscope. If you're having power quality problems, you need either a UPS or a line conditioner.

## Electrostatic Discharge (ESD) Problems

ESD occurs when two items with dissimilar static electrical charges are brought together. Nature doesn't like things to be unequal, so static electrical charges will "jump" from the item with more electrons. This jump is seen as an electrical spark and thus is called an electrostatic discharge. ESD can damage electronic components because the several thousand electrons moving through delicate circuit junctions of silicon chips render the chips useless.

Static can be damaging to equipment and uncomfortable for users at the same time. For example, one worker had the habit of walking around the office without shoes. Walking across a nylon carpet in cotton socks created an immense static charge. When he got within 15 centimeters (not a typo) of the keyboard, the static charge jumped from his fingers to the keyboard. This not only caused him considerable pain, but it also burned out one of the horizontal scan rows on the keyboard, destroying it forever. Fortunately, the computer was properly grounded; otherwise, much more damage could have been done.

 Properly grounding equipment can prevent static, as can maintaining room humidity in the 40–60 percent range.

## Electromagnetic Interference (EMI) Problems

EMI occurs when magnetic fields intersect network or computer cables, causing interference in the cables. Motors and transformers, which are ubiquitous in an office (in air conditioners, heaters, and so on), are a typical source of EMI. A common mistake is to run network cable through an elevator shaft or through a ceiling that hides a bank of transformers in fluorescent lights.

Finding the source of EMI can be a challenge. The best approach is to follow a cable with an inexpensive compass, noting strong, odd needle movement. When you find the source of the EMI, you can protect the cable against it by either replacing the cable with a shielded cable (or fiber-optic cable, which is immune to both EMI and RFI) or by moving the cable far away from the source of the EMI.

## Radio Frequency Interference (RFI) Problems

RFI occurs when radio signals interfere with the normal operation of electronic circuits (computers in particular). Everyday sources of RFI include television and radio transmitters, which by nature create a specific radio frequency as part of the transmission process. Other sources are two-way radios and cellular phones.

The only way to protect against both EMI and RFI is to use shielded network cables. Shielded cable, as used in shielded twisted-pair (STP) and coaxial cable, can reduce the effects of RFI. You could also use fiber-optic cable, which is immune to EMI and RFI, throughout your entire network, although this option can get a little pricey.

 **Real World Scenario**

### "Let's Be Careful Out There!"

In one of the strangest cases of RFI I have ever seen, a server was resetting almost every night, right about 3 AM, while doing a tape backup. Changing the tape drive, the power supply, and other components were of no avail. The log files showed that the tape drive was operating normally and that the server would simply go down and restart, returning to normal operation.

Frustrated with dead ends, an engineer was on-site at 3 AM to observe the failure. He noticed that a police patrol car was parked nearby, radioing in status reports. Separated only by a wall, the server didn't have a chance with 25 watts of VHF radio signal being transmitted from only a few meters away. The radio signal was resetting the server, and once the policeman was done filing reports, the RFI was gone and the server restarted.

## Climate Problems

Network devices (including computers and servers) are very sensitive to temperature extremes and can fail prematurely if subjected to them. The environment for network devices should be roughly the same as that for human beings. Keep the temperature consistently at 70 degrees Fahrenheit, and keep the relative humidity between 40 and 60 percent. Maintaining consistent temperature and humidity can be a challenge because every computer constantly generates heat. Larger companies usually place network equipment in a special room that is climate controlled.

 Even if your company can't provide a climate-controlled server room, you can do at least one thing to avoid climate problems: never put servers in a network closet without ventilation. It is better to put servers out in the open, locked to a desk, than to lock them up in an unventilated closet. Also, never put an electronic device of any kind directly in front of a heat source, such as a space heater. This can cause the components to fail prematurely because excessive heat can damage electronic components.

## Error Messages and Log Files

A careful perusal of error messages and log files can give you a good sense of the health of a network. This is important because you may not want to add a new network device to a network that is experiencing problems. Log files record every action that occurs on a computer. For example, a log file can contain a record of who logged in to the network when, from which machine, and at what time. Figure 6.3 shows a sample log file.

Each network operating system includes special tools for creating and maintaining log files. In Windows NT and later, for example, you use Event Viewer (as shown in Figure 6.3) to display System Logs, Security Logs, and Application Logs. NetWare tracks events in the `ABEND.LOG`, `SYS$LOG.ERR`, and `CONSOLE.LOG` files. In Chapter 10, "Network Troubleshooting," we'll look at log files and error messages in detail.

**FIGURE 6.3** A sample log file from the Windows NT Event Viewer

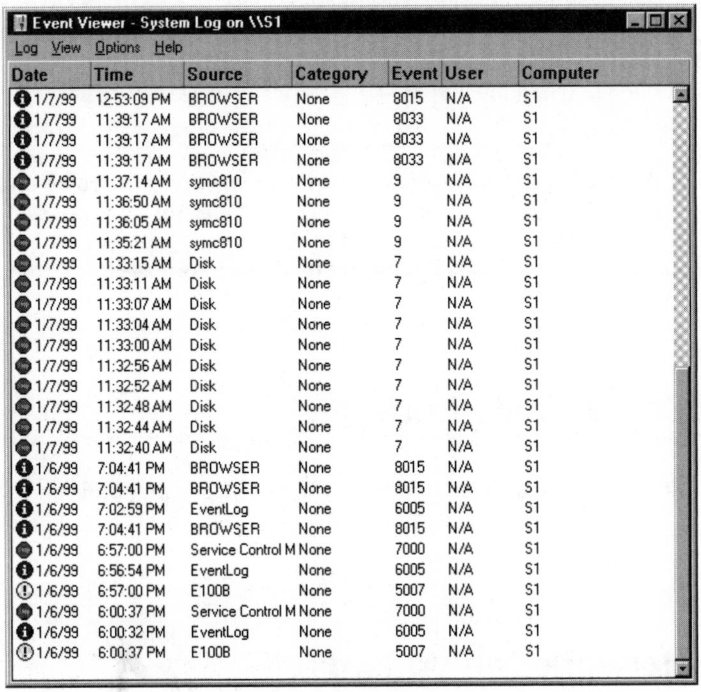


| Date | Time | Source | Category | Event | User | Computer |
|---|---|---|---|---|---|---|
| 1/7/99 | 12:53:09 PM | BROWSER | None | 8015 | N/A | S1 |
| 1/7/99 | 11:39:17 AM | BROWSER | None | 8033 | N/A | S1 |
| 1/7/99 | 11:39:17 AM | BROWSER | None | 8033 | N/A | S1 |
| 1/7/99 | 11:39:17 AM | BROWSER | None | 8033 | N/A | S1 |
| 1/7/99 | 11:37:14 AM | symc810 | None | 9 | N/A | S1 |
| 1/7/99 | 11:36:50 AM | symc810 | None | 9 | N/A | S1 |
| 1/7/99 | 11:36:05 AM | symc810 | None | 9 | N/A | S1 |
| 1/7/99 | 11:35:21 AM | symc810 | None | 9 | N/A | S1 |
| 1/7/99 | 11:33:15 AM | Disk | None | 7 | N/A | S1 |
| 1/7/99 | 11:33:11 AM | Disk | None | 7 | N/A | S1 |
| 1/7/99 | 11:33:07 AM | Disk | None | 7 | N/A | S1 |
| 1/7/99 | 11:33:04 AM | Disk | None | 7 | N/A | S1 |
| 1/7/99 | 11:33:00 AM | Disk | None | 7 | N/A | S1 |
| 1/7/99 | 11:32:56 AM | Disk | None | 7 | N/A | S1 |
| 1/7/99 | 11:32:52 AM | Disk | None | 7 | N/A | S1 |
| 1/7/99 | 11:32:48 AM | Disk | None | 7 | N/A | S1 |
| 1/7/99 | 11:32:44 AM | Disk | None | 7 | N/A | S1 |
| 1/7/99 | 11:32:40 AM | Disk | None | 7 | N/A | S1 |
| 1/6/99 | 7:04:41 PM | BROWSER | None | 8015 | N/A | S1 |
| 1/6/99 | 7:04:41 PM | BROWSER | None | 8015 | N/A | S1 |
| 1/6/99 | 7:02:59 PM | EventLog | None | 6005 | N/A | S1 |
| 1/6/99 | 7:04:41 PM | BROWSER | None | 8015 | N/A | S1 |
| 1/6/99 | 6:57:00 PM | Service Control M | None | 7000 | N/A | S1 |
| 1/6/99 | 6:56:54 PM | EventLog | None | 6005 | N/A | S1 |
| 1/6/99 | 6:57:00 PM | E100B | None | 5007 | N/A | S1 |
| 1/6/99 | 6:00:37 PM | Service Control M | None | 7000 | N/A | S1 |
| 1/6/99 | 6:00:32 PM | EventLog | None | 6005 | N/A | S1 |
| 1/6/99 | 6:00:37 PM | E100B | None | 5007 | N/A | S1 |

## Current Configuration and Baselines

Of particular value when you are upgrading a network or installing new hardware or software are the *server and client configuration* documents. If these have been properly maintained, they include information about the current hardware configuration (including I/O address, IRQ, DMA, and memory address), the installed software, any patches, and any special settings.

Configuration documentation should also include *cable maps* that indicate each network cable's source (workstation/server) and destination (typically, a port in a hub), as well as where each network cable runs. (We'll discuss cabling in detail in Chapter 10.)

*Baseline* documentation indicates how the network normally runs. It includes network traffic statistics, server utilization trends, and processor performance statistics. Baselines indicate how things currently are, not how they should be. Creating and maintaining these types of documents provides a valuable reference point should a client or server fail or malfunction after an upgrade.

## Other Documentation

You have at your disposal three more resources that can be of value before, during, and after upgrading or installing new hardware or software:

- README files
- The manufacturer's technical support CD-ROM
- The manufacturer's technical support website

We discuss all of these in detail in Chapter 10.

**NOTE** All three of these resources can come in handy when you are unable to get through to technical support phone numbers. But some people feel that talking with a human is worth the effort it sometimes takes. Be aware that this is not necessarily free. See Chapter 10 for more information.

# Wireless Networking

Wireless networks have become widespread and are found in both public and commercial settings. As a matter of fact, it is now possible to find wireless networks in many public spaces like coffee shops, malls, airports, and hotels. To that end, the entry level technician should know about the various wireless network components and their installation factors.

## Wireless Network Components

Wireless networks are a little less complex than their wired counterparts. They require fewer components to operate properly. There are two main devices that can be found in a small wireless network: a wireless access point and a wireless NIC. In order to understand proper wireless network installation, you should understand the basics of these two components.

### Wireless Access Points (WAPs)

For a majority of wired networks, there is a central component, like a hub or a switch, that connects the nodes together and allows them to communicate. Wireless networks are similar in that they have a component that connects all wireless devices together. That device is known as a *wireless access point (WAP)*. Its function is to operate as a hub of sorts for the wireless devices. It has at least one antenna (sometimes two for better reception) and a port to connect the wireless AP to a wired network. Figure 6.4 shows an example of a wireless access point.

**FIGURE 6.4**    A wireless access point

One way of thinking of a WAP is as a bridge between the wireless clients and the wired network. In fact, an WAP can be used as a wireless bridge (depending on the settings) to bridge two wired network segments together.

In addition to the stand-alone WAP, there is a WAP that includes a built-in router that can be used to connect both wired and wireless clients to the Internet. This device is usually known as a wireless router. Wireless routers usually act as Network Address Translation (NAT) servers by using the one ISP-provided global IP address to multiplex multiple local IP addresses (often handed out to inside clients by the wireless router from a pool in the 192.168.x.x range). Therefore, the subscriber need not change their service with the ISP in order to increase the number of devices that can simultaneously access the Internet.

## Wireless NIC

Every station that wants to connect to a wireless network will need a *wireless network interface card (NIC)*. In most respects, a wireless NIC does the same job as a traditional NIC, but instead of having a socket to plug some cable into, the wireless NIC will have a radio antenna. In addition to the different types of wireless networking (discussed in the next section), wireless NICs (like other NICs) can also differ in which type of connection they use to connect to the host computer. Figure 6.5 shows an example of a wireless NIC.

**FIGURE 6.5** A wireless NIC

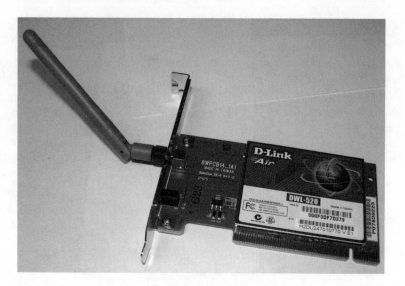

There are wireless adapters that are not NICs. For example, Linksys makes an external USB wireless adapter for notebooks. It is not a NIC because it isn't an expansion card (the *C* in NIC), so they are generally referred to as "adapters." Additionally, NICs also come in the form of PC cards, generally for laptops, not just conventional expansion cards.

## Wireless Antenna Characteristics

Wireless antennas act as both transmitters and receivers. There are two broad classes of antennas on the market, *omni directional* (*Omni*, or point-to-multipoint) and *directional* (*Yagi* or point-to-point). As a general rule, Yagi antennas have greater range than Omni antennas of equivalent gain because Yagis focus all their power in a single direction whereas Omnis must disperse the same power in all directions at once. The drawback of using a directional antenna, though, is that more care must be taken to align communication points, generally making Yagi a good choice only for point-to-point bridging of access points. Most WAPs use Omnis because clients and other APs could be in any direction at any given moment. A non-networking example of an Omni antenna is the FM antenna on your automobile. The orientation of your car does not affect the reception of the signal. The television aerials that some of us are old enough to remember rotating into a specific direction for a certain channel (how many of you labeled your set-top antenna dial for the actual TV stations you could receive?) are examples of Yagi antennas.

Omnis and Yagis are both rated according to their signal gain with respect to an actual or theoretical laboratory reference antenna. These ratings are relative indicators of the corresponding production antenna's range. Range is also affected by the bit rate of the underlying technology, with higher bit rates extending shorter distances. Remember, a Yagi will always have a longer range than an equivalently rated Omni, but the straight-line Yagi will be limited in coverage area.

Manufacturers rate these antennas in units of decibel isotropic (dBi) or decibel dipole (dBd), based on the type of reference antenna (isotropic or dipole) of equivalent frequency operation used to rate the production antenna. A positive value for either unit of measure represents a gain in signal strength with respect to the reference antenna. *Webster's* defines *isotropic* as "exhibiting properties (as velocity of light transmission) with the same values when measured along axes in all directions." Isotropic antennas are not able to be produced in reality, but their properties can be engineered from antenna theory for reference purposes.

As a practical example, consider Cisco Systems's series of Aironet Access Point (indoor) and Bridge (outdoor) antennas. Table 6.1 illustrates the effect gain ratings and attempted bit rates have on range limitations.

**TABLE 6.1**    Wireless Antenna Types and Ranges

| Model | Gain | Indoor Range at 1Mbps | Indoor Range at 11Mbps | Outdoor Range at 2Mbps | Outdoor Range at 11Mbps |
|---|---|---|---|---|---|
| AIR-ANT2410Y-R | 10dBi | 800ft | 230ft | Not Specified | Not Specified |
| AIR-ANT1728 | 5.2dBi | 497ft | 142ft | Not Specified | Not Specified |
| AIR-ANT4941 | 2.2dBi | 350ft | 130ft | Not Specified | Not Specified |
| AIR-ANT2506 | 5.2dBi | Not Specified | Not Specified | 5000ft | 1580ft |
| AIR-ANT24120 | 12dBi | Not Specified | Not Specified | 24,288ft | 7392ft |

The rule of thumb is that antennas operating with frequencies below 1GHz are measured in dBd while those operating above 1GHz are measured in dBi. As this is not always the case, you may find the need to compare the strength of one antenna, measured in dBd, with another, measured in numerically equivalent dBi, in order to determine which is stronger. That's why it's important to know that a particular numerical magnitude of dBd is more powerful than the same numerical magnitude of dBi. The good news is that the relationship between the two is linear, making the conversion quite simple. At the same operating frequency, a dipole antenna has about 2.2dB gain over a 0dBi theoretical isotropic antenna. Therefore, you can easily convert from dBd to dBi by adding 2.2 to the dBd rating. Conversely, subtract 2.2 from the dBi rating to produce the equivalent dBd rating.

Taking into account what you've learned about the difference between Omni and Yagi antennas and the difference between dBd and dBi gain ratings, you should be able to compare the relative range of transmission of one antenna with respect to another based on a combination of these characteristics. By way of example, the following four antenna ratings are given in relative order from greatest to least range:

7dBd Yagi (equivalent to a 9.2dBi Yagi)

7dBi Yagi (longer range than 7dBi Omni)

4.8dBd Omni (equivalent to a 7dBi Omni)

4.8dBi Omni (equivalent to a 2.6dBd Omni)

# Wireless Network Installation

Now that you understand the basic components involved in a wireless network, it's time to learn about their actual installation. Although we've stated earlier that wireless networks contain fewer components and are less complex, there are several major factors that figure into a wireless network installation:

- Wireless LAN standards

- Installation type

- Signal degradation (Site Survey)

## Wireless LAN Standards

Although wireless LANs have been around for only a relatively short time (in networking terms), there are many standards that have been ratified that deal with them. The majority of the technology in use today for wireless LANs is based on the IEEE 802.11 series of standards, although a slightly misaligned niche market exists for infrared and Bluetooth networking as well. More suited to LAN networking than infrared, Bluetooth, and the original 802.11 standard, the three most commonly used 802.11 standards today are as follows:

- IEEE 802.11a

- IEEE 802.11b

- IEEE 802.11g

All three of these wireless versions are technically subgroups of the 802.11 working group. Even though they are in the same group, they are fundamentally different, as you will see.

### Infrared Networking

One type of wireless networking that doesn't receive much attention is infrared wireless. Infrared wireless uses the same basic transmission method as many television remote controls, infrared technology. Infrared is used primarily for short distance, point-to-point communications, like those between a peripheral and a PC. The largest use of infrared wireless is for peripherals using the IrDA standard.

A little-known fact about infrared is that the original IEEE 802.11 wireless standard specified a somewhat limited baseband infrared medium in addition to the more common *Direct Sequence Spread Spectrum (DSSS)* and *Frequency Hopping Spread Spectrum (FHSS)* modulation techniques.

IrDA stands for Infrared Data Association, which is the standards body that develops the IrDA standard for point-to-point, peer-to-peer communications over infrared radiation. Infrared equipment that uses the IrDA standard can be found in many places, including cell phones, handheld PDAs and computers, keyboards, and so on.

The standard specifies a data transmission rate of 16Mbps (that will soon be increased to over 100Mbps with updates to the standard) and a maximum range of about 1 meter (1m). As you can see, although it possesses significant throughput, the range is lacking for a wireless LAN standard for large LANs.

## Bluetooth Networking

One of the newest wireless standards is the wireless networking standard known as Bluetooth. It was designed to replace the myriad cords on an average computer user's desk. Cords for things like keyboards, mice, and headphones can all be eliminated. The standard allows for these many different types of peripherals to all be able to communicate wirelessly with a host device, like a computer. For example, a popular Bluetooth accessory is the wireless headset for cellular phones. It's battery powered and will communicate directly with the phone wirelessly.

Bluetooth has a total maximum throughput of 1Mbps. It isn't a speed demon as far as throughput is concerned, but it is still more than enough for peripheral communications like mice, keyboards, and headphones, and it is possible for two Bluetooth devices to network to each other in a peer-to-peer fashion. But, as with infrared, it is impractical to build an entire multistation wireless LAN using the Bluetooth technology.

## 802.11

The original 802.11 standard specified a somewhat impractical recommendation, in terms of data rates, with regard to the bandwidth-hungry mentality of its contemporary LANs. In 1997, IEEE specified what is now referred to as 802.11-1997, a wireless LAN standard with a bandwidth of 2Mbps (with the ability to fall back to 1Mbps in noisy environments) when using DSSS modulation and a bandwidth of 1Mbps when using FHSS modulation. Even when using FHSS, the standard allows for possible 2Mbps operation in environments in which the noise level is below an acceptable threshold. Both the DSSS and FHSS methods operate in the unlicensed 2.4GHz frequency range. 802.11-1997 has since been updated by 802.11-1999, the supplements to which have given rise to the newer, more common standards of 802.11a, 802.11b, and 802.11g.

## 802.11a

The IEEE 802.11a standard is an extension to the IEEE 802.11 standard that specifies a wireless radio frequency LAN technology that provides for up to 54Mbps of available throughput.It uses the 5GHz radio frequencies (regulated) and OFDM for data encoding. It has a maximum range of 250ft (76m) indoors and approximately 1000ft (305m) outdoors.

## Wireless LAN Modulation Techniques

While a complete discussion of the technical workings of the wireless modulation techniques is beyond the scope of the objectives of the Network + exam and of this Study Guide, it is still important that you are aware of the mating of these techniques with their corresponding 802.11 standards.

### DSSS

DSSS is one of the modulation techniques specified by the original IEEE 802.11 standard and the one chosen for use in the widely accepted IEEE 802.11b standard. IEEE 802.11 uses Differential Binary Phase Shift Keying (DBPSK) for 1Mbps DSSS and Differential Quadrature Phase Shift Keying (DQPSK) for 2Mbps DSSS. The DSSS defined in IEEE 802.11b uses the Complementary Code Keying (CCK) modulation technique, making 5.5Mbps and 11Mbps data rates. All three modulation schemes are compatible and can coexist by using 802.11-standardized rate-switching procedures. DSSS creates a redundant bit pattern for each bit that is transmitted, increasing DSSS's resistance to interference. The benefit is that if one or more bits in the bit pattern are damaged in transmission, the original data might be recoverable from the redundant bits.

### FHSS

Although it's the original modulation technique specified by the IEEE 802.11 standard, FHSS is not the modulation of choice for vendors or the 802.11 working group. As very few vendors support FHSS in 802.11 products, it seems DSSS has become the preferred modulation standard. Continued developments within 802.11 favor DSSS. FHSS modulates the data signal with a carrier signal that changes (hops) in a random yet predictable sequence of frequencies, over time These changes also occur over a wide frequency band. A spreading, or hopping, code determines the transmission frequencies. The receiver is set to the same code, allowing it to listen to the incoming signal at the right time and frequency to properly receive the signal. Manufacturers use 75 or more frequencies per transmission channel. The maximum dwell time, or time spent during a hop at a particular frequency, has been established by the FCC at 400ms.

### OFDM

802.11a uses *Orthogonal Frequency Division Multiplexing (OFDM),* with a system of 52 carriers (sometimes referred to as "subcarriers")modulated by BPSK or QPSK. OFDM's spread spectrum technique distributes the data over these 52 carriers, which are spaced apart at precise frequencies. This spacing helps prevent demodulators from seeing frequencies other than their own. OFDM is resistant to RF interference, exhibiting lower multipath distortion. For more information on OFDM, check out the OFDM Forum's website at www.ofdm-forum.com.

The IEEE 802.11a standard was released at approximately the same time as 802.11b. However, 802.11b received more attention because 802.11a equipment was released approximately two years after the introduction of the 802.11b equipment and because of 802.11b's lower equipment cost. Plus, 802.11a has shorter range due to its higher frequency (higher frequencies attenuate sooner), and also due to the higher frequency, its signal is interfered with more easily.

But, on the plus side, because it uses regulated frequencies, there is less chance of standard devices like microwaves and such interfering with the wireless signal.

## 802.11b

The IEEE 802.11b standard has been given credit for the explosion of wireless networking. The equipment is cheap (and getting cheaper) and provides for decent network access speeds. It's easy to set up and use and is readily available. 802.11a and 802.11b were created at approximately the same time, but the 11b standard got the spotlight as the preferred LAN standard (primarily because of cost and the late introduction of 11a equipment).

The IEEE 802.11b standard specifies a wireless radio frequency LAN technology that provides for up to 11Mbps of available throughput. It uses the 2.4GHz radio frequencies (unregulated) and Direct Sequence Spread Spectrum (DSSS) for data encoding. It has a maximum range of 300ft (91m) indoors and about 1500ft (457m) outdoors.

 Even though they are subsets of the same standard, IEEE 802.11a and 802.11b are incompatible.

### So What Is Wi-Fi?

You may have seen products that are 802.11b compliant with a small sticker on them that says "Wi-Fi." You might be able to guess that this rather odd phrase stands for Wireless Fidelity, but you may not know what its implications are. Simply put, that sticker indicates that the product in question has passed certification testing for 802.11b interoperability by the Wi-Fi Alliance. This nonprofit group was formed to ensure that all 802.11b wireless devices would communicate seamlessly. So, Wi-Fi is a good thing.

## 802.11g

The most recent player in the 802.11 standards game is the IEEE 802.11g standard. It is kind of a "best of both worlds" standard. It includes the high data rate (54Mbps) of 802.11a with the stability and wide product base of 802.11b. Plus, it is backward compatible with 802.11b (alas, not so with 802.11a).

The IEEE 802.11g standard specifies a wireless radio frequency LAN technology that provides for up to 54Mbps of available throughput. It uses the 2.4GHz radio frequencies (unregulated) and both DSSS and OFDM for data encoding. It has a maximum range of 300ft (91m) indoors and about 1500ft (457m) outdoors

 It is important to note that most 802.11g devices are compatible with 802.11b devices. For example, a 802.11b NIC will work with an 802.11g access point (at the lower, 802.11b speed, of course) and vice versa.

Table 6.2 summarizes these IEEE 802.11 wireless LAN standards in comparison to Bluetooth, a possible interferer.

**TABLE 6.2**     Bluetooth and Wireless LAN Standards

| Standard | Max Throughput | Encoding Scheme | Frequency Band(s) | Typical Max Range (Indoors) | Typical Max Range (outdoors) |
|----------|---------------|-----------------|-------------------|----------------------------|------------------------------|
| Bluetooth | 1Mbps | FHSS | 2.4GHz | 328ft/100m | N/A |
| 802.11 | 1-2Mbps | FHSS/DSSS | 2.4GHz | 328ft/100m | 1500ft/457m |
| 802.11a | 54Mbps | OFDM | 5GHz | 250ft/76m | 1000ft/305m |
| 802.11b | 11Mbps | DSSS | 2.4GHz | 328ft/100m | 1500ft/457m |
| 802.11g | 54Mbps | OFDM/DSSS | 2.4GHz | 328ft/100m | 1500ft/457m |

# Installation Type

Let's say you just bought a wireless NIC for your laptop and a WAP. What can you do with them? Well, that all depends on the type of installation you are going to do with these devices. There are two major installation types: ad-hoc and infrastructure mode. Each 802.11 wireless network device is capable of being installed in one of these two modes.

## Ad-Hoc Mode

The simplest installation type for wireless 802.11 devices is ad-hoc mode. In this mode, the wireless NICs (or other devices) can communicate directly without the need for a WAP. A good example of this is two laptops with wireless NICs installed. If both cards were set up for ad-hoc mode, they could connect and transfer files (assuming the other network settings, such as protocols, were set up correctly).

To set up a basic ad-hoc wireless network, all you need are two wireless NICs and two computers. Install the cards into the computers according to the manufacturer's directions. During the installation of the software, you will be asked at some point if you want to set up the NIC in ad-hoc mode or infrastructure mode. For an ad-hoc network, choose the ad-hoc mode setting. Then bring the computers within range (90–100m) of each other. The computers will "see" each other and you will be able to connect to each other.

In order to transfer files, both computers will need to have security settings that will allow it.

Figure 6.6 shows an example of an ad-hoc wireless network. Note the absence of an access point.

**FIGURE  6.6**    A wireless network in ad-hoc mode

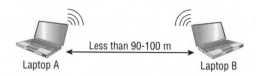

**Infrastructure Mode**

The most common use for wireless networking equipment is to provide the wireless equivalent of a wired network. To do this, all 802.11 wireless equipment has the ability to operate in what is known as infrastructure mode. In this mode, NICs will only communicate with an access point (instead of each other as in ad-hoc mode). The access point will facilitate communication between the wireless nodes as well as communication with a wired network (if present). In this mode, wireless clients appear to the rest of the network as standard, wired nodes.

Figure 6.7 shows a typical infrastructure mode wireless network. Note the access point and that it is connected to the wired network.

**FIGURE  6.7**    A wireless network in infrastructure mode

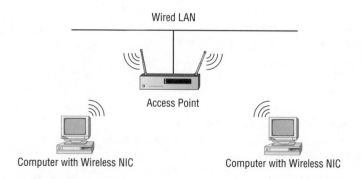

When configuring a client for wireless infrastructure mode, you need to understand a couple of basic wireless concepts: SSID and security. The SSID (short for Security Set Identifier) is the unique 32-character identifier that represents a particular wireless network. All devices participating in a particular wireless network must be configured with the same SSID. If a wireless network is to have more than one access point that provides access to the same wireless network, the access points must all have the exact same SSID.

Multiple access points with the same SSID spread over a large area allow a user to move around that area while maintaining a connection to the wireless network. This process is called *roaming*.

Because most access points are configured by default to broadcast their SSID so wireless clients can browse and find them, and because wireless signals can travel long distances (even outside of a building), security is extremely important on wireless LANs. To that end, most access points have one or more of the following security measures in place:

**WEP** Short for Wired Equivalent Privacy, this protocol, when enabled, requires that both access point and workstation are configured with the same 64-bit, 128-bit, 152-bit, or 256-bit encryption key in order to communicate. This key is manually configured by the network administrator and usually comprises a string of alphanumeric or hexadecimal characters.

You may also see WEP referred to as the Wired Equivalency Protocol, although that is not the original term for which the acronym was used.

**MAC List** Some WAPs are capable of restricting which clients can connect to the AP by keeping track of authorized MAC addresses. The administrator configures the AP with the list of all the MAC addresses of wireless NICs that are authorized to connect to that AP. If a NIC with a MAC address not on the AP's MAC list tries to connect, it will be rejected.

**Disabling SSID Broadcast** By default, WAPs broadcast their SSID to make it easier for clients to find them. For example, Windows XP has a built-in utility that allows users to browse for WAPs. However, you can turn this feature off. You then must configure each client with the SSID of the WAP that client will connect to.

---

 **Real World Scenario**

**War Driving**

Wireless networks are everywhere these days. Electronics retailers are selling wireless access points for less than $100 and they are flying off the shelves. You can find WAPs in public places like shopping malls, coffee shops, airports, and hotels. In some cities, you can walk in a downtown area and find WAPs in almost every business.

This proliferation of WAPs has led to a new hobby for the technologically savvy with time on their hands: war driving. This is the practice of driving around in a car with a laptop, a wireless NIC, and a high gain antenna to locate open WAPs (especially those with high-speed Internet access). There are various software programs that make this process easier (some even have Global Positioning System (GPS) interface software to make relocating the open access point again even easier). War drivers can be a threat because they can potentially access anything on your wireless LAN (and anything it's attached to). In addition, they are potentially consuming resources on your network. But, the threat is low in most cases. If you notice slow-moving vehicles outside your home or business (especially those with computer equipment inside), you might be the target of a war driver.

These features by themselves aren't completely secure, but using multiple wireless security features together will make a wireless LAN much more secure.

## Signal Degradation

Another factor to consider when installing a wireless network is signal degradation. Because the 802.11 wireless protocols use radio frequencies, the signal strength varies according to many factors. The weaker the signal, the less reliable the network connection will be, and thus the less usable as well. These factors are included in the following list:

**Distance**   This one should be fairly obvious. The farther away from the WAP you get, the weaker the signal. Most APs have a very limited maximum range (less than 100m for most systems). To some degree, this can be extended using amplifiers or repeaters or using different antennas.

**Walls**   The more walls a wireless signal has to pass through, the more attenuated (reduced) the signal becomes. Also, the thicker the wall, the more it interrupts the signal. In an indoor office area with lots of walls, the range of wireless could be a low as 25m.

**Protocols Used**   Another factor that determines the range of wireless LAN is the protocol used. The various wireless 802.11 protocols have different maximum ranges. As discussed earlier in Table 6.2, you can see that the maximum effective range varies with the 802.11 protocol used.

**Interference**   The final factor that affects wireless performance is outside interference. Since 802.11 wireless protocols operate in the 900 MHz, 2.4GHz, 5GHz range, interference can come from several sources, including other wireless devices, such as Bluetooth, cordless telephones, microwave ovens (a huge adversary of 802.11b and 802.11g), cell phones, other wireless LANs, and any other device that transmits radio frequency (RF) near the frequency bands that the 802.11 protocols use.

## Hardware Installation

The installation of 802.11 equipment is fairly simple. There are really two main types of components in 802.11 networks: WAPs and NICs. Wireless NIC installation is just like installing any other network card (which you will learn later in this chapter). But, once it's installed, you must connect to a WAP.

WAP installation is fairly simple as well. Take it out of the box, connect the antenna(e), if necessary, and power, and place the WAP where it can reach the most clients. This last part is probably the trickiest. You must place the WAP in such a way that it is servicing the most clients. This will involve a little common sense and a little trial and error. Knowing that walls obstruct the signal, wide open spaces are better indoors. Also, it should be placed away from sources of RF interference, so right near all the other office equipment is probably not the best place for an AP. You might have to move the AP around a bit to get the most signal strength for all the clients that need to use it.

Once you have the hardware installed, it is time to configure it properly.

## Hardware/Software Configuration

Now that you have both the AP and NIC installed, you must configure them to work together. This isn't as tricky as it sounds. Most wireless equipment is designed to work almost without configuration. The only things you need to configure are customization settings (name, network address, etc.) and security settings.

### NIC Configuration

Windows XP includes software to automatically configure a wireless connection and it installs this software automatically when you install a wireless NIC. The first time you reboot after the installation of the NIC, you will see a screen like the one shown in Figure 6.8. This is the Windows wireless configuration screen. From this screen, you can see any available wireless networks and configure how a computer connects to them. You can also configure several of the properties for how this wireless NIC connects to a particular wireless network:

**Use Windows to Configure My Wireless Settings**  This check box determines whether or not Windows XP will configure the wireless settings. When it's unchecked, Windows XP will need an external program to configure how it connects to a wireless network, as is the case with some wireless NICs that have their own software program for this purpose. It is usually best to let Windows XP manage your wireless settings.

**Available Networks**  This list shows of all the wireless networks within range. The networks are listed by their SSID. From this list, you can choose which network you wish to connect to, and you can configure how your workstation connects by clicking the Configure button. If you don't see the wireless network you are looking for, and you are in range, click the Refresh button.

**Preferred Networks**  This list details any wireless networks you have connected to before and want to connect to again automatically. If there is more than one wireless network in range, this list determines the order in which the workstation will try to connect to them. You can change this order using the Move Up and Move Down buttons.

In addition to the general configuration, you may have to configure the encryption for the connection (if the wireless connection you are using requires it). To set up how your workstation uses encryption for a particular connection, from the screen shown in Figure 6.8, click the SSID of the wireless network you want to configure, and then click Configure. You will then see the screen shown in Figure 6.9.

From this screen, you can configure several parameters for the specific connection:

**Network Name**  If for some reason the SSID of the WAP changes, you can change the name of the WAP you are connecting to in this field. Just delete the old one and type in the new name.

**Wireless Network Key (WEP)**  This section contains all the parameters for configuring encryption for this connection. If the network you are connecting to uses WEP encryption, this is the section where you will click the check boxes and configure how the wireless connection uses WEP, the key it uses, and what type of key it is. The following parameters are in this section:

**Data Encryption (WEP Enabled)**    If the network uses a key to encrypt data sent over the network, you should make sure this box is checked (it is checked by default). You will then need to specify the key in the box labeled Network Key. You will also need to specify what type of key it is (ASCII or hex) by selecting the appropriate item from the drop-down list.

**Network Authentication (Shared Mode)**    If your WAP uses shared mode authentication, you must check this box to ensure that your workstation will authenticate to the WAP using the shared key. Often, the key is provided automatically by the WAP during the response to the initial request. If this is the case, you must check the checkbox labeled The Key Is Provided for Me Automatically (the default). Otherwise, uncheck it and enter the key and related information in the appropriate boxes.

**This Computer Is a Computer-to-Computer (Ad Hoc) Network**    Check this check box if you are connecting to another computer instead of an access point.

Once you have changed any settings you need to, click OK to save the changes and finish the configuration.

**FIGURE   6.8**    Windows XP wireless configuration screen

**FIGURE 6.9**    Configuring encryption

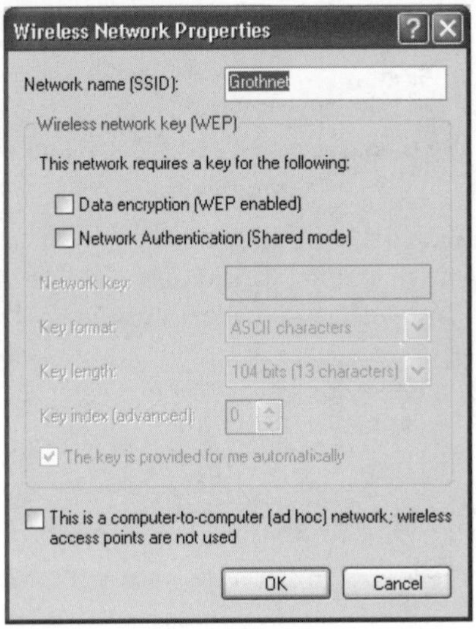

## WAP Configuration

In addition to configuring the workstation(s), you must configure the WAP. There are literally hundreds of different WAPs out there, and each uses a different method to configure its internal software. But, for the most part, they follow some general patterns.

First of all, out of the box, the WAP should come configured with an IP address (usually something similar to 192.168.1.1; check the documentation that comes with the AP to be sure). You can take the WAP out of its box, plug it into a power outlet, and connect it to your network. But, in order for it to work, you've got to configure its IP address scheme to match your network's. To do that, you've usually got to do a little sleight of hand. Start by configuring a workstation on the wired network with an IP address (192.168.1.2 or similar) and subnet mask on the same subnet as the WAP's. You should then be able to connect to the AP to begin the configuration progress. Usually this is done either with a web browser or with a manufacturer-supplied configuration program.

Once you have successfully connected to the WAP, you can configure its parameters. The following are a few parameters common to WAPs that must be configured at a minimum for the AP to work properly.

Some of these parameters may require a complete WAP restart once they've been changed and this can interrupt your connection to the WAP (it may even require you to completely change your IP address on your workstation).

**SSID**   As discussed earlier, this is the name of the wireless network that this AP will advertise. If this new WAP is to be part of an existing wireless network, it should be configured with the same SSID as the existing network. In a network with only one WAP, you can think of the SSID as the "name" of the AP.

 The SSID should not be confused with the WEP passphrase. See the discussion on WEP later in this section for details.

**WAP IP Addresses**   Even though most WAPs come preconfigured with an IP address, it may not match the wired network's IP addressing scheme. To that end, you should configure the WAP's IP addresses (including the address, subnet mask, and default gateway addresses) to match the wired network it is to be connected to.

**Operating Mode (Access Point or Bridge)**   Access points can operate in one of two main modes: *Access Point mode* or *Bridging mode*. Access Point mode allows the WAP to operate as a traditional access point to allow a wireless client transparent access to a wired network. On the other hand, two WAPs set to Bridging mode provide a wireless bridge between two wired network segments.

**Password**   Every access point has some kind of default password that is used to access the WAP's configuration. However, for security reasons, you should change this as soon as you are able to connect to and configure the WAP.

**Wireless Channel**   802.11 wireless networks can operate on different channels to avoid interference. Most wireless WAPs can be set to work on a particular channel from the factory, so for security reasons, you should change it as soon as you can.

**WEP**   This is not a requirement, per se, but enabling it is advisable. WEP security is one of those parameters that should be enabled as soon as you turn the WAP on. WEP allows data to be encrypted before being put over the wireless connection. Configuring WEP means enabling it and choosing a key to be used for the connections.

 You will likely be asked to enter one or more human-readable passphrases, which are considered to be *shared keys,* or secret passwords that are never sent over the wire. After entering each one, you will generally click a button to initiate a one-way hash to produce a WEP key of a size related to the number of bits of WEP encryption you choose. Entering the same passphrase on a wireless client causes the hash (not the passphrase) to be sent from the wireless client to the AP during a connection attempt. Most configuration utilities allow multiple keys to be generated in case the administrator is granting temporary access to the network and does not wish to divulge the primary passphrase. This key can be deleted after the temporary access is no longer needed without affecting access by primary LAN participants.

**Hotel Wireless**

For the last few years or so, I've been consulting with local hotels about the best way to offer in-room high-speed Internet. As you can well imagine, if your competitor is offering Internet, you'd better as well. Now most hotels in Fargo, ND can't afford to completely wire every room with Ethernet. With 100 rooms (on average) and an average cost of $105 per "drop," just the cabling installation could run into $10,000 easily.

I was able to help local hotels install wireless Internet in the main areas of the hotel and in a majority of the rooms for under $1,000. I simply installed an RF access point in the first floor and by using special antennas, could get signal reception in almost all of the rooms in the hotel. Now, they didn't all have the same signal level. The farther a guest was from the access point, the weaker the signal. And, there were some rooms that were too far away from the access point to get a useable signal. But considering the price difference, many hotels were able to take advantage of the features of wireless networking.

# Workstation Configuration

In addition to knowing how to configure a station's hardware, you must be able to configure a Windows workstation to connect to the different types of network operating systems (NOSes) that might be on your network. For the Network+ exam, you should be able to configure these workstations to connect to the following operating systems:

- Windows NT/2000 servers
- NetWare
- UNIX/Linux
- Macintosh

The process for configuring Windows to connect to these various operating systems is basically the same for all server OSes (only the workstation software component differs very slightly), so we'll just cover the two most popular client operating systems' network configurations.

## Configuring a Windows 9x Network

The configuration of a Windows 9x network centers on the Control Panel's Network program. From this one interface, you can configure client software, protocols, NICs, and the network services you want this machine to perform. To access the Network program, select Start ➤ Settings ➤ Control Panel and double-click Network in the Control Panel window that appears. Windows 9x will display the Network window. The Network window has three areas of interest: the Components list, the Primary Logon list, and the File and Printer Sharing button.

If you already have some networking components installed, you can simply right-click the Network Neighborhood icon on your Desktop and choose Properties from the pop-up menu.

## Networking Components

First, let's review the four basic types of networking components that can be added in the Network panel, as shown in Figure 6.10. This screen can be reached by clicking Add on the Configuration tab.

**FIGURE 6.10**    The Select Network Component Type window

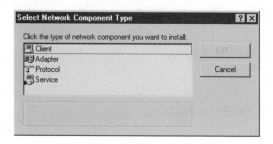

The networking components are as follows:

**Client**    As mentioned before, the client is software that allows your machine to talk to servers on the network. Each server vendor uses a different way of designing its network access. Therefore, if a computer needs to get to both a Novell and a Microsoft network, the computer must have two pieces of client software installed, one for each type of server. The three network client groups supported by Windows 9*x* are for Microsoft, Novell, and Banyan servers.

UNIX/Linux clients are also supported natively, but they use their own set of tools (e.g., Ping, nslookup, etc.) and don't require the installation of a client piece in this area.

**Adapter**    The *adapter* is, technically, the peripheral hardware that installs into your computer, but in this case, it refers to the software that defines how the computer talks to that hardware. If you do not have the proper adapter software installed, your PC will not be able to talk properly to the NIC, and you will not be able to access the network until you change the adapter to one that is compatible with the hardware. It is often best to think of an adapter as simply a network driver, which is what it really is. Many adapters are supported by Windows 95, and Windows 98 and the more recent versions support even more, with support for more recent hardware. Adapter drivers can also be downloaded from most NIC vendors' websites.

**Protocol**   Once the client service and the adapter are installed, you have cleared a path for communication from your machine to network servers. The *protocol* is the computer language that you use to facilitate communication between the machines. If you want to talk to other people, you have to speak their language. Computers are no different. Among the languages available to Windows 9x are NetBEUI, NWLink (IPX/SPX), and TCP/IP.

**Service**   A *service* is a component that gives a bit back to the network that gives it so much. Services add functionality to the network by providing resources or doing tasks for other computers. In Windows 9x, services include file and printer sharing for Microsoft or Novell networks.

### Installing Components

Let's suppose you want to connect to Microsoft servers on your network (including Windows XP, 2000 Server, 2000 Professional, Windows NT, or Windows 9x with sharing enabled). To connect to this network, you must have at least the following three components (services, the fourth component, are not required at this point):

- A client, such as Client for Microsoft Networks
- A protocol (whichever protocol is in use on the network; generally TCP/IP)
- An adapter (whatever is in the PC)

To install a client and protocol for use with your network adapter, follow these steps:

1. Click the Add button toward the bottom of the Network window. This will display the screen shown previously in Figure 6.10.

2. In this screen you can choose what type of item you are going to install. In this example, you're installing the Client for Microsoft Networks, so click Client and then click Add.

3. You will see a screen similar to the one in Figure 6.11. This screen is the standard "pick your component" screen that Windows 9x uses. On the left, select the company whose software (or driver) you want to install (in this example, Microsoft). When you have selected a manufacturer, a list of the software that Windows 9x can install from that company appears on the right.

4. Click Client for Microsoft Networks when it appears in the right pane, and then click OK. Windows 9x will bring you back to the Configuration tab of the Network program.

5. Once you have a client installed, you can verify that the protocol you need is present. TCP/IP generally installs by default, but this is not always so. If it is not present, click Add on the Configuration tab. In the Select Network Component Type window, select Microsoft in the Manufacturers list and TCP/IP in the Network Protocols list. Click OK to complete the installation.

 When it is first installed, TCP/IP is configured to expect that a special server, called a Dynamic Host Configuration Protocol (DHCP) server, is available on the network to provide it with information about the network. If a DHCP server is not available, the protocol will not function properly. Consult your administrator to see whether the network uses DHCP or static addressing. In static addressing, all TCP/IP settings must be manually added, and in this case, you will need additional information from the administrator.

The list of components should reflect your additions and show which network components are currently installed on this machine. If there are a number of components, a scroll bar appears on the right side of the screen. The scroll bar allows you to see all of the clients, network adapters, protocols, and services that might be installed. Once the client and protocol are installed, you will have all the software you need to connect to the network. At this point, just a few choices remain. Don't close that Network program yet!

**FIGURE 6.11** Selecting the software you want to install

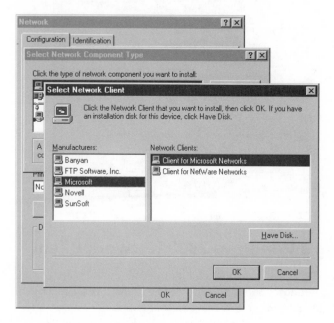

## Determining Your Primary Logon

A Windows 9x workstation can support multiple simultaneous network types. For example, a user can log in to both Novell and Microsoft networks, assuming that both network clients are installed and configured correctly. The Primary Network Logon drop-down list determines which network type you will log on to first. If you have not yet installed a network client, this list will only give you one option: Windows Logon.

We have already installed a Microsoft network client, so select the Client for Microsoft Networks as the primary logon, as displayed in Figure 6.12.

Once you have made this selection, click OK. The Network program will close, and you will be asked to restart the computer so that the new settings can take effect. (You may also be asked for the location of any files that Windows can't find, so you may have to insert your Windows CD.) Until you reboot, the network will not function. When the machine restarts, the network should be available.

**FIGURE 6.12** Choosing a primary network logon

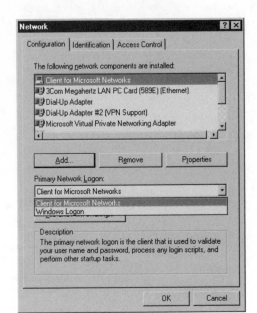

## Configuring a Windows 2000 Network Client

For the most part, the concepts behind configuring Windows 9x are the same as the concepts for configuring in Windows 2000. You still need a client, a protocol, and an adapter, for instance, but the difference is in how they are configured.

First, the Network program is now called Network and Dial-up Connections and is organized differently. When you first access the Network and Dial-up Connections window, you will see that, instead of a list of all components, you are greeted simply by a Make New Connection icon and a Local Area Connection icon, as shown in Figure 6.13.

If you do not see a local area connection, your NIC or your modem is either not present or not functioning properly. If you see more than one LAN connection, it means that you have multiple NICs installed. (Windows 2000 Server, for example, can support multiple NICs.)

To add client software and protocols, right-click the LAN connection and select Properties. You should find that everything you need is in place because the client and IP are installed by default on the LAN adapter.

**FIGURE 6.13**     The Network and Dial-up Connections window

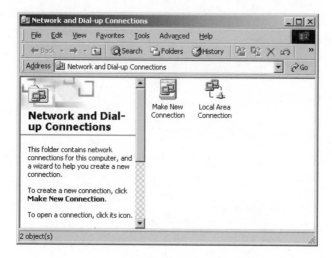

 File and Printer Sharing for Microsoft Networks is also installed by default. To disable it, clear the check mark next to the service. To remove it completely, click Uninstall.

You can also add additional clients, protocols, and services. Windows 2000 supports the same components that Windows 9x supports, plus some additions. (The only component not supported in 2000 that is in 9x is the Banyan client.) Once you have verified that the Client for Microsoft Networks and TPC/IP are installed, click OK. You should not have to reboot after making changes to the network settings in Windows 2000.

## Configuring Windows Clients for NetWare Network Access

Both Windows 9x and Windows 2000 handle the addition of a network client for NetWare in similar ways. Add (for Windows 9x) or install (for Windows 2000) the client, and the NetWare-compatible NWLink protocol will be automatically installed for you as well (Figure 6.14). Once you have these, you will be presented with a NetWare logon option screen on startup, where you can choose which NetWare server or tree you wish to log on to (Figure 6.15).

**FIGURE   6.14**   Network and Dial-up Connections with the NetWare client and NWLink installed

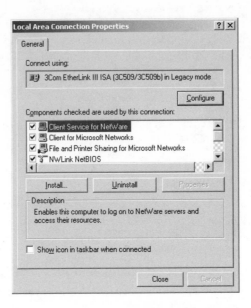

**FIGURE   6.15**   The NetWare default server/tree option screen

The tree is a group of machines that share security and configuration information. Both Novell's NDS and Microsoft's Active Directory use tree structures to store information and authenticate users. To access the NetWare tree more efficiently, frequent NetWare users should download the newest version of NetWare's own client software for 9x/2000. It is available at www.novell.com/download/.

# Network Installation Tools

When installing network components, oftentimes you will have to use some very specialized tools. These tools are used mainly in the telecommunications industry. In the following sections, you will learn about the most common network installation tools:

- Wire crimper
- Media tester (including copper and fiber-optic)
- Punchdown tool

## Wire Crimper

A *wire crimper* (or crimper as it is more commonly known) is a hand tool found in most network technicians' tool bags. Crimpers are primarily used for attaching ends onto different types of network cables by a process known as crimping. Crimping involves using pressure to press some kind of metal teeth into the inner conductors of a cable. An example of a crimper is shown in Figure 6.16.

Contrast this with punching down, which involves pushing the conductor into the metal teeth.

**FIGURE 6.16**    An example of a crimper

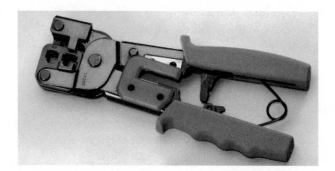

Many network technicians will make patch cables with a crimper. They will take a small piece of Category 5 UTP and crimp two RJ-45 ends on it to make the cable. There are crimpers for the other types of cable as well. There are even crimpers available for crimping on fiber-optic ends.

# Media Testing Tools

The best method for addressing a faulty cable installation is to avoid the problem in the first place by purchasing high-quality components and installing them carefully. But no matter how careful you are, problems are bound to arise. The following sections cover the tools that you can use to test cables both at the time of their installation and afterward, when you're troubleshooting cable problems. Cable testing tools can range from simple, inexpensive mechanical devices to elaborate electronic testers that automatically supply you with a litany of test results in an easy-to-read pass/fail format.

The following sections list the types of tools that are available for both copper and fiber-optic cable testing. This is not to say that you need all of the tools listed here. In fact, some of the following sections attempt to steer you away from certain types of tools. In some cases, there are both high-tech and low-tech devices available that perform roughly the same function, and you can choose which you prefer according to the requirements of your network, your operational budget, or your temperament. Some of the tools are extremely complicated and require extensive training to use effectively, while others are usable by anyone who can read.

You should select the types of tools you need based on the descriptions of cable tests given earlier in this chapter, the test results required by the standards that you're using to certify your network, and the capabilities of the people who will be doing the actual work—not to mention the amount of money you want to spend.

## Wire Map Testers

A wire map tester is a device that transmits signals through each wire in a copper twisted-pair cable to determine if it is connected to the correct pin at the other end. Wire mapping is the most basic test for twisted-pair cables because the eight separate wire connections involved in each cable run are a common source of installation errors. Wire map testers detect transposed wires, opens (broken or unconnected wires), and shorts (wires or pins improperly connected to each other)—all problems that can render a cable run inoperable.

Wire map testing is nearly always included in multifunction cable testers, but in some cases it may not be worth the expense to spend thousands of dollars on a comprehensive device. Dedicated wire map testers are relatively inexpensive (from $200 to $300) and enable you to test your installation for the most common faults that occur during installations and afterward. If you are installing voice-grade cable, for example, a simple wire mapping test may be all that's needed. There are also slightly more expensive (under $500) devices that do wire map testing in addition to other basic functions, such as TDR length testing.

A wire map tester consists of a remote unit that you attach to the far end of a connection and the battery-operated, handheld main unit that displays the results. Typically, the tester displays various codes to describe the type of faults that it finds. In some cases, you can purchase a tester with multiple remote units that are numbered so that one person can test several connections without constantly traveling back and forth from one end of the connections to the other to move the remote unit.

**WARNING** The one wiring fault that is not detectable by a dedicated wire map tester is split pairs, because even though the pinouts are incorrect, the cable is still wired straight through. To detect split pairs, you must use a device that tests the cable for the near-end crosstalk that split pairs cause.

## Continuity Testers

A continuity tester is an even simpler and less expensive device than a wire map tester. It is designed to check a copper cable connection for basic installation problems, such as opens, shorts, and crossed pairs. At $50 to $200, these devices usually cannot detect more complicated twisted-pair wiring faults such as split pairs, but they are sufficient for basic cable testing, especially for coaxial cables, which have only two conductors that are not easily confused by the installer. Like a wire map tester, a continuity tester consists of two separate units that you connect to each end of the cable to be tested. In many cases, the two units can snap together for storage and easy testing of patch cables.

## Tone Generators

The simplest type of copper cable tester is also a two-piece unit and is called a tone generator and probe, also called a "fox and hound" wire tracer. This type of device consists of one unit that you connect to a cable with a standard jack, or to an individual wire with alligator clips. This unit transmits a signal over the cable or wire. The other unit is a penlike probe that emits an audible tone when touched to the other end of the cable or wire or even to its insulating sheath.

This type of device is most often used to locate a specific connection in a punchdown block. For example, some installers prefer to run all of the cables for a network to the central punchdown block without labeling them and then to use a tone generator to identify which block is connected to which wall plate and label the punchdown block accordingly. You can also use the device to identify a particular cable at any point between the two ends. Because the probe can detect the cable containing the tone signal through its sheath, it can help you to locate one specific cable out of a bundle in a ceiling conduit or other type of raceway. You just need to connect the tone generator to one end and touch the probe to each cable in the bundle until you hear the tone.

In addition, by testing the continuity of individual wires using alligator clips, you can use a tone generator and probe to locate opens, shorts, and miswires. An open wire will not produce a tone at the other end, a short will produce a tone on two or more wires at the other end, and an improperly connected wire will produce a tone on the wrong pin at the other end.

This process is extremely time-consuming, however, and it's nearly as prone to errors as the cable installation itself. You either have to continually travel from one end of the cable to the other to move the tone generator unit or use a partner to test each connection, keeping in close contact using radios or some other means of communication in order to avoid confusion. When you consider the time and effort involved, you will probably find that investing in a wire map tester is a more practical solution.

## Optical Loss Test Set

In most cases, you'll need both an optical power meter and a test source in order to properly install and troubleshoot a fiber-optic network, and you can usually save a good deal of money and effort by purchasing the two together. This practice ensures that you're purchasing units that both support the wavelengths and power levels you need and are calibrated for use together. You can purchase the devices together in two ways: as a single combination unit called an optical loss test set (OLTS) or as separate units in a fiber-optic test kit.

An OLTS is generally not recommended for field testing because it is a single unit. While useful in a lab or for testing patch cables, two separate devices would be needed to test a permanently installed link because you have to connect the light source to one end of the cable and the power meter to the other. However, for fiber-optic contractors involved in large installations, it may be practical to give workers their own OLTS so that they can work with a partner and easily test each cable run in both directions.

Fiber-optic test kits are the preferable alternative for most fiber-optic technicians because they include a power meter and light source that are designed to work together, usually at a price that is lower than the cost of two separate products. Many test kits also include an assortment of accessories needed to test a particular type of network, such as adapters for various types of connectors, reference test cables, and a carrying case. Prices for test kits can range from $500 to $600 for basic functionality to as much as $5,000 for a comprehensive kit that can test virtually every type of fiber-optic cable.

Communications can be a vital element of any cable installation in which two or more people are working together, especially when the two ends of the permanent cable runs are a long distance apart, as on a fiber-optic network. Some test sets address this problem by incorporating voice communication devices into the power meter and light source, using the tested cable to carry the signals.

## Multifunction Cable Testers

The most heavily marketed cable testing tools available today are the multifunction cable scanners, sometimes called certification tools. These are devices that are available for both copper and fiber-optic networks. They perform a series of tests on a cable run, compare the results against either preprogrammed standards or parameters that you supply, and display the outcome as a series of pass or fail ratings. Most of these units perform the basic tests called for by the most commonly used standards—such as wire mapping, length, attenuation, and NEXT for copper cables—and optical power and signal loss for fiber-optic. Many of the copper cable scanners also go beyond the basics to perform a comprehensive battery of tests, including propagation delay, delay skew, PS-NEXT, ELFNEXT, PS-ELFNEXT, and return loss.

The primary advantage of this type of device is that anyone can use it. You simply connect the unit to a cable, press a button, and read off the results after a few seconds. Many units can store the results of many individual tests in memory, download them to a PC, or output them directly to a printer.

This primary advantage, however, is also the primary disadvantage of this type of device. The implication behind these products is that you don't really have to understand the tests being performed, the results of those tests, or the cabling standards used to evaluate them. The interface insulates you from the raw data, and you are supposed to trust the manufacturer implicitly and believe that a series of pass ratings means that your cables are installed correctly and functioning properly.

The fundamental problem with this process, however, is that the standards used to assess the test results gathered by the device are not necessarily reliable. Some units claim to certify Category 6 and Category 7 cables, for example, when standards for these cables have not yet been ratified. One must even question the validity of the testers that claim to certify Category 5e cables, since this standard was ratified only recently. When evaluating products like these, it's important to choose units that are upgradable or manually configurable so that you can keep up with the constantly evolving standards.

This configurability can lead to another problem, however. In many cases, it isn't difficult to modify the testing parameters of these units to make it easier for a cable to pass muster. For example, simply changing the NVP for a copper cable can make a faulty cable pass the unit's tests. An unscrupulous contractor can conceivably perform a shoddy installation using inferior cable and use his own carefully prepared tester to show the client a list of perfect "pass" test results.

As another example, some of the more elaborate (and more expensive) fiber-optic cable testers attempt to simplify the testing process by supplying main and remote units that contain both an integrated light source and semiconductor detector and then by testing at the 850nm and 1300nm wavelengths simultaneously. This type of device enables you to test the cable in both directions and at both wavelengths simply by connecting the two units to either end of a cable run. There is no need to use reference test cables to swap the units to test the run from each direction or run a separate test for each wavelength.

However, these devices, apart from costing several times as much as a standard power meter and light source combination ($4,000 or more, in some cases), do not compare the test results to a baseline established with that equipment. Instead, they compare them to preprogrammed standards, which, when it comes to fiber-optic cables, can be defined as somewhat loose. The result is a device that is designed for use primarily by people who really don't understand what they are testing and who will trust the device's pass or fail judgment without question, even when the standards used to gauge the test results are loose enough to permit faulty installations to receive a pass rating.

This is not to say that these multifunction devices are completely useless. In fact, they can be an extremely efficient means of testing and troubleshooting your network. The important thing to understand is what they are testing and to either examine the raw data gathered by the unit or verify that the standards used to formulate the pass/fail results are valid. The prices of these products can be shocking, however. The cost of both copper and fiber-optic units can easily run up to several thousand dollars, with top-of-the-line models exceeding $5,000.

## Punchdown Tool

Most networks today are built using twisted-pair cable of some sort. This cable is usually terminated in wiring closets using a tool known as a *punchdown tool*. It is called that because, essentially, the tool punches down the wire into some kind of insulation displacement connector (IDC). IDCs make contact by cutting through, or displacing, the insulation around a single conductor inside a twisted-pair cable. The punchdown tool pushes a conductor between the sides of a "V" inside an IDC (see Figure 6.17), allowing the small metal "knife" inside the connector to make contact with the inner conductor inside the wire.

**FIGURE 6.17**   Using a punchdown tool

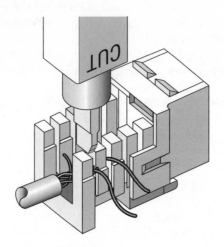

There are different blades and different types of punchdown tools. The most common is the punchdown with replaceable blades for the different types of connectors (either 66 or 110). Figure 6.18 shows an example of one of these types of punchdown tools.

**FIGURE 6.18**   An example of a punchdown tool

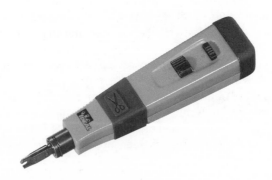

# Summary

In this chapter, you learned about the various Network+ concepts that relate to network installation. First of all, you learned about the various prerequisites that must be considered before you start to install a network, such as standard operating procedures (SOPs) and the environmental impact of network and computer installations.

This chapter covered, in detail, the intricacies of wireless networking, including the main standards, infrared, Bluetooth, and the 802.11 recommendations, as well as their similarities and differences. You also learned about the different types of devices present in these technologies and how to configure them, as well as the classifications of their antennas.

Probably the most important skill for a network installer to have is the ability to install the most common network connectivity device, the network interface card, or NIC. In this chapter, you learned how to properly configure and install a NIC into a PC.

Once you install the NIC, it is important to know how to configure the workstation to connect to various network operating systems. In this chapter, you learned how to add network components and get them functional on Windows systems.

Finally, you learned about the various types of tools and testers used when installing a network. You learned about crimpers and punchdown tools as well as the testers used to test a network installation.

# Exam Essentials

**Specify the general characteristics (for example, carrier speed, frequency, transmission type, and topology) of the wireless technologies.**   It is crucial for you to familiarize yourself with the similarities and differences between the three common 802.11 standards—802.11a, 802.11b, and 802.11g—as well as being able to trace their lineage back to the original 802.11 standard and compare them with related technologies, such as infrared and Bluetooth.

**Identify factors that affect the range and speed of wireless service (for example, interference, antenna type, and environmental factors).**   You must be able to identify the characteristics of wireless technologies that make them susceptible to interference and degradation from environmental factors as well as how the type of antenna used will affect signal range and device orientation. Knowing the difference between Omni and Yagi antennas, as well as understanding their gain ratings, will aid in this objective.

**Be able to select the appropriate NIC and configuration settings (e.g., IRQ, full/half duplex, speeds, etc.).**   Every NIC has certain hardware settings. These include IRQ, I/O address, duplex (full or half), and speed (10, 100, or 1000, depending on the card). In order to successfully install a NIC, you must—either through software or manually by DIP switches or jumpers—set these parameters to appropriate values.

**Be able to configure the appropriate computer/host name and username.**   This can be done using the Network program in Windows 9*x* or Network and Dial-up Connections in Windows

2000. To access each area, simply right-click Network Neighborhood or My Network Places on the Desktop, and then select Properties.

**Be able configure a workstation to connect to various kinds of servers using Windows as the client.** This is done in Windows 9*x* using the Network application. This application has three main parts that must be in place: the client, the NIC driver, and the protocol. The client is specific to the operating system you are connecting to, the NIC is specific to the brand/type of NIC installed in the computer, and the protocol must be the same one running on the server you want to connect to. Windows 2000 when configured as a client, the parts are the same, but the Network application is instead called the Network and Dial-up Connections window.

**Know what a punchdown tool, tone generator, media tester, and wire crimpers are used for.** Punchdown tools are used to connect cables to punchdown panels. Tone generators are used to locate a single cable within a bundle. Media testers are used to test the potential transmission quality of a network cable, and wire crimpers are used to squeeze, or crimp, connectors to the end of a cable, thus allowing a connection to be made.

# Review Questions

1. Which piece of software allows the computer's operating system to access the NIC hardware?

   **A.** NIC driver

   **B.** Operating system driver

   **C.** System driver

   **D.** Protocol driver

2. Which encoding scheme does IEEE 802.11b use?

   **A.** OFDM

   **B.** DSSS

   **C.** ABDR

   **D.** TCPA

3. Which antenna type is considered directional because it focuses all of its transmission or reception power in a single general direction?

   **A.** Yagi

   **B.** dBd

   **C.** dBi

   **D.** Omni

4. Which of the following technologies is ideal for wireless cord replacement but not as great for wireless LAN implementation?

   **A.** IEEE 802.11g

   **B.** Infrared

   **C.** Bluetooth

   **D.** 802.11a

5. If you were going to make a 100Base-TX patch cable, which tool would you use?

   **A.** Screwdriver

   **B.** Punchdown tool

   **C.** Wire crimper

   **D.** Tone generator

6. Which of the following antennas has the greatest range?

   **A.** 7dBd Omni

   **B.** 9dBi Omni

   **C.** 9dBi Yagi

   **D.** 7dBd Yagi

**7.** What is the maximum throughput of Bluetooth?

   **A.** 1Mbps

   **B.** 10Mbps

   **C.** 11Mbps

   **D.** 100Mbps

**8.** Which of the following IEEE 802.11 standards uses frequencies in the range of 5GHz?

   **A.** 802.11

   **B.** 802.11a

   **C.** 802.11b

   **D.** 802.11g

**9.** Which of the following wireless technologies has the second highest bit rate?

   **A.** 802.11

   **B.** 802.11a

   **C.** Bluetooth

   **D.** 802.11b

   **E.** 802.11g

**10.** What is the result of updating an old NIC driver on a system?

   **A.** It can correct bugs.

   **B.** It can be a good way to look like you are doing useful work.

   **C.** It can act as a protocol converter.

   **D.** All of the above.

**11.** 11. Which parameter uniquely identifies a wireless network?

   **A.** Node ID

   **B.** MAC Address

   **C.** SSID

   **D.** LAD ID

**12.** Plug and Play expansion cards sometimes have problems working correctly with _____ _____ expansion cards.

   **A.** PCI

   **B.** Token Ring

   **C.** Legacy ISA

   **D.** EISA

**13.** The SSID on a wireless LAN is most like _____.

   **A.** a password

   **B.** a secret hash

   **C.** an advertised name

   **D.** an encrypted hexadecimal number

**14.** Which type of wireless LAN mode allows two or more devices to share resources without the use of an access point?

   **A.** Ad-hoc

   **B.** Splitterless

   **C.** Infrastructure

   **D.** Nonpoint

**15.** You are a consultant. You have been asked to find out where a particular "mystery jack" originates and what path the cable takes to get there. Which network installation tool would you most likely use?

   **A.** Wire crimper

   **B.** Punchdown tool

   **C.** Media tester

   **D.** Tone generator/tone locator

**16.** Every day around noon, 802.11b wireless LAN users located near the break room complain of slow network performance and lost connectivity. What is the most likely cause of this degradation?

   **A.** Too many people in the break room using cell phones

   **B.** A microwave oven that gets a lot of use

   **C.** The lights in the break room, which are off before lunchtime

   **D.** The users having line-of-sight connectivity to the access point in the break room, which gets blocked by people in the break room

**17.** Which network component "shares out" a printer so that printing services can be provided to the entire network?

   **A.** Print server

   **B.** Print facilitator

   **C.** PCONSOLE.EXE

   **D.** Print manager

**18.** Which of the following power conditions occurs when the voltage level increases quickly and falls just as quickly?

    **A.** Surge

    **B.** Spike

    **C.** Brownout

    **D.** Blackout

**19.** Which power condition occurs when the voltage level increases quickly and remains at the high level for an extended period of time (several seconds)?

    **A.** Surge

    **B.** Spike

    **C.** Brownout

    **D.** Blackout

**20.** Which power condition occurs when the voltage level drops below 120 volts and stays below for an extended period of time?

    **A.** Surge

    **B.** Spike

    **C.** Brownout

    **D.** Blackout

# Answers to Review Questions

1.  A. The NIC driver is a software component that an operating system uses to interface with the NIC hardware.

2.  B. 802.11b uses Direct Sequence Spread Spectrum (DSSS) for data encoding. 802.11a and 802.11g both use Orthogonal Frequency Division Multiplexing (OFDM)

3.  A. Yagi, or directional, antennas focus all of their power in one general direction, making them a logical choice for WAP-to-WAP (point-to-point stationary) bridging but not so great for WAP-to-client (point-to-multipoint mobile) connectivity. Omni antennas are a better choice for the latter. dBd and dBi are relative units of measure for antenna gain.

4.  C. Bluetooth is used for wireless cord replacement for devices, such as keyboards and mice, but falls short in bandwidth and range for wireless LAN implementation. Infrared is used more for line-of-sight short-range serial connectivity between two devices.

5.  C. A 100Base-TX patch cable is a piece of cable with an RJ-45 connector on each end. These connectors must be crimped, and the only tool that can do that is a wire crimper.

6.  D. Keep in mind that you must add 2.2 to the numerical value to convert dBd to dBi. Therefore, even though 9 is greater than 7, both the Omni and Yagi antennas measured in dBd have gain equivalent to 9.2dBi. This makes answers A and D numerically equivalent and superior to B and C. What makes D the correct answer is that Yagi antennas reach farther than Omni antennas of equivalent gain, but they do so in only one general direction.

7.  A. The maximum speed for the Bluetooth wireless technology is 1Mbps.

8.  B. Only 802.11a uses the regulated 5GHz frequency range, making it more expensive, shorter reaching, and easier to interfere with, but in less competition for its frequency bands.

9.  D. Kind of a trick question, this one assumes even though 802.11a and 802.11g tie for the top spot, there is still a "second place" up for grabs, unlike your golf leader board. In that case, the 11Mbps of 802.11b places it handily above the original 802.11 and Bluetooth standards.

10. A. Updating older drivers on a system can correct various bugs. When a hardware manufacturer detects a bug in a driver, it develops and releases a new version to correct the problem.

11. C. The SSID uniquely identifies a wireless network. Any access point part of the same network needs to be configured with the same SSID.

12. C. Because Plug and Play expansion cards automatically assign a computer's resources, they can be set to a resource that conflicts with a Legacy ISA card (which doesn't always register itself with the Plug and Play software).

13. C. The SSID on a wireless LAN is advertised to the medium so that any client that is within range can display the SSID as a LAN name, allowing the user to choose to connect to this wireless LAN from a list and not need to secretly know the SSID. It is the SSID that unifies the devices into a wireless LAN. After that decision, it may be necessary to provide WEP authentication information, but that has nothing to do with the SSID itself.

**14.** A. Ad-hoc networks allow multiple devices to intercommunicate without going through an access point, while infrastructure mode requires the use of an access point. *Splitterless* is an ADSL term, and *nonpoint* is not a valid term.

**15.** D. A tone generator puts a signal on the particular cable being located and the tone locator contains a very sensitive sensor and speaker. When the tone locator is passed near the signal-carrying cable, it emits a sound, indicating that the cable is near. Although a media tester tests cable, it tests only the possible transmission quality of the cable; you would have to find the cable first in order to use it.

**16.** B. Many microwaves operate at the frequency of one of the channels in the 2.4GHz range, leading to interference with 802.11b and 802.11g network equipment. Cell phones and lights do not interfere with wireless LANs. Because wireless LANs in the 802.11 family use RF, being in the line of sight with the access point is not an issue.

**17.** A. The only network component listed that actually provides network printing service to network clients is the print server.

**18.** B. Spikes are an overvoltage condition in which the power level quickly increases and then decreases just as quickly. A brownout is an inverted surge, and a blackout is a total loss of power for several seconds, several minutes, or several hours.

**19.** A. Surges are an overvoltage condition in which the power level increases quickly and stays at a higher level for several seconds. A brownout is an inverted surge, and a blackout is a total loss of power for several seconds, several minutes, or several hours.

**20.** C. Brownouts are an undervoltage condition in which the voltage level drops and stays low for several seconds. During a brownout, the lights usually dim and then become bright again.

# Chapter 7

# WAN and Remote Access Technologies

---

## THE FOLLOWING NETWORK+ EXAM OBJECTIVES ARE COVERED IN THIS CHAPTER:

✓ **2.14 Identify the basic characteristics (for example, speed, capacity, and media) of the following WAN (wide area network) technologies:**

- Packet switching
- Circuit switching
- ISDN (Integrated Services Digital Network)
- FDDI (Fiber Distributed Data Interface)
- T1 (T-carrier level 1)/E1/J1
- T3 (T-carrier level 3)/E3/J3
- OC-*x* (optical carrier)
- X.25

✓ **2.15 Identify the basic characteristics of the following internet access technologies:**

- *x*DSL (digital subscriber line)
- Broadband Cable (cable modem)
- POTS/PSTN (plain old telephone service/Public Switched Telephone Network)
- Satellite
- Wireless

✓ **2.16 Define the function of the following remote access protocols and services:**

- RAS (Remote Access Service)
- PPP (Point-to-Point Protocol)
- SLIP (Serial Line Internet Protocol)
- PPPoE (Point-to-Point Protocol over Ethernet)

- PPTP (Point-to-Point Tunneling Protocol)
- VPN (virtual private network)
- RDP (Remote Desktop Protocol)

✓ **3.4 Given a remote connectivity scenario comprising a protocol, an authentication scheme, and physical connectivity, configure the connection. Includes connection to the following servers:**

- UNIX/Linux/Mac OS X Server
- NetWare
- Windows
- AppleShare IP (Internet Protocol)

Remote access technologies allow users to access your network and its services from a computer outside the network. For example, users can check e-mail and keep in touch with the office while on the road. The need for remote access has increased during the last few years because many employees now work out of their homes and telecommute instead of working at a desk in a cubicle. Today, many employees travel with laptops, and many hotels and motels are equipped with second phone lines or Internet connections.

Before employees can telecommute, however, both their equipment and the corporate network must be set up for remote access. This involves acquiring the appropriate hardware, installing the appropriate software, configuring this hardware and software, and ensuring that the proper protocols are in place. In this chapter, we'll look at these requirements from the standpoint of what you, as a network administrator, will need to know in the workplace and for the Network+ exam.

# Remote Access Connection Configuration Requirements

Remote access requires two basic components: a remote computer and a remote access system on the network (typically a computer or device running special software called the Remote Access Server). The remote computer connects to the remote access server and then operates just as it would if it were a workstation on the network.

This section covers only one type of remote access configuration, a dial-up connection over an analog phone line, once more popular than the now common VPN connections that are made from the equivalent of a standard LAN connection; however, each network operating system (NOS) has many options for remote access to your network. Check your NOS documentation for these options.

In the following sections, we will discuss the hardware and software requirements for setting up a remote access connection using a modem over an analog phone line.

# Hardware Requirements

The device most commonly used to connect computers over a public analog phone line is a *modem* (a contraction of *MOdulator/DEModulator*). A sending modem converts digital signals from the computer into analog signals that can be transmitted over telephone lines and other analog media. On the receiving end, the modem changes the analog signals back to digital signals. Because telephone lines can be found almost everywhere, this method of remote communication is readily available to everyone with access to a phone line.

Modems change the digital ones and zeros into analog signals that can be transmitted over telephone lines. The pattern of these analog signals encodes the data for transmission to the receiving computer. The receiving modem then takes the analog signals and turns them back into ones and zeros. This method is slower than a completely digital transmission, but data can travel over longer distances with fewer errors.

A modem can be either internal or external. The key difference between the two is the amount of configuration required. You must configure internal modems with an IRQ and an I/O address, as well as a virtual COM port address, to ensure that they function properly. External modems simply hook to a serial port and don't require nearly as much configuration.

## Configuring an Internal Modem

*Internal modems* are on expansion cards that fit into a computer's expansion bus. To that end, the modem you install must be designed to work in the type of expansion bus slot in the computer. Configuring an internal modem is much like configuring any other hardware device. You must set the IRQ, I/O address, and virtual COM port so that they don't conflict with other devices.

The only one of these configuration parameters that you haven't seen before is the virtual COM port. A *virtual COM* port is a logical designation given by the operating system for a serial port. A computer can have only two physical serial ports, but it can have as many as four logical ports. Each physical port must be associated with a logical port so that the operating system can use it. The same is true for modems (since they are, in fact, serial devices). You must set a modem to use a COM port that is not being used by any other device.

Each COM port shares an IRQ address with another port. COM1 and COM3 share IRQ 4, and COM2 and COM4 share IRQ 3. If two devices are set to different COM ports (COM1 and COM3, for example) but have the same IRQ, the modem may not function properly. It is usually best to set an internal modem to COM4 because COM1 is most likely to be in use, while COM2 (which shares the IRQ with COM4) is less likely to be used. Table 7.1 lists the virtual COM ports, their associated IRQs, and default I/O addresses. Note which COM ports share IRQ addresses.

## Configuring an External Modem

Although almost all modems used today are internal, there are some situations in which external modems may be more appropriate (such as modem pools). Also, some people prefer external modems because they can see the modem's status lights. Most internal modems use software status lights, which don't work if the hardware or software is failing. When using external modems, you have two considerations: available serial ports and the UART type.

**TABLE 7.1**     COM Port IRQ and Default I/O Addresses

| Port | IRQ | I/O |
|------|-----|-----|
| COM1 | 4 | 3F8 |
| COM2 | 3 | 2F8 |
| COM3 | 4 | 3E8 |
| COM4 | 3 | 2E8 |

### Available Serial Ports

With the large number of external serial expansion devices available—including modems, cameras, and printers—a spare serial port is often not available, making the use of an internal modem one of your only solutions. Universal Serial Bus (USB) allows up to 127 devices (including modems) to be chained off of a single USB port. This technology eliminates the need for multiple serial ports on a computer, as well as the need to use an internal modem.

### UART Type

UART stands for Universal Asynchronous Receiver-Transmitter and is the chip that manages serial communications. Each set of serial ports shares a UART. The type of UART chip determines the maximum port speed that a particular serial port can handle. There are two main types: the 8250 series and the 16550 series. The primary difference between them is the capacity of the port buffers. Internal modems have built-in, high-speed UART chips, so this isn't an issue with internal modems.

The 8250 chips have 8-bit buffers that are limited to a maximum speed of 9600bps and are typically found in PCs manufactured before 1986 (before the IBM AT).

Starting with the IBM AT, computers have the faster 16450 and 16550 UARTs. These chips use 16-bit buffers and transmit data at a maximum speed of 115,200bps. Any modem faster than 9600bps that will be connected to a PC for remote access requires the use of 16550 UARTs in the PC to get the maximum possible speed. Otherwise, connection speed will be limited to the fastest output speed of the 8250 UART, 9600bps.

## Software Requirements

When configuring a workstation for remote access, you must configure the software to recognize the modem in addition to configuring the hardware. In Windows 2000, for example, you do so using Device Manager. To open the Device Manager, follow these steps:

1.  Choose Start ➢ Control Panel ➢ System to open the System Properties dialog box

2.  Choose the Hardware tab and click the Device Manager button.

Additionally, you must configure the software to initiate and maintain the connection. This means configuring the dialer software (the client software that uses a local modem to dial the remote access server) and the network protocols that the communications will use, including the following:

- Transmission Control Protocol/Internet Protocol (TCP/IP)
- Internet Packet eXchange (IPX)
- Point-to-Point Protocol (PPP)
- Point-to-Point Tunneling Protocol (PPTP)
- Layer 2 Tunneling Protocol (L2TP)

Even if the hardware is configured properly, the software may not initiate a connection.

# Remote Access Connection Methods

Because a computer using remote access is not a part of your network, it will not use local area network (LAN) technologies to connect to the network. The remote computer will instead use other kinds of connection methods to connect to the LAN, including the following:

- Public Switched Telephone Network (PSTN, also called plain old telephone service, or POTS)
- Integrated Services Digital Network (ISDN)
- Other digital connection methods (including one of the digital subscriber lines, or DSLs, broadband cable, and T-series connections)

## The Public Switched Telephone Network (PSTN)

The portion of the PSTN that runs from your house to the rest of the world is known as *plain old telephone service (POTS)*. It is the most popular method for connecting a remote user to a local network because of its low cost, ease of installation, and simplicity. However, your connection to the PSTN may be ISDN, DSL, cellular, or some other method.

Two key concepts when discussing PSTN are public and switched. *Public,* of course, is the opposite of *private* and means that, for a fee, anyone can lease the use of the network, without the need to run cabling. The term *switched* explains how the phone system works. Although one or more wires are connected to your home and/or office, they are not always in use. In effect, your wiring and equipment is *offline,* or not part of the network. Yet, in this offline state, you have a standing reservation so that you can join at almost any time. Your identification for this reservation is your phone number, which is what makes the phone companies a viable communications network. You initiate a connection by dialing a phone number. Can you see how it would be technically impractical if every phone number were connected all the time? The backbone cabling issues would be almost impossible.

Let's take an example from the U.S. telephone system. (The actual numbering sequence varies in other countries, though the concept is identical.) The phone company runs a cable consisting of a pair of copper wires (called the *local loop*) from your location (called the *demarcation point,* or *demarc* for short) to a phone company building called the *Central Office (CO).* All the pairs from all the local loop cables that are distributed throughout a small regional area come together at a central point, similar to a patch panel in a UTP-based LAN.

This centralized point has a piece of equipment attached, which is called a switch. The switch functions almost exactly like the switches mentioned in Chapter 2, "The OSI Model," in that a communications session, once initiated by dialing the phone number of the receiver, exists until the "conversation" is closed. The switch can then close the connection. On one side of the switch is the neighborhood wiring. On the other side are lines that may connect to another switch or to a local set of wiring. The number of lines on the other side of the switch depends on the usage of that particular exchange. Figure 7.1 shows a PSTN system that utilizes these components.

When you want to make a call, you pick up the phone. This completes a circuit, which in most cases gives you a dial tone. The tone is the switch's way of saying, "I'm ready to accept your commands." Failure to get a dial tone indicates either a break in the equipment chain or that the switch is too busy at the moment processing other commands. In many areas of the world, you may hear a fast on-and-off tone after giving a command string (phone number) to the local switch. This means that other switches with which the local switch is attempting to communicate are too busy right now. Recently, this has been replaced with a localized voice, which typically says, "We're sorry. All circuits are busy. Hang up and try your call later." This happens frequently on holidays or during natural disasters. The phone company in a local area uses only a few wires (called *trunk lines*) for normal capacity and some auxiliary lines for unexpected usage. This is because wiring and switches are very expensive. It is a trade-off between 100-percent uptime and keeping the costs of leasing the connection from the phone company affordable.

**FIGURE 7.1**    A local connection to the PSTN

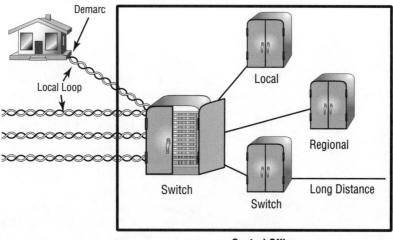

**WARNING**    Use caution when working with bare phone wires because they may carry a current. In POTS, the phone company uses a battery to supply power to the line, which is sometimes referred to as *self-powered*. It isn't truly self-powered, however, because the power comes from the phone system.

As a remote access connection method, POTS has many advantages:

- It is inexpensive to set up. Almost every home in the United States has or can have a telephone connection.
- There are no LAN cabling costs.
- Connections are available in many countries throughout the world.

POTS is a popular remote access connection method because few minor disadvantages are associated with it. The disadvantages are limited bandwidth, and thus a limited maximum data transfer rate, and the inferior analog signal when compared to digital methods, such as ISDN and DSL. At most, 53Kbps (limited by the FCC) data transmissions are possible though rarely achieved by the traveling user connecting remotely to the corporate network. These days, to gain access to corporate remote access services, many travelers use VPN connections over hotel or other public wired or wireless networks, which most often connect to service providers using DSL or T-carrier digital circuits.

## Integrated Services Digital Network (ISDN)

ISDN is a digital, point-to-point network capable of maximum transmission speeds of about 2Mbps (Primary Rate Interface [PRI]), although speeds of 128Kbps (Basic Rate Interface [BRI]) are more common in a small-office, home-office (SOHO) environment.

**NOTE**    In this section, the BRI circuit will be used as a reference.

Because it is capable of much higher data rates at a fairly low cost, ISDN is becoming a viable remote user connection method, especially for those who work out of their homes. ISDN uses the same UTP wiring as POTS, but it can transmit data at much higher speeds. But that's where the similarity ends. What makes ISDN different from a regular POTS line is how it uses the copper wiring. Instead of carrying an analog (voice) signal, it carries digital signals. This is the source of several differences.

A computer connects to the 128Kbps ISDN line via an ISDN *Terminal Adapter,* or *TA* (often incorrectly referred to as an ISDN modem). An ISDN TA is not a modem because it does not convert a digital signal from the computer to an analog signal on the subscriber line; ISDN signals are digital on the subscriber line. A TA is technically an ISDN-compatible device that has one or more non-ISDN ports for devices like computer serial interfaces and RJ-11 analog phones, allowing these non-ISDN devices access to the ISDN network.

An ISDN line has two types of channels. The data is carried on special *Bearer channels,* or *B channels,* each of which can carry 64Kbps of data. A BRI ISDN line has two B channels. One channel can be used for a voice call while the other is being used for data transmissions, and this occurs through time division multiplexing on one pair of copper wires. The second type of channel is also multiplexed onto the one copper pair, is used for call setup and link management, and is known as the *signaling channel,* or *D channel* (also referred to as the *Delta channel*). This channel has only 16Kbps of bandwidth.

To maximize throughput, the two B channels are often combined into one data connection for a total bandwidth of 128Kbps. This is known as *BONDING* (which stands for Bandwidth on Demand Interoperability Group) or *inverse multiplexing.* This still leaves the D channel free for signaling purposes. In rare cases, you may see user data, such as credit card verification, on the D channel. This was introduced as an additional feature of ISDN, but it hasn't caught on.

These are the main advantages of ISDN:

- It has a fast connection.
- It offers higher bandwidth than POTS. BONDING yields 128Kbps bandwidth.
- There is no conversion from digital to analog.

However, ISDN does have a few disadvantages:

- It's more expensive than POTS.
- Specialized equipment is required at the phone company and at the remote computer.
- Not all ISDN equipment can connect to every other type of equipment.
- ISDN is a type of dial-up connection, and therefore, the connection must be initiated.

# Other Digital Options

Digital connections provide one main benefit to remote access users: increased bandwidth over older technologies. The digital nature of ISDN and other digital connection types makes them excellent choices for remote access connections. The following are some of the more important types:

- *x*DSL
- Cable modem (broadband cable)
- Frame Relay
- T-series
- Asynchronous Transfer Mode (ATM)
- Fiber Distributed Data Interface (FDDI)

## *x*DSL Technology

*x*DSL is a general category of copper access technologies that has become popular because it uses regular PSTN phone wires to transmit digital signals and is extremely inexpensive compared with the other digital communications methods. *x*DSL implementations cost hundreds of dollars instead of the thousands that you would pay for a dedicated, digital point-to-point link (such as a T1). They include digital subscriber line (DSL), high data-rate digital subscriber line

(HDSL), single-line digital subscriber line (SDSL), very high data-rate digital subscriber line (VDSL), and asymmetric digital subscriber line (ADSL), which is currently the most popular.

It is beyond the scope of this book to cover all of the DSL types.

ADSL has become the most popular *x*DSL because it focuses on providing reasonably fast upstream transmission speeds (up to 640Kbps) and very fast downstream transmission speeds (up to 9Mbps). This makes downloading graphics, audio, video, and data files from any remote computer very fast. The majority of Web traffic, for example, is downstream. The best part is that ADSL works on a single phone line without losing voice call capability. This is accomplished with what is called a *splitter,* which enables the use of multiple frequencies on the POTS line.

As with ISDN, communicating via *x*DSL requires an interface to the PC. All *x*DSL configurations require a DSL modem, called an *endpoint,* and a network interface card (NIC) in the computer. The NIC is able to be connected directly to the DSL modem using a straight-through Ethernet UTP patch cord with standard RJ-45 connectors on each end, but if other connecting devices are between the computer and the cable modem, either a special switchable port or an Ethernet crossover cable will be required for proper functionality. Figure 7.2 shows a typical DSL modem installation.

## Cable Modem

Another digital remote access connection device is the cable modem. A *cable modem* is a device that is used to connect computers and other devices to a cable television data network. Cable modem technology is one example of high-speed Internet access, also known as *broadband Internet access* (a.k.a. "broadband"). Because the cable company already has a cabled infrastructure in most cities, it was a natural choice to bring high-speed Internet connections to homes. The cable television companies got together and developed the *Data over Cable Service Interface Specification (DOCSIS)* that, among other things, specifies how to allow data services over a cable system. Most cable modems adhere to this standard.

**FIGURE 7.2**    A DSL modem's connections

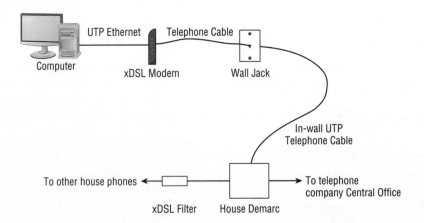

**FIGURE 7.3**    A cable modem's connections

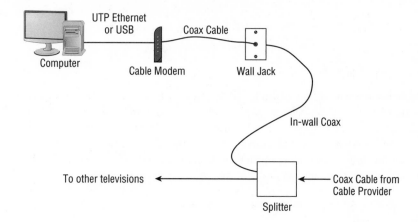

Cable modems are simply small boxes that have a cable connection and a connection to the computer (as shown in Figure 7.3). There are two ways to connect a cable modem to a computer: USB and Ethernet (usually 10Base-T). Most cable modems can use either one of these methods and some modems have both types.

If you are going to connect the cable modem via USB, simply install the software driver for the cable modem on the computer, and then plug in the cable modem. The computer will detect the modem and configure it automatically.

If you are using Ethernet to connect, you must have an Ethernet NIC in your computer that is properly installed and configured. Then, once the NIC is installed, all you need to do is connect the cable modem to the NIC with an appropriate 10Base-T patch cable (RJ-45 connector on both ends, usually supplied with the cable modem). The thing to keep in mind is that the cable modem's Ethernet connection is physically and electronically the same as a *medium dependent interface-crossover (MDI-X)* port on a hub or switch, meaning that you can connect your computer, which has a *medium dependent interface (MDI)* to the cable modem with a straight-though cable.

If you are using a hub or switch on your network and you have the cable modem plugged into the hub or switch, you may experience a connectivity issue because you are connecting an MDI-X port to an MDI-X port, facing the transmit wire pair on one device to the transmit wire pair on the other device. The receive wire pairs are facing each other as well. If either your cable modem or your hub or switch has a switchable port, toggle the associated button from the MDI-X setting to the MDI setting so that the transmit and receive pairs are swapped in the electronics of the one device, making a proper connection between the devices. You'll notice your Link LEDs on the switch port and on the cable modem illuminate in approval. If you cannot find such a button on either device, it will be necessary to use an Ethernet crossover cable to connect the switch or hub to the cable modem. This is no different from connecting two hubs or switches back to back.

For more information on the DOCSIS specification and cable modem technology, visit www.cablemodem.com.

## Frame Relay Technology

Frame Relay is a wide area network (WAN) technology in which variable-length packets are transmitted by switching. *Packet switching* involves breaking messages into chunks at the sending device. Each packet can be sent over any number of routes on its way to its destination. The packets are then reassembled in the correct order at the receiver. Because the exact path is unknown, a cloud is used when creating a diagram to illustrate how data travels throughout the service. Figure 7.4 shows a Frame Relay WAN connecting smaller LANs.

**FIGURE 7.4**    A typical Frame Relay configuration

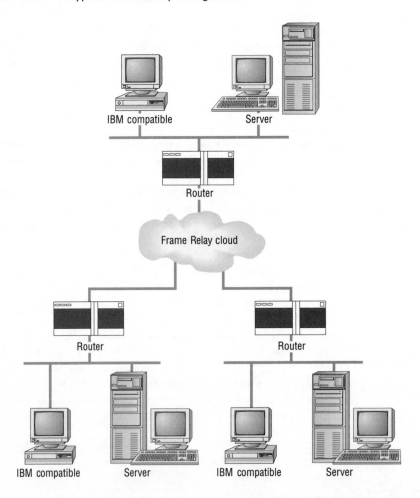

Frame Relay uses permanent virtual circuits (PVCs). PVCs allow virtual data communications circuits between sender and receiver over a packet-switched network. This ensures that all data that enters a Frame Relay cloud at one side comes out at the other over a similar connection.

The beauty of using a shared network is that sometimes you can get much better throughput than you are paying for. When signing up for one of these connections, you specify and pay for a Committed Information Rate (CIR), or in other words, a minimum bandwidth. If the total traffic on the shared network is light, you may get much faster throughput without paying for it. Frame Relay begins at this CIR speed and can reach as much as 1.544Mbps, the equivalent of a T1 line, which we'll discuss next.

As noted in this section, packet switching, used by technologies such as Frame Relay, X.25, and ATM, breaks conversations between devices into pieces, transmitting each piece independently. As a result, there is no reason to dedicate resources to a single conversation. Contrast this technology with *circuit switching*, in which a dedicated path from sender to receiver is established and maintained throughout the conversation. Circuit switching is used by POTS and ISDN; a number is dialed and the connection between endpoints is established based upon the digits dialed and maintained until either end terminates the conversation. Certain resources are dedicated to each circuit-switched conversation for its duration.

## T-Series Connections

The T-series connections are digital connections that you can lease from the telephone company. They can use regular copper pairs like regular phone lines, or they can be brought in as part of a backbone (also called a trunk line). At this point, T-series connections use time division multiplexing (TDM) to divide the bandwidth into channels of equal bit rate.

The T-series connection types are denoted by the letter *T* plus a number. Each connection type differs in its speed and in the signal used to multiplex the channels. Table 7.2 lists some of the T-series connections and their maximum data rates. The most commonly used T-series lines are T1 and T3.

**TABLE 7.2**   T-Series Connections

| Connection | Maximum Speed |
| --- | --- |
| T1 | 1.544Mbps |
| T1C | 3.152Mbps |
| T2 | 6.312Mbps |
| T3 | 44.736Mbps |
| T4 | 274.176Mbps |

### The T1 Connection

A T1 is a 1.544Mbps digital connection that is typically carried over two pairs of copper wires. This 1.544Mbps connection uses a signal known as a digital signal level 1 (DS1) and aggregates 24 discrete, 64Kbps channels that use a signal known as a digital signal level 0 (DS0). Each channel can carry either voice or data. In the POTS world, T1 lines are used to convert and bundle analog phone conversations over great distances due to the better quality of a digital signal and using much less wiring than would be needed if each pair carried only one call. This splitting into independent channels also allows a company to combine voice and data over one T1 connection or to use the T1 as if it were an unchannelized 1.544Mbps pipe. You can also order a fractional T1 (FT1) circuit, which is delivered on a T1 but does not allow the use of all 24 channels.

The European version of the T1 is the E1, which operates at 2.048Mbps. You may also see the J1, which is the Japanese version of the T1 and operates at 1.544 Mbps, just like the T1.

 **Real World Scenario**

**What's a Good Speed for a Business?**

Many of you who are in charge of setting up your company's Internet connection may think that a T1 is the best speed for your business. Unfortunately, T1 connections to the Internet are very expensive. If your business is selling Internet connections (such as an ISP), you could justify spending the money on it. Or, if you have many users (more than 50), you could also make a case for buying one. Otherwise, you may want to check out alternatives for your business that have a similar speed but a lower cost, such as DSL, a cable modem, or ISDN.

### The T3 Connection

A T3 line works similarly to a T1 connection but carries a whopping 44.736Mbps. This is equivalent to 28 T1 circuits (or a total of 672 DS0 channels). This service uses a signal known as the digital signal level 3 (DS3), which is not the same as the DS1 signal and is generally delivered on fiber-optic cable. Many local ISPs have T3 connections to their next-tier ISPs. Also, very large multinational companies use T3 connections to send voice and data between their major regional offices.

As with the T1, the T3 has a European counterpart, the E3, which operates at 34.368Mbps. The Japanese Digital Hierarchy specifies the J3 circuit, which operates at 32.064Mbps.

## Asynchronous Transfer Mode (ATM)

*Asynchronous transfer mode (ATM),* not to be confused with automated teller machines, first emerged in the early 1990s. ATM was designed to be a high-speed communications protocol that does not depend on any specific LAN topology. It uses a high-speed cell-switching technology that can handle data as well as real-time voice and video. The ATM protocol breaks up transmitted data into 53-byte cells. A *cell* is analogous to a packet or frame, except that an ATM cell is always fixed in length, whereas a frame's length can vary.

ATM is designed to switch these small cells through an ATM network very quickly. It does this by setting up a virtual connection between the source and destination nodes; the cells may go through multiple switching points before ultimately arriving at their final destination. The cells may also arrive out of order, so the receiving system may have to reassemble and correctly order the arriving cells. ATM, like Frame Relay, is a connection-oriented service in contrast to most Data Link protocols, which are best-effort delivery services and do not require virtual circuits to be established before transmitting user data.

Data rates are scalable and start as low as 1.5Mbps, with speeds of 25Mbps, 51Mbps, 100Mbps, 155Mbps, and higher. The common speeds of ATM networks today are 51.84Mbps and 155.52Mbps. Both of these speeds can be used over either copper or fiber-optic cabling. An ATM with a speed of 622.08Mbps is also becoming common but is currently used exclusively over fiber-optic cable. ATM supports very high speeds because it is designed to be implemented by hardware rather than software; faster processing speeds are therefore possible. Fiber-based service-provider ATM networks are running today at data rates of 10Gbps are becoming more and more common.

In the U.S., the standard for synchronous data transmission on optical media is *Synchronous Optical Network (SONET);* the international equivalent of SONET is Synchronous Digital Hierarchy (SDH). SONET defines a base data rate of 51.84Mbps; multiples of this rate are known as optical carrier (OC) levels, such as OC-3, OC-12, and so on. Table 7.3 gives common OC levels and their associated data rates.

**TABLE 7.3**   Common Optical Carrier Levels (OC-*x*)

| Level | Data Rate |
| --- | --- |
| OC-1 | 51.84Mbps |
| OC-3 | 155.52Mbps |
| OC-12 | 622.08Mbps |
| OC-48 | 2.488Gbps |
| OC-192 | 9.953Gbps |

### Fiber Distributed Data Interface (FDDI)

The Fiber Distributed Data Interface (FDDI) is a network technology that uses fiber-optic cable as a transmission medium and dual counter-rotating rings to provide data delivery and fault tolerance. FDDI was developed as a way to combine the high-speed capabilities of fiber-optic cable and the fault tolerance of IBM's Token Ring technologies. An FDDI network is based on a standard introduced by the ANSI X3T9.5 committee in 1986. It defines a high-speed (at 100Mbps), token-passing network using fiber-optic cable. In 1994, the standard was updated to include copper cable (called CDDI, or Copper Distributed Data Interface). FDDI was slow to be adopted but has found its niche as a reliable, high-speed technology for backbones and high-bandwidth applications that demand reliability.

FDDI is similar to Token Ring in that it uses token passing for permission to transmit. Instead of a single ring, however, FDDI uses two rings that counterrotate. That is, the token is passed clockwise in one ring and counterclockwise in the other. If a failure occurs, the counter-rotating rings can join together, forming a ring around the fault and thus isolating the fault and allowing communications to continue.

Additionally, stations on an FDDI network can be categorized as either *dual-attached station (DAS)* or *single-attached station (SAS)*. DASes are attached to both rings, whereas SASes are attached to only one of the rings. DASes are much more fault tolerant than SASes.

# Remote Access Protocols

A remote access protocol manages the connection between a remote computer and a remote access server. These are the primary remote access protocols that are in use today:

- Serial Line Internet Protocol (SLIP)
- Point-to-Point Protocol (PPP) and Point-to-Point Protocol over Ethernet (PPPoE)
- Point-to-Point Tunneling Protocol (PPTP)
- Remote Access Services (RAS)
- Remote Desktop Protocol (RDP)

## Serial Line Internet Protocol (SLIP)

In 1984, students at the University of California, Berkeley, developed SLIP for UNIX as a way to transmit TCP/IP over serial connections (such as modem connections over POTS). SLIP operates at both the Physical and Data Link layers of the OSI model. Today, SLIP is found in many network operating systems in addition to UNIX. It is being used less frequently with each passing year, though, because it lacks features when compared with other protocols. Although a low overhead is associated with using SLIP and you can use it to transport TCP/IP over serial connections, it does no error checking or packet addressing and can be used only on serial connections. SLIP is used today primarily to connect a workstation to the Internet or to another network running TCP/IP.

SLIP does not support encrypted passwords and therefore transmits passwords in clear text, which is not secure at all.

Setting up SLIP for a remote connection requires a SLIP account on the host machine and usually a batch file or a script on the workstation. When SLIP is used to log in to a remote machine, a terminal mode must be configured after login to the remote site so that the script can enter each parameter. If you don't use a script, you will have to establish the connection and then open a terminal window to log in to the remote access server manually.

 It is difficult to create a batch file that correctly configures SLIP. Our advice is to avoid SLIP whenever possible. Also, many modern operating systems, such as Windows 2000 Server, don't support inbound SLIP connections. Windows 2000, however, still supports outbound SLIP to allow connections to UNIX machines.

## Point-to-Point Protocol (PPP) and PPPoE (Point-to-Point Protocol over Ethernet)

PPP is used to implement TCP/IP; it is the protocol that establishes a connection over point-to-point links (for example, dial-up and dedicated leased lines). It is most commonly used for remote connections to ISPs and LANs.

PPP uses the Link Control Protocol (LCP) to communicate between PPP client and host. LCP tests the link between client and PPP host and specifies PPP client configuration. Through LCP, PPP also supports authentication negotiation, as well as negotiation of encryption and compression between client and server, using compression control protocols (CCPs) and encryption control protocols (ECPs). PPP can support several network protocols through the use of protocol-specific network control protocols (NCPs), and because it features error checking and can run over many types of physical media, PPP has almost completely replaced SLIP. In addition, PPP can automatically configure TCP/IP and other protocol parameters through the use of the IP control protocol (IPCP) NCP. On the downside, high overhead is associated with using PPP, and it is not compatible with some older configurations.

From the technician's standpoint, PPP is easy to configure. Once you connect to a router using PPP, the router assigns all other TCP/IP parameters. This is typically done with the Dynamic Host Configuration Protocol (DHCP). DHCP is the protocol within the TCP/IP protocol stack that is used to assign TCP/IP addressing information, including host IP address, subnet mask, and DNS configuration. This information can be assigned over a LAN connection or a dial-up connection. When you connect to an ISP, you are most likely getting your IP address from a DHCP server.

To configure a Windows 2000 Professional client to dial up a remote access server and connect using PPP, follow these steps:

1. Choose Start ➤ Programs ➤ Accessories ➤ Communications ➤ Network and Dial-up Connections to open the Network and Dial-up Connections window.

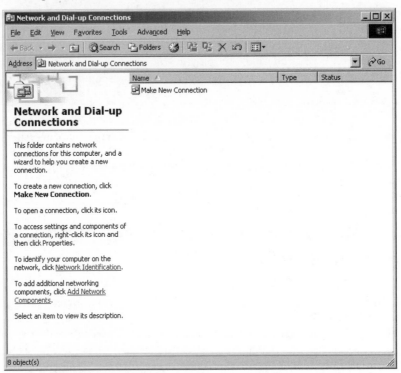

2. Double-click Make New Connection to open the Network Connection Wizard.

**3.** Click Next to display the Network Connection Type window.

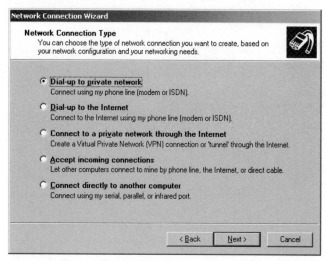

**4.** Select the type of connection you would like to establish and click Next. In this example, Dial-up to Private Network is used to establish a PPP connection. For this option, the next window is the Phone Number to Dial window.

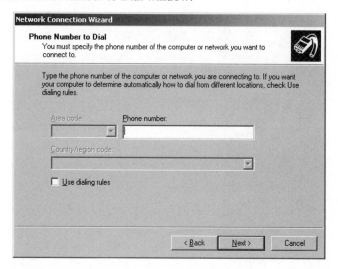

**5.**  Enter the phone number of the remote access server you wish to dial. Check the Use Dialing Rules box if you need to change the area code or country code. Then click Next to display the Connection Availability window.

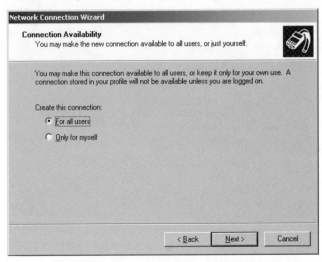

**6.**  Select whether to create the connection for the currently logged-in user or for all users. Then click Next to display the Completing the Network Connection Wizard window.

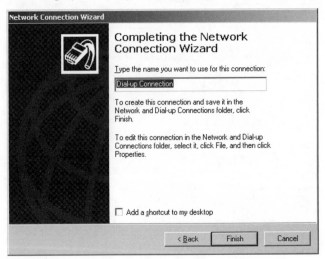

**7.** Enter a descriptive name for your connection and check the Add a Shortcut to My Desktop box if you wish. Click Finish to display the Connect dialog window. This is the same window that displays when you double-click the connection you just created in the Network and Dial-up Connections window.

**8.** Close this window for now and notice that the Network and Dial-up Connections window now shows your newly created connection.

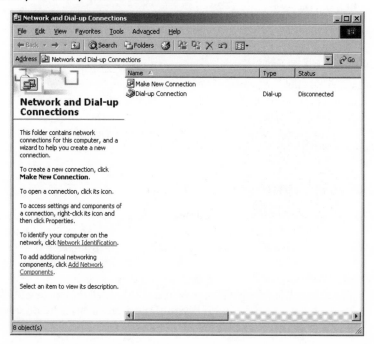

**9.** From the Network and Dial-up Connections window, right-click the connection you just made, choose Properties from the shortcut menu, and then click the Networking tab.

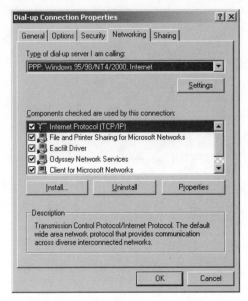

**10.** From the Type of Dial-up Server I Am Calling drop-down list, choose PPP: Windows 95/98/NT4/2000, Internet.

**11.** Check or clear the components you will or won't be using to connect to the server using PPP. You may also install additional components and change the properties of components.

**12.** Click OK to save the settings.

You can now double-click the connection you made in the Network and Dial-up Connections window, enter your username and password, and click Dial to establish the connection.

There is a version of PPP called PPP over Ethernet (PPPoE) that allows the authentication methods of PPP to be used over Ethernet and high-speed Internet connections so individual users can be authenticated for Internet access over a shared medium like Ethernet or DSL.

## Point-to-Point Tunneling Protocol (PPTP)

PPTP is the Microsoft-created protocol based on PPP. It is used to create virtual connections across the Internet using TCP/IP and PPP so that two networks can use the Internet as their WAN link and yet retain private network security. PPTP is both simple and secure.

To use PPTP, you set up a PPP session between the client and server, typically over the Internet. Once the session is established, you create a second dial-up session that dials through the existing PPP session using PPTP. The PPTP session tunnels through the existing PPP connection, creating a secure session. In this way, you can use the Internet to create a secure session between the client and the server. Also called a *virtual private network (VPN)*, this type of connection is very inexpensive when compared with a direct connection.

PPTP is a good idea for network administrators who want to connect several LANs but don't want to pay for dedicated leased lines. But, as with any network technology, there can be disadvantages:

- PPTP is not available on all types of servers.

- PPTP is not a fully accepted standard.

- PPTP is more difficult to set up than PPP.

- Tunneling can reduce throughput.

See Chapter 8 for a discussion on the Layer 2 Tunneling Protocol (L2TP), which is an IETF-standardized tunneling protocol that provides security and privacy as PPTP does. Starting with Windows 2000, Microsoft operating systems offer the choice of L2TP and PPTP.

You can implement PPTP in two ways. First, you can set up a server to act as the gateway to the Internet and the one that does all the tunneling. The workstations will run normally without any additional configuration. You would normally use this method to connect entire networks. Figure 7.5 shows two networks connected using PPTP. Notice how the TCP/IP packets are tunneled through an intermediate TCP/IP network (in this case, the Internet).

**FIGURE 7.5**    A PPTP implementation connecting two LANs over the Internet

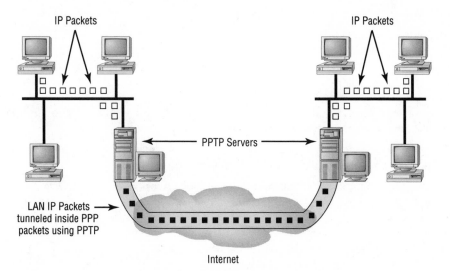

The second way to use PPTP is to configure a single, remote workstation to connect to a corporate network over the Internet. The workstation is configured to connect to the Internet via an ISP, and the VPN client is configured with the address of the VPN remote access server, as shown in Figure 7.6. PPTP is often used to connect remote workstations to corporate LANs when a workstation must communicate with a corporate network over a dial-up PPP link through an ISP and the link must be secure.

**FIGURE 7.6**    A workstation is connected to a corporate LAN over the Internet using PPTP.

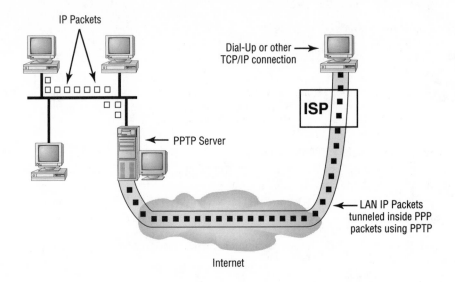

 Windows 98, NT4, 2000, and XP include PPTP. You must add it to Windows 95.

To configure a Windows 2000 Professional client to create a VPN connection using PPTP over a PPP connection to a remote access server, follow these steps:

1.  Choose Start ➢ Programs ➢ Accessories ➢ Communications ➢ Network and Dial-up Connections to open the Network and Dial-Up Connections window.

2.  Double-click Make New Connection to open the Network Connection Wizard.

3.  Click Next to display the Network Connection Type window.

**4.** Select the type of connection you would like to establish and click Next. In this example, Connect to a Private Network through the Internet is used to create a VPN connection. For this option, the next window is the Public Network window.

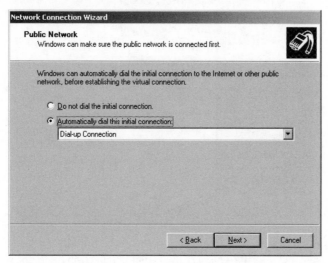

**5.** Select the connection to establish the PPP connection or choose not to dial an initial connection. Then click Next to display the Destination Address window.

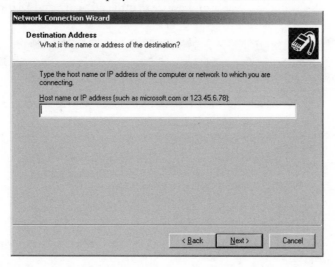

**6.** Enter the host name or IP address of the VPN server to which you wish to connect. This name or address must be reachable through the PPP connection you specified in the Public Network window or to which you intend to connect manually. Then click Next to display the Connection Availability window.

**7.**   Select whether to create the connection for the currently logged-in user (Only for Myself) or for all users. Then click Next to display the Completing the Network Connection Wizard window.

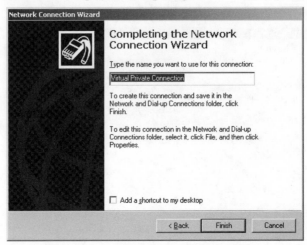

**8.**   Enter a descriptive name for your connection and check the Add a Shortcut to My Desktop box if you wish. Click Finish to display the Initial Connection dialog box. This is the same dialog box that displays when you double-click the VPN connection you just created in the Network and Dial-up Connections window when the PPP connection was not yet established. Close this window for now and notice that the Network and Dial-up Connections window now shows your newly created VPN connection.

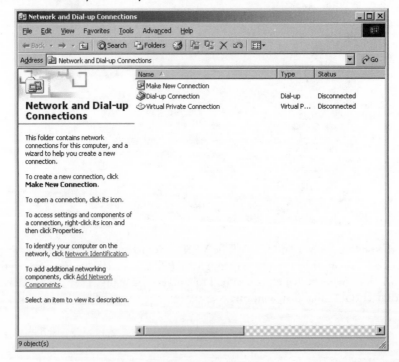

9.  From the Network and Dial-up Connections window, right-click the connection you just made, choose Properties from the shortcut menu, and then click the Networking tab.

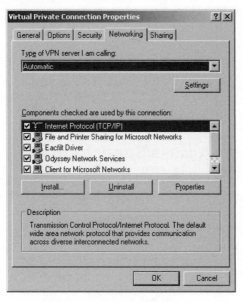

10. From the Type of VPN Server I Am Calling drop-down list, you can choose either PPTP or L2TP. However, we recommend you leave the default Automatic setting because the best matching protocol will be selected automatically, either PPTP or L2TP.

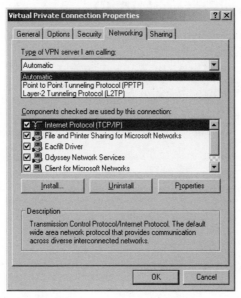

**11.** Check or clear the components you will or won't be using to connect to the VPN server. You may also install additional components and change the properties of components. Note that these components are independent of the ones you specified for the PPP connection through which the VPN is tunneled.

**12.** Click OK to save the settings.

You can now double-click the VPN connection you made in the Network and Dial-up Connections window, choose to connect to the PPP connection through which you wish to tunnel (which may involve dialing up a remote access server, requiring you to first enter your username and password), and click Dial to establish the connection.

## Windows Remote Access Services (RAS)

Both Windows NT and Windows 2000 include technology to allow users to dial up a server and connect to not only that server, but also to that server's host network. This technology is known as RAS. RAS is used in smaller networks where a dedicated dial-up router is not practical or possible. In a RAS setup, you can basically connect a modem to a Windows NT or Windows 2000 server and, by way of the RAS, configure that modem as dial-out only, dial-up only, or a combination.

It is important to note that RAS, without help, provides access to only the LAN to remote users; it does not allow LAN users to use the modem to, say, dial their AOL account. For that, they would need Microsoft's Shared Modem Services, which comes with the Small Business Server edition of Windows NT. Windows 2000, however, comes with the ability to share outbound connections. This is set up with Windows 2000's RRAS utility.

## Remote Desktop Protocol (RDP)

The Remote Desktop Protocol (RDP) is very similar to the Independent Computing Architecture (ICA) protocol used by Citrix products. As a matter of fact, RDP is used to access Windows Terminal Services, a close relative of the Citrix WinFrame product line. RDP performs the same basic functions as ICA, but it does it with a lot less functionality. RDP provides remote access for Windows clients only, whereas ICA provides it for multiple platforms, including DOS, Linux, Macintosh and many others. ICA is also a much more full-featured platform, including support for automatic client updates, publishing an application to a web browser, and much more.

For more information on the differences between RDP and ICA, check out www.purenetworking.net/RDPvsICA.htm.

# Summary

In this chapter, you learned about the different technologies used to access networks remotely. You learned about the different connection methods—like ISDN, FDDI, ATM, dial-up, xDSL, and T1—as well as the different protocols that are used (including PPP, PPTP, and RAS). You also learned about the proper way to configure a workstation using VPN to connect to a network over the Internet.

# Exam Essentials

**Be able to differentiate the kinds of WAN and remote access technologies.** You must be able to tell the different speeds and capacities of the different remote access and WAN technologies, as well as the media over which they are implemented. Tables 7.2 and 7.3 give speeds for some of these items.

**Be able to describe each of the various remote access components.** These include the following: Remote Access Service (RAS), Point-to-Point Protocol (PPP), and Point-to-Point Tunneling Protocol (PPTP). Other protocols include SLIP, PPPoE, and RDP.

**Identify the basic characteristics of various Internet access technologies.** These include DSL, broadband cable, and POTS. It is important to know the differentiating features of these access technologies. Know their advantages and disadvantages so you can know the best use of each.

**Be able to configure remote access on a Windows machine to connect to various types of servers using different protocols.** Depending on the operating system, there are different methods for configuring a client machine for remote access to a particular server.

# Review Questions

1. A computer service center gets a call from a customer complaining that they just bought a new computer and Ethernet switch for their home LAN. Everything worked fine until they plugged the existing computer, the new computer, and DSL modem into the switch. When asked if there were any LEDs lit on the switch, the customer says only the LEDs for the ports leading to the computers are lit. What's the problem?

   **A.** The extra computer is causing a power sag, disabling all devices.

   **B.** The NIC card in the new computer is defective, causing the switch not to power up.

   **C.** Either the switch port or the DSL modem port connected to each other must be switched to MDI mode, but not both.

   **D.** The DSL modem should connect to the computer and the computer to the switch.

2. Which of the following is not a characteristic of PPP?

   **A.** PPP supports DHCP.

   **B.** PPP establishes the connection to the RAS server.

   **C.** PPP takes the place of TCP/IP over dial-up and leased lines.

   **D.** PPP can negotiate encryption and compression.

3. Which option lists the correct order of cable modem components from the computer to the outside cable?

   **A.** NIC, RG-6 coax, cable modem, UTP, wall outlet

   **B.** Cable modem, RG-6, wall outlet, UTP, NIC

   **C.** NIC, UTP, cable modem, RG-6, wall outlet

   **D.** NIC, cable modem, UTP, wall outlet, RG-6

4. Which transport protocol does PPTP use?

   **A.** IPX/SPX

   **B.** SNA

   **C.** AppleTalk

   **D.** TCP/IP

5. Which of the following is the greatest advantage of PSTN (POTS)?

   **A.** Readily available

   **B.** Greater than 64Kbps data rates

   **C.** Fault tolerant

   **D.** Not available in all markets

**6.** Which of the following is an advantage of ISDN? (Choose the best answer.)

   **A.** Readily available

   **B.** Easy to configure

   **C.** Least expensive implementation

   **D.** Greater than 64Kbps possible

**7.** Which WAN technology uses digital signaling from sender to receiver?

   **A.** X.25

   **B.** POTS

   **C.** X2

   **D.** Kflex

   **E.** T-series

**8.** The UART in your PC is an 8250. You have installed an external ISDN Terminal Adapter on your computer. You are not getting the full speed of an ISDN line. You must replace the UART with which chip set?

   **A.** 8550

   **B.** 11500

   **C.** 12550

   **D.** 16550

**9.** Which of the following components is necessary for remote asynchronous connection?

   **A.** Keyboard

   **B.** Modem

   **C.** Mouse

   **D.** Monitor

**10.** What must be set on an internal modem to use it in a PC? (Choose all that apply.)

   **A.** COM port

   **B.** I/O address

   **C.** DMA Channel

   **D.** IRQ

**11.** You bought a Windows 2000 computer by mail order. You can see that the modem is installed because you have plugged a phone line into the RJ-11 modem jack. Everything else has worked from the first time you plugged in the modem, but the modem fails to respond. What should you check next?

   **A.** Device Manager

   **B.** Explorer

   **C.** The vendor's website

   **D.** The Start menu

**12.** You have a server with two external modems. The modems work one at a time but not together. COM1 is set to IRQ 4, I/O 3F8h. COM2 is configured for IRQ 3, I/O 3F8h. What should you do to ensure that both modems work simultaneously?

**A.** Change the IRQ of modem 1.

**B.** Change the I/O address of COM2.

**C.** Change the IRQ of modem 2.

**D.** Change the COM port of modem 2.

**13.** Which of the following protocols works at both the Physical and Data Link layers of the OSI model?

**A.** SLIP

**B.** PPP

**C.** TCP/IP

**D.** PPTP

**14.** What is the name of the 128Kbps two-wire digital circuit that is coming into your home, over which you can have 64Kbps of data throughput and a voice conversation simultaneously or no voice conversation while you run data at 128Kbps?

**A.** ISDN PRI

**B.** POTS

**C.** T1

**D.** ISDN BRI

**15.** A computer store customer comes in requesting a device that will allow their analog phone and their computer to use their ISDN BRI circuit. What should the salesperson sell them?

**A.** A cable modem

**B.** A terminal adapter

**C.** A DSL modem

**D.** An ISDN adapter

**16.** Which of the following circuits has the highest possible bit rate?

**A.** T3

**B.** ADSL

**C.** OC-1

**D.** Broadband cable

**17.** You want to order analog ISDN. You call around and can't seem to find the equipment you want. What could be the possible reason for this?

    **A.** Everyone is out of stock because of unexpected customer demand.

    **B.** ISDN equipment is only available in PC card format.

    **C.** You must order this with external termination.

    **D.** You can't order analog ISDN.

**18.** Which of the following is a remote access protocol that supports the negotiation of such features as compression, encryption, and authentication?

    **A.** PPP

    **B.** SLIP

    **C.** X.25

    **D.** T1

**19.** What is the Microsoft TCP/IP protocol that can be used over the Internet to create a secure virtual network?

    **A.** SLIP

    **B.** PPTP

    **C.** TCP

    **D.** HTTP

**20.** What is the standard I/O port of COM3?

    **A.** 2E8

    **B.** 2F8

    **C.** 3E8

    **D.** D.3F8

# Answers to Review Questions

**1.** C. It's perfectly fine to include a hub or switch in your DSL or cable modem network. However, without a router implementing NAT, generally only one computer can access the Internet at a time because the service provider dynamically assigns only one IP address to a subscriber. But that's not the problem in this case. The problem described here arises when you try to connect two ports in the MDI-X state to each other. MDI-X is the usual state for switch, hub, and DSL/cable modem ports. Therefore, interconnecting any two of these devices will require connectivity on one side to a switchable port so a straight-through cable can be used to communicate. If no such port exists, an Ethernet crossover cable must be used between the MDI-X ports. The power in this situation is probably fine because the LEDs are lit for the switch ports leading to the computers, which have MDI ports that connect to switches, hubs, and broadband modems using regular straight-through cables.

**2.** C. PPP certainly supports TCP/IP and the exchange that must occur in this environment between client and server, but it does not ever take the place of TCP/IP. The other options are characteristics of PPP.

**3.** C. The NIC card in your computer connects to your cable modem's Ethernet port with UTP cable. The modem then connects to the wall outlet with RG-6 or CATV coaxial cable, which interconnects to the permanently wired cable company feed for the room in which the cable modem is installed. Eventually a splitter will be reached, but there should be only one splitter between the cable company's drop and the cable modem. Any additional splitting should be done on the TV side of the first splitter.

**4.** D. The Point-to-Point Tunneling Protocol uses TCP/IP as a transport.

**5.** A. The major advantage to the Public Switched Telephone Network (or POTS, the plain old telephone service) is that it is readily available in almost every part of the world.

**6.** D. Of the advantages listed, the one most often associated with ISDN is the higher bandwidth available.

**7.** E. The T-series of WAN connection (such as T1, T3, and so on) uses digital signaling completely, from sending hardware to receiving hardware.

**8.** D. For the serial buffers to keep up with the high bandwidth of ISDN connections, you must have a 16-bit UART on the serial port that the Terminal Adapter is connected to. The only true 16-bit UART listed is the 16550.

**9.** B. Although a keyboard, a mouse, and a monitor are required for browsing the Web, the only one absolutely required for a remote asynchronous connection is a modem.

**10.** A, B, D. When you install an internal modem into a PC, the COM port, I/O address, and IRQ must be set. This is done either manually, as in the case of most ISA cards, or automatically, as in the case of PCI.

**11.** A. Device Manager is the built-in utility for Windows 2000 that shows whether or not a particular device is installed correctly.

**12.** B. The I/O addresses of both modems are conflicting because they are the same. If you change the I/O address of COM2, both modems will work at the same time.

**13.** A. The SLIP protocol specifies both a Data Link portion and a Physical portion. The Physical portion specifies that the protocol will work only over a serial link.

**14.** D. A 23B+D ISDN PRI is delivered over a T1 circuit, which is a four-wire service. PRIs have 23 64Kbps B channels and 1 64Kbps D channel. It is the ISDN BRI circuit that is delivered to the customer on a single copper pair, boasting a 2B+D service with 128Kbps combined bandwidth on the B channels and a 16Kbps D channel, all on one copper pair. POTS can do analog voice or data, but not both simultaneously and not digitally.

**15.** B. A terminal adapter is an ISDN-compliant device that allows non-ISDN devices, such as computers and analog phones, to gain access to the ISDN network. *ISDN adapter* is a somewhat generic term relating to an expansion card that only serves to make a computer ISDN-compliant.

**16.** C. The only two contenders here are the T3 and the OC-1 circuits, but the OC-1 edges the T3 out by about 7Mbps, with the T3 running at about 45Mbps and the OC-1 having about a 52Mbps bit rate.

**17.** D. ISDN is a digital services network. There is no such thing as analog ISDN.

**18.** A. PPP supports the negotiation of each of these features, while SLIP, an older, more primitive remote access protocol, does not. X.25 and T1 are protocols used to support remote access but are not themselves capable of providing these features.

**19.** B. The Point-to-Point Tunneling Protocol (PPTP) allows you to create a secure virtual connection between two points by tunneling one protocol inside another. Usually, a PPP connection is opened over a TCP/IP link.

**20.** C. Every COM port is assigned a default I/O port. The default I/O port of COM3 is 3E8.

# Chapter

# 8

# Network Access and Security

---

## THE FOLLOWING NETWORK+ EXAM OBJECTIVES ARE COVERED IN THIS CHAPTER:

✓ **2.17 Identify the following security protocols and describe their purpose and function:**

- IPSec (Internet Protocol Security)
- L2TP (Layer 2 Tunneling Protocol)
- SSL (Secure Sockets Layer)
- WEP (Wired Equivalent Privacy)
- WPA (Wi-Fi Protected Access)
- 802.1x

✓ **2.18 Identify authentication protocols (for example, CHAP [Challenge Handshake Authentication Protocol], MS-CHAP [Microsoft Challenge Handshake Authentication Protocol], PAP [Password Authentication Protocol], RADIUS [Remote Authentication Dial-In User Service], Kerberos, and EAP [Extensible Authentication Protocol]).**

✓ **3.2 Identify the basic capabilities needed for client workstations to connect to and use network resources (for example, media, network protocols, and peer and server services).**

✓ **3.5 Identify the purpose, benefits, and characteristics of using a firewall.**

✓ **3.6 Identify the purpose, benefits, and characteristics of using a proxy service.**

✓ **3.7 Given a connectivity scenario, determine the impact on network functionality of a particular security implementation (for example, port blocking/filtering, authentication, and encryption).**

✓ **3.12 Identify the purpose and characteristics of disaster recovery.**

- Backup/restore
- Offsite storage
- Hot and cold spares
- Hot, warm, and cold sites

There are two prerequisites that you should keep in mind when you access a resource on the network: network access and the proper security clearance. These items work together to allow you access to a particular resource.

The first of these two topics that you need to consider is network access. Network access involves installing client software on your computer. This software gives your computer the instructions that it needs to be able to access the network.

Network security involves ensuring that only authorized users have access to the network and that they access it only in authorized ways. You want to ensure that hardware, software, and data are available to authorized users when they are needed, but you also want to ensure that hardware, software, and data are not compromised or threatened. In addition to providing network access, client software works with the network operating system to provide network security.

As a network administrator, you can create an effective security plan in a number of ways and by using a variety of tools and procedures. Some of these are practical, commonsense safeguards, and others involve implementing protective systems and technologies. Although numerous recent examples indicate that almost no network is completely immune to security breaches, taking advantage of the measures in this chapter gives you a head start.

You'll start by learning the different types of clients and how they are installed. You'll then learn some of the simplest of security measures, usernames and passwords, and see both good and bad examples. You'll then move on to the more complex ways to secure your network—firewalls and proxies. Finally, you'll learn about some threats that may exist for your network. The Network+ exam covers all of these topics.

One aspect we don't discuss in this chapter is physical security, which the Network+ exam doesn't include. But remember: If someone can walk in and take your server or backup tapes, you don't have much security at all. In the real world, you'll want to ensure that all appropriate and necessary physical mechanisms are in place to protect your network.

This chapter only discusses the offsite storage portion of objective 3.12. The rest of that objective is covered in Chapter 9.

# Accessing Network Resources

Generally speaking, computers don't know how to access the various resources on your network. Each workstation OS (such as DOS and Windows 95/98, for example) knows how to access only its own local resources (such as local printers and local disk storage). For this reason, network operating systems use various methods to enable workstations to access network resources.

Windows 95/98 computers can use both the various built-in software clients and third-party client software to achieve network connectivity. As a network administrator, you'll need to tailor the connection software to your network. This is known as *proper client selection*. Once the client and the server are communicating, the PC can connect to network directories. Drive mappings allow reproducible connections from the local workstation to a network drive. Additionally, local print jobs on the PC are redirected instead of being sent out of a physical LPT port. The job is then sent to a network printer. This is achieved through printer port captures. Let's look at each of these in detail.

## Client Selection

A workstation communicates with the server over a certain protocol using client software. The protocol might be IPX/SPX (Internet Packet eXchange/Sequenced Packet eXchange), TCP/IP, or NetBEUI. Protocols are separate from the client software, but in some instances, the installation of protocols is integrated into the installation of client software.

In Windows 95/98, installed protocols and clients are listed together. To display a listing of the protocol(s) and client(s) currently installed, follow these steps:

1. Choose Start ➢ Settings ➢ Control Panel to open Control Panel.

2. Double-click Network to open the Network dialog box.

Installed clients are listed in the Configuration tab, at the top of the list above installed protocols and network adapters.

## Installing the Windows 95/98 and NT/2000 Client

Not surprisingly, Windows 95/98 comes with a client to connect to Microsoft servers and PCs. The Client for Microsoft Networks is the preferred client to access Microsoft networks. You also need this client to run the server tools for Windows NT/2000 on a Windows 95/98 computer to be able to perform domain administrative tasks.

Additionally, the network administrator will also have to authenticate (provide username and password at a login screen) again when using the server tools versions of administrative utilities on a Windows 95/98 machine. Therefore, the best combination for a network administrator's desktop machine is Windows NT/2000 Workstation or Server with the Client for Microsoft Networks.

Follow these steps to install the Microsoft Client for Networks on a Windows 95/98 computer:

1. Be sure that your network interface card (NIC) is properly installed and configured. The operating system must already recognize the card. Locate your Windows 95/98 CD and have it ready.

2.  Connect your network cable, and ensure that the link light on the NIC is on.

3.  Make sure that you are at the Windows 95/98 Desktop.

4.  Choose Start ➢ Settings ➢ Control Panel to open Control Panel.

5.  Double-click Network to open the Network dialog box.

6.  Click Add to open the Select Network Component Type dialog box.

7.  Click the Client icon in the list, and then click Add to open the Select Network Client dialog box.

8.  In the Manufacturers box, click Microsoft.

9.  In the Network Clients box, click Client for Microsoft Networks, and then click OK.

10. Click OK in the Network dialog box.

11. Place the Windows 95/98 CD in the drive if prompted to do so. Locate the install CAB files, and click OK if prompted. The Copying Windows Files screen opens and then closes.

12. In the System Settings Change dialog box, click Yes. The system will now reboot.

## Installing the NetWare Client

You have two options for setting up user workstations to connect to a NetWare network:

- Novell NetWare Client

- Microsoft Client for NetWare Networks

The one you select depends on your network and users. If you have a predominantly Windows NT network, the Microsoft client might better fit your needs. If you have a NetWare network or a hybrid network with a substantial Novell base, you need to use the Novell client; the latest version is available from Novell. Stay away from the clients distributed with Microsoft Windows 95/98 and NT/2000.

You can find the Novell Client for NetWare on the following:

- Novell's website at www.novell.com

- NetWare Client CD as part of the NetWare installation CD set or floppies (only with older versions)

- The ZENworks CD

- The SYS volume of a NetWare server

What happens when you lose connectivity with your NetWare server and you need to install client software? If you are using IPX/SPX without a web proxy server, downloading the software from the Novell website is out. Many companies place software media under lock and key and require support staff to install from the network. If that is the case with your company, that cuts out installing from CDs and floppies. The SYS volume is useless if you can't access the server. To avoid these problems, place a copy of the client installation software on your local PC the first time you connect to a NetWare server.

Regardless of the vendor you choose, a good practice is to download the installation files for your operating system (CABs for Windows 95/98, i386 directory for NT), the client software, the video drivers, and the NIC drivers as soon as you connect to a server.

Don't forget about yourself. The best combination for the network administrator's computer is a Windows 95/98 or NT/2000 operating system with the Novell NetWare Client. Novell Directory Services (NDS) takes care of authentication, thus addressing network security. Use Windows NT/2000 if you want additional security on your local machine. As an administrator, you have no choice about the client. Without Novell's client, you will not get the full functionality of the NetWare Administrator utility, and besides, Novell's client is free.

To install the Novell Client for NetWare on a Windows 95/98 computer, follow these steps:

1.  Download the latest Novell Client for NetWare from the Novell website, and run the self-extracting file. Or insert your NetWare Client CD.

2.  Double-click the `setup.exe` file. (This is true for the non-ZENworks version of the client software.) The Novell client license agreement window opens.

3.  Read the license agreement, and then click Yes to accept the agreement and to open the Welcome dialog box.

4.  In the Select an Installation Option section, click Typical.

5.  Click Install to open the Building Driver Information Database and Copying Files windows.

6.  You'll be asked if you want to set the preferred server properties for NetWare 3.*x* servers or the preferred tree, context, and server properties for NetWare 4.*x* and later servers.

    ▪ If you click Yes, you will have an opportunity to set these properties in the Novell NetWare Client Properties dialog box. Click OK when you finish entering the information, and the installation continues.

    ▪ If you click No, the installation continues.

On Windows 95/98 computers, some files need to be copied from the Windows 95/98 CABs. If these are not in the `Windows\Options\Cabs` directory, you will be prompted to insert the Windows 95/98 installation CD.

7.  When the installation is finished and you are prompted to restart the computer, click Reboot.

Be sure that your IPX/SPX or TCP/IP protocol stacks are properly configured. See Chapter 3 for details.

# Installing the UNIX Client

Windows 95/98 needs the client portion of the Network File System (NFS) to connect to the UNIX NFS. If a computer has this client installed, *NFS Client*—or similar wording—will appear in the listing in the Network dialog box.

 Windows 95/98 computers without an NFS client can connect directly to a UNIX system that is running Samba. Samba is a free server-based solution that uses Server Message Blocks (SMBs) to allow Microsoft clients to see the UNIX file system. Samba is available from `ftp://samba.anu.edu.au/pub/samba/`. Samba is designed for UNIX servers and will not install on a Windows 95/98 PC.

The client portion of NFS is currently available only from third-party vendors. No NFS client is distributed with Windows 95/98 or NT/2000. Two popular NFS client vendors are Sun and NetManage. Sun Microsystems offers server and client products for connectivity from a UNIX server to a PC. Its client-based product is Solstice NFS Client. NetManage offers several products, including Chameleon UNIX Link. You should select the vendor and product based on your individual needs and budget and after evaluating the demo software. Since third-party options tend to be more popular than their primary vendor counterparts, we're going to demonstrate the installation of NetManage's Chameleon.

 You can get a demo of Chameleon from the NetManage website at `www.netmanage.com`. This is a demo; after 30 days, the software ceases to function.

To install the NetManage Chameleon UNIX Link on a Windows 95/98 PC, follow these steps:

1. Double-click `setup.exe` in the `Cham_95\NFS` directory. This directory is on your CD or in your download directory after extraction. The NetManage Setup and License Notice windows open.

2. Read the License Notice, and click Accept to open the Setup Option dialog box.

3. Click Typical, and then click Next to open the Serial Number dialog box.

4. Enter your serial number and key in their fields, and then click Next to open the Select Directory dialog box.

 The serial number and key are typically included on a document that comes with the software. You can also obtain them from the website where you downloaded the free software (usually called a "demo" key).

5. Verify the installation directory. By default it is `C:\NETMANAG.95`. If you want to install to a different directory, enter the path or browse to the directory. When you are finished, click Next. Files are installed when the Copy Files dialog box opens.

6.   The Building Driver Information Database and Copying Files windows open. You may be prompted for your Windows 95/98 CD if the CAB files are not on your local hard drive.

7.   The Information screen opens, telling you that it will now install support programs. Click OK to open the Choose Program Destination Location dialog box.

8.   Click Next. The NetManage Setup window tells you that components are being installed.

9.   In the Finish window, click Finish. The NetManage Setup window opens, telling you that you must restart Windows for the changes to take effect.

10.  Click Yes to restart Windows.

## Selecting a Primary Client

Now you have connections to your NT, NetWare, and UNIX servers. Next, you must determine which one will be the primary client on your Windows 95/98 machines. The first question you must ask yourself is, Which servers do your users most often access? For your CAD/CAM engineers, it may be UNIX; for web design, it could be either NT or NetWare. Each user will want their favorite servers to appear first in the Network Neighborhood. As an administrator, you will want to gain quick access to the network you spend the most time managing. The network administrator can set a primary type of client to speed access and searches.

To set a primary client on a Windows 95/98 PC, follow these steps:

1.   Choose Start ➢ Settings ➢ Control Panel to open Control Panel.

2.   Double-click Network to open the Network dialog box with the Configuration tab selected. Notice the Client for Microsoft Networks, the NetManage UNIX Link NFS Client, and the Novell NetWare Client appear at the top of the dialog box.

3.   Click the drop-down button to the right of the Primary Network Logon text field to display the drop-down list.

4.   Scroll down through the options, and select the primary client of your choice. Your selection now appears in the Primary Network Logon text field.

5.   Click OK to save the change. The System Settings Change dialog box opens, asking you to restart your computer.

6.   Click Yes to restart your computer.

# Managing User Account and Password Security

Usernames and passwords are key to network security, and you use them to control initial access to your system. Although the network administrator assigns usernames and passwords, users can generally change their passwords. Thus, you need to ensure that users have information about what constitutes a good password. In the following sections, we'll look at the security issues related to user accounts and passwords, including resource-sharing models and user account and password management.

# Network Resource-Sharing Security Models

You can secure files that are shared over the network in two ways:

- At the share level
- At the user level

Although user-level security provides more control over files and is the preferred model, implementing share-level security is easier for the network administrator. Let's examine these two security models and their features.

## Share-Level Security

In a network that uses share-level security, you assign passwords to individual files or other network resources (such as printers) instead of assigning rights to users. You then give these passwords to all users who need access to these resources. All resources are visible from anywhere in the network, and any user who knows the password for a particular network resource can make changes to it. With this type of security, the network support staff will have no way of knowing who is manipulating each resource. Share-level security is best used in smaller networks, where resources are more easily tracked.

Windows 95/98 and Windows NT/2000/2003 support share-level security.

## User-Level Security

In a network that uses user-level security, rights to network resources (such as files, directories, and printers) are assigned to specific users who gain access to the network through individually assigned usernames and passwords. Thus, only users who have a valid username and password and have been assigned the appropriate rights to network resources can see and access those resources. User-level security provides greater control over who is accessing which resources because users do not share their usernames and passwords with other users (or at least they shouldn't). User-level security is, therefore, the preferred method for securing files.

Windows NT/2000/2003, NetWare, and UNIX support user-level security.

# Managing Accounts

First and foremost, you manage access to network resources through a user account and the rights given to that account. The network administrator is charged with the daily maintenance of these accounts. Common security duties include renaming accounts and setting the number of concurrent connections. You can also specify where users can log in, how often they can log in, at what times they can log in, how often their passwords expire, and when their accounts expire.

## Disabling Accounts

When a user leaves the organization, you have three options:

- Leave the account in place.
- Delete the account.
- Disable the account.

If you leave the account in place, anyone (including the user to whom it belonged) can log in as that user if they know that user's password. Therefore, leaving the account in place is a security breach. Deleting the account presents its own set of problems. If you delete an account and then create a new one, the numeric ID associated with that user (UID in UNIX, SID in Windows Server) is lost. It is through this number that passwords and rights to network resources are associated with the user account. If you create a new user account with the same name as the user account you deleted, the identification number of the new account will be different from that of the old account, and thus none of the settings of the old account will be in place for the new account.

 This same concept holds true for NetWare, although NetWare does not use a number to uniquely identify each entity. Each NDS object (including users) is a unique object ID.

Your best practice is to disable an account until a decision has been made as to what should happen to it. Perhaps you'll want to simply rename the account when a new person is hired. When you disable an account, it still exists but no one can use it to log in. You might also disable an account (rather than deleting it) if someone leaves for an extended period (for example, on maternity/paternity leave or medical leave). In most network operating systems, disabling an account involves changing a setting to say something like Account Disabled.

## Disabling Temporary Accounts

Because of the proliferation of contract and temporary employees in the information technology industry, you need to know how to manage temporary accounts. A temporary account is used for only a short period (less than a month or so) and then disabled.

Managing the accounts of temporary employees is easy. You can simply set the account to expire on the employee's anticipated last day of work. The network operating system then disables, but does not delete, these accounts on the expiration date.

## Setting Up Anonymous Accounts

Anonymous accounts provide extremely limited access for a large number of users who all log in with the same username, which is often Anonymous or Guest. An anonymous login is frequently used to access FTP files. You log in with the username Anonymous and enter your e-mail address as the password.

Users don't necessarily enter their correct e-mail address. If you really want to know where on the Internet the user is located, use third-party software to verify IP addresses and Internet domain names.

Avoid using anonymous accounts for regular network access. If someone is using an anonymous account, you cannot track who manipulated a file. Windows NT/2000/2003 comes with the anonymous account Guest disabled. NetWare does not automatically create a guest account. You should not change these default setups.

Some web servers create an Internet user account to allow anonymous access to the website. The Internet user account is automatically created and allowed to access the web server over the network. The password is always blank. You never see a request to log in to the server. This is done automatically. Without this account, no one would be able to access your web pages.

Do not rename the Internet user account or set a password. If you do so, the general public will not be able to view your website. If you want to secure documents, use another web server, secure HTTP, Windows NT domain and file security, or NetWare Directory Services security.

## Limiting Connections

You may want to limit the number of times a user can connect to the network. Users should normally be logged in to the network for only one instance because they can only be in one place at a time. If the system indicates they are logged in from more than one place, someone else might be using their account. When you limit concurrent connections to one, only a single user at a single workstation can gain access to the network using a particular user account. Some users, however, might need to log in multiple times in order to use certain applications or perform certain functions. In that case, you can allow the user to have multiple concurrent connections.

Limiting the location from which a user logs in can be important also because typical users shouldn't log in to the network from any place but their own workstation. Although in theory this is true, it is not often implemented in most corporations. Users move stations, often not taking their computers with them. Or they have to log in at someone else's station to perform some function. Unless you require really tight security, this restriction requires too much administrative effort. Both NetWare and Windows NT/2000/2003 can limit which station(s) a user is allowed to log in from; however, by default, user accounts are not restricted in this respect. This is probably acceptable in most cases. If you really want to tighten security, restrict users to logging in from their assigned workstations. By default, Windows NT/2000/2003 servers do not allow a regular user to log in at the console because most users should not be working directly on a server. They can do too much damage accidentally. In NetWare, the console interface is entirely different and is not used to access network resources, so this is not an issue.

## Renaming the Maintenance Account

Network operating systems automatically give the network maintenance (or administration) account a default name. In Windows NT/2000/2003, this account is named Administrator; in UNIX, it is Root; and in NetWare, it is Admin. If you don't change this account name, hackers already have half the information they need to break in to your network. The only thing they're missing is the password.

Rename the account to something innocuous or use the same naming convention that is used for regular users. For example, jmorris is a much better choice than super. Here is a list of common names that you should not use:

- Admin
- Administrator
- Analyst
- Audit
- Comptroller
- Controller
- Manager
- Root
- Super
- Superuser
- Supervisor
- Wizard
- Any variation on the above

# Managing Passwords

Like any other aspect of network security, passwords must be managed. Managing passwords involves ensuring that all passwords for user accounts follow security guidelines so that they cannot be easily guessed or cracked, as well as implementing features of your network operating system to prevent unauthorized access.

## What Makes a Strong Password?

Generally speaking, a strong password is a combination of alphanumeric and special characters that is easy for you to remember and difficult for someone else to guess. Unfortunately, many users try to make things easy on themselves and choose passwords that are easy to guess. Let's look at some characteristics of strong passwords.

### Minimum Length

Strong passwords should be at least eight characters, if not more. They shouldn't be any longer than 15 characters so that they are easy to remember. You need to specify a minimum length for passwords because a short password is easily cracked. For example, there are only so many combinations of three characters. The upper limit depends on the capabilities of your operating system and the ability of your users to remember complex passwords. Users will forget passwords that are too long, so you must balance ease of remembrance with the level of security you need to implement.

## The Weak List

Here are some passwords that you should never use:

- The word *password*
- Proper names
- Your pet's name
- Your spouse's name
- Your children's names
- Any word in the dictionary
- A license plate number
- Birth dates
- Anniversary dates
- Your username
- The word *server*
- Any text or label on the PC or monitor
- Your company's name
- Your occupation
- Your favorite color
- Any of the above with a leading number
- Any of the above with a trailing number
- Any of the above spelled backward

There are others, but these are the most commonly used weak passwords.

## Using Characters to Make a Strong Password

Difficult-to-crack passwords do not have to be difficult to remember, and they should include a combination of numbers, letters, and special characters (not just letters, not just numbers, not just special characters, but a combination of all three). Special characters are those that cannot be considered letters or numbers (for example, $ % ^ # @). An example of a strong password is tqbf4#jotld. Such a password may look hard to remember, but it is not. You may remember the following sentence, which uses every letter in the English alphabet: The quick brown fox jumped over the lazy dog. Take the first letter of each word, put the number 4 and a pound (#) symbol in the middle, and you have a strong password.

To consistently get strong passwords, you can use auditing tools, such as a crack program that tries to guess passwords. If you use strong passwords, the crack program should have great difficulty guessing them. Use special characters and numbers in the middle of the password, for example, under43gate@w#ay. Do not use just a regular word preceded by or ending with a special character. Good crack programs strip off the leading and trailing characters in their decryption attempts.

Here are a few examples of strong passwords:

- run4!cover
- iron$steel4
- four$score

**WARNING**   Never write your password on a note and stick it under your keyboard or on your monitor. This is the most common network security breach.

## Password Management Features

All network operating systems (including NetWare, UNIX, and Windows NT/2000/2003) include functions for managing passwords so that the system remains secure and passwords cannot be easily hacked with crack programs. These functions include automatic account lockouts and password expiration.

### Automatic Account Lockouts

Hackers (as well as users who forget their passwords) attempt to log in by guessing a user's password. To ensure that a password can't be guessed by repeatedly inputting different passwords, most network operating systems have a feature that allows an account to be disabled, or locked out, after several unsuccessful login attempts. Once this feature is enabled on an account, the user cannot log in to that account even if the correct password is entered. This feature prevents a potential hacker from running an automated script to continuously attempt logins using different character combinations for the password.

After a lockout is activated, to log in successfully the user must ask the network support staff to unlock the account if the network operating system doesn't unlock it after a preset period. In high-security networks, it is usually advisable for an administrator to manually unlock every locked account rather than letting the network operating system do it automatically. In this way, the administrator is notified of a possible security breach.

**WARNING**   Be careful not to lock yourself out. With many network operating systems, only administrators can reset passwords. If you are the administrator and you lock yourself out, only another administrator can unlock your account. If you are the only administrator, you have a problem. Many network operating system vendors do have solutions to this problem, but the solution will cost you.

### Password Expiration

Passwords, even the best ones, do not age well over time. Eventually someone will guess or crack a password if it never changes. The chance of someone guessing your password (and the impact if it is guessed) is reduced if passwords are set to expire after a certain amount of time. After this time (which varies and can be set by the administrator), the old password is considered invalid and a new one must be specified. This new password is valid until it expires and another password must be specified.

Most organizations set up passwords to expire every 30 days. After that, users must reset their passwords immediately or during the allotted grace period. Some systems give the user a few grace logins after the password has expired. As the administrator, you should limit this grace period to a number of times or days.

 Each network operating system specifies a password expiration period. If your organization's policy states that users must change their passwords every 30 days, check to see if your operating system is enforcing that. For example, in NetWare the default expiration date is every 40 days and therefore might need to be changed.

## Unique Passwords and Password Histories

In older versions of many network operating systems, users could reset their passwords to their original form after using an intermediary password for a while. More recent network operating systems prevent this practice by using password histories.

A *password history* is a record of the past several passwords used by the user. When the user attempts to use any password stored in the password history, the password fails. The operating system then requests a password change again. When implementing a password history policy, be sure to make the password history large enough to contain at least a year's worth of password changes. For a policy that enforces passwords with a standard 30-day life span, a history of 12 or 13 passwords will suffice.

Advanced users know about the history feature. Creating a good password takes some time. Once a user finds a password, the human tendency is to want to keep it and use it for everything, which is counter to good security policy. If a user really likes a particular password or does not want to remember a new one, they will try to find a way around password histories. For example, one user admitted changing their password as many times as it took to defeat the history log and then changing it one last time back to the original password. This can take less than five minutes of a user's time.

Administrators can force users to change their passwords so that they are unique. The latest operating systems require unique passwords. All passwords are stored, and depending on the network operating system, more than 20 passwords can be stored. Reverting to any of the previous passwords is not allowed.

# Using Firewalls

It is popular these days to connect a corporate network to the Internet. By connecting your *private network* (only authorized users have access to the data) to a *public network* (everyone connected has access to the data), you introduce the possibility for security break-ins. For this reason, firewalls are implemented. A *firewall* protects a private network from unauthorized users on a public network.

Firewalls are usually a combination of hardware and software. The hardware is typically a computer or a dedicated piece of hardware (often called a black box) that contains two network cards. One connects to the public side; the other, to the private side. The software controls how the firewall operates and protects your network. It examines each incoming and outgoing packet and rejects any suspicious packets. In general, firewalls work by allowing only packets that pass security restrictions to be forwarded through the firewall.

The Network+ certified system administrator usually does not have the resources to design, install, and manage a firewall. These sections are to help you work in an environment where a firewall is already installed. You might also work as part of a team to install or upgrade your company's firewall solution. These sections will give you the tools you need to understand the basic operation of a firewall.

Firewalls can be placed on top of an existing operating system or be self-contained. Black box systems are proprietary systems that have external controls and are not controlled by the operating system. If you want to use a general-purpose operating system, you have two options: UNIX and Windows. Both can support third-party firewall products. Novell makes its own firewall product, BorderManager, which is excellent and runs on NetWare. But at the time of this writing, there are few third-party firewall products for NetWare.

All Windows NT firewalls should be installed on Windows Server computers rather than on Windows Workstation computers.

## Firewall Technologies

There are many firewall technologies, and they differ in the method they use to restrict information flow. Some, such as access control lists and dynamic packet filtering, are themselves used as firewalls. Others, such as proxies and demilitarized zones, are implemented with other firewall technologies to make a more robust, complete implementation.

**FIGURE 8.1**    Two networks with an ACL-enabled router

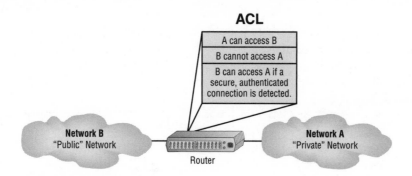

## Access Control Lists (ACL)

The first form of defense for every network connected to the Internet is access control lists (ACLs). These lists reside on your routers and determine which machines (that is, which IP addresses) can use the routers and in what direction. ACLs have been around for decades and have other uses apart from a firewall. Figure 8.1 shows how these lists prevent users on Network B from accessing Network A.

Note that data from users in Network A can pass through the router into Network B. IP spoofing attacks (in which someone, presumably a hacker, pretends to have a network address on the inside of a firewall to gain access to a network) can still occur if a user in Network B pretends to be located in Network A. (We'll discuss IP spoofing later in this chapter.)

## The Demilitarized Zone (DMZ)

Most firewalls in use today implement a feature called a DMZ, which is a network segment that is neither public nor local, but halfway between. People outside your network primarily access your web servers, FTP servers, and mail-relay servers. Because hackers tend to go after these servers first, you should place them in the DMZ. A standard DMZ setup has three network cards in the firewall computer. The first goes to the Internet. The second goes to the network segment where the aforementioned servers are located, the DMZ. The third connects to your intranet.

When hackers break into the DMZ, they can see only public information. If they break into a server, they are breaking into a server that holds only public information. Thus, the entire corporate network is not compromised. Last, no e-mail messages are vulnerable; only the relay server can be accessed. All actual messages are stored and viewed on e-mail servers inside the network. As you can see in Figure 8.2, the e-mail router, the FTP server, and the web server are all in the DMZ, and all critical servers are inside the firewall.

**FIGURE 8.2** A firewall with a DMZ

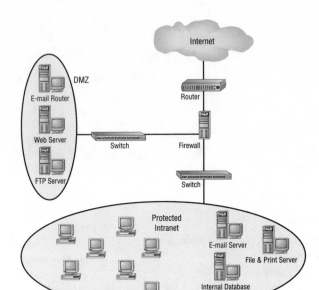

## Protocol Switching

Protocol switching protects data on the inside of a firewall. Because TCP/IP is the protocol used on the Internet, many external types of attacks, including the Ping of Death and SYN floods (discussed later in this chapter), are based on this protocol stack.

You can choose between two common approaches:

- Use a different protocol (not TCP/IP) on the internal network inside the firewall. For example, IP-based attacks aimed at your development server will never have any effect if you are using IPX on the internal network side of a router. This approach makes a router a natural firewall.

- Use TCP/IP on both the internal network and the Internet, and use a different protocol in a dead zone between them. For example, switch from IP to IPX in a dead zone, and then switch back to IP again once inside your network.

You can see both approaches in Figure 8.3. Notice the position of the dead zone between two of the routers, and also notice that the only protocol on the inside of either router is IPX. Any TCP/IP packet from the Internet is unable to pass into the local network because of the difference in protocols.

In both approaches, only the internal network is protected. You still need a firewall to handle any attacks on your network's access point and protocol-switching device.

**FIGURE 8.3**    Protocol switching with and without a dead zone

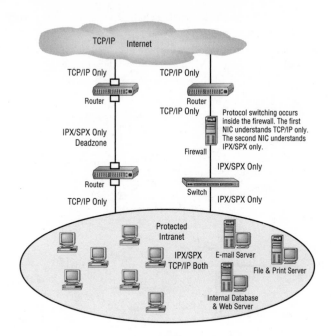

## Dynamic Packet Filtering

*Packet filtering* is the ability of a router or a firewall to discard packets that don't meet certain criteria. Firewalls use *dynamic packet filtering* to ensure that the packets they forward match sessions initiated on their private side. A *dynamic state list* (also known as a *state table*), held on a firewall, keeps track of all communications sessions between stations inside the firewall and stations outside the firewall. This list changes as communications sessions are added and deleted. Dynamic state lists allow a firewall to filter packets dynamically.

In dynamic packet filtering, only packets for current (and valid) communications sessions are allowed to pass. Someone trying to play back a communications session (such as a login) to gain access will be unsuccessful if the firewall is using dynamic packet filtering with a dynamic state list because the data sent would not be recognized as part of a currently valid session. The firewall will filter out (or "drop") all packets that don't correspond to a current session using information found in the dynamic state list. For example, a computer in Network A requests a Telnet session with a server in Network B. The firewall in between the two keeps a log of the communication packets that are sent each way. Only packets that are part of this current communication session are allowed back into Network A through the firewall.

Figure 8.4 shows a failed attempt to infiltrate a network that is protected with a dynamic state list. Notice that the hacker attempts to insert a packet into the communication stream but fails because they did not have the correct packet number. The firewall was waiting for a specific order of packets, and the hacker's packet was out of sequence.

## Proxy Servers

*Proxy servers* (also called proxies, for short) act on behalf of a network entity (either client or server) to completely separate packets from internal hosts and from external hosts. Let's say an internal client sends a request to an external host on the Internet. The request is first sent to a proxy server, where it is examined, broken down, and handled by an application. That application then creates a new packet requesting information from the external server. Figure 8.5 shows the process. Note that this exchange is between applications at the Application layer of the OSI model.

**FIGURE 8.4**    A hacker denied by a dynamic state list

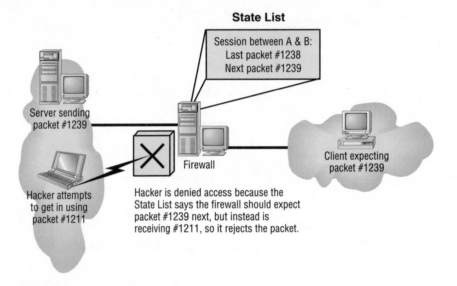

**State List**

Session between A & B:
Last packet #1238
Next packet #1239

Server sending packet #1239

Firewall

Client expecting packet #1239

Hacker attempts to get in using packet #1211

Hacker is denied access because the State List says the firewall should expect packet #1239 next, but instead is receiving #1211, so it rejects the packet.

**FIGURE 8.5**    A packet going to a proxy

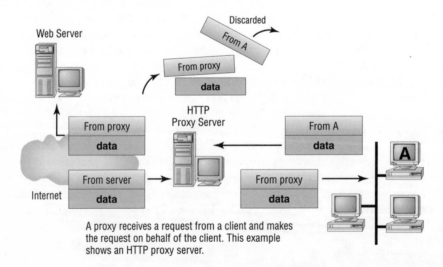

Web Server

Discarded

From A

From proxy
**data**

From proxy
**data**

HTTP Proxy Server

From A
**data**

From server
**data**

From proxy
**data**

Internet

A

A proxy receives a request from a client and makes the request on behalf of the client. This example shows an HTTP proxy server.

Proxies are good firewalls because the entire packet is dissected and each section can be examined for invalid data at each layer of the OSI model. For example, a proxy can examine a packet for information contained in everything from the packet header to the contents of the message. Attachments can also be checked for viruses. Messages can be searched for keywords that might indicate the source of a packet.

You can use this type of searching to prevent sensitive information from exiting your organization with the outbound data stream. If your sensitive documents contain a header or footer that includes the words *MyCompanyName Confidential,* you can set up your proxy server software to search for those keywords. This level of detailed searching degrades performance, however, because it is more time-intensive than checking state lists.

There are many types of proxy servers:

**IP Proxy**    An *IP proxy* hides the IP addresses of all stations on the internal network by exchanging its IP address for the address of any requesting station. You do not want a hacker to know IP addresses specific to your internal network. Web servers on the Internet will also be unable to determine the specific IP address from which a request is being sent. All communications look as if they originate from the proxy server. This type of proxy is also known as a *Network Address Translation (NAT) proxy.*

**Web (HTTP) Proxy**    *Web proxies* (also called HTTP [Hypertext Transfer Protocol] proxies) handle HTTP requests on behalf of the sending workstation. When a web proxy is implemented correctly, a client's web browser asks a web server on the Internet for a web page using an HTTP request. Because the browser is configured to make HTTP requests using an HTTP proxy, the browser sends the request to the proxy server. The proxy server changes the From address of the HTTP request to its own network address and sends it to the Internet web server. The response to the HTTP request goes directly to the proxy (because it replaced the sender's address with its own). The proxy server then replaces its address with the address of the original sender, and the response is delivered to the original sender.

The most popular implementation of a web proxy is a *proxy cache server.* This server receives an HTTP request from a web browser and then makes the request on behalf of the sending workstation. When the requested page is returned, the proxy server caches a copy of the page locally. The next time someone requests the same web page or Internet information, the page can be delivered from the local cache instead of the proxy server having to formulate a new request to the web server on the Internet. This speeds up web surfing for commonly accessed pages. Web proxies can also increase network security by filtering out content that is considered insecure, such as executables, scripts, or viruses.

**FTP Proxy**    FTP proxies handle the uploading and downloading of files from a server on behalf of a workstation. An FTP proxy operates in a fashion similar to that of a web proxy. As with web proxies, FTP proxies can filter out undesirable content (viruses and the like).

**SMTP Proxy**    SMTP proxies handle Internet e-mail. Here, the actual contents of the packet and mail can be automatically searched. Any packets or messages that contain material that is not considered secure can be blocked. Many SMTP proxies allow network virus protection software to scan inbound mail.

Not every firewall falls into a category. Traditional firewall vendors are adding features to their firewalls to make them difficult to classify. Vendors who traditionally offered packet-filtering solutions are now also offering proxy solutions, and vendors who traditionally offered proxy solutions are now also offering packet-filtering solutions. The network administrator can now get a packet-filtering firewall and a proxy firewall combined into one product. Dual-style firewalls are considered hybrids.

## Security Protocols

The security of data that is traversing the Internet is of prime concern to many people, including business owners. For the most part, data is sent across the Internet without any encryption or security. Sensitive data, however, is usually sent using one of several different security protocols. Security protocols are those sets of conditions or rules that define how a secure connection is maintained when transmitting data via an unsecure medium (like the Internet or a wireless connection). The Network+ exam tests your knowledge of several:

- Layer 2 Tunneling Protocol (L2TP)
- Internet Protocol Security (IPSec)
- Secure Sockets Layer (SSL)
- Kerberos
- Wired Equivalent Privacy (WEP)
- Wi-Fi Protected Access (WPA)
- 802.1x
- Password Authentication Protocol (PAP)
- Challenge Handshake Authentication Protocol (CHAP)
- Microsoft Challenge Handshake Authentication Protocol (MS-CHAP)
- Remote Authentication Dial-In User Service (RADIUS)

### L2TP

The Layer 2 Tunneling Protocol (L2TP) is a protocol that was designed by the Internet Engineering Task Force (IETF) and supports non-TCP/IP protocols in virtual private networks (VPNs) over the Internet. It's a combination of the Microsoft Point-to-Point Tunneling Protocol (PPTP) and Cisco's Layer 2 Forwarding (L2F) technology. Because it operates at the Data Link layer (layer 2) of the OSI model, it supports many different protocols, such as IPX and Apple-Talk. It's a good protocol to implement when you have two non-TCP/IP networks that need to be connected via the Internet.

## IPSec

IP Security, or IPSec, is a security protocol designed by the IETF to provide authentication and encryption over the Internet. IPSec works at the Network layer of the OSI model (layer 3) and secures all applications that operate above it (layer 4 and above). Additionally, because it was designed by the IETF and designed to work with IPv4 and IPv6, it has broad industry support and is quickly becoming the standard for VPNs on the Internet. However, if you need to run IPX versions of NetWare through VPN tunnels across the Internet, PPTP would be your best bet because PPTP is based on PPP, which supports IPX through its IPX Control Protocol (IPXCP).

## SSL

The Secure Sockets Layer (SSL) security protocol was developed by Netscape for integration into its Navigator browser. SSL is based on RSA public key encryption and is used to provide secure Session layer connections over the Internet between a web browser and web server. It is service independent, so many different network applications can be secured using SSL. The HTTP Secure (HTTPS) protocol is based on SSL. Eventually, SSL was merged with other Transport layer security protocols by the IETF to form a new protocol called Transport Layer Security (TLS).

## Kerberos

Kerberos is not just a protocol, but an entire security system. Created at MIT, it establishes a user's identity when they first log on to a system that uses Kerberos. That identity and its security credentials are then used throughout an entire logon session. It uses strong encryption to encrypt all transactions and communication. This encryption is freely available, and the source code for it can be freely downloaded from many different sites on the Internet.

## WEP

Wired Equivalent Privacy (WEP) is used to provide basic security for a wireless 802.11b local area network. The WEP protocol is used to encrypt data being transmitted over a wireless 802.11b network. It is a lower-layer security protocol and it encrypts the data before transmission using an algorithm known as RC4. To encrypt the data, a string of characters known as a key is used. The key is made up of a random number known as the Initialization Value (IV) plus a string of text chosen by the administrator or user that sets up WEP on a device. The keys used to encrypt the data stream are usually 40, 64, or 128 bits long.

## WPA

Wi-Fi Protected Access (WPA) is a standard that improves upon the original design of WEP. It was designed to be compatible with WEP-enabled hardware and software and can be implemented usually with a simple software upgrade. In order to provide this enhanced security, WPA adds two main components: TKIP and user authentication. Temporal Key Integrity Protocol (TKIP) encrypts the keys so they are more difficult to intercept by an eavesdropper. WPA's user authentication uses the Extensible Authentication Protocol (EAP), which is a form of public key encryption, to ensure that the user using the wireless network is a valid user.

## EAP

Extensible Authentication Protocol (EAP) is an extension to PPP that provides a host of additional authentication methods for remote access clients. Examples include smart cards, certificates, Kerberos, and biometric schemes, such as retinal scans and fingerprint and voice recognition. While EAP itself does not provide mutual authentication, enhanced forms of the protocol do. For example, EAP-TLS and EAP-TTLS, a tunneled version of EAP-TLS, creates a secure tunnel through which to run password-based versions of EAP, such as EAP-MD5.

## 802.1x

Even the IEEE recognizes the potential security holes in wireless networking. To that end, it has designed the IEEE 802.1x standard as a method for authenticating wireless users. 802.1x is an open framework designed to support multiple authentication schemes. Before a client (known as a *supplicant* in 802.1x parlance) can communicate on a wireless network, it asks the access point (known as an *authenticator*) for permission to enter and provides its credentials. The access point passes those credentials to a centralized authentication server (like a RADIUS server or similar). The server sends back an accept message to the access point if the authentication method is successful, and the access point will allow the user to connect to the wireless network.

It is important to note that 802.1x will allow no access to any wireless ports of any kind (except for 802.1x/EAP during authentication) until the user is authenticated. Also, encryption is not required for use with 802.1x. It is an authentication method only, but it can provide significant security measures, even without WEP keys.

## PAP

Of all the authentication schemes in use today, the Password Authentication Protocol (PAP) is arguably the simplest. In PAP, pairs of usernames and passwords are used. When a client wants to authentication to a server, for example, the client will send the username and password to the server over the network. The username and password are sent in clear text, that is to say, unencrypted. The server receives the username and password and compares them to an encrypted, locally stored table of username-password pairs. If the username and password are a match, the client is authenticated.

Although it is simple, PAP is easily cracked because the username and password are sent in easily readable text form over the network. Anyone with a simple "sniffing" program can intercept a username and password.

## CHAP

The Challenge Handshake Authentication Protocol (CHAP) is a significant improvement over PAP. In CHAP, the username and password never cross the wire. Instead, both the client and server are configured with the same text phrase (known as a *shared secret*). When a client requests to be authenticated, the server sends out a random value (known as a *nonce*) plus an ID value to the client. The client takes these two strings and concatenates them with the shared secret and then generates a one-way hash value using the MD5 encryption algorithm. This hash value is transmitted back to the server (which has performed the same algorithm using the same values and same shared secret). The server compares the hash received from the client with the hash value it has calculated. If they match, the client is authenticated.

### MS-CHAP

Microsoft has its own variation of CHAP known as Microsoft Challenge Handshake Authentication Protocol (MS-CHAP). It works basically the same way as CHAP, except for a couple of items. First of all, CHAP requires that the shared secret be stored locally in clear text. Microsoft decided to take out that requirement and encrypt the secret locally. While CHAP provides authentication of the client by the server only, MS-CHAP version 2 is capable of mutual authentication so that the client can be sure the server is legitimate as well. Version 1 of the protocol, however, was not capable of mutual authentication. Also, the encryption method used to generate the one-way hash in MS-CHAP is DES. Finally, as you may have already guessed, MS-CHAP doesn't work on Linux or other platforms; it's a Windows-only protocol.

### RADIUS

Even though its name suggests it, the Remote Authentication Dial-In User Service (RADIUS) is not a dial-up server. Although that may have been its origins (dial-up authentication in ISPs), it has blossomed into more of a verification service. RADIUS is an authentication and accounting service. It is used for authenticating users over various types of links, including dial-up. Many ISPs use a RADIUS server to provide a central location for all of the usernames and passwords of their clients. All of the dial-up modem banks are then configured to pass authentication requests to the RADIUS server.

It is also used in firewalls. If a user wants to access a particular TCP/IP port, they must provide a username and password. The firewall then contacts the RADIUS server to verify the credentials given. If successful, the user is granted access to that port.

## Comparing Firewall Operating System Platforms

Most firewalls are implemented as a combination of hardware and software. The hardware is typically a server-class machine. The software is usually specially written and sits on top of a network operating system. Firewalls are typically dedicated computers (that is, they don't do file/print serving or perform any other network function).

Let's briefly look the major network operating systems and, and how each implements a firewall.

 Remember that in addition to firewall software, you need at least two NICs (some firewall products use three) to have a functional firewall.

### The UNIX Operating System

UNIX is the network operating system on which the Internet is based and, as such, is also the network operating system on which firewalls are based. In UNIX, you can unload and lock down individual services. This means that you can configure a UNIX server so that only the firewall service is up and running. Proponents of UNIX argue that it is more secure than other operating systems because nonessential services can be removed, though knowledgeable Microsoft or Novell administrators can do the same with Windows and NetWare.

To support multiple segments, the firewall needs a number of network interface cards. An advantage of using UNIX-based firewalls is that they allow the most network cards (more than 32). NetWare has a practical limit of 16, and Windows is currently limited to 4.

As you learned in Chapter 5, UNIX is a command-line-based operating system and thus doesn't lend itself to be the most friendly firewall platform in the world. However, since the introduction of the X Window interface (and firewall software's adoption of it), UNIX-based firewalls have become easier to use.

Finally, because firewalls must examine hundreds, even thousands, of packets per second, speed is a major factor in all firewall platforms. Many companies make security products for both UNIX and Windows NT/2000. UNIX implementations tend to be significantly faster than Windows NT/2000 implementations. If you're communicating over a T1 line, however, platform speed won't create a bottleneck. This only becomes a problem when your corporation gets into the higher connection speeds that T3, OC3, and other connections provide (and therefore your firewall must be examining more packets per second). In these cases, you should consider UNIX-based firewall implementations.

## NetWare

NetWare, through the leverage of NDS, provides for easy network administration through NetWare Administrator, the graphical utility that runs on Windows 95/98 and Windows NT/2000. The primary firewall is Novell's own product, BorderManager. BorderManager installs onto NetWare servers and has a NetWare Administrator snap-in. With this feature, you can continue to use familiar NetWare tools to manage the many aspects of your network, including the firewall.

As a firewall platform NetWare offers two major benefits: speed (which is discussed shortly) and client compatibility. NetWare is compatible with just about every client platform, including Mac OS, Windows 95/98, Windows NT/2000, DOS, and OS/2. NetWare (with BorderManager) can offer firewall protection for all of these client platforms.

BorderManager integrates with NDS and thus can be managed with NetWare's single administration utility, NetWare Administrator. This makes BorderManager an easy-to-use firewall product, especially for experienced NetWare network administrators.

NetWare's core operating system has been optimized for the Intel platform, which is cheap and widely available. Apart from UNIX running on a RISC processor, NetWare is considered by the IT industry to be the fastest, and most efficient, network operating system. BorderManager running on NetWare is one of the fastest firewall software packages available.

## Windows

As Windows becomes more and more popular, firewall developers are porting their software from UNIX to Windows. However, because of security problems associated with Windows (see the WinNuke discussion later in this chapter), it doesn't rival UNIX or NetWare for firewall installations. As these problems are solved (through patches and other fixes, and likely in future editions of Windows), Windows NT and 2000 will gain ground in the firewall market.

Most third-party, Windows-based firewalls can integrate with Windows Domain/Active Directory security. This allows proxies to use Windows usernames and passwords.

The primary advantage of a Windows firewall is that it can be managed through a graphical user interface, as can Windows itself. Windows servers (and thus firewalls based on them) are more intuitive to the general user than a UNIX operating system, with almost the same level of features. If your network support staff is well versed in Windows, the learning curve for a new firewall will not be as steep as that for another operating system.

Windows, however, isn't the fastest network operating system platform, mainly because of the overhead required to maintain the graphical interface; thus, firewalls running on it aren't the fastest. To address this issue, some firewall vendors are adding hardware accelerator cards to increase firewall throughput. Microsoft is advancing the line of Windows servers to utilize more than a dozen CPUs and gigabytes of memory in one box so that performance can be increased to much higher levels. These new features will make Windows NT much faster and thus more effective as a firewall platform. With the advent of Windows 2000 servers, high-end throughput speeds are possible.

## The Black Box

A black box firewall implementation is your fourth choice. You do not know what operating system is inside the box, but it is definitely not Windows. It might be a special implementation of UNIX or a completely proprietary system. These implementations tend to have the fastest throughput because they are designed specifically as firewalls rather than as file and print network operating systems that run firewall software. Cisco's PIX Firewall is an example of a proprietary black box system.

The major feature of a black box firewall is simplicity. You don't have to worry about extraneous features such as file or print services. The box is only a firewall, not a server and a firewall.

Ease of use is not, however, a feature of a black box, which often lacks a screen or an input device. The administrator must rely on connecting to the black box using an external keyboard or terminal to change firewall configuration data. This is not typically a problem with firewalls that don't require significant configuration (as in simpler network implementations). In this case, once the firewall is configured, you can pretty much leave it alone.

Given the dedicated nature of black box firewalls (they aren't used to provide other network services) and that they are designed from the ground up as firewalls, they are often very efficient and fast. They use RISC processors and operating systems designed specifically for a firewall. Unfortunately, black boxes cannot be upgraded easily and often must be replaced as new technology is released.

# Understanding and Defending against Hacker Attacks

You can view the interaction between a hacker and a network administrator in different ways. You can see a harmless game of cat and mouse or a terrorist attack on national security. In either case, a person attempts to break into or crash your system. You, as the network administrator, work at preventing and tracking the attacks.

In the following sections, you will learn about common network attacks and the techniques used to guard against them.

# Hacker Tools: Common Network Attacks

Network attacks that are directed by a hacker are called directed attacks. For example, a Win-Nuke packet (generated by the WinNuke utility, discussed later in this chapter) sent by a hacker to a specific machine is considered a directed attack. Viruses are traditionally not directed attacks. The virus is unknowingly copied from user to user. Viruses are some of the most prevalent attacks used on the Internet. In the following sections, we'll discuss some of the techniques that hackers commonly use to attack a network. Then we'll discuss some tools and procedures you can use to defend against them.

Traditional viruses are covered in Chapter 9, "Fault Tolerance and Disaster Recovery."

## IP Spoofing

*IP spoofing* is the process of sending packets with a fake source address, pretending that the packet is coming from within the network that the hacker is trying to attack. The address can be considered stolen from the hacker's target network. A router (even a packet-filtering router) is going to treat this packet as coming from within the network and will let it pass; however, a firewall can prevent this type of packet from passing into the secured network. Figure 8.6 shows a hacker attempting an IP spoof. Notice that the hacker with the spoofed IP address is denied access to the network by the firewall.

**FIGURE 8.6**   IP spoofing

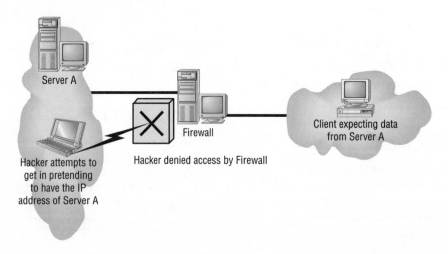

## The Ping of Death

The *Ping of Death* is a type of *denial of service (DoS) attack*. A DoS attack prevents any users, even legitimate ones, from using the system. Ping is primarily used to see if a computer is responding to IP requests. Normally, when you ping a remote host, four normal-sized Internet Control Message Protocol (ICMP) packets are sent to the remote host to see if it is available. In a Ping of Death attack, a very large ICMP packet is sent to the remote host, whose buffer is flooded by this packet. Typically, this causes a system to reboot or hang. Patches to prevent a Ping of Death attack from working are available for most operating systems.

## WinNuke

WinNuke was a Windows program that sends special TCP/IP packets with an invalid TCP header. Windows 95/98 and Windows NT/2000 computers would crash when they received one of these packets because of the way the Windows 95/98 or Windows NT/2000 TCP/IP stack handled bad data in the TCP header. Instead of returning an error code or rejecting the bad data (Microsoft calls it out-of-band data), it sends the computer to the Blue Screen of Death (BSoD). Figuratively speaking, the hacker causes the computer to blow up, or to be nuked. This type of attack does not affect Macs, UNIX boxes, and NetWare servers. Patches and service packs for the affected Microsoft products have long since quelled the threat that out-of-band data once posed.

## SYN Flood

A *SYN flood* is also a DoS attack because it can barrage the receiving machine with dozens of meaningless packets. In normal communications, a workstation that wants to open a TCP/IP communication with a server sends a TCP/IP packet with the SYN flag set to 1. The server automatically responds to the request, indicating that it is ready to start communicating. Only new communications use SYN flags. If you are in the middle of a file download, SYNs are not used. A new SYN packet is used only if you lose your connection and must reestablish communications.

To initiate a SYN flood, a hacker sends a barrage of SYN packets. The receiving station normally can't help itself and tries to respond to each SYN request for a connection. The receiving device soon expends its resources trying to reply, and all incoming connections are rejected until all current connections can be answered. The victim machine cannot respond to any other requests because its buffers are overfilled, and it therefore rejects all packets, including valid requests for connections. Patches that can help with this problem are available for the various network operating systems.

# Intruder Detection: Defense Techniques

There are three main types of intruder detection and defense:

- Active detection involves constantly scanning the network for possible break-ins.
- Passive detection involves logging all network events to a file.
- Proactive defense involves using tools to shore up your network walls against attack.

## Real World Scenario

### Why We Have Firewalls

In the early days of the Internet, firewalls weren't necessary. Internet users more or less behaved themselves and operated on the honor system. Plus, there were very few Fortune 500 companies who connected their entire corporate network to the Internet. However, as the Internet grew, many large companies realized they could communicate better if they connected their network directly to the Internet. At the same time, some users realized they could gain wealth or other consideration by getting into a company's network and stealing data from it. Firewalls were designed in response to this threat. As the saying goes, a few bad apples spoil the whole bunch.

## Active Detection

Active detection is analogous to a security guard walking down the hallway rattling doors. The guard is checking for a break-in. Special network software can search for hackers trying known attack methods and for suspicious activity as hackers travel over the network. Some sophisticated active systems actually take action, such as shutting down the communications sessions that the hacker is using, as well as e-mailing or paging you. Some packages go as far as trying to cripple the computer from which the hacker is attacking. Cisco's NetRanger, Memco's SessionWall, and Snort are all forms of active intrusion-detection software.

## Passive Detection

Video cameras are an example of passive intrusion-detection systems. Their counterparts in networking are files that log events that occur on the network. Tripwire for UNIX systems is one of the earliest programs of this type. With passive detection systems, files and data are looked at and checksums are calculated for each file and piece of data. These checksums are then stored in a log file. If the network administrator notices a security breach on the network, they can access the log files to find clues regarding the security breach.

## Proactive Defense

The main feature of the proactive defense is to make sure your network is invulnerable to attack. You can do this through research and maintenance. You must stay current on all known security holes on your network. You can use tools such as SATAN to find the holes in your security walls and plug them with software patches. Unfortunately, before you can patch a hole, it must be discovered. And the war against attackers is ongoing. As soon as you patch a hole, the hacker will find and exploit two other weaknesses. It usually takes some time for a patch to be developed, and in that time, companies lose resources to a hacker.

# DoD Security Standards

The U.S. Department of Defense (DoD) gave responsibility for computer security to the National Security Agency (NSA) in 1981 via directive 5215.1, and the National Computing Security Center (NCSC) was formed. The NCSC website states the center's mission as "technical standards and criteria for the security evaluation of trusted computer systems that can be incorporated into the Department of Defense component life-cycle management process."

In the following sections, we will briefly examine some NCSC standards and their impact on network security. The Network+ exam asks you to identify each level.

You can find the evaluation criteria for the DoD computer standards (called the Rainbow Series because of the color of the books) at www.radium.ncsc.mil/ tpep/library/rainbow.

## Trusted Computer System

The NCSC first released *A Trusted Computer System Evaluation Criteria (TCSEC)* in 1983 for stand-alone, non-networked computers. The current DoD Standard release is 5200.28-STD and is commonly referred to as the Orange Book. The Orange Book defines the standard parameters of a trusted computer in several classes, indicated by letter and number: the higher the letter, the higher the certification. For example, class A is the highest class and class D is the lowest class. The most publicized class is C2, Controlled Access Protection, which indicates that, within the Trusted Computer guidelines, the computer must have accountability for the data. In other words, each person who uses the computer must have a unique username and password, and the use of a file can be traced to that user. This is the highest NCSC class for local operating systems. Higher-level classes require that operating systems be specifically written to incorporate security-level information as the data is input.

Generally speaking, a stand-alone computer system can qualify for Trusted Computer certification if it meets the objectives in DoD document 5200.28-STD and passes the DoD's evaluation process. Several vendors put their operating systems through this process. Although Microsoft makes the operating systems for the majority of desktop computers, only its Windows NT product has been submitted and approved for the Trusted Computer certification.

For the exam, you must know that both Windows NT Server and Workstation have C2-level Trusted Computer (Orange Book) certification. If the computer on which Windows NT Server is installed is connected to a network, however, it loses the C2 Trusted Computer certification.

## Trusted Network Interpretation

In 1987, the NCSC released enhanced testing criteria based on the Orange Book standard. The new standard, NCSC-TG-005, is called the Red Book and is the *Trusted Network Interpretation Environmental Guideline (TNIEG)*. Trusted computers are addressed in the Orange Book. The Red Book defines the certification criteria for trusted networks. They both use the D through A levels. As with the C2 class in the Trusted Computer implementation, the C2 class is the highest class for generic network operating systems. Higher-level classes require that operating systems be specifically written to incorporate security-level information as the data is input.

With a C2 Trusted Network certification, network operating systems must provide a unique user account for each person on the network and provide accountability for the information the user uses. Additionally, the network communications must be secure.

Currently, several network operating systems are under evaluation for C2 Trusted Network certification. However, the only currently available network operating system that has achieved C2 Trusted Network certification is NetWare 4.

## Certified Operating Systems and Networks

Not all versions of an operating system are certified. This is the case even within the same vendor's product line. The NCSC requires that products adhere to a specific implementation in order to maintain their security certification. Be sure to check these out if you want to take advantage of the security rating.

There are no A-level certified Microsoft Windows, Novell NetWare, or UNIX operating systems yet. C1 has been discontinued as a certification.

The Cray Research and Harris Computer Systems versions of UNIX are B-level certified. UNIX and Windows NT 3.5 are Trusted Computer (Orange Book) certified (C level). NetWare is certified C2 Red Book, allowing it to operate as a trusted network. Tables 8.1 and 8.2 list the Microsoft Windows, Novell NetWare, and UNIX products that are certified as C2 and above as of this writing.

To verify security certification or check out officially released documents or books, go to the NCSC website at www.radium.ncsc.mil/tpep/epl/index.html. Products may be added or removed by the National Security Agency at any time. The tables here are for informational purposes only.

**TABLE 8.1**  National Security Agency Trusted Products: B-Level Certified

| Certification | Operating System | Vendor | Product Version(s) |
|---|---|---|---|
| B3 Orange Book | UNIX | Wang Government Services, Inc. | XTS-200 STOP 3.1E and 3.2E; XTS-300 STOP 4.1, 4.1a, and 4.4.2 |
| B2 Orange Book | UNIX | Trusted Information Systems, Inc. | Trusted XENIX 3 and 4 |
| B1 Orange Book | UNIX | Amdahl Corporation | UTS/MLS, Version 2.15+ |
| B1 Orange Book | UNIX | Compaq | ULTRIX MLS+ Version 2.1 on VAX Station 3100 |
| B1 Orange Book | UNIX | Harris Computer Systems Corporation | CX/SX 6.1.1 and 6.2.1 |
| B1 Orange Book | UNIX | Hewlett-Packard Corporation | HP-UX BLS release 8.04 and 9.0.9+ |
| B1 Orange Book | UNIX | Silicon Graphics, Inc. | Trusted IRIX/B release 4.0.5EPL |
| B1 Red Book | UNIX | Cray Research, Inc. | Trusted UNICOS 8 release 8.0.2 |
| B1 Red Book | UNIX | Harris Computer Systems Corporation | CX/SX with LAN/SX 6.1.1 and 6.2.1 |

**TABLE 8.2**  National Security Agency Trusted Products: C-Level Certified

| Cert. | OS | Vendor | Product Version(s) |
|---|---|---|---|
| C2 Orange Book | UNIX | IBM | RS/6000 Distributed System |
| C2 Orange Book | Windows NT | Microsoft Corporation | Windows NT Server and Workstation, Version 3.5 with Service Pack 3 |
| C2 Red Book | NetWare | Novell, Inc. | NetWare 4 Network System Architecture and Design and NetWare 4.11 |
| C2 Red Book | Proprietary | SISTex, Inc. | Assure EC 4.11 for Novell |

Assure EC 4.11 for Novell is included in Table 8.2 because it has ties to Windows 3.*x*, Windows 95/98, and NetWare. The NSA has certified SISTex's product as being the trusted workstation component of a NetWare 4/4.11 network. The Assure workstation can run DOS and Windows 3.*x* programs. Windows 95/98 is allowed, although it was not specifically tested. Assure is not a Microsoft or Novell product; however, this operating system/hardware combination works with both companies' products.

# Understanding Encryption

Occasionally, company data has to be sent over public networks, such as the Internet, and just about anyone with the desire to do so (including a company's competitors) can view the data in transit. Companies that want to ensure that their data is secure during transit encrypt their data before transmission. Encryption is the process that encodes and decodes data. The encrypted data is sent over the public network and is decrypted by the intended recipient. Generally speaking, encryption works by running the data (represented as numbers) through a special encryption formula (called a *key*). Both the sender and the receiver know the key. The key, generally speaking, is used to encrypt and decrypt the data.

The NSA has classified encryption tools and formulas as munitions since 1979 and therefore regulates them. The agency is concerned that unfriendly nations, terrorists, and criminals will use encrypted communications to plan crimes and go undetected. You can export weak encryption methods, but they cannot compete commercially with the tools designed overseas.

One way to measure an encryption algorithm is by its bit strength. Until 1998, only software with 40-bit strength and less could be exported. That limit has been increased to 56-bit strength and then 128-bit strength by special consideration of the U.S. Department of Commerce.

To ensure the security of monetary transfers, the NSA allows U.S. banks to use more secure encryption methods. Banks need to communicate with their overseas branches, customers, and affiliates.

## Uses for Encryption

In internal networks, some encryption is necessary, such as encrypting passwords that are being sent from workstation to server at login. This is done automatically by many modern network operating systems. Some older network utilities such as FTP and Telnet don't have the ability to encrypt passwords. Encryption is also used by many e-mail systems, giving the user the option to encrypt individual or all e-mail messages. Third-party software packages, such as PGP, can provide data encryption for e-mail systems that don't natively have the ability to encrypt. Encryption is also used for data transmission over VPNs, using the Internet to connect remote users securely to internal networks. Finally, encryption has become important with the advent of e-commerce, online banking, and online investing. Buying products and handling finances online would not be possible if the data sent between all involved parties over the Internet were not encrypted.

# How Encryption Works

The encryption process involves taking each character of data and comparing it against a key. For example, you could encrypt the following string of data in any number of ways:

The quick brown fox

For sample purposes, let's use a simple letter-number method. In this method, each letter in the alphabet corresponds to a particular number. (You may have used this method as a kid when you got a decoder wheel in your Cracker Jack or breakfast cereal box.) If you use a straight alphabetic-to-number encryption (for example, A=1, B=2, C=3, and so on), the data translates into the following:

20 8 5 17 21 9 3 11 2 18 15 23 14 6 15 24

You can then transmit this series of numbers over a network, and the receiver can decrypt the string using the same key in reverse. From left to right, the number 20 translates to the letter *T,* 8 to *H,* 5 to *E,* and so on. Eventually, the receiver gets the entire message:

The quick brown fox

Most encryption methods use much more complex formulas and methods. Our sample key was about 8 bits long; some keys are extremely complex and can be a maximum of 128 bits long. The larger the key (in bits), the more complex the encryption—and the more difficult it is to crack.

# Encryption Keys

To encode a message and decode an encrypted message, you need the proper encryption key or keys. The *encryption key* is the table or formula that defines which character in the data translates to which encoded character. Encryption keys fall into two categories: public and private. Let's look at how these two types of encryption keys are used.

## Private Key Encryption

Private keys are known as *symmetrical keys.* In private key encryption technology, both the sender and receiver have the same key and use it to encrypt and decrypt all messages. This makes it difficult to initiate communication the first time. How do you securely transmit the single key to each user? You use public keys, which we'll discuss shortly.

### The Data Encryption Standard (DES)

International Business Machines (IBM) developed one of the most commonly used private key systems, DES. In 1977, the United States made DES a government standard, defined in the Federal Information Processing Standards Publication 46-2 (FIPS 46-2).

DES uses lookup table functions and is incredibly fast when compared with public key systems. A 56-bit private key is used. RSA Data Systems issued a challenge to break the DES. Several Internet users worked in concert, each tackling a portion of the 72 quadrillion possible combinations. The key used in RSA's challenge was broken in June 1997, after searching only 18 quadrillion keys out of the possible 72 quadrillion. The plain-text message read, "Strong cryptography makes the world a safer place."

### Skipjack and Clipper

The replacement for DES might be the NSA's recent algorithm called *skipjack*. Skipjack is officially called the Escrowed Encryption Standard (EES), defined in FIPS 185, and uses an 80-bit key rather than the DES 56-bit key. The functions and complexity of each algorithm are different as well. Skipjack was supposed to be integrated into the clipper chip.

A *clipper chip* is a hardware implementation of skipjack. Clipper chips were proposed for use in U.S. telephone lines, but many civil liberties and privacy activists became upset because the U.S. government would be able to decrypt secure telephone conversations.

## Public Key Encryption

Public key encryption, or a Diffie-Hellman algorithm, uses two keys to encrypt and decrypt data: a public key and a private key. The receiver's public key is used to encrypt a message to the receiver. The message is sent to the receiver, who can then decrypt the message using the private key. This is a one-way communication. If the receiver wants to send a return message, the same principle is used. The message is encrypted with the original sender's public key (the original sender is now going to be the receiver of this new message) and can only be decrypted with their private key. If the original sender does not have a public key, a message can still be sent with a digital certificate (also sometimes referred to as a digital ID). The digital ID verifies the sender of the message.

Figure 8.7 shows public-key-encrypted communication between two people, User X and User Y.

**FIGURE 8.7** Public key encryption

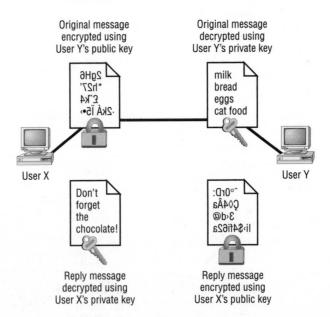

The term *Diffie-Hellman* refers to all public key algorithms. Whitfield Diffie and Martin Hellman from the Stanford Research Institute invented public key encryption. They introduced the dual key concept in their 1976 paper, "New Directions in Cryptography."

### RSA Data Security

Rivest, Shamir, and Adleman (RSA) encryption is a public key encryption algorithm named after the three scientists from the Massachusetts Institute of Technology (MIT) who developed it. They created a commercial company in 1977 to develop asymmetric keys and received several U.S. patents. Their encryption software is used in several products today, including Netscape Navigator and Novell's latest NetWare Client.

 For more information on RSA Data Security, go to www.rsa.com.

### Pretty Good Privacy (PGP)

PGP is an encryption utility based on public key encryption. In the early 1990s, Phil Zimmerman, also from MIT, wrote the majority of the code for this freely available version of public key encryption. The software was designed to encrypt data for e-mail transmission. Zimmerman compared e-mail to postcards. As the e-mail message is passed from server to server on the Internet, anyone can read it, just as anyone can read a postcard as it travels through the postal service. He compared an encrypted message to a letter mailed inside an envelope.

Zimmerman distributed the software for personal use only and restricted commercial use. The name PGP denotes that nothing is 100-percent secure. Both RSA Data Security and the U.S. federal government had problems with Zimmerman's product. RSA complained about patent infringement (a license fee is now paid to RSA). The government decided to prosecute Zimmerman for exporting munitions grade software; however, the charges were eventually dropped. Many years later, PGP and other public-key-related products are readily available.

# Security Policies

A *security policy* defines how security will be implemented in an organization, including physical security, document security, and network security.

Security policies must be implemented completely because random implementation is similar to blocks of Swiss cheese. Some areas are covered, and others are full of holes. Before a network can be truly secure, the network support staff must implement a total network security policy that includes posting company information on bulletin boards, clean desks, audits, recording, and the consequences of not complying with the security policy.

## Security Audit

A security audit is a review of your network to identify components that aren't secure. Although you can do a security audit yourself, you can also contract an audit with a third party. This is a good idea if you want the level of security to be certified. A consultant's audit is a good follow-up to an internal audit.

Government agencies may also require that your network be certified before granting you contract work, especially if the work is considered confidential, secret, or top secret.

## Clean Desk Policy

A clean desk policy does not mean that employees must wipe the bread crumbs from their last lunch. (Being clean with food is still a good idea. Mice and ants are difficult to get rid of once an infestation occurs.) A clean desk policy means that all important documents, such as books, schematics, confidential letters, and the like, are removed from a desk (and locked away) when employees leave their workstations. This goes for offices, laboratories, workbenches, and desks and is especially important for employees who share space. It is easy to grab something off someone's desk without that person's knowledge, and most security problems involve people on the inside. Implementing a clean desk policy is the number-one way to reduce such breaches.

The International Computer Security Association (www.icsa.net) reports that as much as 80 percent of all network break-ins occur from within the company by employees. Thus, protecting your data with a firewall is just the beginning of establishing network security.

For a clean desk policy to be effective, users must clean up their desks every time they walk away from them, without exception. The day this is not done will be the day when prospective building tenants are being shown the layout of the building and an important document ends up missing. Additionally, workstations should be locked to desks, and you should spot-check to help enforce the clean desk policy. Spot-check randomly, for example, before the company picnic or before a child-at-work day.

The ICSA is a vendor-neutral organization that certifies the functionality of security products as well as makes recommendations on security.

## Recording Equipment

Recording equipment, such as tape recorders and video cameras, can contain sensitive, confidential information. A security policy should prohibit their unauthorized presence and use. This could also include small memory devices like USB flash memory keychains.

When you walk into almost any large technology company, you are confronted with signs. A common sign is a camera with a circle surrounding it and a slash through the center of the circle. The text below the sign usually indicates that you cannot bring any recording devices onto the premises. This applies to, but is not limited to, still cameras, video cameras, and tape recorders of any kind.

The NSA recently updated its policy to disallow the Furby doll on government premises. Why would a government not allow dolls on its premises? Well, the Furby doll has a sophisticated computer inside with a digital recording device. The doll repeats what it hears at an interval of time later. This is quite harmless in the playroom at a children's daycare center. A recording of conversations at the NSA, however, cannot be allowed.

## Other Common Security Policies

Security policies can cover hundreds of items. Here are some of the more common:

**Notification**   What good is a security policy if no one knows about it? Give users a copy of the security policy when you give them their usernames and passwords. Computers should also display a shortened version of the policy when a user attempts to connect; for example, "Unauthorized access is prohibited and will be prosecuted to the fullest extent of the law." One hacker argued that since a computer did not tell him otherwise, anyone was free to connect to and use the system.

**Equipment Access**   Disable all unused network ports so that nonemployees who happen to be in the building cannot connect a laptop to an unused port and gain access to the network. Also, place all network equipment under lock and key.

**Wiring**   Network wires should not run along the floor where they can be easily accessed. Routers, switches, and concentrators should also not be hooked up in open office space. They should be in locked closets or rooms, with access to those rooms controlled by badge-swiping systems.

**Door Locks/Swipe Mechanisms**   Be sure that only a few, key people know the combination to the cipher lock on data center doors or that only the appropriate people have badges that will allow access to the data center. Change lock combinations often, and never leave server room doors open or unlocked.

**Badges**   Require everyone to wear an ID badge, including contractors and visitors, and assign appropriate access levels to contractors, visitors, and employees.

**Tracking**   Require badge access to all entrances to buildings and internal computer rooms. Track and record all entry and exit to these rooms.

**Passwords**   Reset passwords at least every month. Train everyone on how to create strong passwords. Set BIOS passwords on every client and server computer to prevent BIOS changes.

**Monitor Viewing**   Block computer monitors so that visitors or people looking through windows can't see them. Be sure that unauthorized users/persons cannot see security guard stations and server monitors.

**Accounts**   Each user should have their own, unique user account, and employees should not share user accounts. Even temporary employees should have their own account. Otherwise, you will not be able to isolate a security breach.

**Testing**   Review and audit your network security at least once a year.

**Background Checks**   Do background checks on all network support staff. This may include calling their previous employers, verifying their college degrees, requiring a drug test, and checking for any criminal background.

**Firewalls**   Use a firewall to protect all Internet connections, and use the appropriate proxies and dynamic packet-filtering equipment to control access to the network. Your firewall should provide as much security as your company requires and your budget allows.

**Intrusion Detection**   Use intrusion-detection and logging software to determine a breach of security. Be sure that you are logging the events you want to monitor.

**Cameras**   Cameras should cover all entrances to the building and the entire parking lot. Be sure that cameras are in weather-proof and tamper-proof housings, and review the output at a security monitoring office. Record everything on extended-length tape recorders.

**Mail Servers**   Provide each person with their own e-mail mailbox, and attach an individual network account to each mailbox. If several people need to access a mailbox, do not give all of them the password to a single network account. Assign privileges to each person's network account. You can then track activity to a single person, even with a generic address such as info@mycompany.com.

**DMZ**   Use a demilitarized zone for all publicly viewable servers, including web servers, FTP servers, and e-mail relay servers. Do not put them outside the firewall. Servers outside the firewall defeat the purpose of the firewall.

**Mail Relay**   Use a mail-relay server for e-mail. E-mail traffic should not go straight to your production servers. That would enable a hacker to directly access your server as well. Use a relay server in a DMZ.

**Patches**   Make sure that the latest security updates are installed after being properly tested on a nonproduction computer.

**Backups**   Store backup tape cartridges securely, not on a shelf or table within reach of someone working at the server. Lock tapes in a waterproof, fireproof safe, and keep at least some of your backups off site.

**Modems**   Do not allow desktop modems for any reason. They allow users to get to the Internet without your knowledge. Restrict modem access to approved server-based modem pools.

**Guards**   In some cases, security guards are necessary. Guards should not patrol the same station all the time. As people become familiar with an environment and situation, they tend to become less observant about that environment. Thus, it makes sense to rotate guards to keep their concentration at the highest possible levels. Guards should receive sufficient breaks to ensure alertness. All patrol areas should be covered during shift changes, rotations, and breaks. Guards should also receive periodic training. Test to ensure that guards can recognize a threat and take appropriate action.

**WARNING**    Covering all these bases does not ensure that your network or facility is secure. This is just a starting point to head you in the right direction.

# Breaking Policy

A security policy is not effective unless it is enforced, and enforced consistently. You cannot exempt certain individuals from policies or the consequences of breaking them. Your network users need to have a clearly written document that identifies and explains what users are and are not allowed to do. Additionally, it is important to state that breaking the policy will result in punishment, as well as which types of policy breaks result in which kind of punishment. Punishment may vary, depending on the severity of the incident. If a policy is broken, the appropriate punishment should be administered immediately.

## Major Infractions

As far back as the mid-1980s, employees were being immediately terminated for technology policy infractions. One employee was immediately terminated from a large computer company when pornography was found on his computer's hard drive. A manager and a security guard visited the employee. The manager informed the employee that he was being summarily terminated. The guard was there to ensure that the employee touched only personal items. The manager logged out the computer session. The former employee could now touch no computer equipment, including storage media such as floppy disks. The manager then informed the guard that the employee had one hour to vacate the premises.

## Minor Infractions

A lesser infraction might be accidentally corrupting your desktop computer by installing software from the Internet. Beta products, new releases of software, and patches need to be tested by the IS department before implementation. One episode of downloading and installing a beta release of a web browser invoked action at a national telephone company. After an employee installed the beta version and rebooted, the production Windows NT server became inoperable. The employee's Internet FTP privileges were revoked for three months.

# The Exit Interview

The exit interview is the process in which employers ask employees who are leaving the company about their employment experience. The exit interview is used to minimize risks whether the employee is leaving under favorable circumstances or is being terminated. During the exit interview, a manager, a human resources representative, a network administrator, and a security guard may be involved to different extents.

### Returning and Logging Property

When an employee leaves the company, all company property needs to be turned in and logged. This includes, but is not limited to, cellular phones, pagers, toolkits, keys, badges, security tokens, models, and all documents. Obviously, coffee mugs and photos of the spouse do not count. The manager, security guard, or both handle this, depending on whether the employee is being terminated or leaving voluntarily.

### Disabling Accounts

The information systems division or department needs to disable all accounts immediately, including those for network and voice mail. This should coincide with the announcement that the employee is leaving (either voluntarily or forcefully). This is especially important when the employee has access to sensitive documents. Even if the person is leaving under favorable conditions, they may still be able to log in and copy data to floppy disks to take with them for their own use. Common practice has extended this from just system administrators to everyone.

Salespeople can easily hurt a company by taking client information with them. One salesperson accessed his former company's voice mail system and stole sales leads. For total security, you need to look beyond the obvious disgruntled ex-network administrator who demolishes your website after leaving.

# Summary

In this chapter, you learned about various technologies used to provide access to a network as well as those used to secure a network. You learned about the various types of clients that exist for a network, how they are installed, and how they provide a computer with network access. Then you learned about the proper (and not so proper) usage and types of usernames and passwords. You also learned about some devices used to secure a network, namely firewalls and proxies. Finally, you learned about some of the security threats that exist within any company.

# Exam Essentials

**Be able to identify proper security implementation procedures.**   Security implementation is primarily a matter of allowing people who should access something the ability to do so and preventing nonauthorized users from accessing the same thing. It also involves doing so with a minimum of steps and fuss. Network security involves such procedures as securing the workstations and servers, setting proper passwords, and providing proper network protection.

**Be able to identify the different types of firewall technologies.**   Firewall technologies include true NAT, proxy, access control list, and dynamic packet filtering.

**Be able to identify the need for a firewall.**   Any network that is connected directly to the Internet needs some kind of firewall to protect the entire network from potential attack from somewhere on the Internet.

**Be able to identify the different types of proxy servers.**   A proxy server acts on behalf of a client. Most often, a proxy server is characterized by the service or protocol it is "proxying" (e.g., HTTP proxy for HTTP requests).

**Be able to predict the impact of implementing a particular security scenario on network functionality.**   Any increase in network security decreases the speed of a user's network access because they have one more level of security to get through before they can do their job. Therefore, the tighter the security, the less functionality you can get out of a network but the more network stability you will achieve.

**Be able to differentiate between a proxy and Network Address Translation (NAT).**   Proxy servers act on behalf of a client, whereas NAT simply changes "from" addresses as the packets pass through the proxy server.

# Review Questions

1. Which of the following is the most appropriate name for the network administration account?

    **A.** super

    **B.** superuser

    **C.** tswilliam

    **D.** administrator

    **E.** the original name

2. Which type of firewall checks for a current communication and the next packet needed?

    **A.** Access control lists

    **B.** Member control lists

    **C.** Static state lists

    **D.** Dynamic packet filtering

    **E.** Proxy

3. Which of the following protocols provide mutual authentication? (Choose all that apply.)

    **A.** EAP

    **B.** EAP-TLS

    **C.** CHAP

    **D.** MS-CHAP

4. Which of the following is a function of L2TP?

    **A.** L2TP allows layer 2 communication over twisted pair.

    **B.** L2TP creates a secure connection over the Internet.

    **C.** L2TP offers secure tunneling for TCP/IP, IPX, and others.

    **D.** L2TP provides authentication of remote access users.

5. For security reasons, where should you store backup tapes? (Choose all that apply.)

    **A.** Next to the server

    **B.** Next to the monitor

    **C.** In a drawer

    **D.** Locked in a cabinet

    **E.** Sealed in an envelope

    **F.** Off site

**6.** Which operating systems have achieved a National Security Agency certification allowing them to be used in a networked B- or C-level certified environment? (Choose all that apply.)

   **A.** UNIX

   **B.** NetWare

   **C.** Windows

   **D.** Linux

**7.** Which group of books does the DoD publish that deal with network security?

   **A.** The Rainbow Series

   **B.** The Colored Book Series

   **C.** The Orange Book Series

   **D.** The Red Book Series

   **E.** The Brown Book Series

**8.** Which government agency did the U.S. Department of Defense (DoD) task to handle computer security certification?

   **A.** EPA

   **B.** DOE

   **C.** DIS

   **D.** DSS

   **E.** NSA

**9.** What is the Diffie-Hellman algorithm used to do?

   **A.** Encrypt data using public key cryptography

   **B.** Encrypt data using private key cryptography

   **C.** Encrypt data using symmetric cryptography

   **D.** Run a key manager that distributes tokens

   **E.** Revoke distributed security tokens

**10.** What is the strongest bit-strength encryption that the U.S. government normally allows to be exported?

   **A.** 32-bit

   **B.** 40-bit

   **C.** 64-bit

   **D.** 128-bit

   **E.** 250-bit

   **F.** 256-bit

**11.** Which type of security uses a file that identifies predefined IP addresses that are allowed to send data through a router?

**A.** Access control lists

**B.** Dynamic state list

**C.** Proxy

**D.** Interpreter

**E.** Translator

**12.** Which of the following passwords are considered weak? (Choose all that apply.)

**A.** tempest4@wiND

**B.** gwashington

**C.** MargeS

**D.** MSmith

**E.** os2Cys&BtDel?

**F.** wwater7D$walkEr

**13.** How often should regular users be forced to reset their passwords?

**A.** Never

**B.** Every day

**C.** Once a week

**D.** Once a month

**E.** Once a semester

**F.** Once a fiscal quarter

**14.** Which of the following are good criteria for a strong password? (Choose all that apply.)

**A.** Three characters or longer

**B.** Eight characters or longer

**C.** Using both alphanumeric and special characters

**D.** Using the license plate number of your truck

**E.** Using words not found in a dictionary

**15.** What is the proper action to take before you leave your workstation? You are going to get a glass of water and will return in five minutes.

**A.** Power down your workstation.

**B.** Log out.

**C.** Unplug the monitor.

**D.** Unplug the computer.

**16.** Whose accounts should immediately be disabled when their employment is terminated? (Choose all that apply.)

   **A.** Secretaries

   **B.** Lab assistants

   **C.** Engineers

   **D.** Managers

   **E.** Security guards

   **F.** Network administrators

**17.** What should be collected in an exit interview of a terminated employee? (Choose all that apply.)

   **A.** Schematics

   **B.** Blood sample

   **C.** Coffee mug

   **D.** Office keys

   **E.** Badge

   **F.** Pager

   **G.** Spouse's photo

**18.** What types of recording devices are typically allowed inside technology companies?

   **A.** The Furby doll

   **B.** Handheld still cameras

   **C.** Mounted company security video cameras

   **D.** Dictation tape recorders

   **E.** Newspaper reporter tape recorders

**19.** Active intrusion-detection systems have which of the following characteristics? (Choose all that apply.)

   **A.** Scanning communications in near real time

   **B.** Recording actions of attackers without raising an alarm

   **C.** Acting to terminate the communications of the attacker

   **D.** Shutting themselves down to hide from the attacker

   **E.** Shutting down the entire network to protect against attacks

**20.** Which of the following attacks affects only Windows operating systems?

   **A.** PingNuke

   **B.** Ping of Death

   **C.** WinNuke

   **D.** Win of Death

   **E.** SYNNuke

   **F.** SYN of Death

# Answers to Review Questions

1. C. It's considered a "best practice" to not use the names super, superuser, or administrator because those are default accounts. The best choice is to pick a user and give them administrative privileges. Then, delete, rename, or disable the built-in administration accounts.

2. E. A proxy provides firewall services by keeping track of all communications sessions and fetching the next packets.

3. B, D. EAP and CHAP provide only client authentication, while EAP-TLS and MS-CHAP provide authentication of the client to the server as well as authentication of the server to the client.

4. B. L2TP provides a secure VPN connection over the Internet for TCP/IP only. In order to provide such a service to IPX, a protocol such as PPTP should be used. RADIUS, for example, not L2TP, provides verification services for dial-in users.

5. D, F. The best location for backup tapes is in a locked cabinet off site. These practices make it difficult for someone to steal the backups as well as provide protection of the tapes in case of fire or other catastrophe.

6. A, B. Of the operating systems listed, only UNIX and NetWare have been certified for use in a networked environment. Windows NT 3.5 and 4.0 were certified, but only as a workstation environment.

7. A. The Rainbow Series is the series of books that the DoD publishes for standards of secure networking.

8. E. The National Security Agency (NSA) is responsible for handling computer security certification.

9. A. Diffie-Hellman is a public key cryptography algorithm.

10. B. As this book went to press, a 40-bit encryption algorithm was the strongest you could export. That restriction is currently being revised.

11. A. Access control list security uses a file (the ACL) that identifies which addresses can send data through a particular firewall or router.

12. B, C, D. The best passwords are those that don't use any part of a person's name or a dictionary word. Thus, since options B, C, and D all are essentially usernames, they would be considered weak passwords.

13. D. It has been found that, for ease of remembrance and maximum possible security, a user should be forced to change their password at least once a month (or every 30 days). Any sooner and the user will forget their new password frequently; any later and they may complain that they would just like to keep their same password all the time (and it would increase the chance an unauthorized user might guess the password).

**14.** B, C, E. The best passwords are eight characters or longer; use numbers, letters, and special characters; and are words not necessarily found in a dictionary. Any word that can be found in a dictionary, is a proper name, or is another name of sentimental value is considered a bad/weak password.

**15.** B. It would be inefficient to shut down your workstation or unplug the computer because it takes so long to restart it. Unplugging the monitor would still leave the computer accessible (an intruder could simply plug it back in). The only convenient way to secure the computer for that short a time is to simply log out.

**16.** A, B, C, D, E, F. For security reasons, all accounts should be disabled when the employee quits or is terminated. You don't necessarily have to delete the account, but it should be disabled so that the employee can't use it.

**17.** A, D, E, F. Any item that could be used to gain access to a company's resources should be collected during the exit interview of an employee. Keys, badges, and important papers (like schematics) should be obtained along with any company property (intellectual or otherwise).

**18.** C. For an absolutely secure installation, the only recording devices that should be on the premises are company-owned and -operated devices like security cameras.

**19.** A, C. Active intrusion systems detect intrusions or possible intrusions the moment they occur and take actions to prevent the intrusion. These systems, if working correctly, should affect only the intruder.

**20.** C. Although many of these attacks can affect Windows systems, only one—WinNuke—was designed specifically to attack Windows systems. It works because of a bug in the Windows TCP/IP stack.

# Chapter 9

# Fault Tolerance and Disaster Recovery

Computers are not perfect. They can (and do) have problems that affect their users' productivity. These problems range from small errors to total system failure. Errors and failures can be the result of environmental problems, hardware and software failure, hacking (malicious, unauthorized use of a computer or a network), and natural disasters.

In all cases, you can take measures to minimize the impact of computer and network problems. These measures fall into two major categories: fault tolerance and disaster recovery. *Fault tolerance* is the capability of a computer or a network system to respond to a condition automatically, usually resolving it, and thus reducing the impact on the system. If fault tolerance measures have been implemented, it is unlikely that a user would know that a problem existed. *Disaster recovery*, as its name suggests, is the ability to get a system functional after a total system failure (a disaster for a company and the network administrator) in the least amount of time. Strictly speaking, if enough fault tolerance methods are in place, you shouldn't need disaster recovery.

Both methods are important and are implemented on most, if not all, networks. Because of this, the Network+ exam will test you on your knowledge of the most popular implementations of fault tolerance and disaster recovery. In this chapter, we will look at the following:

- How to assess fault tolerance and disaster recovery needs

- Power management

- Disk system fault tolerance methods

- Backup considerations

- Virus protection

# Assessing Fault Tolerance and Disaster Recovery Needs

Before implementing fault tolerance or disaster recovery, you should determine how critical your systems are to daily business operations. Additionally, you should determine how long each system could afford to be nonfunctional (down). Making these determinations will dictate which fault tolerance and disaster recovery methods you implement and to what extent. The more vital the system, the greater lengths (and, thus, the greater expense) you should go to in order to protect it from downtime. Less-critical systems may call for simpler measures. For example, banks, insurance companies, the U.S. government, and airlines all run highly critical computer and network systems. Thus, they all have complex and expensive fault tolerance and disaster recovery systems in place.

In terms of how fault tolerance and disaster recovery are implemented, sites can be described as hot, warm, or cold. As the temperature decreases, so does the level of fault tolerance and disaster recovery that are implemented at a site.

# Hot Site

In a hot site, every computer system and piece of information has a redundant copy (possibly multiple redundancies). This level of fault tolerance is used when systems must be up 100 percent of the time. Hot sites are strictly fault-tolerant implementations, not disaster recovery implementations (as no downtime is allowed). Budgets for this type of fault-tolerant implementation are typically large.

In a system that has 100-percent redundancy, the redundant system(s) will take over for the failed system without any downtime. The technology used to implement hot sites is *clustering*, which is the process of grouping multiple computers in order to provide increased performance and fault tolerance.

Although servers are commonly clustered, workstations are normally not because they are simple and cheap to replace. Each computer in the cluster is connected to the other computers in the cluster by high-speed, redundant links (usually multiple fiber-optic cables). Each computer runs special clustering software that makes the cluster of computers appear as a single entity to clients.

There are two levels of cluster service: failover and true.

## Failover Clustering

A failover cluster includes two entities (usually servers). The first is the active device (the device that responds to network requests), and the second is the failover device. The *failover device* is an exact duplicate of the active device, but it is inactive and connected to the active device by a high-speed link. The failover device monitors the active device and its condition by using what is known as a heartbeat. A *heartbeat* is a signal that comes from the active device at a specified interval. If the failover device doesn't receive a heartbeat from the active device in the specified interval, the failover device considers the active device inactive, and the failover device comes online (becomes active) and is now the active device.

When the previously active device comes back online, it starts sending out the heartbeat. The failover device, which currently is responding to requests as the active device, hears the heartbeat and detects that the active device is now back online. The failover device then goes back into standby mode and starts listening to the heartbeat of the active device again.

In a failover cluster, both servers must be running failover clustering software, such as Novell's System Fault Tolerance, Level III (SFTIII), Standby Server and High Availability Server (with Novell's High Availability software, either of the servers can fail and the other will take over), and Microsoft Cluster Server (MSCS) for Windows NT servers. This functionality is built into Microsoft Windows 2000 and later operating systems. Each software package provides failover functionality.

Here are some advantages of this approach to fault tolerance:

- Resources are almost always available. This approach ensures that the network service(s) that the device provides will be available as much as 99 percent of the time. Each network service and all data are exactly duplicated on each device, and when one experiences problems, the other takes over for virtually uninterrupted service.

- It is relatively inexpensive when compared with true clustering (discussed in the next section).

But, as with any technology, there are disadvantages, and failover clustering has its fair share:

- There is only one level of fault tolerance. This technology works great if the active device fails, but if the failover device fails as well, the network will totally lose that device's functionality.

- There is no load balancing. Servers in a failover-clustering configuration are in either active or standby mode. There is no balancing of network service load across both servers in the cluster. The active server responds to network requests, and the failover server simply monitors the active server, wasting its processor resources.

- Failover clusters take anywhere from a few seconds to a few minutes to detect and recover from a failed server, a delay referred to as cutover time. During cutover time, the server can't respond to network client requests, so the server is effectively down. This time is indeed short, but nevertheless, clients can't get access to their services in the meantime.

- Hardware and software must be exactly duplicated. In most failover configurations, the hardware for both active and failover devices must be *identical*. If it's not, the transition of the failover device to active device may be hindered. These differences may even cause the failover to fail. This is a disadvantage because it involves checking all aspects of the hardware. (For servers, this means disk types and sizes, NICs, processor speed and type, and RAM.)

 Even though Microsoft Cluster Server (MSCS) is described earlier as a failover clustering technology, it does have some capability for load balancing (according to Microsoft). It currently supports only a two-device configuration, so it primarily fits into this category of clustering.

## True Clustering

True clustering differs from failover clustering in two major ways:

- It supports multiple devices.
- It provides load balancing.

In true clustering (also called *multiple server clustering*), multiple servers (or any network devices) act together as a kind of super server. True clusters must provide load balancing. For example, 20 servers can act as one big server. All network services are duplicated across all servers, and network requests are distributed across all servers. Each server is connected to the other servers through a high-speed, dedicated link. If one server in the cluster malfunctions, the other servers automatically take over the burden of the failed server. When the failed server comes back online, it resumes responding to requests as part of the cluster. This technology can provide greater than 99-percent availability for network services hosted by the cluster.

Several advantages are associated with true clustering:

- There is more than 99-percent availability for network services. With multiple servers, the impact of a single server, or even more than one server, in the cluster going down is minimized because other servers take over the functionality.

- It offers increased performance. Because each server is taking part of the load of the cluster, much higher total performance is possible.

- There is no cutover time. Because multiple servers are always responding to network requests, true clusters don't suffer from the cutover time even when a server goes down. The remaining servers do receive an increased load, and clients may see a Server Busy or Not Found error message if they should, by some chance, try to communicate with the server that is going down. But if the user tries the operation again, one of the remaining servers will respond to the request.

- It provides for replication. If the clustering software in use supports it, a few servers can be located offsite in case the main site is destroyed by fire, flood, or other disaster. Because there is a replica (copy) of all data in a different location, this technology is known as *replication*.

But these advantages don't come without a price. Here are a couple of disadvantages to true clustering:

- The more servers, the more complex the cluster. As you add servers to the cluster to increase performance, you also increase the complexity. For this reason, most clustering software is limited to a maximum of 64 servers. As technology develops, this limit will increase. The minimum number of servers in a true cluster is 2.

- It is much more expensive. Because of the hardware involved and the complexity of the clustering software, true clustering requires a serious financial commitment. To justify the expense, ask the keepers of the purse strings how much money would be lost if the system were down for a day.

## Warm Site

In a warm site, the network service and data are available most of the time. The data and services are less critical than those in a hot site. With hot-site technologies, all fault tolerance procedures are automatic and are controlled by the NOS. Warm-site technologies require a little more administrator intervention, but they aren't as expensive.

The most commonly used warm-site technology is a duplicate server. A *duplicate server*, as its name suggests, is one that is currently not being used and is available to replace any server that fails. When a server fails, the administrator installs the new server and restores the data; the network services are available to users with a minimum of downtime. The administrator sends the failed server out to be repaired. Once the repaired server comes back, it is now the spare server and is available when another server fails.

Using a duplicate server is a disaster recovery method because the entire server is replaced but in a shorter time than if all the components had to be ordered and configured at the time of the system failure. The major advantage of using duplicate servers rather than clustering is that it's less expensive. A single duplicate server costs much less than a comparable clustering solution.

Corporate networks don't often use duplicate servers, and that's because there are some major disadvantages associated with using them:

- You must keep current backups. Because the duplicate server relies on a current backup, you must back up every day and verify every backup, which is time-consuming. To stay as current as possible, some companies run continuous backups.

- You can lose data. If a server fails in mid-afternoon and the backup was run the evening before, you will lose any data that was placed on the server since the last backup. This may not be a big problem on servers that aren't updated frequently.

## Cold Site

A cold site cannot guarantee server uptime. Generally speaking, cold sites have little or no fault tolerance and rely completely on efficient disaster recovery methods to ensure data integrity. If a server fails, the IT personnel will do their best to recover and fix the problem. If a major component needs to be replaced, the server stays down until the component is replaced. Errors and failures are handled as they occur. Apart from regular system backups, no fault tolerance or disaster recovery methods are implemented.

This type of site has one major advantage: It is the cheapest way to deal with errors and system failures. No extra hardware is required (except the hardware required for backing up). Any disadvantages of implementing a cold site would stem from having an application that cannot afford the downtime associated with service-affecting faults and disasters.

The term *nearline* refers to a storage method that is neither online nor offline but somewhere in the middle, like tape backup. It involves material that is not likely to be needed except in cases of disaster recovery. While there is not a one-to-one correspondence between any type of site (hot, warm, or cold) and nearline storage, which is not actively accessed during normal operation, you can see that nearline storage comes in handy when recovering from disasters in warm and cold sites.

# Power Management

A key element of any fault tolerance plan is a power management strategy. Electricity powers the network, switches, hubs, PCs, and computer servers. Variations in power can cause problems ranging from a reboot after a short loss of service to damaged equipment and data. Fortunately, a number of products are available to help protect sensitive systems from the dangers of lightning strikes, dirty (uneven) power, and accidental power cable disconnection, including surge protectors, Standby Power Supplies, Uninterruptible Power Supplies, and line conditioners. What you use depends on how critical your system is (whether you decide that it is a hot, warm, or cold site). At a minimum, you should connect individual workstations to surge protectors, and network hardware and servers should use Uninterruptible Power Supplies or line conditioners. Critical operations, such as ambulance corps and hospitals, typically go one step further and also have a gas-powered backup generator to provide long-term supplemental power to all systems.

# Surge Protectors

Surge protectors (also commonly referred to as *surge suppressors*) are typically power blocks or power strips with electronics that limit the amount of voltage, current (amps), and noise that can get through to your equipment. They are designed to protect your equipment from long-lasting increases in voltage (surges) and high, short bursts of voltage (spikes). The unit does not provide any power, however. Rather, it blocks harmful electricity from reaching your equipment. The surge protector detects a surge or a spike and clamps down on the incoming voltage, reducing it to safe levels. If the surge is large enough, it can trip the built-in safety mechanism. You may then lose power and have to reset the equipment you are protecting. Common causes of surges and spikes are fluctuations in power from the electricity company, additions of equipment to the power grid by customers, and natural storms.

## Level of Protection

Unfortunately, surge protectors provide only a limited amount of protection. Surge protectors are simple devices that can only protect against large spikes and surges. Small increases in voltage are allowed to pass. These small increases may not cause immediate damage, but over time, they can damage sensitive computer equipment. It is definitely better to have a surge protector than not have one, but the surge protector must be of high quality (these usually cost more than $30).

**WARNING**    The $5.99 power strips you find at Wal-Mart and similar stores are not true surge protectors. They are simply multiple-outlet strips with a single circuit breaker and provide only the most basic protection. Don't use them with computer equipment.

## Common Components/Features

Tripp Lite's Isobar and American Power Conversion's (APC's) SurgeArrest are two leading surge protector products. When selecting a surge protector, look for these components and features:

**Active Protection Light**    When this light is illuminated, the unit is properly functioning. It should be on at all times.

**Site Wiring Fault Light**    When this light is illuminated, there is a wiring fault in the circuit to which the surge protector is connected. This light should be off at all times.

**Ground**    Make sure that the unit has three prongs on the plug, the third (middle) plug being for ground. If the ground is missing, the user can receive a lethal shock. This may seem obvious, but it is important to remember.

**IEEE 587 Category A (ANSI/IEEE C62.41) Let-Through Rating**   Check the value of the IEEE 587 A Let-Through rating. This value indicates how much voltage is let through when the surge protector clamps down on the incoming spike or surge. The lower this rating, the lower the voltage that is let through and the better you are protected. A 330V rating is excellent protection.

**UL Listing**   Underwriters Laboratories Inc. is an independent testing laboratory that certifies electrical equipment specifications. A UL listing indicates that the surge protector meets national electrical code and safety standards.

**Circuit Breaker**   This button pops out after a large spike or surge. When the circuit breaker trips, you will lose all power to your equipment. Press the button back in to reset the surge protector.

**Additional Ports**   New protectors protect much more than power cables. Today's surge protectors have RJ-45 and coaxial connectors for protecting network cards from extremely high surges. Also, RJ-11 and ISDN ports protect modems from telephone pole lightning strikes (which can follow the phone line right into the modem, thus damaging it).

## Battery Backup Systems

Battery backup systems protect computer systems from power failures. There are several different types of power failures, including brownouts and blackouts. A brownout is when the power level falls to a lower level and stays there for several seconds (or longer). This may eventually lead to a blackout, or total loss of power.

 Brownouts and blackouts were covered in Chapter 6, "Wired and Wireless Networks."

Battery backup systems use a battery to power the computer and its assorted peripherals. Generally speaking, when these devices are activated due to a power failure, they permit the user to save data and initiate a graceful shutdown of the system. They normally aren't used to run the system for an extended period (unless the units use a *very* large-capacity battery).

 Never plug a laser printer or copier into a battery backup device. These devices draw tremendous amounts of current when they are turned on (much more than any computer or network device ever would draw). If you do this, you could permanently damage or disable your battery backup device.

There are two main types of battery backup systems:

- Standby Power Supply (SPS)
- Uninterruptible Power Supply (UPS)

## Standby Power Supply (SPS)

A Standby Power Supply (SPS) contains a battery, a switchover circuit, and an inverter (a device to convert the DC voltage from the battery into AC voltage that the computer and peripherals need). The outlets on the SPS are connected to the switching circuit, which is in turn connected to the incoming AC power (called line voltage). The switching circuit monitors the line voltage. When it drops below a factory-preset threshold, the switching circuit switches from line voltage to the battery and inverter. The battery and inverter power the outlets (and, thus, the computers or devices plugged into them) until the switching circuit detects that line voltage is present again at the correct levels. The switching circuit then switches the outlets back to line voltage.

 Power output from battery-powered inverters isn't exactly perfect. Normal power output alternates polarity 60 times a second (60 Hertz). When graphed, this output looks like a sine wave. Output from inverters is stepped to approximate this sine wave output, but it really never duplicates it. Today's inverter technology can come extremely close, but the differences between inverter and true AC power can cause damage to computer power supplies over the long run.

### Level of Protection

SPS can provide some protection against power outages (more so than surge protectors, at any rate). Unfortunately, because the switching circuit must switch between power sources, there is a short period of time when the outlets have no power. Computers and network devices can usually handle this infinitesimally short period of time without power, but they don't always handle it gracefully. Some devices will lock up or experience errors. Others can even reboot (thus negating the reason for having a battery backup system).

For this reason, SPS has never been really popular with computer and electronic equipment users. They are inexpensive and they can provide a basic level of protection, but this is usually not sufficient for hot sites that require 100-percent uptime.

### Common Components/Features

Most Standby Power Supplies will have one or more of these features or components:

**Multiple Outlets**   Each SPS will have at least one outlet for connecting computers or network devices to the SPS. Most have multiple outlets. The number of outlets depends on the capacity of the battery, the inverter, and the switching circuit in the SPS.

**Line Voltage Indicator**   This light or indicator, when illuminated, indicates that the SPS is receiving sufficient AC line voltage to power the equipment plugged into the SPS.

**Battery Power Indicator**   This light or indicator, when illuminated, indicates that the equipment plugged into the SPS is running off the battery and inverter in the SPS. When this indicator is initially illuminated, a beep will sound, warning that power to the SPS has failed.

**System Management Port**   This is usually a standard serial port (although USB ports are becoming more popular). It allows the SPS to connect to the host computer (or server) it is protecting. The host computer runs SPS management software that gathers statistics about the power the SPS is using and providing. Also, when a power failure occurs, this port is used to send a signal from the SPS informing the management software on the host computer that the power to the SPS has failed. The management software can then initiate a graceful shutdown of the workstation computer or server.

## Uninterruptible Power Supply (UPS)

An Uninterruptible Power Supply (UPS) is another type of battery backup often found on computers and network devices today. It is similar to an SPS in that it has outlets, a battery, and an inverter. The similarities end there, though. A UPS uses an entirely different method to provide continuous AC voltage to the equipment it supports.

In a UPS, the equipment is always running off the inverter and battery. A UPS contains a charging/monitoring circuit that charges the battery constantly. It also monitors the AC line voltage. When a power failure occurs, the charger just stops charging the battery. The equipment never senses any change in power. The monitoring part of the circuit senses the change and emits a beep to tell the user the power has failed.

### Level of Protection

A UPS provides a significant amount of protection against many types of power problems because the computer is always running off the battery and inverter. Problems with the input line voltage don't really affect the output voltage. They only affect the efficiency of the charging circuit. A UPS is the most popular form of power protection because it provides significant protection at a fairly low cost.

### Common Components/Features

When buying a UPS, you must look for the features that will solve your particular power problems or that meet your needs in general. Here are some of the features a UPS includes:

**Multiple Outlets**   Each UPS will have at least one outlet for connecting computers or network devices to the UPS. Most have multiple outlets. The number of outlets depends on the capacity of the battery, inverter, and switching circuit in the UPS.

**Line Voltage Indicator**   This light or indicator, when illuminated, indicates that the UPS is receiving sufficient AC line voltage to power the charging circuit of the UPS.

**Battery Power Indicator**   This light or indicator, when illuminated, indicates that the equipment plugged into the UPS is running off the battery and inverter in the UPS and that the charging circuit is not active. When this indicator is initially illuminated, a beep will sound, warning that power to the UPS has failed.

**System Management Port**   This was once usually a standard serial port, with USB ports becoming more popular in recent years. It allows the UPS to connect to the device it is protecting. The host computer runs UPS management software that gathers statistics about the power the UPS is using and providing. Also, when a power failure occurs, this port is used to send a signal to the management software on the host computer that the power to the UPS has failed. The management software can then initiate a graceful shutdown of the workstation computer or server.

## Line Conditioners

The AC voltage that powers our everyday devices comes from power sources usually located far from where we use it. The power is conducted through wires and stepping stations over many miles on its trip from where it's generated to where it's used. At any point along this trip, erroneous electrical patterns or signals that computers may not be able to handle properly can be introduced into the power. These erroneous signals are known as *line noise* and can cause many types of problems, including random lockups, random reboots, and system crashes.

All power signals have varying degrees of line noise. In areas that have particularly bad line noise, a device known as a *line conditioner* is used. This device filters out the erroneous signals in the power, leaving the devices it supplies with clean, 110-volt, 60Hz power.

Line conditioners are complex (and thus expensive) devices that incorporate a number of power-correction technologies to provide electronic devices with clean power. Some of these technologies are UPS, surge suppression, and power filtering.

### Level of Protection

Line conditioners provide the highest level of power protection for electronic devices. Hot sites will have a large line conditioner (or multiple line conditioners) that service every computer in an organization. These conditioners are often wired directly into the electrical system of a company. Special outlets (with markings that indicate they are protected outlets) are wired in each room. Wires from these outlets lead directly back to the line conditioner. These devices are usually cost-prohibitive for smaller companies or for a single computer, although some small companies will invest in a small line conditioner for their main server if it is a critical server.

### Common Components/Features

Line conditioners usually have control panel interfaces. Some manufacturers replace the control panel interface with a computer and power management software. These interfaces can report both incoming and outgoing voltages, as well as any problems the interfaces might be experiencing themselves. These devices are so complex and large that they typically require large cooling fans and an adequate supply of cool air.

# Disk System Fault Tolerance

A hard disk is a temporary storage device, and every hard disk will eventually fail. The most common problem is a complete hard-disk failure (also known as a hard-disk crash). When this happens, all stored data is irretrievable. Therefore, if you want your data to be accessible 90 to 100 percent of the time (as with warm and hot sites), you need to use some method of disk fault tolerance. Typically, disk fault tolerance is achieved through disk management technologies such as mirroring, striping, and duplexing drives and provides some level of data protection. As with other methods of fault tolerance, disk fault tolerance means that a disk system is able to recover from an error condition of some kind.

The following methods provide fault tolerance for hard-disk systems:

- Mirroring
- Duplexing
- Data striping
- Redundant Array of Independent (or Inexpensive) Disks (RAID)

> ### Understanding Disk Volumes
>
> Before you read about the various methods of providing fault tolerance for disk systems, you should know about one important concept: volumes. When you install a new hard disk into a computer and prepare it for use, the NOS sets up the disk so that you can store data on it in a process known as formatting. Once this has been achieved, the NOS can access the disk. Before it can store data on the disk, it must set up what is known as a volume. A *volume,* for all practical purposes, is a named chunk of disk space. This chunk can exist on part of a disk, can exist on all of a disk, or can span multiple disks. Volumes provide a way of organizing disk storage, as you can see in this illustration:
>
>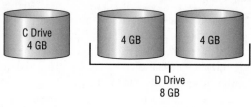

## Disk Mirroring

Mirroring a drive means designating a hard-disk drive in the computer as a mirror or duplicate to another, specified drive. The two drives are attached to a single disk controller. This disk fault tolerance feature is provided by most network operating systems. When the NOS writes data to the specified drive, the same data is also written to the drive designated as the mirror. If the first drive fails, the mirror drive is already online, and because it has a duplicate of the information contained on the specified drive, the users won't know that a disk drive in the server has failed. The NOS notifies the administrator that the failure has occurred. The downside is that if the disk controller fails, neither drive is available. Figure 9.1 shows how disk mirroring works.

The drives do not need to be identical, but it helps. Both drives must have the same amount of free space to allow a mirror to be formed. For example, you have two 4GB drives; one has 3GB free, and the other has 2GB free. You can create one 2GB mirrored system.

## Disk Duplexing

As with mirroring, duplexing also saves data to a mirror drive. In fact, the only major difference between duplexing and mirroring is that duplexing uses two separate disk controllers (one for each disk). Thus, duplexing provides not only a redundant disk, but a redundant controller and data ribbon as well. Duplexing provides fault tolerance even if one of the controllers fails. Figure 9.2 shows a duplexed disk system. Compare this with Figure 9.1. Notice that there is now an extra disk controller in the system.

Mirroring is an implementation of RAID level 1, which is discussed in detail later in this chapter.

Duplexing is also an implementation of RAID level 1.

**FIGURE 9.1**   Disk mirroring

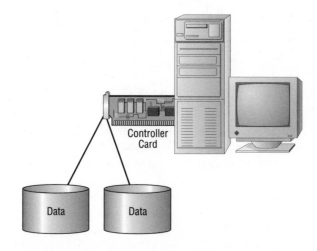

**FIGURE 9.2**   Disk duplexing

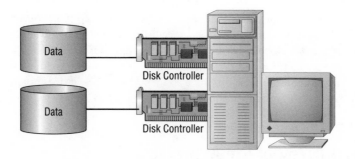

**FIGURE 9.3** How disk striping works

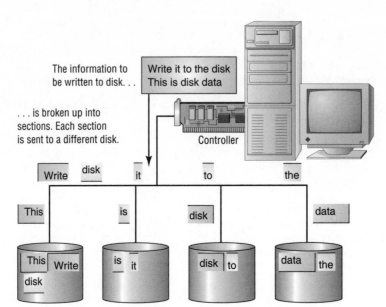

Each disk holds a piece of the original information.

## Disk Striping

From a performance point of view, writing data to a single drive is slow. When three drives are configured as a single volume, information must fill the first drive before it can go to the second and fill the second before filling the third. If you configure that volume to use disk striping, you will see a definite performance gain. Disk striping breaks up the data to be saved to disk into small portions and sequentially writes the portions to all disks simultaneously in small areas called stripes. These stripes maximize performance because all of the read/write heads are working constantly. Figure 9.3 shows an example of striping data across multiple disks. Notice that the data is broken into sections and that each section is sequentially written to a separate disk.

Striping data across multiple disks improves only performance; it does not improve fault tolerance. To add fault tolerance to disk striping, it is necessary to use parity. Disk striping is also known as RAID level 0.

## Redundant Array of Inexpensive (or Independent) Disks (RAID)

RAID is a technology that uses an array of less-expensive hard disks instead of one enormous hard disk and provides several methods for writing to those disks to ensure redundancy. (The term *independent* found favor as the cost of larger disks became less prohibitive and skewed with regard to how much larger they were than the drives of a more common or average size for the day.) Those methods are described as *levels,* and each level is designed for a specific purpose:

**RAID 0 (Commonly Used)**  This method is the fastest because all read/write heads are constantly being used without the burden of parity or duplicate data being written. A system using this method has multiple disks, and the information to be stored is striped across the disks in blocks without parity. This RAID level only improves performance; it does not provide fault tolerance.

**RAID 1 (Commonly Used)**  This level uses two hard disks, one mirrored to the other (commonly known as mirroring; duplexing is also an implementation of RAID 1). This is the most basic level of disk fault tolerance. If the first hard disk fails, the second automatically takes over. No parity or error-checking information is stored. Rather, the drives have duplicate information. If both drives fail, a new drive must be installed and configured and the data must be restored from a backup. RAID 1 has the least processing overhead of the more popular RAID levels that provide fault tolerance (compared with RAID 3 and RAID 5, for example).

**RAID 2**  At this level—which is no longer recommended for reasons stated later—individual bits are striped across multiple disks. Multiple redundancy drives in this configuration are dedicated to storing error correcting code (ECC), a method of error correction found built in to modern hard drives, without the use of RAID. If any data drive fails, the data on that drive can be rebuilt from ECC data stored on the redundancy drive. Two of the better known configurations included an array of 10 data disks and 4 ECC disks and an array of 32 data disks and 7 ECC disks. Due to requirements that are incredibly difficult and expensive to implement, such as specialized controller hardware to synchronize the spindles of all disks in the array, this is not a commonly used implementation.

**RAID 3**  At this level, data is striped across multiple hard drives using a parity drive (similar to RAID 2). The main difference is that the data is striped in bytes, not bits as in RAID 2. This configuration is popular because more data is written and read in one operation, increasing overall disk performance.

---

 **Real World Scenario**

**Parity Information**

*Parity,* as it relates to disk fault tolerance, is a general term for the fault tolerance information computed for each chunk of data written to a disk. This parity information can be used to reconstruct missing data should a disk fail. Striping can use parity or not, but if the striping technology doesn't use parity, you won't gain any fault tolerance. When striping is used with parity, the parity information is computed for each block and written to the drive.

The advantage to using parity with striping is gaining fault tolerance. If any part of the data gets lost or destroyed, the information can be rebuilt from the parity information. The downside to using parity is that computing and writing parity information reduces the total performance of a disk system that uses striping. The parity information also reduces the total amount of free disk space.

**RAID 4**    This level is similar to RAID 2 and 3 (striping with parity drive), except that data is striped in blocks, which facilitates fast reads from one drive. RAID 4 is the same as RAID 0, with the addition of a parity drive. This is not a popular implementation.

**RAID 5 (Commonly Used)**    At this level, the data and parity are striped across three or more drives. This allows for fast writes and reads. The parity information is written with the data across all drives in the array as opposed to the dedicated parity drive of RAID 4. So, if any one disk fails, the drive can be replaced and its data can be rebuilt from the data and parity data stored on the other drives. This works well if one disk fails. If more than one disk fails, however, the data will need to be recovered from backup media. While a minimum of three disks is required, five or more disks are most often used.

**RAID 6**    RAID 6 is similar to RAID 5. It is less popular, however, due to the need for specialized, usually more expensive controllers and the loss of an additional drive for its cause. RAID 6 uses RAID 5 as a basis but duplicates the parity information, saving the second copy on a different drive from the one on which the first copy was saved. This implementation requires an additional drive over RAID 5 but can handle the simultaneous failure of two drives.

There are other levels of RAID, including RAID 53, 7, and 10, but because they are less popular, we won't discuss them here.

### Hot and Cold Spares

With disk fault tolerance, and RAID specifically, it is often desirable to have spare disks available to replace any that have failed. That is, after all, the point of having redundant disks. These disks can be categorized as either hot or cold spares. A *cold spare* is a component that is a duplicate of an existing, currently functioning component that can be swapped in if the functioning component fails. The main thing that makes a cold spare a cold spare is that the system must be brought down to replace the malfunctioning component with the spare. A *hot spare*, on the other hand, is ready to run and will automatically take over the non-functioning component upon its failure so that no service is interrupted.

Disks are not the only thing that can have hot or cold spares. As a matter of fact, entire computers can have spares. Clustering is one example of having a hot spare computer. Also, NICs commonly have hot spares.

# Backup Considerations

Although you can never be completely prepared for every natural disaster or human foible that can bring down your network, you can make sure that you have a solid backup plan in place to minimize the impact of lost data. Even if the worst happens, you don't have to lose days or weeks of work, provided that you have a solid plan in place. A *backup plan* is the set of guidelines and schedules that determine which data should be backed up and how often. A backup plan includes information such as the following:

- What to back up
- Where to back it up
- When to back up
- How often to back up
- Who should be responsible for backups
- Where media should be stored
- How often to test backups
- The procedure to follow in case of data loss

The following sections cover some of the items that are contained in a common backup plan:

- Backup media options
- Backup utilities
- Backup types
- Tape rotation schedule

## Backup Media Options

When you back up your network's data, you must have something on which to store it; this is called the backup medium. You have several options:

- Small-capacity removable disks
- Large-capacity removable disks
- Removable optical disks
- Magnetic tape

Let's examine the advantages and disadvantages of each type, starting with small-capacity removable disks.

### Small-Capacity Removable Disks

Small-capacity disks are magnetic media disks that have a capacity of less than 1GB and can be removed from their drives and replaced as they get filled. They are popular because of their low cost and ease of use. Additionally, because they are inexpensive, many computers come with one or more of these drives. Table 9.1 lists some examples of this type of backup medium and their popular capacities.

**TABLE 9.1** Popular Small-Capacity Removable Disks

| Medium | Capacity |
| --- | --- |
| Floppy disk | 1.44MB, 2.88MB |
| SyQuest cartridges | 44MB, 88MB, 105MB, 200MB, 230MB |
| Iomega Zip disk | 100MB, 250MB, 750MB |
| Imation SuperDisk | 120MB |
| Removable hard-disk drive | Varies |

## Large-Capacity Removable Disks

Large-capacity removable disks are virtually the same as small-capacity removable disks except they can store more data (more than 1GB per disk). The drives and media cost more, but the increase in capacity easily offsets the increased cost. Large-capacity removable disks are good for backing up a workstation that has only one or two disks. You can also use them to back up a server, but because they don't have the capacity to back up a server with a single removable disk (multiple disks would be required for each backup), their use is limited. Table 9.2 lists a few of the common large-capacity removable disks and their capacities.

**TABLE 9.2** Popular Large-Capacity Removable Disks

| Medium | Capacity |
| --- | --- |
| Iomega Jaz | 1GB, 2GB |
| Sharq | 1.5GB |
| SyQuest cartridges | 1GB, 1.5GB |
| Removable hard-disk drive | Varies |

## Removable Optical Disks

Removable optical disks use a laser (or some kind of light beam) to read and write information stored on a removable disk. They typically have large capacities and are fairly slow (more than 100 milliseconds as opposed to less than 50 milliseconds for magnetic) access times. The advantage to optical disks is that the capacities start at about 128MB and go up from there (650MB is a common size). There are even special optical jukeboxes, containing hundreds of disks and a robotic arm to select disks and put them in the drive(s), that have capacities in the hundreds of terabytes (1 terabyte is 1024 gigabytes). Table 9.3 lists some of the popular optical formats and their capacities.

**TABLE 9.3**    Popular Removable Optical Disk Capacities

| Medium | Common Capacities |
|---|---|
| CD-ROM, CD-R, CD-RW | 650MB |
| Magneto Optical disk | 650MB, 1.3GB, 4.6GB |
| DVD-ROM, DVD-R, DVD-RW, DVD+R, DVD+RW | 4.7GB, most commonly up to 17GB |

CD-R and CD-RW are writeable CD-ROM implementations. DVD-ROMs have similar varieties, with the newer +R/RW versions having more capacity than the -R/RW versions.

## Magnetic Tape

Magnetic tape is the oldest and most popular backup medium for offline (not readily accessible) data storage. It stores data in the form of magnetically oriented metal particles (either copper oxide or chromium dioxide) on a polyester tape. It is popular because it is simple, inexpensive, and has a high capacity. Most networks use a magnetic tape backup of some kind. Table 9.4 lists a few of the most common magnetic tape backup technologies and their common capacities.

**TABLE 9.4**    Common Magnetic Tape Capacities

| Technology | Common Capacities |
|---|---|
| QIC | 100MB to gigabytes and up |
| DDS Cartridges for DAT drives | 2–40 gigabytes (varies with drive) |
| DLT (Digital Linear Tape) | 35GB and up |
| AIT | 25GB, 50GB |

## Backup Utilities

A backup utility is a software program that can archive the data on a hard disk to a removable medium. Backup utilities can compress data before they store it, making it more efficient to use a backup program to archive data than to simply copy it to the backup medium.

**Real World Scenario**

**Copying Workstation Data to the Network**

Servers must be backed up because they contain all the data for the entire network. In most networks, workstations are not backed up because they usually don't contain any data of major importance. (Individual workstations would be backed up only if the users are trained improperly and don't store all their data on the network.) But, users can mistakenly save their data to their local workstation. Also, user application configuration data is normally stored on the workstation. If a workstation's hard disk goes down, the configuration is lost.

For backups to be successful, users need to ensure that all necessary data is located on the network. You can do this in two ways: user training and folder replication. Training is time-consuming and costly, but productive in the long run. Users should understand the general network layout and know how to save their data in the proper place. This keeps all user data centralized and makes it easy for the administrator to back it up.

When you replicate folders, client platforms that support replication will share their hard disks (or portions of them) with the rest of the network. The network backup software then backs up those portions of the workstation that the administrator specifies.

---

Most operating systems include backup utilities, but these are usually simple programs that lack the advanced features of full-fledged, third-party programs (such as Seagate Backup Exec and Computer Associates's ARCserve):

- Windows operating systems have a built-in backup program with user-friendly backup and restoration utilities for applications and data as well as system state. It's called, simply, Backup.

- Novell's NetWare comes with SBACKUP.

- Unix comes with a command-based tape archive utility called tar.

All of these backup utilities are good for an initial backup of your system. For a complete set of features including scheduling and managing tape sets, purchase a third-party product that fits your platforms and specific backup requirements.

## Backup Types

After you choose your backup medium and backup utility, you must decide what type of backup to run. The types vary by how much data they back up each time and by how many tapes it takes to restore data after a complete system crash. There are three backup types:

- Full
- Differential
- Incremental

## Full Backup

In a full backup, all network data is backed up (without skipping any files). This type of backup is straightforward because you simply tell the software which servers (and, if applicable, workstations) to back up and where to back up the data and then you start the backup. If you have to do a restore after a crash, you have only one set of tapes to restore from (as many tapes as it took to back up everything). Simply insert the most recent full backup into the drive and start the restore.

If you have a tape system with a maximum capacity of half the size of all the data on your server, the backup utility will stop the backup halfway through and ask you to insert the next tape. Normally, full backups take several hours, and most companies can't afford to have a user sit in front of the tape drive and change tapes. So you need a backup drive and medium with enough capacity or a backup system that can automatically change its own tapes (such as a DAT autoloader).

Figure 9.4 shows the amount of data backed up each day in a full backup scheme. Note that if you are working with 10GB of data, approximately 10GB is stored on a new tape each night, along with any additional data from that day. However, you are basically backing up the same data each day.

**FIGURE 9.4**     The amount of data backed up with a full backup

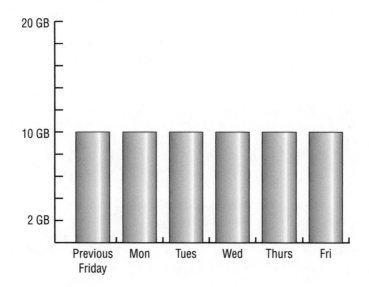

## Differential Backup

In a differential backup strategy, a single, full backup is done typically once a week. Every night for the next six nights, the backup utility backs up all files that have changed since the last full backup (the actual differential backup). After a week's worth of differential backups, another full backup is done, starting the cycle all over again. With differential backups, you use a maximum of two backup sessions to restore a file or group of files.

### Real World Scenario

#### Data Backups

I've been to several small businesses that don't make backups because they either don't have a backup mechanism, don't know how, or just plain don't want to. Whenever I consult with a small business on a backup system, I try to make a recommendation that best fits their particular data needs and the experience level of the owners or persons responsible for the data integrity of the company. For example, if they aren't very tech-savvy, I'll set up an automatic full backup system (assuming they have the money and full backup is practical) so all they have to do is rotate one tape. If they have very little money, I'll recommend a large-capacity external USB or FireWire hard drive. In any case, I always recommend that backups be the responsibility of one main person. That doesn't mean they can't delegate their duties (if necessary), just that that one person be responsible for ensuring that the backups get done.

Here's how it works: The backup utility keeps track of which files have been backed up through the use of the archive bit, which is simply an attribute that indicates a file's status with respect to the current backup type. The archive bit is cleared for each file backed up during the full backup. After that, any time a program opens and changes a file, the NOS sets the archive bit, indicating that the file has changed and needs to be backed up. Then each night, in a differential backup, the backup program copies every item that has its archive bit set, indicating the file has changed since the last full backup. The archive bit is not touched during each differential backup.

When restoring a server after a complete server failure, you must restore two sets of tapes: the last full backup and the most current differential backup. A full restoration may take longer, but each differential backup takes much less time than a full backup. This type of backup is used when the amount of time each day available to perform a system backup (called the *backup window*) is less during the week and more on the weekend.

Figure 9.5 shows the amount of data being backed up each day in a differential backup. Notice that the amount of data becomes gradually larger every day as the number of files that need to get backed up increases. Remember that the archive bit isn't cleared each day. By the end of the week, therefore, the files that changed at the beginning of the week may have been backed up several times, even though they haven't changed since the first part of the week.

## Incremental Backup

In an incremental backup, a full backup is used in conjunction with daily partial backups to back up the entire server, thus reducing the amount of time it takes for a daily backup. With an incremental backup, the weekly full backup takes place as it does during a differential backup, and the archive bit is cleared during the full backup. The incremental, daily backups back up only the data that has changed since the *last* backup (*not* the last full backup). The archive bit is cleared each time a backup occurs. With this method, only files that have changed since the previous day's backup are backed up. Each day's backup is a different size because a different number of files are modified each day.

**FIGURE 9.5**     The amount of data backed up in a differential backup

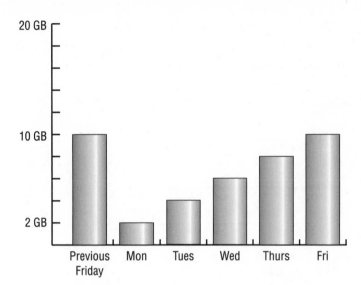

This method provides the fastest daily backups for networks whose daily backup window is extremely small. However, the network administrator does pay a price for shortened backup sessions. The restores made with this method after a server failure take the longest of the three methods. The full backup set is restored plus every tape from the day of the failure back to the preceding full backup.

Figure 9.6 shows the incremental backup scenario. Note that not only is the amount of data backed up each day different, as is the case with differential and full backups, but it is also much smaller than with a differential or full backup. Furthermore, unlike the other two backup types, incremental backups never back up the same information twice.

Each backup type is used for a different purpose. Full backups are used when restore time is at a premium. Incremental backups are used when backup time is at a premium. Differential backups are a compromise between the two methods. Table 9.5 summarizes the backup types.

**TABLE 9.5**     Backup Types

| Type | What Is Backed Up | Archive Bit Cleared? | Number of Sets to Restore after Server Crash |
|------|-------------------|----------------------|----------------------------------------------|
| Full | All data on the server (network) | Y | Full only |
| Differential | Data since the last full backup | N | Full plus last differential |
| Incremental | Data since the last backup | Y | Full plus every daily incremental since last full backup |

**FIGURE 9.6** The amount of data backed up with an incremental backup

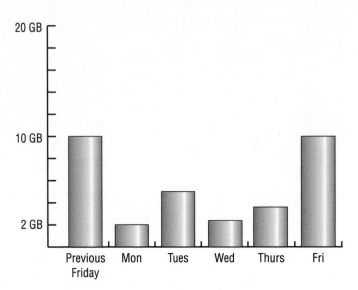

## Tape Rotation Schedule

Rotating backup tapes is the most practical way to manage a tape backup scheme, since the costs of using a new tape each day are prohibitive. Do not use a different tape each day. Instead, reuse tapes from previous months and weeks. We will look at some simple rotations, such as weekly, along with some rather complicated schemes.

### Weekly Rotation

In a weekly rotation, you use a different backup tape or tapes for each day of the week. Weekly rotations are the simplest to understand and set up. You first assign a tape to each weekday and label the tape with the name of the day. You have five tapes, and you overwrite each tape as the day of the week comes again. The furthest you can go back to do a restore is one business week. On Friday, before the backup, you can go back to any day for one week, but no further.

### Monthly Rotation

Rotating tapes on a monthly basis allows you to restore data for an entire month. Managing this type of backup scheme is more complicated because you must keep track of many more tapes. A straightforward solution is to assign 31 tapes and do a full backup each day. This becomes unwieldy if a full backup takes many tapes. For example, a thousand-user corporation's e-mail, file, and print servers can take multiple high-capacity DLT tapes per session.

Most of your restore requests will be reported shortly after a file is accidentally deleted or corrupted. Take your typical user who accidentally deletes their home directory. Using a GUI interface, this is as easy as right-clicking a folder and then left-clicking Delete. The user will immediately call network support and plead for quick rescue. In this case, you only have to go back to the previous day's tape. To plan for this scenario, have daily backups that go back a week. Supplement this with a weekly backup for an entire month.

In this configuration, you would use no more than nine tapes. You will use one tape for each day Monday through Thursday (four tapes) and one tape for each Friday of the month (four or five tapes, depending on how many Fridays there are in a month). A maximum of nine tapes will give you daily backups for a week and weekly backups for a month. Label the tapes Monday through Thursday and Friday Week 1 through Friday Week 5.

## Yearly Rotation

You can build a yearly backup on top of the monthly system. You'll need 12 tapes, one for each month, labeled with the names of the months. Rename the last weekly, full backup of each month to the corresponding month. You go from 9 tapes to 21 tapes and gain the capability of going back a year to restore data. Only one day out of each month is available after you go back further than your current month.

## Grandfather-Father-Son Rotation

A standard rotation scheme for tapes is the Grandfather-Father-Son (GFS) method. With this method, daily backups are differential, incremental, or full. Full backups are done once a week. The daily backups are known as the Son. The last full backup of the week is known as the Father. Because the daily tapes are reused after a week, they age only five days. The weekly tapes stay around for a month and are reused during the next month. The last full backup of the month is known as the monthly backup, or the Grandfather. The Grandfather tapes become the oldest, and you retain them for a year before reusing them. Figure 9.7 (on next page) is an example of a GFS tape scheme.

## Long-Term Configurations

In addition to daily, weekly, and yearly backups, some companies, for archival purposes, do an end-of-year backup, which is then kept offsite in long-term storage. They do this to keep a record of the year's financial and transactional data so that they can refer to it in case of tax problems. (The IRS may require businesses to keep transactional data for seven years.)

Some companies do two end-of-year backups—one before closing out the fiscal year and another after closing out. They do this in case they mess up the closing and need to start over. When the closing out is finished, they back up the closed-out system and place the tape in long-term storage.

**FIGURE 9.7**    Grandfather-Father-Son rotation

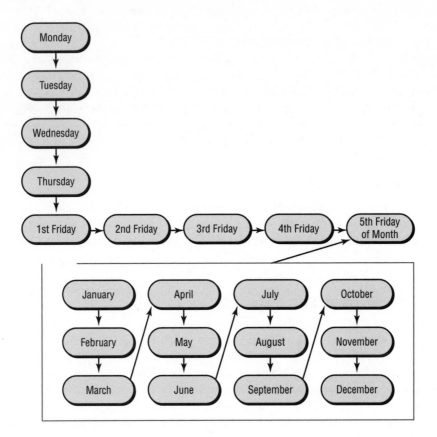

# Virus Protection

A *virus* is a program that causes malicious change in your computer and makes copies of itself. Sophisticated viruses encrypt and hide themselves to thwart detection. There are tens of thousands of viruses that your computer can catch. Known viruses are referred to as being "in the wild." Research laboratories and universities study viruses for commercial and academic purposes. These viruses are known as being "in the zoo," or not out in the wild. Every month, the number of viruses in the wild increases.

Viruses can be little more than hindrances, or they can shut down an entire corporation. The types vary, but the approach to handling them does not. You need to install virus protection software on all computer equipment. This is similar to vaccinating your entire family, not just the children who are going to summer camp. Workstations, personal computers, servers, and firewalls all must have virus protection, even if they never connect to your network. They can still get viruses from removable storage media or Internet downloads.

# Types of Viruses

Several types of viruses exist, but the popular ones are file viruses, macro (data file) viruses, and boot sector viruses. Each type differs slightly in the way it works and how it infects your system. Many viruses attack popular applications such as Microsoft Word, Excel, and PowerPoint; they are easy to use and it's easy to create a virus for them. Because writing a unique virus is considered a challenge to a bored programmer, viruses are becoming more and more complex and harder to eradicate.

## File Viruses

A file virus attacks executable application and system program files, such as those ending in .COM, .EXE, and .DLL. Most of these types of viruses replace some or all of the program code with their own. Only once the file is executed can the virus cause its damage. This includes loading itself into memory and waiting to infect other executables, further propagating its potentially destructive effects throughout a system or network. Examples of file viruses are Jerusalem and Nimda (although Nimda is usually seen as an Internet worm) may also infect common Windows files, as well as files with extensions such as .HTML, .HTM, and .ASP.

## Macro Viruses

A macro is a script of commonly enacted commands that are used to automatically perform operations without a user's intervention. Macro viruses use the Visual Basic macro scripting language to perform malicious or mischievous functions in data files created with Microsoft Office products, for example. Macro viruses are among the most harmless (but also the most annoying). Since macros are easy to write, macro viruses are among the most common viruses and are frequently found in Microsoft Word and PowerPoint. They affect the file you are working on. For example, you might be unable to save the file even though the Save function is working, or you might be unable to open a new document—you can only open a template. These viruses will not crash your system, but they are annoying. Cap and Cap A are examples of macro viruses.

## Boot Sector Viruses

Boot sector viruses get into the master boot record. This is track one, sector one on your hard disk, and no applications are supposed to reside there. The computer at bootup checks this section to find a pointer for the operating system. If you have a multi-operating-system boot between various versions or instances of Windows, for example, this is where the pointers are stored. A boot sector virus will overwrite the boot sector, thereby making it look as if there is no pointer to your operating system. When you power up the computer, you will see a Missing Operating System or Hard Disk Not Found error message. Monkey B, Michelangelo, Stoned, and Stealth Boot are examples of boot sector viruses.

Nearly any virus that falls under one of these three categories can be implemented as a *Trojan Horse*. Just as the Greeks in legend attacked Troy by hiding within a giant horse, a Trojan virus hides within other programs and is launched when the program in which it is hiding is launched. DMSETUP.EXE and LOVE-LETTER-FOR-YOU.TXT.VBS are examples of known Trojan Horses. Displaying extensions for known file types can help you remain vigilant against such naming tricks. These are only a few of the types of viruses out there. For a more complete list, see your antivirus software manufacturer's website, or go to Symantec's website at www.symantec.com.

## Updating Antivirus Components

A typical antivirus program consists of two components:

- The definition files
- The engine

The definition files list the various viruses, their type, and their footprints and specify how to remove them. More than 100 new viruses are found in the wild each month. An antivirus program would be useless if it did not keep up with all the new viruses. The engine accesses the definition files (or database), runs the virus scans, cleans the files, and notifies the appropriate people and accounts. Eventually viruses become so sophisticated that a new engine and new technology are needed to combat them effectively.

Heuristic scanning is a technology that allows an antivirus program to search for a virus even if there is no definition for it. The engine looks for suspicious activity that might indicate a virus. Be careful if you have this feature turned on. A heuristic scan might detect more than viruses; removing harmless code might cause unpredictable results.

For an antivirus program to be effective, you must upgrade, update, and scan in a specific order:

1. Upgrade the antivirus engine.
2. Update the definition files.
3. Create an antivirus emergency boot disk.
4. Configure and run a full on-demand scan.
5. Schedule monthly full on-demand scans.
6. Configure and activate on-access scans.
7. Update the definition files monthly.

**8.** Make a new antivirus emergency boot disk monthly.

**9.** Get the latest update when fighting a virus outbreak.

**10.** Repeat all steps when you get a new engine.

We will look at the first steps in using antivirus software in the following sections. The other steps are beyond the scope of this book.

## Upgrading an Antivirus Engine

An antivirus engine is the core program that runs the scanning process; virus definitions are keyed to an engine version number. For example, a 3.*x* engine will not work with 4.*x* definition files. When the manufacturer releases a new engine, consider both the cost to upgrade and the added benefits.

 Before installing new or upgraded software, back up your entire computer system, including all data.

## Updating Definition Files

Every week you need to update your list of known viruses—called the virus definition files. You can do this manually or automatically through the manufacturer's website. You can use a staging server within your company to download and then distribute the updates, or you can set up each computer to download updates.

## Scanning for Viruses

An antivirus scan is the process in which an antivirus program examines the computer suspected of having a virus and eradicates any viruses it finds. There are two types of antivirus scans:

- On-demand
- On-access

An on-demand scan searches a file, a directory, a drive, or an entire computer. An on-access scan checks only the files you are currently accessing. To maximize protection, you should use a combination of both types.

## On-Demand Scans

An on-demand scan is a virus scan initiated by either a network administrator or a user. You can manually or automatically initiate an on-demand scan. Typically, you'd schedule a monthly on-demand scan, but you'll also want to do an on-demand scan in the following situations:

- After you first install the antivirus software
- When you upgrade the antivirus software engine
- When you suspect a virus outbreak

Before you initiate an on-demand scan, be sure that you have the latest virus definitions.

When you encounter a virus, scan all potentially affected hard disks and any floppy disks that could be suspicious. Establish a cleaning station, and quarantine the infected area. The support staff will have a difficult time if a user continues to use the computer while it is infected. Ask all users in the infected area to stop using their computers. Suggest a short break. If it is lunchtime, all the better. Have one person remove all floppies from all disk drives. Perform a scan and clean at the cleaning station. For computers that are operational, update their virus definitions. For computers that are not operational or are operational but infected, boot to an antivirus emergency boot disk. Run a full scan and clean the entire system on all computers in the office space. With luck, you will be done before your users return from lunch.

## On-Access Scans

An on-access scan runs in the background when you open a file or use a program. For example, an on-access scan can run when you do any of the following:

- Insert a floppy disk
- Download a file with FTP
- Receive e-mail messages and attachments
- View a web page

The scan slows the processing speed of other programs, but it is worth the inconvenience.

A relatively new form of malicious attack makes its way to your computer through ActiveX and Java programs (applets). These are miniature programs that run on a web server or that you download to your local machine. Most ActiveX and Java applets are safe, but some contain viruses or snoop programs. The snoop programs allow a hacker to look at everything on your hard drive from a remote location without your knowing. Be sure that you properly configure the on-access component of your antivirus software to check and clean for all these types of attacks.

There is a host of great shareware and freeware available on the Internet today. Titles include Microsoft AntiSpyware, Spybot Search & Destroy and Ad-Aware, as well as Windows Update.

Many programs will not install unless you disable the on-access portion of your antivirus software. This is dangerous if the program has a virus. Your safest bet is to do an on-demand scan of the software before installation. Disable on-access scanning during installation, and then reactivate it when the installation is complete.

## Emergency Scans

In an emergency scan, only the operating system and the antivirus program are running. An emergency scan is called for after a virus has invaded your system and taken control of a machine. In this situation, insert your antivirus emergency boot disk and boot the infected computer from it. Then scan and clean the entire computer.

Another possibility is to use an emergency scan website like housecall.trendmicro.com. It allows you to scan your computer via a high speed Internet access without using an emergency disk.

If you don't have your boot disk, go to another computer and create one.

# Software Revisions

Patches, fixes, service packs, and updates are all the same thing—free software revisions. These are intermediary solutions until a new version of the product is released. They may solve a particular problem, as does a security patch, or change the way your system works, as does an update. You can apply a so-called hot patch without rebooting your computer; in other cases, applying a patch requires that the server go down.

## Is It Necessary?

Because patches are designed to fix problems, it would seem that you would want to download the most current patches and apply them immediately. That is not always the best thing to do. Patches can sometimes cause problems with existing, older software. Different philosophies exist regarding the application of the newest patches. The first philosophy is to keep your systems only as up-to-date as necessary to keep them running. This is the "if it ain't broke, don't fix it" approach. After all, the point of a patch is to fix your software. Why fix it if it isn't broken? The other philosophy is to keep the software as up-to-date as possible because of the additional features that a patch will sometimes provide.

You must choose the approach that is best for your situation. If you have little time to devote to chasing down and fixing problems, go with the first philosophy. If you always need the latest and greatest features, even at the expense of stability, go with the second.

## Where to Get Patches

Patches are available from several locations:

- The manufacturer's website

- The manufacturer's CD or DVD
- The manufacturer's support subscriptions on CD or DVD
- The manufacturer's bulletin (less frequently an option)

You'll notice in every case that the source of the patch, regardless of the medium being used to distribute it, is the manufacturer. You cannot be sure that patches available through online magazines, other companies, and shareware websites are safe. Also, patches for the operating system are sometimes included when you purchase a new computer.

## How to Apply Patches

Just as you always need to plan for an upgrade, you need to plan for a patch. Never blindly install patches (or any other new software) without examining the potential impact on the network. Although patches are designed to fix known problems, they may create new ones. It is best to try patches on a test network or system before installing them on all systems on the network.

Follow these steps to apply a patch:

1. Research the enhancements and changes that the patch provides. Go to the manufacturer's website, or take a look at the official documentation.

2. Download the patch and related documentation to an isolated test network (or computer if you don't have an entire test network).

3. Decompress any documentation files and read them. (Yes, the manual is something you read *before* installation, not after things crash.)

4. Note the changes, and define a way to test the new features.

5. Install the patch on a test workstation/server.

6. Select the installation method that allows you to save previous configurations so that you can uninstall if necessary.

7. Record any options and your selections, such as retaining or replacing drivers.

8. Reboot the computer.

9. If the operating system does not load or work properly, start over with a clean test machine. Select to keep your original drivers. (NIC drivers are commonly updated and may not work.)

10. Try out the new features. Test all patches to see if they work as advertised.

11. Run the test workstation/server for two weeks. Reboot it and try different tasks during this time.

12. If all goes well, do a limited rollout of the update to your support staff's personal computers and applicable servers, and have them test the patch.

13. After the IS support staff determines the product is safe, do a limited rollout to some users' workstations and applicable servers.

14. Roll out the patch to all production servers and all workstations via an automated procedure.

15. Ensure proper revision control. Make sure that all equipment has the same approved patch.

Remember that these are general steps. Refer to the documentation that comes with the patch (most likely a README.TXT file) for specific instructions on installing a specific patch.

You can see that this process can take a long time, even with multiple test machines and people helping you. The process can be speeded up a little, but do not skip any steps. If at any point you cannot get a system to work, even with changing the install options, stop the installation and refer to the support documentation for the patch to see if you are doing something wrong. Do not roll out a patch until it has been proven stable in all test environments.

If you use your operating system or application CDs to make changes to the operating system or an application after applying the patch, you may overwrite the updates made by the patch. You will need to reapply the patch after accessing these files.

# Summary

In this chapter, you learned about fault tolerance and disaster recovery. Fault tolerance is the ability of a system to resist failures and faults and to recover from them by itself. Disaster recovery is the ability of a system to recover from some kind of disaster where data is lost. Disaster recovery methods are used to replace data that has been lost due to some unforeseen circumstance.

In the first section, you learned about the various ways to assess fault tolerance and disaster recovery needs and the various ways that network systems need fault tolerance and disaster recovery. You learned that the amount of money used to protect data should be proportionate to the value of the data and the ease with which it can be replaced.

In the next section, you learned about the various types of power management that are put in place to prevent problems from happening or to allow a system to recover from a small, power-related fault. These items include UPS, SPS, and surge protectors.

Following power management, you learned that the most critical component of a fault tolerance plan is the amount and type of disk fault tolerance implemented. Types of disk fault tolerance include RAID in its various forms. Additionally, you learned about the different methods of backup and how they apply to disaster recovery.

You also learned how important virus protection is to a network and that, if antivirus measures are in place, fault tolerance and disaster recovery are not needed. Viruses are small programs that can interrupt the normal function of a computer. Viruses can spread on a network like wildfire and must be eliminated before they have a chance to spread and cause damage.

Finally, you learned that, in order to keep systems running with the least amount of problems, a software patch must occasionally be applied. A software patch is a piece of software that temporarily fixes small problems within an existing program until the next major release of the software.

# Exam Essentials

**Be able to explain the proper use of antivirus software**  Antivirus software is specialized software that detects and removes harmful programs called viruses from your computer. It must be updated regularly to be aware of the most common viruses and their behavior.

**Explain when to implement fault tolerance.**  Fault tolerance and disaster recovery must be implemented at some point and to some level on every network. Fault tolerance provides a means by which a computer or network has redundancy or the ability to recover from small faults and to continue providing services during a fault.

**Explain when to implement disaster recovery.**  Disaster recovery typically means recovering after a major disaster, typically by backing up data on a regular basis, so that critical data is not lost.

**Know what a full backup is.**  Each backup type differs primarily in the amount backed up and whether the items being backed up have changed. Full backups typically back up the entire contents of a server, whether they've changed or not.

**Know what an incremental backup is.**  Each backup type differs primarily in the amount backed up and whether the items being backed up have changed. Incremental backups are usually used in conjunction with full backups and back up everything that has changed since the last backup (full or incremental).

**Know what a differential backup is.**  Each backup type differs primarily in the amount backed up and whether the items being backed up have changed. Differential backups are also used in conjunction with a full backup and back up everything that has changed since the last full backup.

**Be able to describe why backups are important.**  Backups are used to have a duplicate copy of any data so that in the case of hardware failure or data loss, the information can be obtained from the backup media.

**Be able to describe different types of backup media.**  The most common backup media are various forms of magnetic tape (DAT, Travan, DLT, etc.) and CD-ROMs (CD-RW, DVD-ROM, etc.). Magnetic tape uses a plastic tape coated with metal oxide particles to store the data. It's inexpensive but has a finite life and relatively slow speed. CD-ROMs have a much longer life and higher speeds but much smaller capacities.

# Review Questions

1. What type of communication does a failover server typically have with the primary server?

   **A.** Total. They are two virtual servers in the same box.

   **B.** The two machines are in different sites connected by a modem.

   **C.** The two machines are in different sites connected by sleeping NICs.

   **D.** A dedicated network cable links the two servers.

   **E.** None. The failover server is on a separate network for protection.

2. What does the failover server listen for to determine if it needs to take over services?

   **A.** Ping

   **B.** Heartbeat

   **C.** Shutdown sequence

   **D.** Startup sequence

   **E.** Telnet session

3. What technology does VMS use to allow multiple servers to access the same resources to provide load balancing and fault tolerance?

   **A.** Clusters

   **B.** Proxies

   **C.** Slave servers

   **D.** Master servers

   **E.** Failover servers

4. What feature or benefit does a backup system give you?

   **A.** A master/slave server combination

   **B.** A clustered network that is up 100 percent of the time

   **C.** Copies of data on tape or removable media

   **D.** A power conditioner

   **E.** A UPS with a built-in surge protector

5. What RAID level provides the fastest access times with no fault tolerance?

   **A.** 0

   **B.** 1

   **C.** 3

   **D.** 5

   **E.** 10

**6.** RAID level 1 is more commonly known as _____.

   **A.** striping

   **B.** striping with parity

   **C.** duplicating

   **D.** mirroring

   **E.** master/slave

**7.** What is the minimum number of hard disks required for RAID 5?

   **A.** One

   **B.** Two

   **C.** Three

   **D.** Four

   **E.** Five

**8.** What are the differences between disk duplexing and disk mirroring? (Choose all that apply.)

   **A.** Disk duplexing uses one controller card, whereas mirroring uses two.

   **B.** Disk duplexing uses two controller cards, whereas mirroring uses one.

   **C.** Disk duplexing is slower because it uses only two disks, whereas mirroring uses three.

   **D.** Disk duplexing is faster because it uses three disks, whereas mirroring uses two.

   **E.** Disk duplexing can have a controller fail and not lose access to data.

   **F.** Mirroring can have a controller fail and not lose access to data.

**9.** The term used to describe various types of viruses being delivered disguised as other program types is _____.

   **A.** encapsulation

   **B.** macro

   **C.** Trojan Horse

   **D.** embedded

**10.** What power management device should be connected to every server?

   **A.** SPS

   **B.** UPS

   **C.** APS

   **D.** USPS

   **E.** SPSS

**11.** What power management device is best suited for noncritical workstations and home stereo equipment?

   **A.** Standby Power Supply (SPS)

   **B.** Uninterruptible Power Supply (UPS)

   **C.** Power conditioner

   **D.** Gas generator

   **E.** Surge protector

**12.** What is a brownout?

   **A.** A long increase in power

   **B.** A change from AC to DC power

   **C.** A reduction in power

   **D.** A short decrease in power

**13.** What is an electrical spike?

   **A.** A long increase in power

   **B.** A change from AC to DC power

   **C.** A reduction in power

   **D.** A short increase in power

**14.** A full backup does what to the archive bit once a backup has completed?

   **A.** Clears it

   **B.** Activates it

   **C.** Nothing

   **D.** Sets it to 100

   **E.** Resets it to 1000

**15.** In which type of backup do you use a maximum of two backup sessions to restore a file or a group of files?

   **A.** Full

   **B.** Partial

   **C.** Incremental

   **D.** Additional

   **E.** Differential

**16.** An incremental backup copies what to tape?

   **A.** Data files only

   **B.** Operating system files only

   **C.** Files with the archive clear

   **D.** Files that have changed since the last full backup only

   **E.** Files changed since the last full or incremental backup

**17.** How does the restore time from a full backup compare with other backup schemes required to fully restore a server?

   **A.** It is the shortest because multiple sessions are accessed.

   **B.** It is the shortest because a single session is accessed.

   **C.** It is the longest because multiple sessions are accessed.

   **D.** It is the longest because a single session is accessed.

   **E.** It takes the same amount of time as all other backup schemes.

**18.** Which fault tolerance mechanism has the least processing overhead?

   **A.** RAID 5

   **B.** RAID 0

   **C.** RAID 3

   **D.** RAID 1

**19.** How often should you update your virus definition files?

   **A.** Daily

   **B.** Weekly

   **C.** Monthly

   **D.** Quarterly

   **E.** Yearly

**20.** You should get your updates from which source(s)? (Choose all that apply.)

   **A.** Manufacturer

   **B.** Online magazine

   **C.** Postal magazine

   **D.** Original equipment manufacturer (OEM)

   **E.** Shareware website

# Answers to Review Questions

1. D. A failover server must have a connection available to the other server in case the other server goes down. Thus, there is a dedicated network between the two to ensure that the other server will be available when the failover occurs.

2. B. Failover servers send a signal to the backup failover server every few seconds. When the backup server detects that the primary server has not sent the signal after a specified time, the failover takes over until the primary comes back online. This signal is known as a "heartbeat."

3. A. VMS clustering makes many servers appear as one. If one server malfunctions, the others will keep functioning, thus allowing no breaks in network services.

4. C. Backup systems are designed to provide a backup copy of existing data in case of system failure. These copies are typically stored on magnetic tape or some other kind of removable media.

5. A. With RAID 0, you use multiple disks as a single volume and the data is striped across all drives. This RAID level gives you increased performance, but it doesn't provide any increased reliability.

6. D. RAID level 1 is more commonly known as mirroring, or duplexing. With mirroring, you have two disks of the same size and data is written to both disks at once. If one fails, the other is available to service disk requests.

7. C. Although five or more disks are commonly used, the minimum number of hard-disk drives needed for a RAID level 5 configuration is three.

8. B, E. By definition, the major differences between disk duplexing and mirroring are that in a duplex configuration, the disks are mirrored but each disk has its own disk controller adapter card installed in the computer. The reason for this is that in a mirrored configuration, if a disk controller fails, both mirrored disks are lost. Duplexing provides an extra level of protection.

9. C. The term Trojan Horse refers to a virus of any type (file, macro, or boot sector) that hides within the code of another program. Macro viruses are actually a specific type of virus that do not hide within another program but instead comprise scripts written into data files.

10. B. An Uninterruptible Power Supply (UPS) provides the most power protection and management features of those listed. It should be connected to every server to protect the server from power problems.

11. E. A surge protector provides only a basic level of protection against specific power overage problems. It won't protect a server against power underage (sags, brownouts, blackouts) problems.

12. D. A brownout occurs when the power dips below standard levels for several seconds and then returns to normal levels.

13. D. A spike is an extremely short increase in power that is immediately followed by a return to normal voltage levels. It gets its name because a graph of this condition looks like a spike.

**14.** A. A full backup will clear the archive bit on every file it backs up.

**15.** E. A differential backup uses a full backup and a daily backup that backs up everything that has changed since the last full backup. When a restore needs to happen, only two tapes will be used.

**16.** E. An incremental backup backs up the files that have changed since the last full or incremental backup. Each time an incremental backup backs up files, it clears the archive bit.

**17.** B. Because you are restoring only a single backup session, it doesn't take as long as it would if you had to restore from either a differential or incremental where you have, at the very least, two sessions.

**18.** D. Compared to the other fault tolerance mechanisms (RAID 3 and RAID 5), RAID 1 involves the least processing but not the least disk overhead. RAID 0 is not a fault tolerance mechanism.

**19.** B. Because new viruses are introduced often (approximately once or twice a month), the generally accepted guideline is to update the virus definition files for your antivirus software approximately once a week.

**20.** A, D. The best places to get updates (such as patches, fixes, and upgrades) for a particular software or hardware item is from either the manufacturer of that item or the OEM distributor. They can provide patches and more on a website or via a CD mailing.

# Chapter 10

# Network Troubleshooting

---

## THE FOLLOWING NETWORK+ EXAM OBJECTIVES ARE COVERED IN THIS CHAPTER:

✓ **4.3 Given a network scenario, interpret visual indicators (for example, link LEDs [light-emitting diodes] and collision LEDs) to determine the nature of a stated problem.**

✓ **4.4 Given a troubleshooting scenario involving a client accessing remote network services, identify the cause of the problem (for example, file services, print services, authentication failure, protocol configuration, physical connectivity, and SOHO [small office, home office] router).**

✓ **4.5 Given a troubleshooting scenario between a client and the following server environments, identify the cause of a stated problem:**

- UNIX/Linux/Mac OS X Server
- NetWare
- Windows
- AppleShare IP (Internet Protocol)

✓ **4.6 Given a scenario, determine the impact of modifying, adding, or removing network services (for example, DHCP [Dynamic Host Configuration Protocol], DNS [Domain Name Service] and WINS (Windows Internet Naming Service]) for network resources and users.**

✓ **4.7 Given a troubleshooting scenario involving a network with a particular physical topology (for example, bus, star, mesh, or ring) and including a network diagram, identify the network area affected and the cause of the stated failure.**

✓ **4.8 Given a network troubleshooting scenario involving an infrastructure (for example, wired or wireless) problem, identify the cause of a stated problem (for example, bad media, interference, network hardware, or environment).**

✓ **4.9 Given a network problem scenario, select an appropriate course of action based on a logical troubleshooting strategy. This strategy can include the following steps:**

- 1. Identify the symptoms and potential causes.
- 2. Identify the affected area.
- 3. Establish what has changed.
- 4. Select the most probable cause.
- 5. Implement an action plan and solution, including potential effects.
- 6. Test the result.
- 7. Identify the results and effects of the solution.
- 8. Document the solution and process.

There is no doubt about it. The only way to get good at trouble-shooting computers and networks is the same way to get good at any other art: practice, practice, practice. And as with any art, you must learn some basic skills before you can start practicing.

This chapter introduces you to some items to keep in mind when troubleshooting networks, as well as the troubleshooting topics covered on the Network+ exam. In this chapter, we'll examine some basic troubleshooting techniques. First, we'll look at how to check quickly for simple problems. Then, we'll discuss a common troubleshooting model that you can use to identify many network problems. Finally, we'll look at some common troubleshooting resources and some tips and tricks that you can use to make troubleshooting easier.

You may notice as you read this chapter that some of the objectives listed at the beginning are not directly covered in this chapter (in particular, objectives 4.6 through 4.9). That is because the background material for troubleshooting is the substance of all the previous chapters.

# Narrowing Down the Problem

Troubleshooting a network problem can be daunting. That's why it's best to start by trying to narrow down the source of the problem. When troubleshooting, there are five questions you should ask yourself:

1. Did you check the simple stuff?
2. Is hardware or software causing the problem?
3. Is it a workstation or server problem?
4. Which segments of the network are affected?
5. Are there any cabling issues?

## Did You Check the Simple Stuff?

The first thing to check, as most people will tell you, is the simple stuff. There's a saying that goes "All things being equal, the simplest explanation is probably the correct one." For computers, it's rather hard to categorize simple stuff because what's simple to one person might be complex to another. We like to define simple stuff (as it relates to troubleshooting) as items that are so obvious that you don't think to check them. When it turns out that one of those items is the problem, your reaction is almost always "Duh!" Almost everyone can agree on a few items that fall into this category:

- Correct login procedure and rights
- Link lights/collision lights
- Power switch
- Operator error

## The Correct Login Procedure and Rights

To gain access to the network, users must follow the correct login procedure exactly. If they don't, they will be denied access. Considering everything that must be done correctly and in the correct order, it's a miracle that anyone logs in to a network correctly at all. There are so many opportunities for making a mistake.

First, a user must enter the username and password correctly. As easy as this sounds, users frequently enter this information incorrectly, don't realize it, and report to the network administrator that the network is broken or that they can't log in. The most common problem is accidentally typing the wrong username or password. In some operating systems, this can happen when you accidentally leave the Caps Lock key pressed. An example of this is Unix, in which passwords are case sensitive; the user will not be able to log in unless their password is in all uppercase letters.

Additionally, in NetWare and Windows, the network administrator can restrict the times and conditions under which users can log in. If a user doesn't log in at the right time or from the right workstation, the network operating system will reject the login request even though it might be a valid request in terms of the username and password being spelled correctly. Additionally, a network administrator might restrict how many times a user can log in to the network simultaneously. If that user tries to establish more connections than are allowed, access will be denied. Any time a user is denied access to the network, they are likely to interpret that as a problem even though the network operating system might be doing what it should.

 **Real World Scenario**

### Can the Problem Be Reproduced?

The first question to ask anyone who reports a network or computer problem is, "Can you show me what 'not working' looks like?" If you can reproduce the problem, you can identify the conditions under which it occurs. And if you can identify the conditions, you can start to determine the source.

Unfortunately, not every problem can be reproduced. The hardest problems to solve are those that can't be reproduced but instead appear randomly.

To test for these types of problems, first check to see if the username and password are being typed correctly and whether or not the Caps Lock key is pressed. Try the login yourself from another workstation (assuming that doesn't violate the security policy). If it works, you might try asking the user to check to see if the Caps Lock light on the keyboard is on (indicating that the Caps Lock key has been pressed). If that doesn't solve the problem, check the network documentation to see if the aforementioned kinds of restrictions are in place.

If intruder detection is enabled on the network, the user's account will be locked after a specified number of incorrect login attempts. In this case, the user cannot log in until the administrator has unlocked the account or until a certain amount of time specified by the administrator has elapsed, after which the account is unlocked.

## The Link and Collision Lights

The *link light* is a small light-emitting diode (LED) found on both the NIC and the hub. It is typically green and is labeled "link" (or some abbreviation). A link light indicates that the NIC and hub (in the case of 10Base-T) are making a logical (Data Link layer) connection. You can usually assume that the workstation and hub are communicating if the link lights are lit on both the workstation's NIC and the hub port to which the workstation is connected.

The link lights on some NICs aren't activated until the driver is loaded. So, if the link light isn't on when the system is first turned on, you may have to wait until the operating system loads the NIC driver.

The *collision light* is also a small LED, typically amber in color. It can usually be found on both Ethernet NICs and hubs. When lit, it indicates that an Ethernet collision has occurred. It is important to know that this light will blink occasionally because collisions are somewhat common on busy Ethernet networks. However, if this light stays on continuously, there are too many collisions happening for legitimate network traffic to get through. This can be caused by a malfunctioning network card or another malfunctioning network device.

Be careful not to confuse the collision light with the network activity or network traffic light (usually green). The network activity light indicates that a device is transmitting. This particular light should be blinking on and off continually as the device transmits and receives data on the network.

## The Power Switch

To function properly, all computer and network components must be turned on and powered up. As obvious as this is, network administrators often hear a user complain, "My computer is on, but my monitor is dark." In this case, our response is to ask, "Is the monitor turned on?" After a pause, the voice on the other end usually says sheepishly, "Oh. Thanks."

Most systems include a power indicator such as a Power or PWR light, and the power switch typically has a 1 or an On indicator. However, the unit could be powerless even if the power switch is in the On position. Thus, you need to check that all power cables are plugged in, including the power strip.

Remember that every cable has two ends, and both must be plugged in to something.

When troubleshooting power problems, start with the most obvious device and work your way back to the power service panel. There could be any number of power problems between the device and the service panel, including a bad power cable, bad outlet, bad electrical wire, tripped circuit breaker, or blown fuse. Any of these items can cause power problems at the device.

## Operator Error

The problem may be that the user simply doesn't know how to perform the operation correctly; in other words, the problem may be due to *operator error (OE)*. Those in the computer and networking industry have devised several colorful expressions to describe operator error:

- EEOC (Equipment Exceeds Operator Capability)
- PEBCAK (Problem Exists Between Chair And Keyboard)
- ID Ten T Error (written as ID10T)

Assuming that all problems are related to operator error, however, is a mistake. Before you attribute any problem to operator error, ask the user to reproduce the problem in your presence, and pay close attention. You may find out that the user is having a problem because they are using an incorrect procedure—for example, flipping the power switch without following proper shutdown procedures. You may also find out that the user was trained incorrectly, in which case you might want to see if others are having the same difficulty. If the problem and solution are not obvious, try the procedure yourself, or ask someone else at another workstation to do so.

This is only a partial list of simple stuff. You'll come up with your own expanded list over time, as you troubleshoot more and more systems.

## Is Hardware or Software Causing the Problem?

A hardware problem typically manifests itself as a device in your computer that fails to operate correctly. You can usually tell that a hardware failure has occurred because you will try to use that piece of hardware and the computer will issue an error indicating that this has happened. Some failures, such as hard-disk failures, may give warning signs—for example, a Disk I/O error or something similar. Other components may just suddenly fail. The device will be operating fine and then simply fail.

The solution to hardware problems usually involves either changing hardware settings, updating device drivers, or replacing hardware. As we have discussed in previous chapters, I/O address, interrupt request lines (IRQ), and direct memory access (DMA) conflicts can cause computers (including workstations and servers) to malfunction. Change the hardware settings to solve these types of problems.

If the hardware has actually failed, however, you must get out your tools and start replacing components. If this is not one of your skills, you can send the device out for repair. In either case, because the system can be down for anywhere from an hour to several days, it's always prudent to have backup hardware on hand.

Software problems are a little more evasive. Some problems might result in General Protection Fault messages, which indicate a Windows or Windows program error of some type. Also, a program might suddenly stop responding (hang), or the entire machine might lock up randomly. The solution to these problems generally involves a trip to the manufacturer's support website to get software updates and patches or to search for the answer in a knowledge base.

Sometimes software will give you a precise message regarding the source of the problem, such as the software is missing a file or a file has become corrupt. In this case, you can either provide the file or, if necessary, reinstall the software. Neither solution takes long, and your computer will be up and running in a short time.

 Sometimes fragmented memory, which occurs after you open and close too many programs, is the source of the problem. The solution may be to reboot the computer, thus clearing memory. Be sure to add this to your network-troubleshooting bag of tricks.

## Is It a Workstation or a Server Problem?

Troubleshooting this problem involves first determining whether one person or a group of people are affected. If only one person is affected, think workstation. If several people are affected, the server or, more generally speaking, a portion of the network is probably experiencing problems.

If a single user is affected, your first line of defense is to try to log in from another workstation within the same group of users. If you can do so, the problem is related to the user's workstation. Look for a cabling fault, a bad NIC, or some other problem.

On the other hand, if several people in a group (such as a whole department) can't access a server, the problem may be related to that server. Go to the server in question and check for user connections. If everyone is logged in, the problem could be related to something else, such as individual rights or permissions. If no one can log in to that server, including the administrator, the server may have a communication problem with the rest of the network. If it has crashed, you might see messages to that effect on the server's monitor or the screen might be blank, indicating that the server is no longer running. These symptoms vary among network operating systems.

## Which Segments of the Network Are Affected?

Making this determination can be tough. If multiple segments are affected, the problem could be a network address conflict. As you may remember from Chapter 4, "TCP/IP Utilities," network addresses must be unique across an entire network. If two segments have the same IPX network address, for example, all the routers and NetWare servers will complain bitterly and send out error messages, hoping that it's just a simple problem that a router can correct. This is rarely the case, however, and thus the administrator must find and resolve the issue. Also keep in mind that the continuous broadcasting of error messages will negatively impact network performance.

If all users of the network are experiencing the problem, it could be related to a different device, such as a server that everyone accesses. Or, a main router or hub could be down, making network transmissions impossible.

Additionally, if the network has WAN connections, you can determine if a network problem is related to the WAN connection by checking to see if stations on both sides can communicate. If they can, the problem isn't related to the WAN. If they can't communicate, you must check everything between the sending station and the receiving one, including the WAN hardware. Usually, the WAN devices have built-in diagnostics that can indicate whether the WAN link is functioning correctly to help you determine if the fault is related to the WAN link or to the hardware involved.

## Are There Any Cabling Issues?

After you determine whether the problem is related to the whole network, to a single segment, or to a single workstation, you must determine whether the problem is related to network cabling. First, check to see if the cables are properly connected to the correct port. More than once, we've seen a wall phone cable plugged into a modem in the In jack.

Additionally, patch cables from workstation to wall jack can and do go bad, especially if they get moved or tripped over often. This problem is often characterized by connection problems. If you test the NIC and there is no link light (discussed earlier in this chapter), the problem could be related to a bad patch cable.

It is also possible to have a cabling problem in the walls where the cabling wasn't installed correctly. If a network cable was run over a fluorescent light, for example, the workstation attached to that cable might have problems only when the lights are on. The problem is that the fluorescent lights produce a large amount of electromagnetic interference (EMI) and can disrupt communications in that cable. This kind of problem may manifest itself only at times when most lights need to be on.

Next, check the medium dependent interface/medium dependent interface-crossover (MDI/MDI-X) port setting on small, workgroup hubs, a potential source of trouble that is often overlooked. This port is used to uplink, for example, to a hub on the network's backbone. The port setting has to be set to either MDI or MDI-X, depending on the type of cable used for the hub-to-hub connection. A crossover cable (discussed later in this chapter) requires that the port be set to MDI; a standard network patch cable requires that the port be set to MDI-X. You can usually adjust the setting via a regular switch or a dual inline package (DIP) switch. Check the hub's documentation.

Some hubs just have a port labeled MDI, since the MDI-X setting is really just another port standard for all intents and purposes. If you connect hubs using a standard patch cable, you must connect the MDI port to a standard (MDI-X) port on the backbone hub.

# Troubleshooting Steps

In the Network+ troubleshooting model, there are eight steps you must follow:

1. Establish symptoms.
2. Identify the affected area.
3. Establish what has changed.
4. Select the most probable cause.
5. Implement a solution.
6. Test the result.
7. Recognize the potential effects of the solution.
8. Document the solution.

To facilitate our discussion of the troubleshooting steps, let's assume that a user has called you, the network administrator, to complain about not being able to connect to the Internet.

## Step 1: Establish Symptoms

Obviously, if you can't identify a problem, you can't begin to solve it. Typically, you need to ask some questions to begin to clarify exactly what is happening. In our example, we should ask the user the following:

- Which part of the Internet can't you access? A particular website? A particular address? Any website?

- Can you use your web browser?

We find out that the user cannot access the corporate intranet or get to any sites on the Internet. He can, however, use his web browser to access the corporate FTP site, which he has bookmarked (by IP address 10.0.0.2). We can, therefore, rule out the web browser as the source of the problem.

## Step 2: Identify the Affected Area

Computers and networks are fickle; they can work fine for months, suddenly malfunction horribly, and then continue to work fine for several more months, never again exhibiting that particular problem. And that's why it's important to be able to reproduce the problem and identify the affected area. Identifying the affected area narrows down what you have to troubleshoot.

One of your goals is to make problems easier to troubleshoot and, thus, get users working again as soon as possible. Therefore, the best advice you can give when training users is that when something isn't working, try it again and then write down exactly what is and is not happening. Most users' knee-jerk reaction is to call you immediately when they experience a problem. This isn't necessarily the best thing to do because your response is most likely, "What were you doing when the problem occurred?" And most users don't know precisely what they were doing at the computer because they were primarily trying to get their job done. Therefore, if you train users to reproduce the problem first, they'll be able to give you the information you need to start troubleshooting it.

In our example, we find out that when the user tries to access the corporate intranet, he gets the following error message:

We're in luck—we can re-create this problem.

It is a definite advantage to be able to watch the user try to reproduce the problem because you can determine whether the user is performing the operation correctly.

## Step 3: Establish What Has Changed

If you can reproduce the problem, your next step is to attempt to determine what has changed. Drawing on your knowledge of networking, you might ask yourself and your user questions such as the following:

**Were you ever able to do this?**   If not, then maybe this is not an operation the hardware or software is designed to do. You can inform the user that the system won't do the operation (or that they may need additional hardware or software to do it).

**If so, when did you become unable to do it?**   If the computer was able to do the operation and then suddenly could not, the conditions that surround this change become extremely important. You may be able to discover the cause of the problem if you know what happened immediately before the change. It is likely that the cause of the problem is related to the conditions surrounding the change.

**Has anything changed since you were last able to do this?**   This question can give you insight into a possible source for the problem. Most often, the thing that changed before the problem started is the source of the problem. When you ask this question of a user, the answer is typically that nothing has changed, so you might need to rephrase it. For example, you can try asking, "Did anyone add anything to your computer?" or "Are you doing anything that's different from the way you normally proceed?"

**Were any error messages displayed?**    This is one of the best indicators of the cause of a problem. Error messages are designed by programmers to help them determine what aspect of a computer system is not functioning correctly. These error messages are sometimes clear, such as "Disk Full" (indicating that the disk cannot store any more files on it because it is full). Or they can be cryptic, such as "A random bit has been flipped in the I/O subsystem of memory junction 44FA380h" (this is a fictitious error, but you may encounter some just as complex). If you get a cryptic error message, you can go to the software or hardware vendor's support website and usually get a translation of the "programmerese" of the error message into English.

**Are other people experiencing this problem?**    This is one question you must ask yourself. That way you might be able to narrow down the cause of the problem to a specific item. Try to duplicate the problem yourself from your own workstation. If you can't duplicate the problem on another workstation, it may be related to only one user or group of users (or possibly their workstations). If more than one user is experiencing this problem, you may know this already because several people will be calling in with the same problem.

**Is the problem always the same?**    Generally speaking, when problems crop up, they are almost always the same problem each time they occur. But their symptoms may change ever so slightly as conditions surrounding them change. A related question is, "If you do $x$, does the problem get better or worse?" For example, you might ask a user, "If you use a different file, does the problem get better or worse?" If the symptoms become less severe, it might indicate that the problem is related to the original file being used.

These are just a few of the questions you can use to isolate the cause of the problem.

In our example, we find out that the problem is unique to one user, indicating that the problem is specific to his workstation. When we watch him as he attempts to reproduce the problem, we notice that he is typing the address correctly. The error message leads us to believe that the problem has something to with Domain Name Service (DNS) lookups on his workstation.

## Step 4: Select the Most Probable Cause

After you observe the problem and isolate the cause, your next step is to select the most probable cause for the problem. Trust me, this gets easier with time and experience.

You must come up with at least one possible cause, even though it may not be correct. And you don't always have to come up with it yourself. Someone else in the group may have the answer. Also, don't forget to check online sources and vendor documentation.

In our example, we determined earlier that the cause was improperly configured DNS lookup on the workstation. The correction, then, is to reconfigure DNS on the workstation.

## Step 5: Implement a Solution

In this step, you implement the solution. In our example, we need to reconfigure DNS on the workstation by following these steps in Windows 2000 Server:

1. Choose Start ➢ Settings ➢ Control Panel ➢ Network and Dial-up Connections to open the Network and Dial-up Connections window.

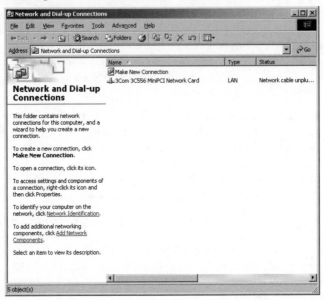

2. Double-click a network adapter in the list to display the Properties tabs for the adapter. The adapter in the previous screen shot is named 3Com 3C556 MiniPCI Network Card.

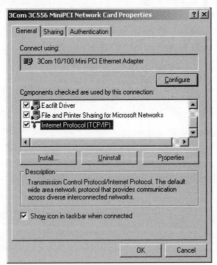

**3.** Double-click the Internet Protocol (TCP/IP) entry in the Components Checked Are Used by This Connection frame. This brings up the Internet Protocol (TCP/IP) Properties window.

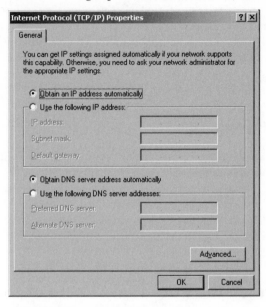

**4.** Note the static/dynamic DNS settings on the General tab. Click the Advanced button to bring up the Advanced TCP/IP Settings window and select the DNS tab.

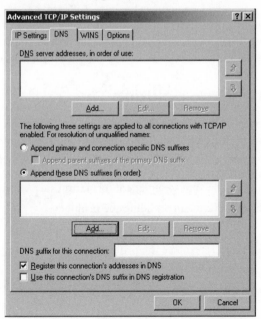

DNS settings are uniform across all adapters. So, using one adapter to access these configuration pages affects the solitary DNS configuration for the entire system. As you can see in the previous screen shot, there are no static DNS settings on this workstation. You should only change such settings when you fully understand the effect of these changes or are told to do so by someone who does. Incorrect configuration of these settings will disable the normal operation of your workstation. We can assume our DNS configuration requires some sort of static changes, such as the specification of DNS suffixes, which can coexist with DHCP-learned DNS settings.

## Step 6: Test the Result

Now that you have made the changes, you must test your solution to see if it solves the problem. In our example, we'd ask the user to try to access the intranet (since that was the problem reported). In general terms, ask the user to repeat the operation that previously did not work. If it works, great! The problem is solved. If it doesn't, try the operation yourself.

If the problem isn't solved, you may have to go back to step 4, select a new possible cause, and redo steps 5 and 6. But it is important to make note of what worked and what didn't so that you don't make the same mistakes twice.

## Step 7: Recognize the Potential Effects of the Solution

A fundamental flaw of any network technician is solving only the one problem and not realizing what other problems that solution may cause. It is possible that the solution may be worse than the problem. As the saying goes, "Sometimes the cure is worse than the disease."

Before fully implementing the solution to a problem, make sure you are completely aware of the potential effects of the solution and the other problems it may cause. If it causes more problems than it fixes, the solution probably isn't the best solution for the problem.

## Step 8: Document the Solution

As you learned in Chapter 6, "Wired and Wireless Networks," network documentation is very important. You'll definitely want to document problems and solutions so that you have the information at hand when a similar problem arises in the future. With documented solutions to documented problems, you can assemble your own database of information that you can use to troubleshoot other problems. Be sure to include information such as the following:

- A description of the conditions surrounding the problem
- The NOS version, the software version, the type of computer, and the type of NIC
- Whether you were able to reproduce the problem
- The solutions you tried
- The ultimate solution

# The Troubleshooter's Resources

In the process of troubleshooting a workstation, a server, or other network component, you have many resources at your disposal. In this section, we'll take a brief look at some of them. Those you use depend on the situation and your personal preferences. You will eventually have your own favorites.

## Log Files

As you learned in Chapter 6, *log files* can indicate the general health of a server. Each log file format is different, but generally speaking, the log files contain a running list of all errors and notices, the time and date they occurred, and any other pertinent information. Let's look at a couple of the log files from the most commonly used network operating systems, NetWare 5 and Windows 2000 Server.

### NetWare Log Files

NetWare uses three log files that can help you diagnose problems on a NetWare server:

- The Console Log file (CONSOLE.LOG)
- The Abend Log file (ABEND.LOG)
- The Server Log file (SYS$LOG.ERR)

Each file has different uses in the troubleshooting process.

### The Console Log file

The Console Log file (CONSOLE.LOG) keeps a history of all errors that have occurred and information that has been displayed on the server's console. It is located in the SYS:\ETC directory on the server and is created and maintained by the utility CONLOG.NLM, which comes with NetWare versions 3.12 and later. You must load this utility manually (or place the load command in the AUTOEXEC.NCF file so that it starts automatically upon server startup) by typing the following at the console prompt:

LOAD CONLOG

Once this utility is loaded, it erases whatever CONSOLE.LOG file currently exists and starts logging to the new file.

> This command works with any version of NetWare, including 3.12 or later. However, if you are using NetWare 5 or later, the LOAD command is optional. It is required in versions 3.12 to 4.1x.

Figure 10.1 shows a sample CONSOLE.LOG file. From this log file, we can tell that someone edited the AUTO-EXEC.NCF file and then restarted the server. This indicates a major change on the server. If we were trying to troubleshoot a server that was starting to exhibit strange problems after a recent reboot, this might be a source to check.

**FIGURE 10.1** A sample CONSOLE.LOG file

```
CONLOG-1.04-10: System console logging started Fri Feb 12 13:52:40 1999.
CONLOG-1.04-9: Logging system console to sys:etc\console.log.
S1:edit autoexec.ncf
Loading module EDIT.NLM
  NetWare Text Editor
  Version 4.15    March 23, 1998
  Copyright 1989-1998 Novell, Inc.  All rights reserved.
File OWL501F.DLL in use by user ADMIN on station 23
File NWCORE32.DLL in use by user ADMIN on station 23
File WANMAN.DLL in use by user ADMIN on station 23
File SLP-SP.ZIP in use by user ADMIN on station 23
*** WARNING *** There are active files open.
Down server? y
IPXRTR: IPX link state router down.
Java: Cleaning up resources, Please Wait.

Module JAVA.NLM unloaded
Notifying stations that file server is down
Dismounting volume DATA

 2-12-1999   1:57:26 pm:    DS-7.9-23
     Bindery close requested by the SERVER


 2-12-1999   1:57:26 pm:    DS-7.9-20
     Directory Services:  Local database has been closed

Dismounting volume SYS
```

**WARNING**  The information in the CONSOLE.LOG file is lost every time the CONLOG.NLM is unloaded and reloaded. It doesn't keep a history of every command ever issued, only those issued since CONLOG.NLM was loaded. However, you can configure the ARCHIVE=YES parameter to configure CONLOG.NLM to keep a history of all the CONLOG files. The first file is saved with a .000 extension, the next with a .001 extension, and so forth. The complete command to run at the console (or add to Autoexec.ncf) is Conlog archive=yes.

## The Abend Log File

This log file registers all Abends on a NetWare server. An Abend (ABnormal END) is an error condition that can halt the proper operation of the NetWare server. Abends can be serious enough to lock the server, or they can simply force an NLM to shut down. You know an Abend has occurred when you see an error message that contains the word *Abend* on the console. Additionally, the server command prompt will include a number in angle brackets (for example, <1>) that indicates the number of times the server has Abended since it was brought online.

Because the server may reboot after an Abend, these error messages and what they mean can be lost. NetWare versions 4.11 and later include a routine to capture the output of the Abend both to the console and to the ABEND.LOG file. ABEND.LOG is located in the SYS:SYSTEM directory on the server.

The ABEND.LOG file contains all the information that is output to the console screen during an Abend, plus much more:

- The exact flags and registers of the processor at the time of the Abend
- The NLMs that were in memory, including their versions, descriptions, memory settings, and exact time and date

Here is a portion of our ABEND.LOG file:

```
************************************************************

Server S1 halted Friday, February 12, 1999   2:37:03 pm
Abend 1 on P00: Server-5.00a: Page Fault Processor
          Exception(Error code 00000002)


Registers:
    CS = 0008 DS = 0010 ES = 0010 FS = 0010 GS = 0010
       SS = 0010
    EAX = 00000000 EBX = D0AC2238 ECX = 0697DEF0
      EDX = 00000009
    ESI = D0C5C040 EDI = 00000000 EBP = 0697DED0
       ESP = 0697DEC0
    EIP = D0AC2232 FLAGS = 00014246
    D0AC2232 C600CC           MOV      [EAX]=?,CC
    EIP in ABENDEMO.NLM at code start +00000232h


Running process: Abendemo Process
Created by: NetWare Application
Thread Owned by NLM: ABENDEMO.NLM
Stack pointer: 697DCE0
OS Stack limit: 697A000
Scheduling priority: 67371008
Wait state: 5050170   (Blocked on keyboard)
Stack: D0AC22C1  (ABENDEMO.NLM|MenuAction+89)
       D1FEA602  (NWSNUT.NLM|NWSShowPortalLine+3602)
       --00000008  ?
       --00000000  ?
       --0697DF20  ?
       --D0134080  ?
       --00000001  ?
```

```
        D1FEA949  (NWSNUT.NLM|NWSShowPortalLine+3949)
        --00000010  ?
        --0697DEF0  ?
        --0697DEF4  ?
        --0697DFAC  ?
        --D0C2E100  (CONNMGR.NLM|WaitForBroadcastsToClear+C90C)
        --00000003  ?
        --00000008  ?
        --00000012  ?
        --00000000  ?
        --00000019  ?
        --00000050  ?
        --000000FF  ?
        --00000001  ?
        --00000010  ?
        --00000001  ?
        --00000000  ?
        --00000011  ?
        --0697DFDC  ?
        --0000000B  ?
        --00000000  ?
        D1FEABD9  (NWSNUT.NLM|NWSShowPortalLine+3BD9)
        --0000000B  ?
        --00000000  ?
        --00000000  ?


Additional Information:
     The CPU encountered a problem executing code in
       ABENDEMO.NLM.  The problem may be in that module
       or in data passed to that module by a process owned
       by ABENDEMO.NLM.


Loaded Modules:
SERVER.NLM       NetWare Server Operating System
   Version 5.00    August 27, 1998
     Code Address: FC000000h  Length: 000A5000h
     Data Address: FC5A5000h  Length: 000C9000h
```

```
LOADER.EXE        NetWare OS Loader
  Code Address: 000133D0h  Length: 0001D000h
  Data Address: 000303D0h  Length: 00020C30h
CDBE.NLM          NetWare Configuration DB Engine
  Version 5.00    August 12, 1998
  Code Address: D0087E000h  Length: 00007211h
  Data Address: D0887000h  Length: 0000684Ch
```

This information can be useful when determining the source of an Abend. For example, anytime you see the words *Page Fault* or *Stack* in the output, the Abend occurred because of something having to do with memory. Usually, it's because a program or process tried to take memory that didn't belong to it (for example, from another program). When NetWare detects this, it shuts down the offending process and issues an Abend.

## The Server Log File

The general Server Log file (SYS$LOG.ERR ), found in the SYS:SYSTEM directory, lists any errors that occur on the server, including Abends and NDS errors and the time and date of their occurrence. An error in the SYS$LOG.ERR file might look something like this:

```
1-07-1999  11:51:10 am:    DS-7.9-17
   Severity = 1  Locus = 17  Class = 19
   Directory Services:  Could not open local database,
    error: -723
```

The Severity, Locus, and Class designations in the second line substitute for lengthy text descriptions of the error and can provide more information:

- Severity indicates the seriousness of the problem.
- Locus indicates which system component is affected by the error (for example, memory, disk, or LAN cards).
- Class indicates the type of error.

Tables 10.1, 10.2, and 10.3 explain the codes used for Severity, Locus, and Class. Based on the information in these tables, we can determine some information about the preceding example of a SYS$LOG.ERR file. A severity of 1 indicates a warning condition (so the problem isn't really serious), a locus of 17 indicates that the error relates to the operating system (which would make sense because this is a Directory Services error), and a class of 19 indicates that the problem is with a domain, meaning that the problem is defined by the operating system but it's not an operating system problem. These designations tell us the reported error is related to NDS and that it's not really serious. In fact, this particular error might occur when you bring up the server and the database hasn't yet been opened by the operating system.

**TABLE 10.1**    **SYS$LOG.ERR** Severity Code Descriptions

| Number | Description |
|--------|-------------|
| 0 | **Informational.** Indicates that the information is non-threatening, usually just to record some kind of entry in the SYS$LOG.ERR file. |
| 1 | **Warning.** Indicates a potential problem that does not cause damage. |
| 2 | **Recoverable.** Indicates that an error condition that can be recovered by the operating system has occurred. |
| 3 | **Critical.** Indicates a condition that should be taken care of soon and that might cause a server failure in the near future. For example, mirrored partitions are out of sync or the Abend recovery routine is invoked. |
| 4 | **Fatal.** Indicates that something has occurred that will cause the imminent shutdown of the server or that a shutdown has occurred. This type of error might occur when a disk driver unloads because of a software failure. |
| 5 | **Operation Aborted.** Indicates that an attempted operation could not be completed because of an error. For example, a disk save could not be completed because the disk was full. |
| 6 | **No NOS Unrecoverable.** Indicates that the operation could not be completed but that it will not affect the operating system. For example, a compressed file is corrupt and unrecoverable. |

**TABLE 10.2**    **SYS$LOG.ERR** Locus Code Descriptions

| Number | Description |
|--------|-------------|
| 0 | Unknown |
| 1 | Memory |
| 2 | File System |
| 3 | Disks |
| 4 | LAN Boards |
| 5 | COM Stacks (Communication Protocols) |

**TABLE  10.2**     **SYS$LOG.ERR** Locus Code Descriptions  *(continued)*

| Number | Description |
| --- | --- |
| 6 | No Definition |
| 7 | TTS (Transaction Tracking System) |
| 8 | Bindery |
| 9 | Station |
| 10 | Router |
| 11 | Locks |
| 12 | Kernel |
| 13 | UPS |
| 14 | SFT_III |
| 15 | Resource Tracking |
| 16 | NLM |
| 17 | OS Information |
| 18 | Cache |
| 19 | Domain |

**TABLE  10.3**     **SYS$LOG.ERR** Class Code Descriptions

| Number | Description |
| --- | --- |
| 0 | Class Unknown |
| 1 | Out of Resources |
| 2 | Temporary Situation |
| 3 | Authorization Failure |
| 4 | Internal Error |

**TABLE 10.3** **SYS$LOG.ERR** Class Code Descriptions *(continued)*

| Number | Description |
|--------|-------------|
| 5 | Hardware Failure |
| 6 | System Failure |
| 7 | Request Error |
| 8 | Not Found |
| 9 | Bad Format |
| 10 | Locked |
| 11 | Media Failure |
| 12 | Item Exists |
| 13 | Station Failure |
| 14 | Limit Exceeded |
| 15 | Configuration Error |
| 16 | Limit Almost Exceeded |
| 17 | Security Audit Information |
| 18 | Disk Information |
| 19 | General Information |
| 20 | File Compressions |
| 21 | Protection Violation |

## Windows 2000 Server Log Files

Windows 2000 Server, like other network operating systems, employs comprehensive error and informational logging routines. Every program and process theoretically could have its own logging utility, but Microsoft has come up with a rather slick utility, Event Viewer, which, through log files, tracks all events on a particular Windows 2000 Server system.

Normally, though, you must be an administrator or a member of the Administrators group to have access to Event Viewer.

To use Event Viewer, follow these steps:

**1.** Choose Start ➢ Programs ➢ Administrative Tools ➢ Event Viewer to open the Microsoft Management Console (MMC) Event Viewer snap-in:

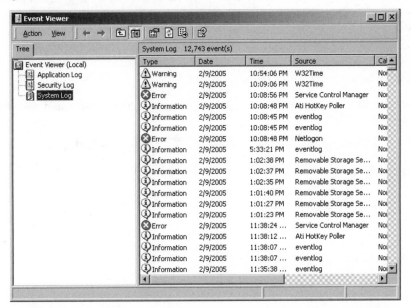

**2.** The System Log displays by default. To view the Application or Security Log, select it from the list in the left frame under the Tree tab.

Using Event Viewer, you can take a look at three types of logs:

- The System Log
- The Security Log
- The Application Log

### The System Log

This log file tracks just about every event that occurs on that computer. It is similar to NetWare's SYS$LOG.ERR file. However, whereas the SYS$LOG.ERR file tracks many categories of errors, the System Log tracks only three main types of events:

- Information (An event occurred, especially a service failure.)
- Warning (An event occurred that could cause problems.)
- Error (A component has failed and needs immediate attention.)

In a log file, the icon that precedes the date indicates the event's type. The previous screen shot shows the three types of events found in the System Log.

Two other types of events (Success Audit and Failure Audit) normally appear only in the Security Log (discussed later in this chapter).

Figure 10.2 shows a sample System Log. The list contains several categories of information, including the date and time the event occurred, the source of the event (which process the event came from), which user (if applicable) initiated the process, the name of the computer the event happened on, and the Event ID number (in the Event column). The Event ID number is the unique error type of a particular event. For an explanation of each Event ID number, check the Help file or go to www.microsoft.com/technet/ and search for "Event ID."

**FIGURE 10.2**   A sample System Log (Note the different error types and event IDs.)

| Date | Time | Source | Category | Event | User | Computer |
|------|------|--------|----------|-------|------|----------|
| 1/7/99 | 12:53:09 PM | BROWSER | None | 8015 | N/A | S1 |
| 1/7/99 | 11:39:17 AM | BROWSER | None | 8033 | N/A | S1 |
| 1/7/99 | 11:39:17 AM | BROWSER | None | 8033 | N/A | S1 |
| 1/7/99 | 11:39:17 AM | BROWSER | None | 8033 | N/A | S1 |
| 1/7/99 | 11:37:14 AM | symc810 | None | 9 | N/A | S1 |
| 1/7/99 | 11:36:50 AM | symc810 | None | 9 | N/A | S1 |
| 1/7/99 | 11:36:05 AM | symc810 | None | 9 | N/A | S1 |
| 1/7/99 | 11:35:21 AM | symc810 | None | 9 | N/A | S1 |
| 1/7/99 | 11:33:15 AM | Disk | None | 7 | N/A | S1 |
| 1/7/99 | 11:33:11 AM | Disk | None | 7 | N/A | S1 |
| 1/7/99 | 11:33:07 AM | Disk | None | 7 | N/A | S1 |
| 1/7/99 | 11:33:04 AM | Disk | None | 7 | N/A | S1 |
| 1/7/99 | 11:33:00 AM | Disk | None | 7 | N/A | S1 |
| 1/7/99 | 11:32:56 AM | Disk | None | 7 | N/A | S1 |
| 1/7/99 | 11:32:52 AM | Disk | None | 7 | N/A | S1 |
| 1/7/99 | 11:32:48 AM | Disk | None | 7 | N/A | S1 |
| 1/7/99 | 11:32:44 AM | Disk | None | 7 | N/A | S1 |
| 1/7/99 | 11:32:40 AM | Disk | None | 7 | N/A | S1 |
| 1/6/99 | 7:04:41 PM | BROWSER | None | 8015 | N/A | S1 |
| 1/6/99 | 7:04:41 PM | BROWSER | None | 8015 | N/A | S1 |
| 1/6/99 | 7:02:59 PM | EventLog | None | 6005 | N/A | S1 |
| 1/6/99 | 7:04:41 PM | BROWSER | None | 8015 | N/A | S1 |
| 1/6/99 | 6:57:00 PM | Service Control M | None | 7000 | N/A | S1 |
| 1/6/99 | 6:56:54 PM | EventLog | None | 6005 | N/A | S1 |
| 1/6/99 | 6:57:00 PM | E100B | None | 5007 | N/A | S1 |
| 1/6/99 | 6:00:37 PM | Service Control M | None | 7000 | N/A | S1 |
| 1/6/99 | 6:00:32 PM | EventLog | None | 6005 | N/A | S1 |
| 1/6/99 | 6:00:37 PM | E100B | None | 5007 | N/A | S1 |

Event Viewer - System Log on \\S1
Log   View   Options   Help

If you want more detail on a specific event, double-click it. Figure 10.3 shows the event detail for the following event (listed in Figure 10.2):

`1/7/9911:33:15 AMDiskNone7N/AS1`

The note in the Description box indicates that Windows 2000 Server found a bad disk block. Even though this is an error event, it is not serious. One bad block is not a problem; several disk blocks starting to go bad at once is a problem. The Data box lists the exact data the Event Viewer received about the error condition. This may be useful in determining the source of the problem. More than likely, if you have a serious problem that you can't fix, this is the information that you will send to the vendor (or to Microsoft) to help troubleshoot the problem.

### The Security Log

This log tracks security events specified by the system's or domain's Audit policy. The Audit policy specifies which security items will be tracked in Event Viewer. To set the local Audit policy on your Windows 2000 workstation, follow these steps:

1. Choose Start ➢ Programs ➢ Administrative Tools ➢ Local Security Policy to open the MMC Local Security Settings snap-in.

**FIGURE 10.3**    The Event Detail dialog box for an event listed in Figure 10.2

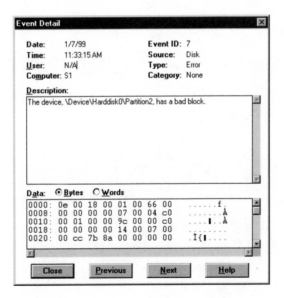

**2.** In the left frame, expand Local Policies and click on Audit Policy to display the local and effective settings for your machine's Audit policy in the right frame:

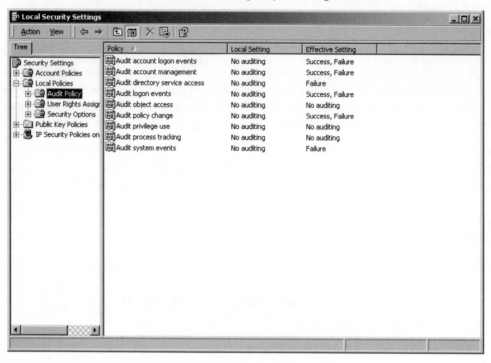

**3.** Double-click the policy you would like to change the auditing for. This brings up the Local Security Policy Setting dialog box for the policy you selected:

4.  Check the Success or Failure check box to track the success or failure of the policy's events. Since these are security settings, most often you'll want to log failures, but you can check both boxes.

5.  Click OK, and the success or failure (or both) of the event will be logged for this system.

After you set the Audit policy for a system, you can view its Security Log. Follow these steps:

1.  Choose Start ➢ Programs ➢ Administrative Tools ➢ Event Viewer to open the Microsoft Management Console (MMC) Event Viewer snap-in.

2.  The System Log displays by default. To view the Security Log, select it from the list in the left frame under the Tree tab:

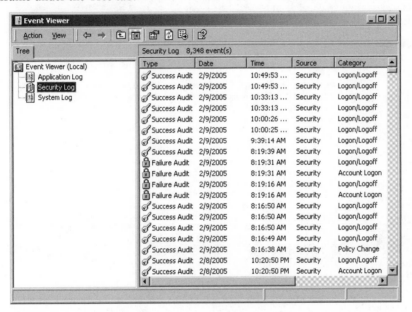

As you can see, this log looks similar to the System Log in most respects. The main differences are the icons and the types of events recorded here. To view the detail for an event, double-click it.

The Security Log displays two types of events:

-   Success Audit (The event passed the security audit.)
-   Failure Audit (The event failed the security audit.)

The previous screen shot shows the icons associated with these two types of events. When an item fails a security audit, something security-related failed. For example, a common entry (assuming the Failure check box is checked in the Local Security Policy Setting dialog box) is a Failure Audit with a value of Logon/Logoff in the category. This means that the user failed to log on.

## The Application Log

This log is similar to the other two logs except that it tracks events for network services and applications (for example, SQL Server and other BackOffice products). It uses the same event types (and their associated icons) as the System Log. Figure 10.4 shows an example of an Application Log.

**FIGURE 10.4**    A sample Application Log

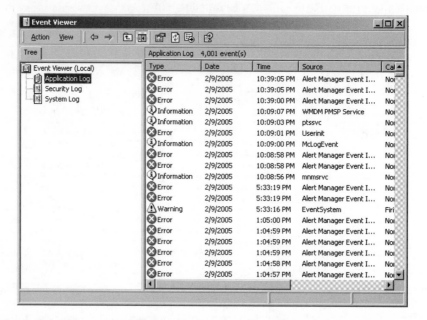

To access the Application Log, in Event Viewer, choose Log ➢ Application. The Source column indicates which service logged which event. For example, in Figure 10.4, you can see three error events that came from Microsoft SQL Server (the MSSQL entry).

All together, the log files present a picture of the general health of a Windows 2000 Server. Generally speaking, if you see an error message, open Event Viewer and check the System Log. If you don't see the event here, check the other two logs.

# Manufacturers' Troubleshooting Resources

In addition to viewing log files, you can use several types of troubleshooting tools that manufacturers make available for their network operating systems. You can use these resources to augment your own knowledge as well as to solve those pesky problems that have no pattern or few recognizable symptoms. Each type of resource provides different information or different levels of support (some of which have been discussed in previous chapters, but their importance to troubleshooting necessitates discussing them again here). Let's examine the most popular:

- README files

- Telephone support
- Technical support CD-ROM
- Technical support website

## README Files

*README files* contain information that did not make it into the manual. The latest information released about the software can often be found in the README files. Also, they may contain tips, default settings, and installation information (so you don't have to read the entire first chapter to install the software).

When troubleshooting application or networking software, check out the README file before you try any of the other manufacturers' resources. It is usually found on the first installation disk or CD.

## Telephone Support

Many people prefer telephone support over other forms of support. You actually get to talk to a human being from the software manufacturer about the problem. Most, if not all, software manufacturers have toll-free support numbers. The people on their end of the line can provide anything from basic how-to answers to complex, technical answers.

Unfortunately, because of their popularity, technical support phone lines are often busy. When the line is finally free, you might, however, find yourself in "voicemail hell." We've all been through it: Press 1 for support for products A, B, and C. Press 2 for Products D, E, and F, and so on and so on. Most people get frustrated and hang up. They prefer to speak with a human being as soon as the call is answered. Today, phone support is often not free (the number to reach support might be, but the support itself is not) but must be purchased via either a time-limited contract or on an incident-by-incident basis. This is particularly true for network operating system software support. To solve this problem, companies have devised other methods, such as the technical support CD-ROM and website, which we will discuss next.

## The Technical Support CD-ROM

With the development of CD-ROM technology, it became possible to put volumes of textual information on a readily accessible medium. The CD-ROM was, thus, a logical distribution vehicle for technical support information. In addition, the CD was portable and searchable. Introduced in the early 1990s, Novell's Network Support Encyclopedia (NSE) CD-ROM was one of the first products of this kind. Microsoft's TechNet came soon after. Both companies charge a nominal fee for a yearly subscription to these CDs (anywhere from $100–$500).

To be sure, the first editions of these products (as with the first editions of most software products) left much to be desired. Search engines were often clumsy and slow, and the CDs were released only about twice a year. As these products evolved, however, their search engines became more advanced, they included more documents, and they were released more often. And, probably most important, manufacturers began to include software updates, drivers, and patches on the CD.

## The Technical Support Website

The technical support CDs were great, but people started to complain (as people are wont to do) that because this information was vital to the health of their network, they should get it for free. Well, that is, in fact, what happened. The Internet proved to be the perfect medium for allowing network support personnel access to the same information that was on the technical support CD-ROMs. Additionally, websites can be instantly updated and accessed, so they provide the most up-to-date network support information. Since websites are hosted on servers that can store much more information than CD-ROMs, websites are more powerful than their CD-ROM counterparts. Because they are easy to access and use and because they are detailed and current, websites are now the most popular method for disseminating technical support information. As examples, you can view Novell's technical support website at `http://support.novell.com` and Microsoft's technical support website (TechNet, a monthly subscription) at `http://support.microsoft.com/servicedesks/technet/`.

# Hardware Network Troubleshooting Tools

In addition to manufacturer-provided troubleshooting tools, there are a few hardware devices we can use to troubleshoot the network. These are actual devices that you can use during the troubleshooting process. Some devices have easily recognizable functions; others are more obscure. The following are four of the most popular hardware tools (and the Network+ exam tests you on them, by the way):

- A crossover cable
- A hardware loopback
- A tone generator
- A tone locator

## The Crossover Cable

Sometimes also called a cross cable, a *crossover cable* is typically used to connect two hubs, but it can also be used to test communications between two stations directly, bypassing the hub. A crossover cable is used only in Ethernet UTP installations. You can connect two workstation NICs (or a workstation and a server NIC) directly using a crossover cable.

A normal Ethernet (10Base-T) UTP cable uses four wires—two to transmit and two to receive. Figure 10.5 shows this wiring, with all wires going from pins on one side directly to the same pins on the other side.

**FIGURE 10.5**   A standard Ethernet 10Base-T cable

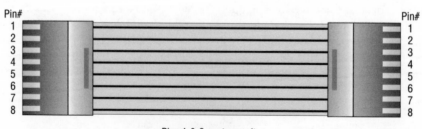

Pins 1 & 2 are transmit.
Pins 3 & 6 are receive.

The standard Ethernet UTP crossover cable used in both situations has its transmit and receive wire pairs crossed so that the transmit set on one side (hooked to pins 1 and 2) is connected to the receive set (pins 3 and 6) on the other. Figure 10.6 illustrates this arrangement. Note that four of the wires are crossed as compared with the straight-through wiring of the standard 10Base-T UTP cable shown earlier in Figure 10.5.

**FIGURE 10.6** A standard Ethernet 10Base-T crossover cable

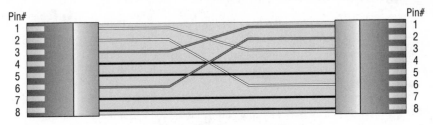

Pins 1 & 2 connect to pins 3 & 6.
Pins 3 & 6 connect to pins 1 & 2.

 Be sure to label a crossover cable as such to ensure that no one tries to use it as a workstation patch cable. If it is used as a patch cable, the workstation won't be able to communicate with the hub and the rest of the network.

You can carry a crossover cable in the tool bag along with your laptop. If you want to ensure that a server's NIC is functioning correctly, you can connect your laptop directly to the server's NIC using the crossover cable. You should be able to log in to the server (assuming both NICs are configured correctly).

## The Hardware Loopback

A *hardware loopback* is a special connector for Ethernet 10Base-T NICs. It functions similarly to a crossover cable, except that it connects the transmit pins directly to the receive pins (as shown in Figure 10.7). It is used by the NIC's software diagnostics to test transmission and reception capabilities. You cannot completely test an NIC without one of these devices.

**FIGURE 10.7** A hardware loopback and its connections

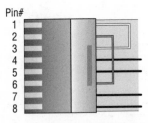

In a loopback, pins 1 & 3 and
pins 2 & 6 are connected.

Usually, the hardware loopback is no bigger than a single RJ-45 connector with a few small wires on the back. If a NIC has hardware diagnostics that can use the loopback, the hardware loopback plug will be included with the NIC. To use it, simply plug the loopback into the RJ-45 connector on the back of the NIC and start the diagnostic software. Select the option in your NIC's diagnostic software that requires the loopback, and start the diagnostic routine. You will be able to tell if the NIC can send and receive data through the use of these diagnostics.

## Tone Generator and Tone Locator

The combination of tone generator and tone locator is used most often on telephone systems to locate cables. Since telephone systems use multiple pairs of UTPs, it is nearly impossible to determine which set of wires goes where. Network documentation would be extremely helpful in making this determination, but if no documentation is available, you can use a tone generator and locator.

Don't confuse these tools with a cable tester that tests cable quality. You use the tone generator and locator only to determine which UTP cable is which.

The *tone generator* is a small electronic device that sends an electrical signal down one set of UTP wires. The *tone locator* is another device that is designed to emit a tone when it detects the signal in a particular set of wires. When you need to trace a cable, hook the generator (often called the *fox*) to the copper ends of the wire pair you want to find. Then move the locator (often called the *hound* because it chases the fox) over multiple sets of cables (you don't have to touch the copper part of the wire pairs; this tool works by induction) until you hear the tone. A soft tone indicates that you are close to the right set of wires. Keep moving the tool until the tone gets the loudest. Bingo! You have found the wire set. Figure 10.8 shows a tone generator and locator and how they are used.

**FIGURE 10.8** Use of a common tone generator and locator

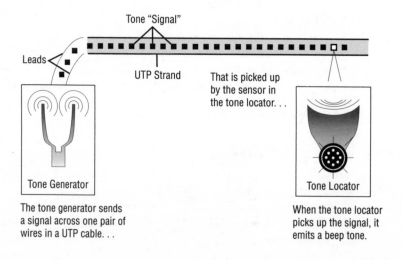

**WARNING** Never hook a tone generator to a cable that is hooked up to either a NIC or a hub! Because the tone generator sends electrical signals down the wire, it can blow a NIC or a hub. That is why tone generators are not usually used on networks. Cable testers are used more often. We'll discuss cable testers later in this chapter.

# Software Troubleshooting Tools

In addition to these hardware troubleshooting tools, you can use software programs to gain information about the current health and state of the network. These tools fall into two main categories:

- Protocol analyzers
- Performance-monitoring tools

We use the term *network software diagnostics* to refer to these tools.

## Protocol Analyzer

Any software that can analyze and display the packets it receives can be considered a *protocol analyzer*. Protocol analyzers examine packets from protocols that operate at the lower four layers of the OSI model (including Transport, Network, Data Link, and Physical) and can display any errors they detect. Additionally, most protocol analyzers can capture packets and decode their contents. Capturing packets involves copying a series of packets from the network into memory and holding the copy so that it can be analyzed.

You could, for example, capture a series of packets and decode their contents to figure out where each packet came from, where it was going, which protocol sent it, which protocol should receive it, and so on. For example, you can find out the following:

- The nature of the traffic on your network
- Which protocol is used most often
- If users are accessing unauthorized sites
- If a particular network card is jabbering (sending out packets when there is no data to send)

Two common examples of protocol analyzers are Sniffer, a Network General product, and Novell's LANalyzer.

## Performance-Monitoring Tools

In addition to protocol analyzers, many network operating systems include tools for monitoring network performance and can display statistics such as the number of packets sent and received, server processor utilization, the amount of data going in and out of the server, and so on. NetWare comes with the `MONITOR.NLM` utility, and Windows 2000 comes with Performance Monitor. Both monitor performance statistics. You can use these utilities to determine the source of the bottleneck when users complain that the network is slow.

To start the MONITOR.NLM utility in NetWare, simply type **load monitor** at the console prompt. To start the Performance Monitor program in Windows 2000, you must first be logged in as Administrator (or a member of the Server Operators group). Once you are logged in, choose Start ➢ Programs ➢ Administrative Tools ➢ Performance.

# Troubleshooting Tips

Now that we have covered the basics of network troubleshooting, we should go over a few troubleshooting tips. These tips will give you more "ammo" while you're hunting for network problems and using the various steps of the troubleshooting model discussed earlier.

## Don't Overlook the Small Stuff

If you'll remember, the first thing we discussed in this chapter was small stuff. Often a problem is caused by something simple, such as a power switch in the wrong position, a card or port not functioning (as indicated by a link light that's not lit), or simply operator error. Even the most experienced administrator has forgotten to turn on the power, left a cable unplugged, or mistyped a username and password.

Finally, make sure that users get training for the systems they use. That may seem like an extra bother, but an hour or two of training goes a long way toward preventing problems. The number of incidents of EEOC will decline with a little user training.

## Prioritize Your Problems

It is unlikely that as a network administrator or technician, you will receive problem calls one at a time. Typically, when you receive one call, you already have three people waiting for service. For this reason, you must learn to prioritize.

You start this process by asking some basic questions of the person reporting the problem so that you can determine its severity. If the current problem is minor and you have two more serious problems already facing you, your priorities are obvious.

You establish priorities to ensure that you spend your time wisely. The order in which you attempt to solve your networking problems, from highest priority to lowest, might look something like this:

- Total network failure (affects everyone)
- Partial network failure (affects small groups of users)
- Small network failure (affects a small, single group of users)
- Total workstation failure (single user can't work at all)
- Partial workstation failure (single user can't do most tasks)
- Minor issue (single user has problems that crop up now and again)

Mitigating circumstances can, of course, change the order of this list. For example, if the president of the company can't retrieve e-mail, you'd take the express elevator to their office as soon as you hang up from the call. Also, a minor, persistent problem might move up the ladder.

Remember also that some simple problems may take more effort than larger problems. You may be able to bring up a crashed server in a matter of minutes, but a user who doesn't know how to make columns line up in Microsoft Word may take up to an hour or longer to train. The latter of these problems might get relegated toward the bottom of the list because of the time involved. It is more efficient to solve problems for a larger group of people than to fix this one user's problem immediately.

Some network administrators list all network service requests on a chalkboard or a whiteboard. They then prioritize them based on the previously discussed criteria. Some larger companies have written support-call tracking software whose only function is to track and prioritize all network and computer problems. Use whatever method makes you comfortable, but prioritize your calls.

## Check the Software Configuration

Often, network problems can be traced to software configuration (as with our DNS configuration example earlier in this chapter). When you are checking for software problems, don't forget to check configuration, including the following:

- DNS configuration
- WINS configuration
- HOSTS file
- AUTOEXEC.BAT (DOS and Windows)
- CONFIG.SYS (DOS and Windows)
- STARTUP.NCF, AUTOEXEC.NCF, and server parameter settings (NetWare)
- The Registry (Windows 95/98/Me and NT and later)

Software configuration settings love to hide in places like these and can be notoriously hard to find (especially in the Registry).

Additionally, in text configuration files, look for lines that have been commented out (either intentionally or accidentally). A command such as REM or REMARK or the asterisk or semicolon characters indicate comment lines in a file.

 The HOSTS file uses a # (pound sign) to indicate a comment line, as does NetWare's NCF files.

## Don't Overlook Physical Conditions

As we discussed in Chapter 6, you want to make sure that from a network design standpoint, the physical environment for a server is optimized for placement, temperature, and humidity.

When troubleshooting an obscure network problem, don't forget to check the physical conditions under which the network device is operating. Check for problems such as the following:

- Excessive heat
- Excessive humidity (condensation)
- Low humidity (leads to ESD problems)
- EMI/RFI problems
- ESD problems
- Power problems
- Unplugged cables

## Don't Overlook Cable Problems

Cables, generally speaking, work fine once they are installed properly. Rarely is the cabling system the problem, unless someone has made some change to it. If you suspect that the cabling system is the problem, try replacing the patch cables at the workstation and hub first. These are easiest to get to (and replace). If that solves the problem, you know the problem was related to the patch cable. It was either faulty or the wrong type.

If the patch cable isn't the problem, use a cable tester (not a tone generator and locator) to find the source of the problem. Wires that are moved can be prone to breaking or shorting. A short can happen when the wire conductor comes in contact with another conductive surface, changing the path of the electrical signal. The signal will go someplace else instead of to the intended recipient. You can use cable testers to test for many types of problems, including these:

- Broken cables
- Incorrect connections
- Interference levels
- Total cable length (for length restrictions)
- Cable shorts
- Connector problems

 As a matter of fact, cable testers are so sophisticated that they can even indicate the exact location of a cable break, accurate to within six inches or better.

## Check for Viruses

Many troubleshooters overlook virus scanning because they assume that the network virus-checking software should have picked up any viruses. To be effective, it must be kept up-to-date. Updates are made available almost daily. As we discussed in Chapter 9, "Fault Tolerance and Disaster Recovery," you must run the virus definition update utility to keep the virus definition file current.

If you are having strange, unusual, irreproducible problems with a workstation, try scanning it with an up-to-date virus scan utility. You'd be surprised how many times people have spent hours and hours troubleshooting a strange problem only to run a virus scan utility, find and clean one or more viruses, and have the problem disappear.

# Summary

In this chapter, you learned about the proper methods of troubleshooting network problems. In the first section, you learned the proper method to start to fix any network problem by eliminating what the problem is *not*. You learned how to narrow the problem down to its essentials and therefore further define it.

Next, you learned a systematic approach to troubleshooting, using an eight-step troubleshooting model to troubleshoot almost any problems you may encounter on your network. After that, you learned about several resources that you can use to help you during the troubleshooting process. You learned about the websites and other support tools available for most vendors' products.

Finally, you learned a few troubleshooting tips that will help make the troubleshooting process go more smoothly. As you venture out into the "real world," keep these tips in mind; they will help make you an expert troubleshooter.

# Exam Essentials

**Know the eight troubleshooting steps, in order.**   The steps, in order, are as follows:

1. Establish symptoms.
2. Identify the affected area.
3. Establish what has changed.
4. Select the most probable cause.
5. Implement a solution.
6. Test the result.
7. Recognize the potential effects of the solution.
8. Document the solution.

**Be able to identify a link light.**   A link light is the small, usually green, LED on the back of a network card. This LED is typically found next to the media connector on a NIC and is usually labeled "Link."

**Understand how proper network use procedures can affect the proper operation of a network.**
If a user is not following a network use procedure properly (e.g., not logging in correctly), that
user may report a problem where none exists. A good network troubleshooter should know
how to differentiate between a network hardware/software problem and a "lack of user training" problem.

**Know how to narrow down a problem to one specific area or cause.**   Most problems can
usually be traced to one specific area or cause. You must be able to determine if a problem is
specific to one user or a bunch of users, specific to one computer or a bunch of computers, and
related to hardware or software. The answers to these questions will give you a very specific
problem focus.

**Know how to detect cabling-related problems.**   Generally speaking, most cabling-related
problems can be traced by plugging the suspect workstation into a known, working network
port. If the problem disappears (or at the very least changes significantly), the problem is related
to the cabling for that workstation.

**Understand viruses completely and the impact they can have on a network.**   Viruses are
small programs that generally serve no useful purpose. Additionally, they self-replicate (make
copies of themselves and put themselves on other systems). Viruses cause problems with computer software, ranging from unstable systems to complete loss of data. Networks make it much
easier for viruses to spread because all of the systems on a network are connected together. Theoretically, if one network-connected computer is infected with a virus, all computers connected
to the same network could potentially be infected in a short period of time.

# Review Questions

1. Which NetWare log file(s) always indicate(s) the time and date at which a failure or an event occurred? (Choose all that apply.)

   **A.** SYS$LOG.ERR

   **B.** CONSOLE.LOG

   **C.** ABEND.LOG

   **D.** SYS$ERR.LOG

2. You have a user who cannot connect to the network. What is the first thing you could check to determine the source of the problem?

   **A.** Workstation configuration

   **B.** Station link light

   **C.** Patch cable

   **D.** Server configuration

3. A user cannot access the local intranet. Which action will *not* help you determine how to narrow the problem down to the intranet?

   **A.** Accessing the intranet from your workstation

   **B.** Accessing the intranet from the user's workstation as yourself

   **C.** Replacing the patch cable on the workstation

   **D.** Asking another user to access the intranet from the problem user's workstation

4. Several users can't log in to the server. Which action would help you to narrow the problem down to the workstations, network, or server?

   **A.** Run tracert from a workstation

   **B.** Check the server console for user connections

   **C.** Run netstat on all workstations

   **D.** Check the network diagnostics

5. Without a _____, you may not be able to perform 100 percent of the network diagnostics for a network card.

   **A.** hardware loopback

   **B.** patch cable

   **C.** crossover cable

   **D.** protocol analyzer

6. A user can't log in to the network. She can't even connect to the Internet over the LAN. Other users in the same area aren't experiencing any problems. You attempt to log in as this user from your workstation with her username and password and don't experience any problems. However, you cannot log in with either her username or yours from her workstation. What is a likely cause of the problem?

   A. Insufficient rights to access the server

   B. A bad patch cable

   C. Server down

   D. Wrong username and password

7. A user is experiencing problems logging in to a Unix server. He can connect to the Internet over the LAN. Other users in the same area aren't experiencing any problems. You attempt logging in as this user from your workstation with his username and password and don't experience any problems. However, you cannot log in with either his username or yours from his workstation. What is a likely cause of the problem?

   A. The Caps Lock key is pressed.

   B. The network hub is malfunctioning.

   C. You have a downed server.

   D. You have a jabbering NIC.

8. Which technical support resource has the most current information and up-to-date drivers and patches?

   A. README file

   B. Technical support CD-ROM

   C. Technical support website

   D. Technical phone support

9. You are troubleshooting your only PC at home at 11:30 on a Sunday night, but you are having trouble connecting to the Internet. You suspect that the modem needs a new driver. Which technical support resource could you possibly use to get the new driver?

   A. README file

   B. Technical support CD-ROM

   C. Technical support website

   D. Technical support phone support

10. Your NetWare 5 server suddenly experienced an error. It then started the shutdown procedure, and the error scrolled off the screen. You didn't have CONLOG.NLM loaded when this happened. Next to the command prompt on the console, there was a number in angle brackets, like this: <2>. Which log file could you look in to determine the source of the problem and the error message that was displayed?

    A. BOOT.LOG

    B. ABEND.LOG

    C. SYS$LOG.ERR

    D. SYS$ERR.LOG

**11.** A user calls you reporting a problem logging in to the corporate intranet. You can access the website without problems using the user's username and password. At your request, the user has tried logging in from other workstations but has been unsuccessful. What is the most likely cause of the problem?

**A.** The user is logging in incorrectly.

**B.** The network is down.

**C.** The intranet server is locked up.

**D.** The server is not routing packets correctly to that user's workstation.

**12.** A user calls you reporting a problem logging in to the corporate intranet. You cannot access the website using the user's username and password, but you can access it when logging in with your username. At your request, the user has tried logging in from other workstations, but without success. What is the most likely cause of the problem?

**A.** The user is logging in incorrectly.

**B.** The user's workstation is misconfigured.

**C.** The intranet server is locked up.

**D.** The user doesn't have the correct rights.

**13.** Which software-troubleshooting tool could you use to determine which protocol is configured with the wrong address?

**A.** Performance-monitoring tools

**B.** Protocol analyzer

**C.** Antivirus checker

**D.** Protocol-layer monitor

**14.** Which hardware-troubleshooting tool(s) could you use to find out where a cable is routed? (Choose all that apply.)

**A.** Crossover cable

**B.** Hardware loopback

**C.** Tone generator

**D.** Tone locator

**15.** Which Windows 2000 log file keeps track of all events, such as login/logout and use of rights?

**A.** Security

**B.** System

**C.** Application

**D.** Console

**16.** Which Windows 2000 utility do you use to manage the major Windows 2000 log files?

**A.** Log File Manager

**B.** Event Viewer

**C.** User Manager

**D.** Server Performance Monitor

**17.** A user calls you complaining that he can't access the corporate intranet web server. You try the same address, and you receive a Host Not Found error. Several minutes later, another user reports the same problem. You can still send e-mail and transfer files to another server. What is the most likely cause of the problem?

**A.** The hub is unplugged.

**B.** The server is not routing protocols to your workstation.

**C.** The user's workstation is not connected to the network.

**D.** The web server is down.

**18.** You are connecting a cubicle farm to your network. You install NICs in all the workstations and run cables to a workgroup hub. You then connect the MDI port on the workgroup hub to the main hub with a standard patch cable. When you power up the cubicle farm computers, none of them can see the servers on the network. What could you replace to solve this problem?

**A.** Hub patch cable

**B.** Workstation patch cables

**C.** Server patch cables

**D.** Workgroup hub

**19.** A user from the accounting department calls complaining that she can't see any servers on the network or log in. Her computer operates fine otherwise. No other users from the accounting department are reporting any problems. What is the first thing you could check?

**A.** Patch cable quality

**B.** Link lights

**C.** Power cables

**D.** Server status

**20.** Several users have complained of the server's poor performance as of late. You know that the memory installed in the server is sufficient. What could you check to determine the source of the problem?

**A.** Server's NIC link light

**B.** Protocol analyzer

**C.** Performance-monitoring tools

**D.** Server's System Log file

# Answers to Review Questions

1. A, C. Because both the SYS$LOG.ERR and ABEND.LOG files log errors that may or may not be critical, it is important that you know when these events occurred. As such, both of these NetWare log files contain date and time stamps for each event.

2. B. The link light indicates that the network card is making a basic-level connection to the rest of the network. It is a very easy item to check, and if the link light is not lit, it is usually a very simple fix (like plugging in an unplugged cable).

3. C. Replacing the patch cable is a much more difficult troubleshooting step than testing intranet access from different workstations. Because workstations are usually grouped together, it would be easier to have many people first try to access at once than to crawl around behind a desk or cubicle to replace a patch cable.

4. B. Although all of these are good tests for network connectivity, checking the server console for user connections will tell you if other users are able to log into the server or not. If they can, the problem is most likely related to one of those users' workstations. If they can't, the problem is either the server or network connection. This helps narrow down the problem.

5. A. A hardware loopback is either a cable or plug that you attach to the network interface on a NIC. The loopback connects a NIC's outputs to its inputs so that you can test the transmission and reception capabilities of the NIC. Without a hardware loopback, you can't run the full batch of tests in the NIC's diagnostics program (since a transmission test is usually part of this batch of tests).

6. B. Because of all the tests given and their results, you can narrow the problem down to the network connectivity of that workstation. And because no other users in her area are having the same problem, it can't be the hub or server. You can log in as the user from your workstation, so you know it isn't a rights issue or username/password issue. The only possible answer listed is a bad patch cable.

7. A. Because other users in the same area aren't having problem, it can't be a downed server, network hub, or jabbering NIC. And because both you and the user can't log in, more than likely it's a problem specific to that workstation. The only one that would affect your ability to log in from that station is the Caps Lock key being pressed. That will cause the password to be in all uppercase (which most server OSes treat as a different password) and thus it will probably be rejected.

8. C. A vendor's technical support website usually has the most current information because the information can be distributed immediately. Most vendors have moved to using a technical support website as opposed to a CD-ROM because it's much cheaper and users prefer it.

9. B. Of those options listed, the only place to get a driver is the technical support CD-ROM or driver CD-ROM that comes with the modem. You could normally get it from the Internet, but your Internet connection is not functioning and you can't call tech support because it's after most tech support's "normal business hours."

**10.** B. The conditions described indicate that the NetWare server experienced an Abend. When this happens, a NetWare 5 server will write the Abend error and the conditions under which the Abend occurred to the ABEND.LOG file. So, of those listed, the best place to look would be the ABEND.LOG file.

**11.** A. Because the user can't log in correctly from any machine, more than likely he is using the wrong procedure for logging in. Because no one else is having that problem (including yourself), the problem must be related to that user.

**12.** D. Because you cannot log in with the user's password from your machine or from any other machine, the problem is most likely related to that particular username. The only answer listed that is specific to the username is that the user doesn't have the correct rights.

**13.** B. A protocol analyzer is a software tool that can be used to examine the details of packets as they travel across the wire. Using this kind of tool, you could examine the addresses of packets as they cross the wire and see which station is configured incorrectly.

**14.** C, D. A tone generator and tone locator can help you find out where cables are routed. The tone generator sends a signal down the wire. The tone locator is run along a wire to test if it contains the signal. Using this tool, you can tell where a cable (the cable that you attach the tone generator to) is running and what path it takes.

**15.** A. The Security Log file in the Event Viewer logs all security-related events, including authentication, rights application, and breaches of those security methods. Each time some kind of security event occurs, the item is written to the Security Log file.

**16.** B. The Event Viewer is the Windows 2000 utility used to manage the major Windows 2000 log files (System, Security, and Application). It is an application that is installed with each installation of Windows 2000 (Start ➤ Programs ➤ Administrative Tools ➤ Event Viewer).

**17.** D. Because other people are experiencing the problem, most likely the problem is either network or server related. Because you can transfer files to and from another server, it can't be the network. Thus, the problem is related to the web server.

**18.** A. The MDI port was designed to uplink one hub to another using a crossover cable. By putting in a standard patch cable, you prevent the hubs from communicating, thus the workgroup cannot communicate with the servers.

**19.** B. The link lights will tell if the computer can communicate with the rest of the network. Although you could check all of these items for this problem, trying the link light(s) on the NIC in the workstation and hub to make sure they can communicate is the first thing to do because it's the simplest.

**20.** C. Performance-monitoring tools can give an idea of how "busy" the server and the rest of the network are. These tools use graphs to indicate how much traffic is going through that server.

# Glossary

**10Base-FL**   An implementation of Ethernet that specifies a 10Mbps (megabits per second) signaling rate, baseband signaling, and fiber-optic cabling.

**10Base-T**   An implementation of Ethernet that specifies a 10Mbps signaling rate, baseband signaling, and twisted-pair cabling.

**access control list (ACL)**   List of rights that an object has to resources in the network. Also a type of firewall. In this case, the lists reside on a router and determine which machines can use the router and in what direction.

**ACK**   *See* acknowledgment.

**acknowledgment (ACK)**   A message confirming that the data packet was received. This occurs at the Transport layer of the OSI model.

**ACL**   *See* access control list.

**Active Directory**   The replacement for NT Directory Service (NTDS) that is included with Windows 2000 and 2003. It acts similarly to Novell Directory Services (NDS) because it is a true X.500-based directory service.

**active hub**   A hub that is powered and actively regenerates any signal that is received. *See also* hub.

**active monitor**   Used in Token Ring networks, a process that prevents data frames from roaming the ring unchecked. If the frame passes the active monitor too many times, it is removed from the ring. Also ensures that a token is always circulating the ring.

**adapter**   Technically, the peripheral hardware that installs into your computer or the software that defines how the computer talks to that hardware.

**address**   Designation to allow PCs to be known by a name or number to other PCs. Addressing allows a PC to transmit data directly to another PC by using its address (IP or MAC).

**address record**   Part of a DNS table that maps an IP address to a domain name. Also known as an A (or host) record.

**Address Resolution Protocol (ARP)**   The Network layer protocol that IP uses to ascertain the MAC address of a known IP address when IP determines that the destination is on the local subnet and communication with the destination must therefore occur at the Data Link layer.

**ad hoc RF network**   A network created when two RF-capable devices are brought within transmission range of each other. A common example is handheld PDAs beaming data to each other.

**ADSL**   *See* asymmetrical digital subscriber line.

**alias record**   *See* CNAME record.

**antivirus**   A category of software that uses various methods to eliminate viruses in a computer. It typically also protects against future infection. *See also* virus.

**AppleShare**   The Macintosh server implementation of the AppleTalk Filing Protocol (AFP).

**Application layer**   The seventh layer of the OSI model, it deals with how applications access the network and describes application functionality, such as file transfer, messaging, and so on.

**ARP table**   A table used by the Address Resolution Protocol (ARP). Contains a list of known TCP/IP addresses and their associated MAC addresses. The table is cached in memory so that ARP lookups do not have to be performed for frequently accessed TCP/IP addresses but aged out so that associations do not become stagnant. *See also* Address Resolution Protocol, media access control, Transmission Control Protocol/Internet Protocol.

**asymmetrical digital subscriber line (ADSL)**   An implementation of DSL where the upload and download speeds are different. *See also* digital subscriber line.

**Asynchronous Transfer Mode (ATM)**   A connection-oriented network architecture based on broadband ISDN technology that uses constant size 53-byte cells instead of packets. Because cells don't change size, they are switched much faster and more efficiently than packets across a network.

**ATM**   *See* Asynchronous Transfer Mode.

**Attachment Unit Interface (AUI) port**   Port on some NICs that allows connecting the NIC to different media types by using an external transceiver.

**B channel**   *See* bearer channel.

**backbone**   The part of most networks that connects multiple segments together to form a LAN. The backbone usually has higher speed than the segments. *See also* segment, local area network.

**backup plan**   Term used to describe a company's strategy to make copies of and restore its data in case of an emergency.

**backup window**   The amount of time that an administrator has available to perform a complete, successful backup.

**bandwidth**   In network communications, the amount of data that can be sent across a wire in a given time. Each communication that passes along the wire decreases the amount of available bandwidth.

**baseband**   A transmission technique in which the signal uses the entire bandwidth of a transmission medium.

**baseline**   A category of network documentation that indicates how the network normally runs. It includes such information as network statistics, server utilization trends, and processor performance statistics.

**bearer channel (B channel)**   The channels in an ISDN line that carry data. Each bearer channel typically has a bandwidth of 64Kbps.

**best effort transmission**   Transmission that occurs between devices without any form of connection establishment or acknowledgment of received data. Best effort transmission is performed by protocols that are both connectionless and unreliable, such as UDP, IP, and Ethernet.

**blackout**   *See* power blackout.

**blank**   These are often referred to as slot covers. If a PC card is removed, there will be an opening in the computer case. This will allow dirt and dust to enter the computer and prevent it from being cooled properly. Some computer cases have the blanks as part of the case and they must be broken off from the case before a bus slot may be used to insert a PC card into it.

**BONDING**   A procedure where two ISDN B channels are joined together to provide greater bandwidth. BONDING stands for Bandwidth ON Demand Interoperability Group, but it's often seen in lowercase as a more generalized term referring to inverse multiplexing.

**bounded media**   A network medium that is used at the Physical layer where the signal travels over a cable of some kind.

**bridge**   A network device, operating at the Data Link layer, that logically separates a single network into segments but lets the two segments appear to be one network to higher-layer protocols.

**broadband**   A network transmission method in which a single transmission medium is divided so that multiple signals can travel across the same medium simultaneously.

**broadcast address**   A special network address that refers to all users on the network. For example, the TCP/IP address 255.255.255.255 is the broadcast address. Any packets sent to that address will be sent to everyone on that LAN.

**broadcast domain**   The collection of all devices that will receive each other's broadcast frames. Each interface on a router terminates a broadcast domain. Routers will not forward broadcasts to other interfaces. They can be made to turn certain broadcasts into unicasts to specific devices, but they will not propagate broadcasts. VLANs created on LAN switches are broadcast domains. Any broadcast created by a device attached to a switch port assigned to a VLAN will be received only by those devices attached to switch ports assigned to the same VLAN.

**brownout**   *See* power brownout.

**burned-in address (BIA)**   Usually a MAC address that has been burned into an EEPROM on a networking device, becoming a permanent physical address for the device.

**bus**   A pathway in a PC that allows data and signals to be transmitted between the PC components. Types of buses include ISA and PCI.

**bus topology**   A topology where the cable and signals run in a straight line from one end of the network to the other.

**cable**   A physical transmission medium that has a central conductor of wire or fiber surrounded by a plastic jacket.

**cable map**   General network documentation indicating each cable's source and destination as well as where each network cable runs.

**cable modem**   A device used to interconnect computing and networking equipment, via Ethernet, with a television cable company's data network through the same cable circuit used to deliver television programming. The standard for data communications over the cable television network is known as the Data over Cable Service Interface Specification (DOCSIS).

**cable tester**   A special instrument that is used to test the integrity of LAN cables. *See also* time-domain reflectometer.

**carrier**   Signal at a frequency that is chosen to carry data. Addition of data to the frequency is modulation and the removal of data from the frequency is demodulation. This is used on analog devices like modems.

**Carrier Sense Multiple Access/Collision Avoidance (CSMA/CA)**   A media access method that sends a request to send (RTS) packet and waits to receive a clear to send (CTS) packet before sending. Once the CTS is received, the sender sends the packet of information.

**Carrier Sense Multiple Access/Collision Detection (CSMA/CD)**   A media access method that first senses whether there is a signal on the wire, indicating that someone is transmitting currently. If no one else is transmitting, it attempts a transmission and listens for someone else trying to transmit at the same time. If this happens, both senders back off and don't transmit again until some specified period of time has passed. *See also* collision.

**categories**   Different grades of cables that determine how much protection is offered against interference from outside the cable. Category 1 allows voice data only. Category 2 allows data transmissions up to 4Mbps. Category 3 allows data transmissions up to 10Mbps. Category 4 allows data transmissions up to 16Mbps. Category 5 allows data transmissions up to 100Mbps.

**Central Office (CO)**   The office in any metropolitan or rural area that contains the telephone switching equipment for that area. The Central Office connects all users in that area to each other as well as to the rest of the PSTN. *See also* Public Switched Telephone Network.

**Challenge Handshake Authentication Protocol (CHAP)**   A client/server authentication method that uses MD5 encryption and a random value to authenticate a client. The authentication server "challenges" the client to come up with the same value based on the random value and the secret shared between client and server.

**Channel Service Unit (CSU)**   Generally used with a T1 Internet line, it is used to terminate the connection from the T1 provider. The CSU is usually part of a CSU/DSU unit. It also provides diagnostics and testing if necessary.

**CHAP**   *See* Challenge Handshake Authentication Protocol (CHAP).

**checkpoints**   A certain part or time to allow for a restart at the last point that the data was saved.

**checksum**     A hexadecimal value computed from transmitted data that is used in error-checking routines.

**circuit switching**     A switching method where a dedicated connection between the sender and receiver is maintained throughout the conversation. POTS and ISDN, for example, establish circuit-switched connections through dialed numbers. *See also* packet switching.

**classful**     Relates to the default characteristics of and constraints placed on an IP address based on the class of address in question. For example, a Class C address, by default, has 24 network bits and 8 host bits, limiting it to no more than 254 hosts per network. Classful defaults are considered in the absence of detailed configuration information, such as a nondefault subnet mask.

**Classless Interdomain Routing (CIDR)**     The new routing method used by InterNIC to assign IP addresses. CIDR can be described as a "slash $x$" network. The $x$ represents the number of bits in the network that InterNIC controls.

**client**     A client is a part of a client/server network. It is the part where the computing is usually done. In a typical setting, a client will use the server for remote storage, backups, or security such as a firewall.

**client/server network**     A server-centric network in which all resources are stored on a file server and processing power is distributed among workstations and the file server.

**clipper chip**     A hardware implementation of the skipjack encryption algorithm.

**clustering**     A computing technology where many servers work together so that they appear to be one high-powered server. If one server fails, the others in the cluster take over the services provided by the failed server.

**CNAME record**     A DNS record type that specifies other names for existing hosts. This allows a DNS administrator to assign multiple DNS host names to a single DNS host. Also known as an *alias record*.

**coaxial cable**     Often referred to as coax. A type of cable used in network wiring. Typical coaxial cable types include RG-58 and RG-62. 10Base-2 Ethernet networks use coaxial cable. Coaxial cable is usually shielded.

**collision**     The error condition that occurs when two stations on a CSMA/CD network transmit data (at the Data Link layer) at the same time. *See also* Carrier Sense Multiple Access/Collision Detection.

**collision domain**     The group of devices whose frames could potentially collide with one another. Each interface on a bridge, switch, or router terminates a collision domain. These devices become responsible for recovering from collisions that occur due to their forwarding of frames out other interfaces.

**collision light**     An LED on a NIC or hub that indicates when a collision has occurred.

**concentrator**     *See* hub.

**connectionless**   Communications between two hosts that have no previous session established for synchronizing sent data. If the service is also unreliable, the data is not acknowledged at the receiving end. This can allow for data loss.

**connectionless services**   *See* connectionless, connectionless transport protocol.

**connectionless transport protocol**   A transport protocol, such as UDP, that does not create a virtual connection between sending and receiving stations before transmitting user data between them. *See also* User Datagram Protocol.

**connection-oriented**   Communications between two hosts that have a previous session established for synchronizing sent data. If the service is also reliable, the data is acknowledged by the receiving device. This allows for guaranteed delivery of data between PCs.

**connection-oriented transport protocol**   A transport protocol that establishes a virtual connection between sending and receiving stations before any user data is transmitted between them. TCP is a connection-oriented protocol. *See also* Transmission Control Protocol.

**controller**   Part of a PC that allows connectivity to peripheral devices. A disk controller allows the PC to be connected to a hard disk. A network controller allows a PC to be connected to a network. A keyboard controller is used to connect a keyboard to the PC.

**Control Panel**   A special window inside Microsoft Windows operating systems (Windows 95 and above) that has icons for all of the configurable options for the system.

**cost**   A value given to a route between PCs or subnets to determine which route may be best. The word *hop* is sometimes used to refer to the number of routers between two PCs or subnets. *See also* hop.

**country codes**   The two-letter abbreviations for countries, used in the DNS hierarchy. *See also* Domain Name Service.

**CRC**   *See* cyclical redundancy check.

**crossover cable**   The troubleshooting tool used in Ethernet UTP installations to test communications between two stations, bypassing the hub. Crossover cables can also be used to interconnect two DTE devices, such as PCs and routers, or two DCE devices, such as hubs and switches. *See also* unshielded twisted-pair cable, medium dependent interface, medium dependent interface-crossover.

**crosstalk**   A type of interference that occurs when two LAN cables run close to each other. If one cable is carrying a signal and the other isn't, the one carrying a signal will induce a "ghost" signal (crosstalk) in the other cable.

**CSMA/CA**   *See* Carrier Sense Multiple Access/Collision Avoidance.

**CSMA/CD**   *See* Carrier Sense Multiple Access/Collision Detection.

**cyclical redundancy check (CRC)**   An error-checking method in data communications that runs a formula against data before transmissions. The sending station then appends the resultant value (called a checksum) to the data and sends it. The receiving station uses the same formula on the data. If the receiving station doesn't get the same checksum result for the calculation, it considers the transmission invalid, rejects the frame, and asks for a retransmission.

**daemon**   Pronounced like "demon," a program that acts like a terminate and stay resident (TSR) application by loading into memory and lurking there for any trigger that calls upon its services.

**datagram**   A unit of data also known as a packet. More commonly, a datagram refers to the data that comes from the application or from UDP.

**Data Link layer**   The second layer of the OSI model. It describes the logical topology of a network, which is the way that packets move throughout a network. It also describes the method of media access. *See also* Open Systems Interconnect.

**Data over Cable Service Interface Specification (DOCSIS)**   *See* cable modem.

**data packet**   A unit of data sent over a network. A packet includes a header, addressing information, and the data itself. A packet is treated as a single unit as it is sent from device to device. Also known as a *datagram*.

**Data Service Unit (DSU)**   It transmits data through a Channel Service Unit (CSU) and is almost always a part of a single device referred to as a CSU/DSU.

**D channel**   *See* delta channel.

**default gateway**   The router that all packets are sent to when the workstation doesn't know where the destination station is or when it can't find the destination station on the local segment.

**delta channel (D channel)**   A channel on an ISDN line used for link management. For Basic Rate Interface (BRI) circuits, the D channel is 16Kbps. For the Primary Rate Interface (PRI), the D channel is 64Kbps. *See also* Integrated Services Digital Network.

**demarcation point (demarc)**   The point on any telephone installation where the telephone lines from the central office enter the customer's premises.

**denial of service (DoS) attack**   Type of hack that prevents any users—even legitimate ones—from using the system.

**destination port number**   The address of the PC to which data is being sent from a sending PC. The port portion allows for the demultiplexing of data to be sent to a specific application.

**DHCP**   *See* Dynamic Host Configuration Protocol.

**digital subscriber line (DSL)**   A digital WAN technology that brings high-speed digital networking to homes and businesses over POTS. There are many types, including HDSL (high-speed DSL) and VDSL (very high data-rate DSL). *See also* plain old telephone service, asymmetrical digital subscriber line.

**Direct Sequence Spread Spectrum (DSSS)**   A modulation technique used by the original IEEE 802.11 standard, as well as by the 802.11b standard. DSSS creates a redundant bit pattern for each bit that is transmitted so that if one or more bits in the bit pattern are damaged in transmission, the original data might be recoverable from the redundant bits. *See also* Frequency Hopping Spread Spectrum, Orthogonal Frequency Division Multiplexing.

**directional antenna (Yagi)**   A point-to-point antenna that, when used as a wireless access point, is not suitable for general client access but rather for point-to-point bridging of access points. *See also* omnidirectional antenna.

**directory**   A network database that contains a listing of all network resources, such as users, printers, groups, and so on.

**directory service**   A network service that provides access to a central database of information, which contains detailed information about the resources available on a network.

**disaster recovery**   The procedure by which data is recovered after a disaster.

**disk striping**   Technology that enables writing data to multiple disks simultaneously in small portions called stripes. These stripes maximize use by having all of the read/write heads working constantly. Different data is stored on each disk and is not automatically duplicated (this means that disk striping in and of itself does not provide fault tolerance).

**distance vector routing protocol**   A route discovery method in which each router, using broadcasts, tells every other router what networks and routes it knows about and the distance to them.

**DIX**   Another name for a 15-pin AUI connector or a DB-15 connector.

**DNS**   *See* Domain Name Service.

**DNS server**   Any server that performs address resolution by translating DNS host names to IP addresses. *See also* Domain Name Service, Internet Protocol.

**DNS zone**   An area in the DNS hierarchy that is managed as a single unit. *See also* Domain Name Service.

**DOCSIS**   *See* cable modem.

**DoD Networking Model**   A four-layer conceptual model describing how communications should take place between computer systems. The four layers are Process/Application, Host-to-Host, Internet, and Network Access.

**domain**   A group of networked Windows computers that share a single SAM database. *See also* Security Accounts Manager.

**Domain Name Service (DNS)**   The network service used in TCP/IP networks that translates host names to IP addresses. *See also* Transmission Control Protocol/Internet Protocol.

**dotted decimal**   Notation used by TCP/IP to designate an IP address. The notation is made up of 32 bits (4 bytes), each byte separated by a decimal. The range of numbers for each octet is 0–255. The leftmost octet contains the high-order bits and the rightmost octet contains the low-order bits.

**DSL**   *See* digital subscriber line.

**DSSS**   *See* Direct Sequence Spread Spectrum.

**D-type connector**   The first type of networking connector, the D-type connector, is used to connect many peripherals to a PC. A D-type connector is characterized by its shape. Turned on its side, it looks like the letter *D* and contains rows of pins (male) or sockets (female). AUI connectors are examples.

**dual-attached stations (DAS)**   Stations on an FDDI network that are attached to both cables for connection redundancy and fault tolerance.

**dumb terminal**   A keyboard and monitor that send keystrokes to a central processing computer (typically a mainframe or minicomputer) that returns screen displays to the monitor. The unit has no processing power of its own, hence the moniker "dumb."

**duplexed hard drives**   Two hard drives to which identical information is written simultaneously. A dedicated controller card controls each drive. Used for fault tolerance.

**duplicate server**   Two servers that are identical for use in clustering.

**dynamic ARP table entries**   *See* dynamic entry.

**dynamic entry**   An entry made in the ARP table whenever an ARP request is made by the Windows TCP/IP stack and the MAC address is not found in the ARP table. The ARP request is broadcast on the local segment. When the MAC address of the requested IP address is found, that information is added to the ARP table. *See also* Internet Protocol, media access control, Transmission Control Protocol/Internet Protocol.

**Dynamic Host Configuration Protocol (DHCP)**   A protocol used on a TCP/IP network to send configuration data, including TCP/IP address, default gateway, subnet mask, and DNS configuration, to clients. *See also* default gateway, Domain Name Service, subnet mask, Transmission Control Protocol/Internet Protocol.

**dynamic packet filtering**   A type of firewall used to accept or reject packets based on the contents of the packets.

**dynamic routing**   The use of route discovery protocols to talk to other routers and find out what networks they are attached to. Routers that use dynamic routing send out special packets to request updates of the other routers on the network as well as to send their own updates.

**dynamically allocated port**   TCP/IP port used by an application when needed. The port is not constantly used.

**EEPROM**   *See* electrically erasable programmable read-only memory.

**electrically erasable programmable read-only memory (EEPROM)**   A special integrated circuit on expansion cards that allows data to be stored on the chip. If necessary, the data can be erased by a special configuration program. Typically used to store hardware configuration data for expansion cards.

**electromagnetic interference (EMI)**   The interference that can occur during transmissions over copper cable because of electromagnetic energy outside the cable. The result is degradation of the signal.

**electronic mail (e-mail)**   An application that allows people to send messages via their computers on the same network or over the Internet.

**electrostatic discharge (ESD)**   A problem that exists when two items with dissimilar static electrical charges are brought together. The static electrical charges jump to the item with fewer electrical charges, causing ESD, which can damage computer components.

**e-mail**   *See* electronic mail.

**EMI**   *See* electromagnetic interference.

**encoding**   The process of translating data into signals that can be transmitted on a transmission medium.

**encryption key**   The string of alphanumeric characters used to decrypt encrypted data.

**endpoint**   The two ends of a connection for transmitting data. One end is the receiver, and the other is the sender.

**ESD**   *See* electrostatic discharge.

**Ethernet**   A shared-media network architecture. It operates at the Physical and Data Link layers of the OSI model. As the media access method, it uses baseband signaling over either a bus or a star topology with CSMA/CD. The cabling used in Ethernet networks can be coax, twisted-pair, or fiber-optic. *See also* Carrier Sense Multiple Access/Collision Detection, Open Systems Interconnect.

**Ethernet address**   *See* MAC address.

**expansion slot**   A slot on the computer's bus into which expansion cards are plugged to expand the functionality of the computer (for example, using a NIC to add the computer to a network). *See also* network interface card.

**extended AppleTalk network**   An AppleTalk network segment that is assigned a 16-bit range of numbers rather than a single 16-bit number.

**Extensible Authentication Protocol (EAP)**   An extension to PPP that supports multiple authentication methods, including Kerberos, passwords, certificates, smart cards, and so on. IEEE 802.1x is the standard that dictates how EAP is used within Ethernet frames.

**extranet**    An intranet interconnected and intercommunicating with networks that are under separate administrative control by way of an arrangement between the administrative entities. *See also* internetwork, intranet.

**failover device**    A device that comes online when another fails.

**failover server**    A hot site backup system in which the failover server is connected to the primary server. A heartbeat is sent from the primary server to the backup server. If the heartbeat stops, the failover system starts and takes over. Thus, the system doesn't go down even if the primary server is not running.

**Fast Ethernet**    The general category name given to 100Mbps Ethernet technologies.

**fault-resistant network**    A network that will be up and running at least 99 percent of the time or that is down less than 8 hours a year.

**fault-tolerant network**    A network that can recover from minor errors.

**FDDI**    *See* Fiber Distributed Data Interface.

**FHSS**    *See* Frequency Hopping Spread Spectrum.

**Fiber Channel**    A type of server-to-storage system connection that uses fiber-optic connectors.

**Fiber Distributed Data Interface (FDDI)**    A network topology that uses fiber-optic cable as a transmission medium and dual, counter-rotating rings to provide data delivery and fault tolerance.

**fiber-optic**    A type of network cable that uses a central glass or plastic core surrounded by a plastic coating.

**file server**    A server specialized in holding and distributing files.

**File Transfer Protocol (FTP)**    A TCP/IP protocol and software that permit the transferring of files between computer systems. Because FTP has been implemented on numerous types of computer systems, files can be transferred between disparate computer systems (for example, a personal computer and a minicomputer). *See also* Transmission Control Protocol/Internet Protocol.

**firewall**    A combination of hardware and software that protects a network from attack by hackers that could gain access through public networks, including the Internet.

**FQDN**    *See* Fully Qualified Domain Name.

**Frame Relay**    A WAN technology that transmits packets over a WAN using packet switching. *See also* packet switching.

**frequency division multiplexing (FDM)**    A multiplexing technique whereby the different signals are sent across multiple frequencies.

**Frequency Hopping Spread Spectrum (FHSS)**    A modulation technique specified by the original IEEE 802.11 standard but not supported by manufacturers. DSSS is the modulation technique of choice by 802.11 equipment makers. FHSS modulates the data signal with a carrier signal that hops through a random, yet predictable, sequence of frequencies. A hopping code determines the transmission frequencies. The receiver is set to the same code, allowing it to listen to the incoming signal at the right time and frequency to properly receive the signal. *See also* Direct Sequence Spread Spectrum, Orthogonal Frequency Division Multiplexing.

**FTP**    *See* File Transfer Protocol.

**FTP proxy**    A server that uploads and downloads files from a server on behalf of a workstation.

**full backup**    A backup that copies all data to the archive medium.

**Fully Qualified Domain Name (FQDN)**    An address that uses both the host name (workstation name) and the domain name.

**gateway**    The hardware and software needed to connect two disparate network environments so that communications can occur.

**global group**    A type of group in Windows NT that is used networkwide. Members can be from anywhere in the network, and rights can be assigned to any resource in the network.

**ground loop**    A condition that occurs when a signal cycles through a common ground connection between two devices, causing electromagnetic interference (EMI). *See also* electromagnetic interference.

**hardware address**    A Data Link layer address assigned to every NIC at the MAC sublayer. The address is in the format *xx:xx:xx:xx:xx:xx*. Each *xx* is a two-digit hexadecimal number. *See also* media access control, network interface card.

**hardware loopback**    A small plug used in a NIC that connects the transmission pins directly to the receiving pins, allowing diagnostic software to test if a NIC can successfully transmit and receive. *See also* network interface card.

**heartbeat**    The data transmissions between two servers in a cluster to detect when one fails. When the standby server detects no heartbeats from the main server, it comes online and takes control of the responsibilities of the main server. This allows for all services to remain online and accessible.

**hop**    One pass through a router. *See also* cost, router.

**hop count**    As a packet travels over a network through multiple routers, each router will increment the hop count field in the packet by one as it crosses the router. It is used to limit the number of routers a packet can cross on the way to its destination.

**host**    Any network device with a TCP/IP network address. *See also* Transmission Control Protocol/Internet Protocol.

**Host-to-Host layer**    A layer in the DoD model that corresponds to the Transport layer of the OSI model. *See also* DoD Networking Model, Open Systems Interconnect.

**HTML**    *See* Hypertext Markup Language.

**HTTP** *See* Hypertext Transfer Protocol.

**hub** A Physical layer device that serves as a central connection point for several network devices. A hub repeats the signals it receives on one port to all other ports. *See also* active hub.

**Hypertext Markup Language (HTML)** A set of codes used to format text and graphics that will be displayed in a browser. The codes define how data will be displayed.

**Hypertext Transfer Protocol (HTTP)** The protocol used for communication between a web server and a web browser.

**IBM data connector** A proprietary data connector created by IBM. This connector is unique because there isn't a male version and female version; any IBM connector can connect with another IBM connector and lock together.

**ICMP** *See* Internet Control Message Protocol.

**IEEE** *See* Institute of Electrical and Electronics Engineers.

**IEEE 802.*x* standards** The IEEE standards for LAN and MAN networking.

**IEEE 802.1 LAN/MAN Management** Standard that specifies LAN/MAN network management and internetworking.

**IEEE 802.2 Logical Link Control** Standard that specifies the operation of the logical link control (LLC) sublayer of the Data Link layer of the OSI model. The LLC sublayer provides an interface between the MAC sublayer and the Network layer. *See also* media access control, Open Systems Interconnect.

**IEEE 802.3 CSMA/CD Networking** Standard that specifies a network that uses Ethernet technology and a CSMA/CD network access method. *See also* Carrier Sense Multiple Access/Collision Detection.

**IEEE 802.5 Token Ring** Specifies a logical ring, physical star, and token-passing media access method based on IBM's Token Ring.

**IEEE 802.10 LAN/MAN Security** A series of guidelines dealing with various aspects of network security.

**IEEE 802.11 Wireless LAN** Defines standards for implementing wireless technologies such as infrared and spread-spectrum radio.

**IETF** *See* Internet Engineering Task Force.

**Institute of Electrical and Electronics Engineers (IEEE)** An international organization that sets standards for various electrical and electronics issues.

**Integrated Services Digital Network (ISDN)** A telecommunications standard that is used to digitally send voice, data, and video signals over the same lines. *See also* delta channel.

**internal bridge** A bridge created by placing two NICs in a computer.

**internal modem**   A modem that is a regular PC card and is inserted into the bus slot. These modems are inside the PC.

**International Organization for Standardization (ISO)**   The standards organization that developed the OSI model. This model provides a guideline for how communications occur between computers.

**Internet**   A global network made up of a large number of individual networks interconnected through the use of public telephone circuits and TCP/IP protocols. *See also* Transmission Control Protocol/Internet Protocol.

**Internet Architecture Board (IAB)**   The committee that oversees management of the Internet. It is made up of two subcommittees: the Internet Engineering Task Force (IETF) and the Internet Research Task Force (IRTF). *See also* Internet Engineering Task Force, Internet Research Task Force.

**Internet Control Message Protocol (ICMP)**   A message and management protocol for TCP/IP. The Ping utility uses ICMP. *See also* Ping, Transmission Control Protocol/Internet Protocol.

**Internet Engineering Task Force (IETF)**   An international organization that works under the Internet Architecture Board to establish standards and protocols relating to the Internet. *See also* Internet Architecture Board.

**Internet Protocol (IP)**   The protocol in the TCP/IP protocol suite responsible for network addressing and routing. *See also* Transmission Control Protocol/Internet Protocol.

**Internet Research Task Force (IRTF)**   An international organization that works under the Internet Architecture Board to research new Internet technologies. *See also* Internet Architecture Board.

**Internet service provider (ISP)**   A company that provides direct access to the Internet for home and business computer users.

**internetwork**   Also known as an internet, for short, the interconnection and intercommunication between autonomous networks. *See also* intranet, extranet.

**Internet Packet eXchange (IPX)**   A connectionless, routable network protocol based on the Xerox XNS architecture. It is the default protocol for versions of NetWare before NetWare 5. It operates at the Network layer of the OSI model and is responsible for addressing and routing packets to workstations or servers on other networks. *See also* Open Systems Interconnect.

**intranet**   Often an internetwork encompassing only networks under a single administrative domain; very often used to refer to a large corporation's internal internetwork. *See also* internetwork, extranet.

**inverse multiplexing**   The network technology that allows one signal to be split across multiple transmission lines at the transmission source and combined at the receiving end.

**IP**   *See* Internet Protocol.

**IP address**  An address that is used by the Internet Protocol and identifies a device's location on the network.

**ipconfig**  A Windows NT utility used to display a machine's current configuration.

**IP proxy**  A server technology that protects your network. With an IP proxy, all communications look as if they originated from a proxy server because the IP address of the user making a request is hidden. IP proxies use a technology known as NAT. *See also* Network Address Translation.

**IP spoofing**  A hacker trying to gain access to a network by pretending their machine has the same network address as the internal network.

**IPX**  *See* Internet Packet eXchange.

**IPX network address**  A number that represents an entire network. All servers on the network must use the same external network number.

**ISDN**  *See* Integrated Services Digital Network.

**ISDN terminal adapter**  The device used on ISDN networks to connect a local network (or single machine) to an ISDN network. It provides power to the line as well as translates data from the LAN or individual computer for transmission on the ISDN line. *See also* Integrated Services Digital Network.

**ISP**  *See* Internet service provider.

**Java**  A programming language, developed by Sun Microsystems, that is used to write programs that will run on any platform that has a Java Virtual Machine installed.

**Java Virtual Machine (JVM)**  Software, developed by Sun Microsystems that creates a virtual Java computer on which Java programs can run. A programmer writes a program once without having to recompile or rewrite the program for all platforms.

**jumper**  A small connector (cap or plug) that connects pins. This creates a circuit that indicates a setting to a device.

**JVM**  *See* Java Virtual Machine.

**kernel**  The core component of any operating system, the kernel handles the functions of memory management, hardware interaction, and program execution.

**key**  A folder in Windows Registry that contains subkeys and values, or a value with an algorithm to encrypt and decrypt data.

**LAN**  *See* local area network.

**LAN driver**  The interface between the NetWare kernel and the NIC installed in the server. Also a general category of drivers used to enable communications between an operating system and a NIC. *See also* network interface card.

**laser printer**   A printer that uses a laser to form an image on a photo-sensitive drum. The image is then developed with toner and transferred to paper. Finally, a heated drum fuses toner particles onto the paper.

**Layer 2 Switch**   A switching hub that operates at the Data Link layer and builds a table of the MAC addresses of all the connected stations. *See also* media access control.

**Layer 3 Switch**   Functioning at the Network layer, a switch that performs the multiport, virtual LAN, data pipelining functions of a standard Layer 2 Switch, but it can also perform basic routing functions between virtual LANs.

**LCP**   *See* Link Control Protocol.

**lease**   In DHCP, the duration of time for which a client is allowed to use the parameters assigned to it by the server. *See also* Dynamic Host Configuration Protocol.

**line conditioner**   A device used to protect against power surges and spikes. Line conditioners use several electronic methods to clean all power coming into the device.

**line noise**   On a power line, any extraneous signal that is not part of the power feed.

**line voltage**   The voltage, supplied from the power company, that comes out at the outlets.

**Link Control Protocol (LCP)**   The protocol used to establish, configure, and test the link between a client and PPP host. *See also* Point-to-Point Protocol.

**link light**   A small light-emitting diode (LED) that is found on both the NIC and the hub. It is usually green and labeled "Link" or something similar. A link light indicates that the NIC and the hub are making a Data Link layer connection. *See also* hub, network interface card.

**link state route discovery**   A route discovery method that transmits special packets (Link State Packets, or LSPs) that contain information about the networks to which the router is connected.

**link state routing**   A type of routing that advertises a router's entire routing table only at startup and possibly at infrequently scheduled intervals. Aside from that, the router sends updates to other routers only when changes occur in the advertiser's routing table.

**link state routing protocol**   A routing protocol whereby the router sends out incremental information only, such as updates to its own routing table.

**Linux**   A version of UNIX, developed by Linus Torvalds. Runs on Intel-based PCs and is generally free. *See also* UNIX.

**local area network (LAN)**   A network that is restricted to a single building, a group of buildings, or even a single room. A LAN can have one or more servers. LANs are defined by the Data Link protocols they run. For example, Ethernet networks are LANs, but PPP networks are not. They are WAN links.

**local groups**   Groups created on individual servers. Rights can be assigned only to local resources.

**local loop**   The part of the PSTN that goes from the Central Office to the demarcation point at the customer's premises. *See also* Central Office, demarcation point, Public Switched Telephone Network.

**log file**   A file that keeps a running list of all errors and notices, the time and date they occurred, and any other pertinent information.

**logical bus topology**   Type of topology in which the signal appears to travel the distance of the cable and is received by all stations on the backbone. Compare to a physical bus topology, in which this is actually the case. Logical bus topologies are most often implemented as physical star topologies. *See also* backbone.

**Logical Link Control (LLC)**   A sublayer of the Data Link layer. Provides an interface between the MAC sublayer and the Network layer. *See also* media access control, topology.

**logical network addressing**   The addressing scheme used by protocols at the Network layer.

**logical parallel port**   Port used by the CAPTURE command to redirect a workstation printer port to a network print queue. The logical port has no relation to the port to which the printer is actually attached or to the physical port. *See also* physical parallel port.

**logical port address**   A value that is used at the Transport layer to differentiate between the upper-layer services.

**logical ring topology**   A network topology in which all network signals travel from one station to another, being read and forwarded by each station.

**logical topology**   Describes the way the information flows. Logical topologies are the same as the physical topologies except that the flow of information, rather than the physical arrangement, specifies the type of topology.

**LSL**   *See* Link Support Layer.

**MAC**   *See* media access control.

**MAC address**   The address that is either assigned to a network card or burned into the NIC. This is how PCs keep track of one another and keep each other separate.

**mail exchange (MX) record**   A DNS record type that specifies the DNS host name of the mail server for a particular domain name.

**MAU**   *See* Multistation Access Unit.

**media access**   The process of vying for transmission time on the network media.

**media access control (MAC)**   A sublayer of the Data Link layer that controls the way multiple devices use the same media channel. It controls which devices can transmit and when they can transmit.

**media converter**   A networking device that converts from one network media type to another—for example, converting from an AUI port to an RJ-45 connector for 10Base-T.

**medium dependent interface (MDI)**    The standard pin configuration for a wiring specification. The transmit and receive pairs of an MDI port are crossed with respect to those of an MDI-X port. MDI is generally considered to be the pin configuration used on the device acting as data terminal equipment (DTE). There is generally one port on Ethernet hubs or switches that can be switched between MDI and MDI-X. Hub or switch ports set for MDI allow the hub or switch to be connected to the standard MDI-X port of another hub or switch without the use of a crossover cable. *See also* medium dependent interface-crossover.

**medium dependent interface-crossover (MDI-X)**    A nonstandard pin configuration for a wiring specification, characterized by reversing the transmit and receive channels with respect to the MDI specification. MDI-X is generally considered to be the pin configuration used on the device acting as data circuit-terminating equipment (DCE). There is generally one port on Ethernet hubs or switches that can be switched between MDI and MDI-X. Hub or switch ports set for MDI allow the hub or switch to be connected to the standard MDI-X port of another hub or switch without the use of a crossover cable. If the switchable port is set for MDI-X, it can be used with a straight-through cable for connection to an end device, such as a PC or router. *See also* medium dependent interface.

**member server**    A computer that has Windows NT server installed but doesn't have a copy of the SAM database. *See also* Security Accounts Manager.

**mesh topology**    A network topology in which there is a connection from each station to every other station in the network.

**Microsoft Challenge Handshake Authentication Protocol (MS-CHAP)**    Microsoft's version of CHAP designed for authentication communications between Windows clients and servers. *See also* Challenge Handshake Authentication Protocol (CHAP).

**modem**    A communication device that converts digital computer signals into analog tones for transmission over the PSTN and converts them back to digital upon reception. The word *modem* is an acronym for *modulator/demodulator*.

**MS-CHAP**    *See* Microsoft Challenge Handshake Authentication Protocol (MS-CHAP).

**multiple-server clustering**    A system in which multiple servers run continuously, each providing backup and production services at the same time. (Expensive servers, therefore, are not sitting around as designated "backup" servers, used only when an emergency arises.) If a server fails, another just takes over, without any interruption of service.

**multiplexing**    A technology that combines multiple signals into one signal for transmission over a slow medium. *See also* frequency division multiplexing, inverse multiplexing.

**multipoint RF network**    A radio frequency (RF) network consisting of multiple stations, each with transmitters and receivers. This type of network also requires an RF bridge as a central sending and receiving point.

**Multistation Access Unit (MAU)**    The central device in Token Ring networks that acts as the connection point for all stations and facilitates the formation of the ring.

**name resolution**   The process of translating (resolving) logical host names to network addresses.

**NAT**   *See* Network Address Translation.

**National Computing Security Center (NCSC)**   The agency that developed the Trusted Computer System Evaluation Criteria (TCSEC) and the Trusted Network Interpretation Environmental Guideline (TNIEG).

**National Security Agency (NSA)**   The U.S. government agency responsible for protecting U.S. communications and producing foreign intelligence information. It was established by presidential directive in 1952 as a separately organized agency within the Department of Defense (DoD).

**nbtstat (NetBIOS over TCP/IP statistics)**   The Windows TCP/IP utility that is used to display NetBIOS over TCP/IP statistics. *See also* network basic input/output system, Transmission Control Protocol/Internet Protocol.

**NCP**   *See* NetWare Core Protocol.

**NCSC**   *See* National Computing Security Center.

**NDPS**   *See* Novell Distributed Print Services.

**NDS**   *See* Novell Directory Services.

**NDS tree**   A logical representation of a network's resources. Resources are represented by objects in the tree. The tree is often designed after a company's functional structure. Objects can represent organizations, departments, users, servers, printers, and other resources. *See also* Novell Directory Services.

**nearline site**   A warm or cold site that uses a storage method that is neither online or offline, but somewhere in the middle, like tape backup. It contains material that is not likely to be needed, except in cases of disaster recovery.

**NetBEUI**   *See* NetBIOS Extended User Interface.

**NetBIOS**   *See* network basic input/output system.

**NetBIOS Extended User Interface (NetBEUI)**   Transport protocol that is based on the NetBIOS protocol and has datagram support and support for connectionless transmission. NetBEUI is a protocol that is native to Microsoft networks and is mainly for use by small businesses. It is a nonroutable protocol that cannot pass over a router but does pass over a bridge since it operates at the Data Link layer. *See also* network basic input/output system.

**NetBIOS name**   The unique name used to identify and address a computer using NetBEUI.

**netstat**   A utility used to determine which TCP/IP connections—inbound or outbound—the computer has. It also allows the user to view packet statistics, such as how many packets have been sent and received. *See also* Transmission Control Protocol/Internet Protocol.

**NetWare**   The network operating system made by Novell.

**NetWare 3.***x*   The version series of NetWare that supported multiple, cross-platform clients with fairly minimal hardware requirements. It used a database called the bindery to keep track of users and groups and was administered with several DOS, menu-based utilities (such as SYSCON, PCONSOLE, and FILER).

**NetWare 4.***x*   The version series of NetWare that includes NDS. *See also* Novell Directory Services.

**NetWare 5.***x*   The version series of NetWare that includes a multiprocessing kernel. It also includes a five-user version of Oracle 8, a relational database, and the ability to use TCP/IP in its pure form.

**NetWare Administrator**   The utility used to administer NetWare versions 4.*x* and later by making changes to the NDS Directory. It is the only administrative utility needed to modify NDS objects and their properties. *See also* Novell Directory Services.

**NetWare Core Protocol (NCP)**   The upper-layer NetWare protocol that functions on top of IPX and provides NetWare resource access to workstations. *See also* Internet Packet eXchange.

**NetWare Link Services Protocol (NLSP)**   Protocol that gathers routing information based on the link state routing method. Its precursor is the Routing Information Protocol (RIP). NLSP is a more efficient routing protocol than RIP. *See also* link state routing.

**NetWare Loadable Module (NLM)**   A component used to provide a NetWare server with additional services and functionality. Unneeded services can be unloaded, thus conserving memory.

**network**   A group of devices connected by some means for the purpose of sharing information or resources.

**Network Address Translation (NAT)**   A TCP/IP service that many routers, firewalls, and IP proxies can provide. NAT translates addresses that are legal for an inside network but illegal for a corresponding outside network into addresses that are legal for the outside network. NAT also resolves the outside addresses back to the inside addresses as return traffic for the originating device comes back from the outside network. *See also* IP proxy.

**network attached storage**   Storage, such as hard drives, attached to a network for the purpose of storing data for clients on the network. Network attached storage is commonly used for backing up data.

**network basic input/output system (NetBIOS)**   A Session layer protocol that opens communication sessions for applications that want to communicate on a network.

**network-centric**   Refers to network operating systems that use directory services to maintain information about the entire network.

**Network File System (NFS)**   A protocol that enables users to access files on remote computers as if the files were local.

**network interface card (NIC)**   Physical device that connects computers and other network equipment to the transmission medium.

**Network layer**   This third layer of the OSI model is responsible for logical addressing and translating logical names into physical addresses. This layer also controls the routing of data from source to destination as well as the building and dismantling of packets. *See also* Open Systems Interconnect.

**network media**   The physical cables that link computers in a network; also known as *physical media.*

**network operating system (NOS)**   The software that runs on a network server and offers file, print, application, and other services to clients.

**network software diagnostics**   Software tools, either protocol analyzers or performance monitoring tools, used to troubleshoot network problems.

**Network Support Encyclopedia (NSEPro)**   *See* Novell Support Connection.

**NFS**   *See* Network File System.

**NIC**   *See* network interface card.

**NIC diagnostics**   Software utilities that verify that the NIC is functioning correctly and test every aspect of NIC operation. *See also* network interface card.

**NIC driver**   *See* LAN driver.

**NLM**   *See* NetWare Loadable Module.

**NLSP**   *See* NetWare Link Services Protocol.

**non-unicast packet**   A packet that is not sent directly from one workstation to another.

**NOS**   *See* network operating system.

**Novell Directory Services (NDS)**   A NetWare service that provides access to a global, hierarchical directory database of network entities that can be centrally managed.

**Novell Distributed Print Services (NDPS)**   A printing system designed by Novell that uses NDS to install and manage printers. NDPS supports automatic network printer installation, automatic distribution of client printer drivers, and centralized printer management without the use of print queues.

**Novell Support Connection**   Novell's database of technical information documents, files, patches, fixes, NetWare Application Notes, Novell lab bulletins, Novell professional developer bulletins, answers to frequently asked questions, and more. The database is available from Novell and is updated quarterly.

**NSA**   *See* National Security Agency.

**N-series connector**   A male/female screw and barrel connector used with Thinnet and Thicknet cabling.

**nslookup**   A utility that allows you to query a name server to see which IP address a name resolves to.

**NT Directory Services (NTDS)**   System of domains and trusts for a Windows NT Server network.

**NTDS**   *See* NT Directory Services.

**object**   The item that represents some network entity in NDS. *See also* Novell Directory Services.

**octet**   Refers to 8 bits; one-fourth of an IP address.

**ODI**   *See* Open Datalink Interface.

**OE (operator error)**   When the error is not software or hardware related, it may be a problem with the user not knowing how to operate the software or hardware. An OE problem can be a serious one.

**OFDM**   *See* Orthogonal Frequency Division Multiplexing.

**offline**   The general name for the condition when some piece of electronic or computer equipment is unavailable or inoperable.

**Omni**   *See* omnidirectional antenna.

**omnidirectional antenna (Omni)**   A point-to-multipoint antenna that provides equal power dispersion in almost all directions. Omni is the primary antenna type used with a wireless access point that is designed to offer service to clients in any direction simultaneously. Contrast with directional Yagi antennas. *See also* directional antenna.

**Open Datalink Interface (ODI)**   A driver specification, developed by Novell, that enables a single workstation to communicate transparently with several different protocol stacks using a single NIC and a single NIC driver.

**OpenLinux**   A version of the Linux network operating system developed by Caldera.

**Open Systems Interconnect (OSI)**   A model defined by the ISO to categorize the process of communication between computers in terms of seven layers. The seven layers are Application, Presentation, Session, Transport, Network, Data Link, and Physical. *See also* International Organization for Standardization.

**Organizationally Unique Identifier (OUI)**   The first 24 bits of a 48-bit MAC address. Each OUI is assigned by the IEEE to a single manufacturer of devices that have MAC addresses assigned to them. As long as the manufacturer does not duplicate the last 24 bits of the MAC address, the assumption is that the entire MAC address will be unique worldwide. However, renegade manufacturers and manufacturing mistakes can result in duplicate MAC addresses. As long as the devices with duplicate addresses do not make it onto the same local network segment (the same IP subnet, for example), this conflict will never be an issue.

**Orthogonal Frequency Division Multiplexing (OFDM)**   A modulation technique used by 802.11a that is implemented with a system of 52 subcarriers. OFDM's spread spectrum technique distributes the data over these 52 subcarriers, which are spaced apart at precise frequencies. This spacing helps prevent demodulators from seeing frequencies other than their own. *See also* Direct Sequence Spread Spectrum, Frequency Hopping Spread Spectrum.

**OSI**   *See* Open Systems Interconnect.

**oversampling**   Method of synchronous bit synchronization in which the receiver samples the signal at a much faster rate than the data rate. This permits the use of an encoding method that does not add clocking transitions.

**overvoltage threshold**   The level of overvoltage that will trip the circuit breaker in a surge protector.

**packet**   The basic division of data sent over a network.

**packet filtering**   A firewall technology that accepts or rejects packets based on their content.

**packet switching**   A method of switching that sends information as potentially smaller discrete packets, each one independently addressed for the intended recipient. Intermediate devices, such as switches and routers, can send these packets along one or more different paths to the same destination, making the autonomy of each packet imperative. A packet-switched connection is virtual and the physical paths are shared, in contrast to the concept of the dedicated paths of circuit switching. *See also* frame relay and circuit switching.

**passive detection**   A type of intruder detection that logs all network events to a file for an administrator to view later.

**passive hub**   A hub that simply makes physical and electrical connections between all connected stations. Generally speaking, these hubs are not powered.

**password history**   List of passwords that have already been used.

**patch**   Software that fixes a problem with an existing program or operating system.

**patch cable**   A central wiring point for multiple devices on a UTP network. *See also* unshielded twisted-pair cable.

**patch panel**   A central wiring point for multiple devices on a UTP network. The patch panel itself contains no electronic circuits. Generally, patch panels are in server rooms or located near switches or hubs to provide an easy means of patching over wall jacks or hardware.

**PDC**   *See* Primary Domain Controller.

**PDU**   *See* protocol data unit.

**peer communication**   The use of headers to allow corresponding protocol processes in two devices to communicate with one another as if there were a direct connection between the devices at the protocol's layer.

**peer-to-peer network**    Computers that are hooked together and have no centralized authority. Each computer is equal and can act as both a server and a workstation.

**peripheral**    Any device that can be attached to a computer to expand its capabilities.

**permanent virtual circuit (PVC)**    A technology used by Frame Relay that allows virtual data communications (circuits) to be set up between sender and receiver over a packet-switched network.

**PGP**    *See* Pretty Good Privacy.

**physical address**    *See* MAC address.

**physical bus topology**    A network that uses one network cable that runs from one end of the network to the other. Workstations connect at various points along this cable.

**Physical layer**    The first layer of the OSI model. This layer controls the functional interface. *See also* Open Systems Interconnect.

**physical media**    *See* network media.

**physical mesh topology**    A network configuration in which each device has multiple connections. These multiple connections provide redundant connections.

**physical parallel port**    A port that is on the back of a computer and allows a printer to be connected with a parallel cable.

**physical port**    An opening that is on a network device and allows a cable of some kind to be connected. Ports allow devices to be connected to each other with cables.

**physical ring topology**    A network topology that is set up in a circular fashion. Data travels around the ring in one direction, and each device on the ring acts as a repeater to keep the signal strong as it travels. Each device incorporates a receiver for the incoming signal and a transmitter to send the data on to the next device in the ring. The network is dependent on the ability of the signal to travel around the ring.

**physical star topology**    Describes a network in which a cable runs from each network entity to a central device called a hub. The hub allows all devices to communicate as if they were directly connected. *See also* hub.

**physical topology**    The physical layout of a network, such as bus, star, ring, or mesh.

**Ping**    A TCP/IP utility used to test whether another host is reachable. An ICMP request is sent to the host, who responds with a reply if it is reachable. The request times out if the host is not reachable.

**Ping of Death**    A large ICMP packet sent to overflow the remote host's buffer. This usually causes the remote host to reboot or hang.

**plain old telephone service (POTS)**    The classic analog circuit commonly used to connect to the Public Switched Telephone Network (PSTN) to make voice calls for conversations and modem and facsimile sessions. *See* asymmetrical digital subscriber line, digital subscriber line, Public Switched Telephone Network.

**plenum-rated coating**    Coaxial cable coating that does not produce toxic gas when burned.

**point-to-point**    Network communication in which two devices have exclusive access to a network medium. For example, a printer connected to only one workstation would be using a point-to-point connection.

**Point-to Point Protocol (PPP)**    The protocol used with dial-up connections to the Internet. Its functions include error control, security, dynamic IP addressing, and support for multiple protocols.

**Point-to-Point Tunneling Protocol (PPTP)**    A protocol that allows the creation of virtual private networks (VPNs), which allow users to access a server on a corporate network over a secure, direct connection via the Internet. *See also* virtual private network.

**polling**    A media access control method that uses a central device called a controller that polls each device in turn and asks if it has data to transmit.

**POP3**    *See* Post Office Protocol version 3.

**port**    A numerical value used in the headers of such protocols as TCP and UDP to signify the identity of the next-highest-layer protocol responsible for the control information that follows the header containing the port number. Using this value, the protocol is able to hand its payload to the appropriate protocol at the next layer higher, creating the appearance of simultaneously multiplexing the PDUs of multiple higher-layer protocols.

**positive forward acknowledgement**    The term used to describe acknowledgement schemes, such as the one used by TCP, that only acknowledge properly received PDUs (no negative acknowledgements to indicate errors in reception) and do so by specifying the next PDU identifier (the sequence number in TCP) the recipient expects to receive, not previously received identifiers.

**Post Office Protocol version 3 (POP3)**    The protocol used to download e-mail from an SMTP e-mail server to a network client. *See also* Simple Mail Transfer Protocol.

**POTS**    *See* plain old telephone service.

**power blackout**    A total loss of power that may last for only a few seconds or as long as several hours.

**power brownout**    A condition in which power drops below normal levels for several seconds or longer.

**power overage**    A condition in which too much power is coming into the computer. *See also* power spike, power surge.

**power sag**    A lower-power condition in which the power drops below normal levels for a few seconds and then returns to normal levels.

**power spike**   A condition in which the power level rises above normal for less than a second and drops back to normal.

**power surge**   A condition in which the power level rises above normal and stays there for longer than a second or two.

**power underage**   A condition in which the power level drops below the standard level. *See also* power sag.

**PPP**   *See* Point-to-Point Protocol.

**PPTP**   *See* Point-to-Point Tunneling Protocol.

**Presentation layer**   The sixth layer of the OSI model; responsible for formatting data exchange such as graphic commands and conversion of character sets. Also responsible for data compression, data encryption, and data stream redirection. *See also* Open Systems Interconnect.

**Pretty Good Privacy (PGP)**   A shareware implementation of RSA encryption. *See also* RSA Data Security, Inc.

**Primary Domain Controller (PDC)**   An NT server that contains a master copy of the SAM database. This database contains all usernames, passwords, and access control lists for a Windows NT domain. *See also* Security Accounts Manager.

**print server**   A centralized device that controls and manages all network printers. The print server can be hardware, software, or a combination of both. Some print servers are actually built into the network printer NICs. *See also* network interface card.

**print services**   The network services that manage and control printing on a network, allowing multiple and simultaneous access to printers.

**private key**   A technology in which both the sender and the receiver have the same key. A single key is used to encrypt and decrypt all messages. *See also* public key.

**private network**   The part of a network that lies behind a firewall and is not "seen" on the Internet. *See also* firewall.

**protocol**   A predefined set of rules that dictates how computers or devices communicate and exchange data on the network.

**protocol address**   A generic term for Network-layer addresses, such as IP or IPX addresses, that alludes to the protocol dependency of the address.

**protocol analyzer**   A software and hardware troubleshooting tool that is used to decode protocol information to try to determine the source of a network problem and to establish baselines.

**protocol data unit (PDU)**   A generic term used to describe the end product of a protocol. It can be thought of as the entire data structure handed down by a protocol to the protocol at the next lowest layer or the information placed on the network media by the Physical layer. A PDU will consist of the original user data and any upper-layer control information (headers and trailers) imposed by upper-layer protocols encapsulated by the control information of the protocol creating the PDU.

**protocol suite** The set of rules a computer uses to communicate with other computers.

**proxy** A type of firewall that prevents direct communication between a client and a host by acting as an intermediary. *See also* firewall.

**proxy cache server** An implementation of a web proxy. The server receives an HTTP request from a web browser and makes the request on behalf of the sending workstation. When the response comes, the proxy cache server caches a copy of the response locally. The next time someone makes a request for the same web page or Internet information, the proxy cache server can fulfill the request out of the cache instead of having to retrieve the resource from the Web.

**proxy server** A type of server that makes a single Internet connection and services requests on behalf of many users.

**PSTN** *See* Public Switched Telephone Network.

**public** For use by everyone. Also a popular name for certain UNIX and FTP folders.

**public key** A technology that uses two keys to facilitate communication, a public key and a private key. The public key is used to encrypt a message to a receiver. *See also* private key.

**public network** The part of a network that is on the outside of a firewall and is exposed to the public. *See also* firewall.

**Public Switched Telephone Network (PSTN)** The U.S. public telephone network. It is also called the plain old telephone service (POTS). *See also* Central Office.

**punchdown tool** A hand tool used to terminate twisted-pair wires on a wall jack or patch panel.

**PVC** *See* permanent virtual circuit.

**QoS** *See* Quality of Service.

**quad decimal** Four sets of octets separated by a decimal point; an IP address.

**quality of service (QoS)** Data prioritization at the Network layer of the OSI model. Results in guaranteed throughput rates. *See also* Open Systems Interconnect.

**radio frequency interference (RFI)** Interference on copper cabling systems caused by radio frequencies.

**RAID** *See* Redundant Array of Independent (or Inexpensive) Disks.

**RAID levels** The different types of RAID, such as RAID 0, RAID 1, etc.

**README file** A file that the manufacturer includes with software to give the installer information that came too late to make it into the software manuals. It's usually a last-minute addition that includes tips on installing the software, possible incompatibilities, and any known installation problems that might have been found right before the product was shipped.

**reduced instruction set computing (RISC)**     Computer architecture in which the computer executes small, general-purpose instructions very rapidly.

**Redundant Array of Independent (or Inexpensive) Disks (RAID)**     A configuration of multiple hard disks used to provide fault tolerance should a disk fail. Different levels of RAID exist, depending on the amount and type of fault tolerance provided.

**regeneration process**     Process in which signals are read, amplified, and repeated on the network to reduce signal degradation, which results in longer overall possible length of the network.

**reliable**     The quality of a protocol that uses acknowledgments to allow the recipient to confirm unerrored receipt of data from a source device. *See also* unreliable.

**remote access protocol**     Any networking protocol that is used to gain access to a network over public communication links.

**remote access server**     A computer that has one or more modems installed to enable remote connections to the network.

**Rendezvous**     An IP-based ZeroConf open service discovery protocol that allows devices to be added to and removed from networks without configuration.

**repeater**     A Physical layer device that amplifies the signals it receives on one port and resends or repeats them on another. A repeater is used to extend the maximum length of a network segment.

**replication**     The process of copying directory information to other servers to keep them all synchronized.

**RFI**     *See* radio frequency interference.

**RG-58**     The type designation for the coaxial cable used in Thin Ethernet (10Base-2). It has a 50-ohm impedance rating and uses BNC connectors.

**RG-62**     The type designation for the coaxial cable used in ARCnet networks. It has a 93-ohm impedance and uses BNC connectors.

**ring topology**     A network topology in which each computer in the network is connected to exactly two other computers. With ring topology, a single break in the ring brings the entire network down.

**RIP**     *See* Routing Information Protocol.

**RISC**     *See* reduced instruction set computing.

**RJ (Registered Jack) connector**     A modular connection mechanism that allows for as many as eight copper wires (four pairs). RJ connectors are most commonly used for telephone (such as the RJ-11) and network adaptors (such as RJ-45).

**roaming profiles**    Profiles downloaded from a server at each login. When a user logs out at the end of the session, changes are made and remembered for the next time the user logs in.

**route**    The path to get to the destination from a source.

**route cost**    How many router hops there are between source and destination in an internetwork. *See also* hop, router.

**router**    A device that connects two networks and allows packets to be transmitted and received between them. A router determines the best path for data packets from source to destination. *See also* hop.

**Routing Information Protocol (RIP)**    A distance-vector routing protocol used by IP and IPX. It uses hops or ticks to determine the cost for a particular route.

**routing**    A function of the Network layer that involves moving data throughout a network. Data passes through several network segments using routers that can select the path the data takes. *See also* router.

**routing protocol**    One of a collection of protocols designed to allow routers to dynamically learn routes from one another, reducing or eliminating the need for manual configuration of routes. Examples of routing protocols are RIP, IGRP and EIGRP, OSPF, IS-IS, BGP, NLSP, and ATM's Private Network-to-Network Interface (PNNI).

**routing table**    A table that contains information about the locations of other routers on the network and their distance from the current router.

**RSA Data Security, Inc.**    A commercial company that produces encryption software. RSA stands for Rivest, Shamir, and Adleman, the founders of the company.

**sag**    *See* power sag.

**SAM**    *See* Security Accounts Manager.

**Secure Hypertext Transfer Protocol (S-HTTP)**    A protocol used for secure communications between a web server and a web browser.

**Security Accounts Manager (SAM)**    A database within Windows NT that contains information about all users and groups and their associated rights and settings within a Windows NT domain. *See also* Backup Domain Controller.

**Security Log**    Log file used in Windows NT and 2000 Event Viewer to keep track of security events specified by the domain's Audit policy.

**security policy**    Rules set in place by a company to ensure the security of a network. This may include how often a password must be changed or how many characters a password should be.

**segment**    A unit of data smaller than a packet. Also refers to a portion of a larger network (a network can consist of multiple network segments). *See also* backbone.

**self-powered**    Term used to describe a device that has its own power.

**sequence number**   A number used to determine the order in which parts of a packet are to be reassembled after the packet has been split into sections.

**Sequenced Packet eXchange (SPX)**   A connection-oriented protocol that is part of the IPX protocol suite. It operates at the Transport layer of the OSI model. It initiates the connection between the sender and receiver, transmits the data, and then terminates the connection. *See also* Internet Packet eXchange, Open Systems Interconnect.

**Serial Line Internet Protocol (SLIP)**   A protocol that permits the sending of IP packets over a serial connection.

**server**   A computer that provides resources to the clients on the network.

**server and client configuration**   A network in which the resources are located on a server for use by the clients.

**server-centric**   A network design model that uses a central server to contain all data as well as control security.

**service**   Services add functionality to a network by providing resources or doing tasks for other computers. In Windows *9x*, services include file and printer sharing for Microsoft or Novell networks.

**service accounts**   Accounts created on a server for users to perform special services; examples of service accounts are backup operators, account operators, and server operators.

**Session layer**   The fifth layer of the OSI model, it determines how two computers establish, use, and end a session. Security authentication and network naming functions required for applications occur here. The Session layer establishes, maintains, and breaks dialogs between two stations. *See also* Open Systems Interconnect.

**share-level security**   In a network that uses share-level security, instead of assigning rights to network resources to users, passwords are assigned to individual files or other network resources (such as printers). These passwords are then given to all users that need access to these resources. All resources are visible from anywhere in the network, and any user who knows the password for a particular network resource can make changes to it.

**shared key**   A password or other object shared by two devices communicating across a link, often used to create a one-way hash that is transmitted and compared by the recipient to a one-way hash it creates using the same shared key. The shared key is generally not sent across the link.

**shell**   UNIX interfaces that are based solely upon command prompts. There is no graphical interface.

**shielded**   Term that describes cabling that has extra wrapping to protect it from stray electrical or radio signals. Shielded cabling is more expensive than unshielded.

**shielded twisted-pair cable (STP)**   A type of cabling that includes pairs of copper conductors, twisted around each other, inside a metal or foil shield. This type of medium can support faster speeds than unshielded wiring.

**S-HTTP** *See* Secure Hypertext Transfer Protocol.

**signal** Transmission from one PC to another. This could be a notification to start a session or end a session.

**signal encoding** The process whereby a protocol at the Physical layer receives information from the upper layers and translates all the data into signals that can be transmitted on a transmission medium.

**signaling method** The process of transmitting data across the medium. Two types of signaling are digital and analog.

**Simple Mail Transfer Protocol (SMTP)** A program that looks for mail on SMTP servers and sends it along the network to its destination at another SMTP server.

**Simple Network Management Protocol (SNMP)** The management protocol created for sending information about the health of the network to network management consoles.

**single-attached station (SAS)** A station on an FDDI network that is attached to only one of the cables. They are less fault tolerant than dual-attached stations.

**skipjack** An encryption algorithm developed as a possible replacement for Data Encryption Standard (DES) and is classified by the National Security Agency (NSA). Not much is known about this encryption algorithm except that it uses an 80-bit key.

**SLIP** *See* Serial Line Internet Protocol.

**SMTP** *See* Simple Mail Transfer Protocol.

**SNMP** *See* Simple Network Management Protocol.

**socket** A combination of a port address and an IP address.

**SONET (Synchronous Optical Network)** A standard in the U.S. that defines a base data rate of 51.84Mbps; multiples of this rate are known as optical carrier (OC) levels, such as OC-3, OC-12, etc.

**source address** The address of the station that sent a packet, usually found in the source area of a packet header.

**source port number** The address of the PC that is sending data to a receiving PC. The port portion allows for multiplexing of data to be sent from a specific application.

**splitter** Any device that electrically duplicates one signal into two.

**SPS** *See* Standby Power Supply.

**SPX** *See* Sequenced Packet eXchange.

**Standby Power Supply (SPS)** A power backup device that has power going directly to the protected equipment. A sensor monitors the power. When a loss is detected, the computer is switched over to the battery. Thus, a loss of power might occur (typically for less than a second).

**star topology**   A network topology in which all devices on the network have a direct connection to every other device on the network. These networks are rare except in very small settings due to the huge amount of cabling required to add a new device.

**state table**   A firewall security method that monitors the states of all connections through the firewall.

**static ARP table entries**   Entry in the ARP table that is manually added by a user when a PC will be accessed often. This will speed up the process of communicating with the PC since the IP-to-MAC address will not have to be resolved.

**static routing**   A method of routing packets; the router's routing is updated manually by the network administrator instead of automatically by a route discovery protocol.

**straight tip (ST)**   A type of fiber-optic cable connector that uses a mechanism similar to the BNC connectors used by Thinnet. This is the most popular fiber-optic connector currently in use.

**subnet mask**   A group of selected bits that identify a subnetwork within a TCP/IP network. *See also* Transmission Control Protocol/Internet Protocol.

**subnetting**   The process of dividing a single IP address range into multiple address ranges.

**subnetwork**   Also referred to as a subnet, for short, a network that is part of another network. The connection is made through a gateway, bridge, or router.

**subnetwork address**   Also referred to as a subnet address, a part of the 32-bit IPv4 address that designates the address of the subnetwork.

**subscriber connector (SC)**   A type of fiber-optic connector. These connectors are square shaped and have release mechanisms to prevent the cable from accidentally being unplugged.

**supernetting**   The process of combining multiple IP address ranges into a single IP network.

**surge protector**   A device that contains a special electronic circuit that monitors the incoming voltage level and then trips a circuit breaker when an overvoltage reaches a certain level called the overvoltage threshold.

**surge suppressors**   *See* surge protector.

**switched**   Term used to describe a network that has multiple routes to get from a source to a destination. This allows for higher speeds.

**symmetrical keys**   Keys that are used to both encrypt and decrypt data.

**SYN flood**   A denial of service attack in which the hacker sends a barrage of SYN packets. The receiving station tries to respond to each SYN request for a connection, thereby tying up all the resources. All incoming connections are rejected until all current connections can be established.

**TA**   *See* terminal adapter.

**TCP**   *See* Transmission Control Protocol.

**TCP/IP** *See* Transmission Control Protocol/Internet Protocol.

**TDMA** *See* Time Division Multiple Access.

**TDR** *See* time-domain reflectometer.

**telephony server** A computer that functions as a smart answering machine for the network. It can also perform call center and call routing functions.

**Telnet** A protocol that functions at the Application layer of the OSI model, providing terminal emulation capabilities. *See also* Open Systems Interconnect.

**template** A set of guidelines that you can apply to every new user account created.

**terminal adapter (TA)** In ISDN, the device (often erroneously referred to as an ISDN modem) that is used to interconnect ISDN-incompatible devices, such as PC serial ports or Ethernet interfaces and POTS phones, to an ISDN network for eventual connection to an ISDN circuit.

**terminal emulator** A program that enables a PC to act as a terminal for a mainframe or a UNIX system.

**terminate and stay resident (TSR)** Software that executes and retains all or a portion of its code in memory, monitoring and waiting for an event to trigger further execution. *See also* daemon.

**terminator** A device that prevents a signal from bouncing off the end of the network cable, which would cause interference with other signals.

**test accounts** An account set up by an administrator to confirm the basic functionality of a newly installed application, for example. The test account has equal rights to accounts that will use the new functionality. It is important to use test accounts instead of administrator accounts to test new functionality. If an administrator account is used, problems related to user rights may not manifest themselves because administrator accounts typically have full rights to all network resources.

**TFTP** *See* Trivial File Transfer Protocol.

**Thick Ethernet (Thicknet)** A type of Ethernet that uses thick coaxial cable and supports a maximum transmissions distance of 500 meters. Also called 10Base5.

**Thin Ethernet (Thinnet)** A type of Ethernet that uses RG-58 cable and 10Base2.

**Time Division Multiple Access (TDMA)** A method to divide individual channels in broadband communications into separate time slots, allowing more data to be carried at the same time. It is also possible to use TDMA in baseband communications.

**time-domain reflectometer (TDR)** A tool that sends out a signal and measures how much time it takes to return. It is used to find short or open circuits. Also called a *cable tester*.

**Time to Live (TTL)**   A field in IP packets that indicates how many routers the packet can still cross (hops it can still make) before it is discarded. TTL is also used in ARP tables to indicate how long an entry should remain in the table.

**token**   The special packet of data that is passed around the network in a Token Ring network. *See* Token Ring network.

**token passing**   A media access method in which a token (data packet) is passed around the ring in an orderly fashion from one device to the next. A station can transmit only when it has the token. If it doesn't have the token, it can't transmit. The token continues around the network until the original sender receives the token again. If the token has more data to send, the process repeats. If not, the original sender modifies the token to indicate that the token is free for anyone else to use.

**Token Ring network**   A network based on a physical star, logical ring topology, in which data is passed along the ring until it finds its intended receiver. Only one data packet can be passed along the ring at a time. If the data packet goes around the ring without being claimed, it is returned to the sender.

**tone generator**   A small electronic device that is used to test network cables for breaks and other problems by sending an electronic signal down one set of UTP wires. Used with a tone locator. *See also* tone locator, unshielded twisted-pair cable.

**tone locator**   A device used to test network cables for breaks and other problems; designed to sense the signal sent by the tone generator and emit a tone when the signal is detected in a particular set of wires.

**topology**   The physical and/or logical layout of the transmission media specified in the physical and logical layers of the OSI model. *See also* Open Systems Interconnect.

**traceroute**   *See* tracert.

**tracert**   The Microsoft-based TCP/IP traceroute command-line utility that shows the user every router interface a TCP/IP packet passes through on its way to a destination. The command `traceroute` is used in such environments as the Cisco IOS CLI. *See also* Transmission Control Protocol/Internet Protocol.

**trailer**   A section of a data packet that contains error-checking information.

**transceiver**   The part of any network interface that transmits and receives network signals.

**transient**   A high-voltage burst of current.

**transmission**   Sending of packets from the PC to the network cable.

**Transmission Control Protocol (TCP)**   The protocol found at the Host-to-Host layer of the DoD model. This protocol breaks data packets into segments, numbers them, and sends them in random order. The receiving computer reassembles the data so that the information is readable for the user. In the process, the sender and the receiver confirm that all data has been received; if not, it is resent. This is a connection-oriented protocol. *See also* connection-oriented transport protocol.

**Transmission Control Protocol/Internet Protocol (TCP/IP)**   The protocol suite developed by the DoD in conjunction with the Internet. It was designed as an internetworking protocol suite that could route information around network failures. Today it is the de facto standard for communications on the Internet.

**transmission media**   Physical cables and/or wireless technology across which computers are able to communicate.

**Transport layer**   The fourth layer of the OSI model, it is responsible for checking that the data packet created in the Session layer was received error free. If necessary, it also changes the length of messages for transport up or down the remaining layers. *See also* Open Systems Interconnect.

**Trivial File Transfer Protocol (TFTP)**   A protocol similar to FTP that does not provide the security or error-checking features of FTP. *See also* File Transfer Protocol.

**Trojan horse**   A virus or other malicious process that hides within another, possibly trusted, program that the user executes without knowing the Trojan horse is embedded. Execution of the host program generally launches the Trojan horse.

**trunk lines**   The telephone lines that form the backbone of a telephone network for a company. These lines connect the telephone(s) to the telephone company and to the PSTN. *See also* Public Switched Telephone Network.

**T-series connections**   A series of digital connections leased from the telephone company. Each T-series connection is rated with a number based on speed. T1 and T3 are the most popular.

**TSR**   *See* terminate and stay resident.

**TTL**   *See* Time to Live.

**twisted-pair cable**   A type of network transmission medium that contains pairs of color-coded, insulated copper wires that are twisted around each other. A twisted-pair cable consists of one or more twisted pairs in a common jacket.

**type**   A DOS command that displays the contents of a file. Also, short for *data type*.

**UDP**   *See* User Datagram Protocol.

**Uniform Resource Locator (URL)**   A URL is one way of identifying a document on the Internet. It consists of the protocol that is used to access the document and the domain name or IP address of the host that holds the document, for example, `http://www.sybex.com`.

**uninterruptible power supply (UPS)**   A natural line conditioner that uses a battery and power inverter to run the computer equipment that plugs into it. The battery charger continuously charges the battery. The battery charger is the only thing that runs off line voltage. During a power problem, the battery charger stops operating and the equipment continues to run off the battery.

**Universal Serial Bus (USB)**   A versatile, chainable serial bus technology that connects up to 127 devices at speeds of 1.5Mbps and 12Mbps (versions 1.0 and 1.1—1.5Mbps is the sub-channel rate), as well as 480Mbps (version 2.0—Hi-Speed USB).

**UNIX**   A 32-bit, multitasking operating system developed in the 1960s for use on mainframes and minicomputers.

**unreliable**   The quality of a protocol that does not use acknowledgments to allow a receiving device to inform the source that it received its transmitted data without error. *See also* reliable.

**unshielded**   Term that describes cabling that has little no wrapping to protect it to protect it from stray electrical or radio signals. Unshielded cabling is less expensive than shielded.

**unshielded twisted-pair cable (UTP)**   Twisted-pair cable consisting of a number of twisted pairs of copper wire with a simple plastic casing. Because no shielding is used in this cable, it is very susceptible to EMI, RFI, and other types of interference. *See also* crossover cable, electromagnetic interference, radio frequency interference.

**upgrade**   To increase an aspect of a PC, for example, by upgrading the RAM (increasing the RAM), upgrading the CPU (changing the current CPU for a faster CPU), etc.

**UPS**   *See* uninterruptible power supply.

**uptime**   The amount of time a particular computer or network component has been functional.

**URL**   *See* Uniform Resource Locator.

**user**   The person who is using a computer or network.

**User Datagram Protocol (UDP)**   Protocol at the Host-to-Host layer of the DoD model, which corresponds to the Transport layer of the OSI model. Packets are divided into segments, given numbers, sent randomly, and put back together at the receiving end. This is a connectionless protocol. *See also* connectionless transport protocol, Open Systems Interconnect.

**user-level security**   A type of network in which user accounts can read, write, change, and take ownership of files. Rights are assigned to user accounts, and each user knows only their own username and password, which makes this the preferred method for securing files.

**vampire tap**   A connection used with Thicknet to attach a station to the main cable. It is called a vampire tap because it has a tooth that "bites" through the insulation to make the physical connection.

**virtual COM**   Serial port that is used as if it were a serial port, but the actual serial port interface does not exist.

**Virtual LAN (VLAN)**   A technology that allows users on different switch ports to participate in their own network separate from, but still connected to, the other stations on the same or connected switch.

**virtual private network (VPN)**   A network that uses the public Internet as a backbone for a private interconnection (network) between locations.

**virus**   A program intended to damage a computer system. Sophisticated viruses encrypt and hide in a computer and may not appear until the user performs a certain action or until a certain date. *See also* antivirus.

**virus engine**   The core program that runs the virus-scanning process.

**volume**   Loudness of a sound, or the portion of a hard disk that functions as if it were a separate hard disk.

**VPN**   *See* virtual private network.

**WAN**   *See* wide area network.

**web proxy**   A type of proxy that is used to act on behalf of a web client or web server.

**web server**   A server that holds and delivers web pages and other web content using the HTTP protocol. *See also* Hypertext Transfer Protocol.

**wide area network (WAN)**   A network that crosses local, regional, and international boundaries.

**Windows Internet Naming Service (WINS)**   A Windows NT service that dynamically associates the NetBIOS name of a host with a domain name. *See also* network basic input/output system.

**Windows 2003**   The latest version of the Windows network operating system from Microsoft.

**Windows NT**   A network operating system developed by Microsoft that uses that same graphical interface as the Desktop environment, Windows 95/98.

**Windows NT 3.51**   The version of Windows NT based on the "look and feel" of Windows 3.*x*. *See also* Windows NT.

**Windows NT 4**   The version of Windows NT based on the "look and feel" of Windows 95/98. *See also* Windows NT.

**Windows NT Service**   A type of Windows program (a file with either an .EXE or a .DLL extension) that is loaded automatically by the server or manually by the administrator.

**Windows XP**   The latest version of the Windows desktop operating system from Microsoft.

**winipcfg**   The IP configuration utility for Windows 95/98 that allows you to view the current TCP/IP configuration of a workstation.

**WinNuke**   A Windows-based attack that affects only computers running Windows NT 3.51 or 4. It is caused by the way that the Windows NT TCP/IP stack handles bad data in the TCP header. Instead of returning an error code or rejecting the bad data, it sends NT to the Blue Screen of Death (BSOD). Figuratively speaking, the attack nukes the computer.

**WINS**   *See* Windows Internet Naming Service.

**wire crimper**   Used for attaching ends onto different types of network cables by a process known as crimping. Crimping involves using pressure to press some kind of metal teeth into the inner conductors of a cable.

**Wired Equivalent Privacy (WEP)**   A security protocol for 802.11b wireless LANs. It gets it name from the fact that this protocol is designed to provide a security level roughly equivalent to a wired LAN. This is done by encrypting the data that is transmitted wirelessly.

**wireless access point (WAP)**   A wireless bridge used in a multipoint RF network.

**wireless bridge**   It performs all the functions of a regular bridge, but it uses RF instead of cables to transmit signals.

**workgroup**   A specific group of users or network devices, organized by job function or proximity to shared resources.

**workstation**   A computer that is not a server but is on a network. Generally a workstation is used to do work, while a server is used to store data or perform a network function. In the most simple terms, a workstation is a computer that is not a server.

**World Wide Web (WWW)**   A collection of HTTP servers running on the Internet. They support the use of documents formatted with HTML. *See also* Hypertext Markup Language, Hypertext Transfer Protocol.

**worms**   Similar to a virus. Worms, however, propagate themselves over a network. *See also* virus.

**WWW**   *See* World Wide Web.

**X Windows**   A graphical user interface (GUI) developed for use with the various flavors of UNIX.

**Yagi**   *See* directional antenna.

**ZeroConf**   Short for Zero Configuration, an IETF initiative chartered to create recommendations for networking devices in small environments so that no configuration is necessary after the devices are interconnected.

# Index

Note to the Reader: Throughout this index **boldfaced** page numbers indicate primary discussions of a topic. *Italicized* page numbers indicate illustrations.

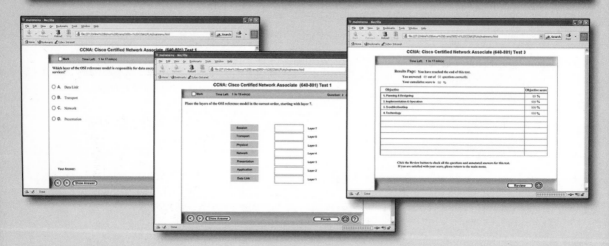